The Films of
STEVEN SPIELBERG

The Films of
STEVEN SPIELBERG

DOUGLAS BRODE

CITADEL PRESS
Kensington Publishing Corp.
www.kensingtonbooks.com

CITADEL PRESS books are published by

Kensington Publishing Corp.
850 Third Avenue
New York, NY 10022

All Kensington titles, imprints, and distributed lines are
available at special quantity discounts for bulk purchases
for sales promotions, premiums, fund raising, educational,
or institutional use. Special book excerpts or customized
printings can also be created to fit specific needs. For details,
write or phone the office of the Kensington special sales
manager: Kensington Publishing Corp., 850 Third Avenue,
New York, NY 10022, attn: Special Sales Department,
phone 1-800-221-2647.

Kensington and the K logo Reg. U.S. Pat. & TM Office
Citadel Press is a trademark of Kensington Publishing Corp.

Design by A. Christopher Simon

First printing November 2000

10 9 8 7 6 5 4 3 2 1

Printed in the United States of America

Library of Congress Cataloging-in-Publication Data

Brode, Douglas, 1943–.
    The films of Stephen Spielberg / Douglas Brode.—Rev. and
updated.
       p.   cm.
    "A Citadel Press book."
    ISBN 0-8065-1951-7 (pbk.)
    I. Spielberg, Steven, 1947–   —Criticism and interpretation.
I. Title.
PN1998.3.S65B76   1998
791.43'0233'092—dc21   98–20239
                                                              CIP

For
IRMA LICHENSTEIN BRODE
and
LEAH POSNER SPIELBERG

strong, supportive Jewish mothers,
equally proud
of their sons' accomplishments

Acknowledgments

With thanks to Anthony Michael Varone for his endless hours as a volunteer research assistant; Mercy Sandberg-Wright for her help in acquiring stills; and John Nucifora of Chimney's Video for supplying all screening tapes; also, to Peter Violas and Kathryn Metherell and to all the people at Amblin Entertainment who took the time to provide information and support, as well as TriStar Pictures, Paramount, Warner Brothers, Universal, M-G-M, United Artists, and Columbia; in New York City, Jerry Ohlinger's Movie Material Store and Photofest; in Los Angeles, Cinema Collectors and Larry Edmond's Bookstore. And also, thanks to Robbie Strauss and James MacKillop.

Contents

The Films of
STEVEN SPIELBERG

THE MAN IN THE HAT: Like so many of his heroes, the young Spielberg liked to sport a jaunty hat while directing, a clear suggestion of the highly personal element in movies that were for so long accepted as mere synthetic entertainments, but which in fact are all serious emotional autobiographies.

Introduction: Citizen Spielberg

Once upon a time, in a fabulous kingdom called Arizona during a mythical age known as the 1950s, six-year-old Steven Spielberg woke in the middle of the night to find his father, barely able to control his excitement, standing in the darkness by the boy's bed. As soon as little Steven's eyes were open, Arnold Spielberg whispered that he should quietly come along. He took the child by the hand and firmly dragged the boy out of the house to the family car. Though the father's manner was calm and gentle, little Steven was terrified, so much so that he acquiesced to everything, even as Arnold wordlessly started the car and drove away from the home where his wife, Leah, and their three daughters remained fast asleep. Unsure whether he was still in bed dreaming or if this were actually happening, Steven cast a backward glance at the house, wondering if he would ever see it or its inhabitants again.

They traveled for a half hour, not saying a word other than the father's single-sentence explanation "I'm taking you to see an extraordinary show!" They did not arrive at a theater, a circus tent, or a theme-park pavilion, but at an isolated stretch on the desert outside Phoenix, where about a hundred people (though there must have appeared to be a thousand to the frightened but now fascinated child) were lying on the ground, on old blankets, staring upward. To Steven, the sky must have looked the way skies do in the films he would begin making some twenty years later: immense, black, star-studded. That is, a night sky filled with wonder, mystery, and potential for magic and menace.

"My first conscious catharsis" is how Spielberg would recollect what he observed. As his father spread out blankets and pillows, they joined the others. People briefly glanced over, saying nothing but smiling knowingly at newcomers, who likewise "understood," one way or another learning of the miraculous, metaphysical thing about to happen, attracted to this isolated place like pieces of metal to a magnet. They observed a meteor shower that either was, or appeared to the child to be, "phantasmagoric." While the city slept, a precious few witnessed proof positive that there was indeed enchantment in the universe.

Two decades later, Spielberg—quickly rising amid the ranks of young Hollywood filmmakers—would recall that scene from childhood and re-create it for his third feature (the first he himself wrote as well as directed), *Close Encounters of the Third Kind.* In that UFO extravaganza, an equally giddy father, Roy Neary (Richard Dreyfuss), drags his family out to see just such a natural phenomenon. By film's end, he realizes that, love them as he may, Roy must leave if he is to ever rediscover the child within himself, the child he has spent most of his adult working and parenting life denying. It's not surprising to learn, then, that several years after the magical real-life moment, Arnold Spielberg likewise left his family.

In its time, *Close Encounters of the Third Kind* was happily accepted as a marvelously crafted crowd pleaser, a wonderful cinematic roller-coaster ride. Today, *Close Encounters of the Third Kind* can still be seen as that, or something more: a thinly disguised emotional autobiography of its author, presented through conventions of an escapist-entertainment genre that allow easy access for the public at large. This would be the modus operandi of Steven Spielberg, filmmaker. "I'm like a kid whose eyes are bigger than his stomach," he giddily announced in 1974, immediately after the release of his first theatrical feature. "There are so many movies I want to make. I used to sit around wondering why nobody would make a movie about this subject or that. Now I can make those missing movies myself."

Missing movies! As if all films—past, present, and future—were part of some huge jigsaw puzzle that collectively added up to our cinematic heritage and he had been assigned to dutifully fill in some missing pieces. Spielberg did not happen to wander into the movie business; he was by his own admission destined for it. He was born on December 18, 1947, in Cincinnati, the oldest of four children (and the only boy) born to Arnold and Leah (Posner) Spielberg. The unique approach he would later take toward filmmaking—a delicate, sometimes uncertain balance between technical know-how and serious artistic ambitions—was dictated by the polar-extreme influences of his parents: Arnold worked as an electrical engineer and, early on, computer expert, while his mother was a former concert pianist. His father taught him technology; his mother, aesthetics.

Spielberg's lifelong love of stories began with his father, who would regale the boy with bedtime tales of his experiences (no doubt, more mythical than real) during World War II. Arnold had served as a radioman aboard a B-25, fighting the Japanese in Burma. Steven acquired two ongoing interests. One was a romanticized notion of the forties as an age of innocence. Throughout his life, as evidenced in his movies, Spielberg measured our own shabby reality against an impossible ideal of the way things used to be. His other fascination was with airplanes. Spielberg began assembling models, normal

From that moment on, Spielberg felt like an outsider. He necessarily developed, from his mother, an optimistic view of a brighter future. That view sustained him through hard times, eventually becoming a basic ingredient in his films. "Looking forward to it!" was, he believes, the first full phrase he uttered as a small child. While still in Ohio, his mother would tell him that in three weeks his grandparents were coming to visit from New Jersey, explaining: "It's something to look forward to." He adopted that saying, made it a key part of his personal shield against encroaching sadness. When, a week later, his mother reminded him that his grandparents would be arriving in two weeks, he finished the sentence for her: "It's something to look forward to."

But there was something bad he always had to look forward to as well: moving again. Years later, Hollywood's hottest moviemaker would reflect on how

STEVEN SPIELBERG, STORYTELLER (photo by David James; courtesy Universal Studios and Amblin Entertainment, Inc.).

enough in and of itself, though he (like his future child-hero in *Empire of the Sun*) became obsessed with them as well as the idea of flight they embodied.

There was a reason why the young Spielberg dreamed of flight, physically and also spiritually. His father, attempting to move up the ladder of success, accepted a succession of executive-level jobs with major firms, so Steven spent most of his early years on the move: in the suburbs of Haddonfield, New Jersey, then eventually on to Scottsdale, Arizona, and nearby Phoenix. Wherever they went, there was always friction between his essentially incompatible parents, no matter how hard they tried to make things work. "I was surrounded by so much negativity when I was a kid," he later recalled, "that I had no recourse but to be positive." Experiences at school were not any better. Once, his gym teacher had a class of fifty children run a mile around the track. Huffing and puffing, all of the students managed to make it except two: a mentally retarded boy and Steven Spielberg, who could see his peers staring at him, laughing, then cheering for the retarded boy to hurry up and cross over the finish line first.

THE KIND OF A BOY YOU ARE, THE KIND OF A MAN YOU'LL BE: As a child (*inset*), young Steven was already immersed in the American car culture; as an Arizona teenager, the Jewish boy learned to successfully assimilate by starring the neighborhood kids in minimovies; as a director, he made such middle-American classics as *Raiders of the Lost Ark* (courtesy Paramount Pictures).

terribly disoriented he constantly felt. "Just when I would find a best friend—at the moment of my greatest comfort and tranquillity—we'd go somewhere else. The older I got, the harder it got." Then Spielberg's eyes brightened as he suddenly sensed that he was now, in fictional contexts, artistically dealing with those experiences by telling stories dear to his heart: "*E.T.* reflects a lot of that. When Elliott finds E.T., he hangs on. He announces in no uncertain terms, 'I'm keeping him.' And he means it."

E.T. was still a long way off, though movies—other people's movies, then his own—were with him early on. At first, his ultrastrict parents shielded him, all but throwing a blanket over the TV set to keep their kids from being exposed to anything unpleasant; they also closely monitored the movies their children were allowed to see. Still, his father took him to his first film at age five: *The Greatest Show on Earth,* Cecil B. DeMille's 1952 Oscarwinning circus epic. It is, perhaps, not coincidental that the film—which so influenced him—was made by a moviemaker who, like Spielberg in his own films, spoke across his own unique cultural identity (DeMille was Episcopalian) in a universal voice that appealed to the vast American masses of all denominations. Moreover, DeMille (like Spielberg) was accused of overt sentimentality, of being more a shameless showman than a true artist, like such contemporaries as Frank Capra, John

Ford and Howard Hawks. In time, critics would make just such charges against Spielberg, unfavorably comparing him with Martin Scorsese and Francis Ford Coppola.

Concerned that his child might be frightened when lions went out of control, Arnold carefully explained to Steven that they were all imprisoned up there on the screen and could not get to him. For a moment, the boy—grasping what a movie was—felt disappointed, cheated that he wasn't going to see a real-live circus, only a representation of one. Then the film began. No matter what his father had said, Spielberg later recalled that DeMille's film was so vivid and believable that "they [the lions] were getting out at me. Ever since [becoming a filmmaker], I've wanted to try to involve the audience as much as I can, so they no longer think they're sitting [passively] in an audience," watching from a distance, but are totally involved in, even transported by, the moviegoing experience.

Within a few years, Spielberg was old enough to attend movies without his father. Often friendless, he frequented the movie houses in those cities in which the family temporarily lived, watching all the Walt Disney pictures, of which his parents approved. Though they forbade him to see creepy films like *I Was a Teenage Werewolf,* he slipped out and caught it, anyway, then felt he was being properly punished when he woke up screaming for the

INDELIBLE INFLUENCES 2: Today, Spielberg's prize possession is the Rosebud sled from *Citizen Kane* (*left*, courtesy R.K.O. Radio Pictures/Turner Film Library), which in Orson Welles's classic represented the child's traumatic moment of separation from his mother. In John Ford's legendary western *The Searchers* (*right*, courtesy Warner Bros.), a child (Natalie Wood), long separated from her family, is finally carried home by a wayward foster-father (John Wayne) and adoptive brother (Jeffrey Hunter).

next several nights. Spielberg soon discovered Forrest J. Ackerman's cult publication *Famous Monsters of Filmland* and began creating makeshift concoctions of makeup with which he experimented on his sisters, lining them up, then transforming their faces into miniversions of Frankenstein, Dracula, and the Wolfman.

It would be wrong, though, to paint an overly pretty picture of this seemingly happy situation or its central character. He loved to ruthlessly torment his kid sisters, perhaps because he believed his parents doted on them and ignored him. He relied on monster-movie mythology to get at the girls. Whenever his mother put little Annie to bed, Steven would slip outside her window and call out in an eerie voice, "I am the MOOOOOON!" The child would scream in terror all night. Once, he cut the head off Nancy's favorite doll and served it to her on a platter, surrounded by neatly arranged lettuce and tomato. His mother admits: "Steven was not a cuddly child."

He was in third grade when he learned firsthand the impact film and TV could have on the popular psyche. Every kid in school had seen Walt Disney's *Davy Crockett*; when, on the playground, Spielberg arrived without the requisite coonskin cap, he was tagged the villainous Santa Anna, at which point pint-sized Alamo defenders came after him with the butts of toy flintlock rifles. He was regularly chased home until he convinced his parents to buy him the proper Disney paraphernalia. He was made aware, early on, of the significance of movie merchandising, an aspect of the film business he and colleague George Lucas would carefully oversee, though more "serious" contemporaries like Scorsese and

Coppola never deigned to involve themselves with such crass commercialism.

From watching movies, Spielberg quickly progressed to making them. He would become the symbol and spokesman for what eventually came to be called postliterate society: intelligent, knowledgeable people who know what they know from movies rather than books. One junior high school incident seems particularly telling: Handed a copy of Nathaniel Hawthorne's *The Scarlet Letter,* Spielberg quickly grew bored and couldn't get through it. However, he set to work drawing little stick-figure cartoons at the bottom edge of every page, creating a makeshift flip book, riffling the pages with his thumb. It wasn't celluloid, but it was a movie.

He went to work on his first film at age thirteen. Leah had given Arnold an 8-mm movie camera for Father's Day, but little Steven assumed responsibility for documenting a summer outing in the Rocky Mountains. He was stunned to realize the sense of control the camera offered him: If he chose to include one of their activities, like swimming, it would be reinforced every time they watched the home movies, thus existing forever. If he cut something away in his makeshift editing room, it was swiftly lost in the mists of time. A filmmaker is, to a degree, a god; his control is complete. That must have held great appeal for a little boy who feared he could not control his daily life.

Understandably, he was totally hooked at that moment, realizing that in addition to restructuring reality, he could also use the camera to create his own world. The man who would initially make his reputation with vehicular crashes started on the road to Hollywood by setting his

electric trains on a track toward one another and recording the results. Claymation stop-action experiments followed, the little movies becoming ever more elaborate and more expensive. To finance his "artistic" career, Steven needed a more prosaic business. He opened a citrus-tree whitewashing and debugging firm, charging seventy-five cents per tree, reckoning that six trees could pay for one roll of film. Living in the West and loving westerns, he created a cowboy picture, a three-and-a-half-minute oater called *The Last Gun,* brought in at a budget of $8.50.

15

Movies, he realized, could pay off: That one earned him his Boy Scout merit badge in photography. Wanting to control distribution as well as direct, he set up screenings for the neighborhood kids in a makeshift theater, charging each a quarter to get in and watch the movies ("starring" themselves), then rushing behind his little homemade concession stand to sell popcorn and beverages. During high school, he went on to shoot another fifteen minimovies. Sometimes filmmaking served as a means of survival: When several bullies began beating up on him, Spielberg cagily convinced them to star in an action flick, *Battle Squad;* if something less than true friends, they were unable to remain hostile while taking direction—under his control.

Meanwhile, the moviemaking grew more ambitious. For one, he talked a hospital administrator into closing off a wing for a location shot. On another, he insisted that the local airport shut down a runway. "No one ever said 'no' to him, and it's a good thing," his mother reflected. "Steven doesn't understand 'no.'" Now, though, it was time for an epic. From his father, Spielberg inherited a love of science fiction and a fascination with astronomy. Their warmest times together were spent gazing at the stars through a homemade reflecting telescope. Volumes of the sci-fi magazine *Analog* were piled high on the back of their porcelain toilet. Containing endless tales of fantasy in other worlds, they represented Arnold Spielberg's still-repressed desire to escape from the mundane. So Steven mounted *Firelight,* a two-and-a-half-hour sci-fi epic feature about several scientists investigating inexplicable lights in the sky. Inspired by B-movies as filtered through his own already sharp consciousness, it was completed at a cost of five hundred dollars.

He was inspired to write it one night while in the process of falling asleep. The boy leaped out of bed, ran for his typewriter, and worked for the next twenty-four hours, not stopping until he had knocked out a 140-page screenplay.

Firelight took a year to complete, since filming was confined to weekends. It was shot silent, though Spielberg had the Eastman lab apply a sound strip and rented a now-antiquated machine called a Bolex Sonerizer. He persuaded his actors (drama students, drafted from Arizona State University) to join him at his makeshift studio, study their own lip movements in the film, rehearse several times, then postsynch the film. More than three hundred dollars of the budget came from his amused and supportive father, who augmented what Steven was able to scrape together from his own now-lucrative business.

Spielberg would later describe *Firelight* as "one of the five worst films ever made anywhere," though he still keeps a print locked away in a desk drawer. The then sixteen-year-old proved to be a natural showman as well as a born filmmaker: He talked a Phoenix theater owner into playing *Firelight,* then arranged for limousines to bring the participants (including his mother, who would be by his side some thirty years later when he received the Best Director Oscar) to opening-night festivities while klieg lights passed across the sky. *Firelight* recouped its entire cost and made him a profit of fifty dollars to boot.

That grand night was the climax of his relatively happy life up until then. The next day, the downslide began; at sixteen, he stepped into the family station wagon and, with a Mayflower truck following behind, trundled off to Saratoga in northern California's Bay Area, near San Jose, where he completed his last year of high school. Spielberg would not discover Orson Welles's 1941 film classic *Citizen Kane* until years later; when he did, he would—like most movie lovers—consider it the greatest film ever made. For Spielberg, though, the intense reaction must have been personal and emotional as well as aesthetic and intellectual. The image of little Charles Foster Kane, suddenly swept away from the West of his happy childhood toward a new, supposedly more sophisticated life—in fact, an ongoing nightmare—had to hit him hard, stirring memories of his own sudden loss. Little Charlie Kane tries to hang on to his Rosebud sled, representing the simplicity and innocence he is being torn away from. Today that bit of movie memorabilia is owned by Steven Spielberg, who tracked it down, bought it, and now considers it his prized possession.

For the first time in his life, Spielberg became intensely aware of himself as a Jew. Before that, he only dimly understood that his parents and grandparents, on both sides, hailed from Odessa, Russia, and a part of Austria once encompassed by Poland. In time, he would set his Oscar-winning Best Picture there, though in those early years, he never even heard the word "Holocaust." On occasion, his parents had referred to "the murdering Nazis." More often, Jewishness embodied itself in sweet, simple actions: his mother making matzo brei one day, salami and egg cooked "pancake" style the next. Today Spielberg prepares those dishes himself, at home, twice a week, though as a good Jewish son, he insists: "My mom makes it much better."

In northern California, however, Jewishness came to mean something other than what he ate for breakfast. That was 1966, reportedly the year when peace and love were manifesting themselves among the young people of America. Apparently, someone forgot to tell that to the youth of Saratoga. Lonely and alienated, Spielberg was abused, verbally and physically. During daily study-hall periods, the overriding quiet was punctured by sounds of pennies tossed at the Jew by teens seated at desks around him. The increasingly unpleasant situation became so intense during gym class that he was forced to stop attending. Though Steven lived within walking distance, his mother deemed it necessary to pick him up after school in her car to protect him from beatings.

There was another reason why life no longer seemed attractive. When he was fourteen, he realized that the friction between his parents was becoming untenable. At fifteen, it became clear they were not going to make it as

a couple; a year after that, they divorced. Spielberg has not chosen to speak publicly about that time except to admit that adjusting to life without a father was one of the most traumatic experiences of his life, perhaps the most disturbing. When graduation time came, he viewed it as an escape from what, for him, had become a teenager's personal Holocaust.

One might assume that Spielberg would have easily won admission to a leading university's film program. The problem was that his all-encompassing dedication to amateur filmmaking caused his grades to suffer; Spielberg considered himself lucky to win a spot at California State College at Long Beach, which at the time did not even offer a single film-history course. Concentrating his efforts on not flunking out, Spielberg temporarily put aside all thoughts of moviemaking, focusing instead on academics. The boy who hated reading chose to major in, of all things, English.

Once he had firmed up an acceptable grade average, however, he was soon back on track. He wanted to be where the serious action was but knew uniformed guards kept the general population from entering movie studios. Spielberg hatched a plan. He bought a ticket for Universal's studio ride, a bus tour which whisked visitors through the working studio. When the tour stopped for them to use the bathroom, Spielberg slipped away from the group, hiding between two soundstages until the others left, then walking around the back lot for hours, discovering an empty office in one of the little bungalows

where producers were quartered. The following day, he put on a suit and tie and, carrying an officious-looking briefcase, somehow bluffed his way past the front-gate guards, appearing to be some mogul's gofer. He walked directly to "his" office and sat down, presumably thinking: Someday all of this will be mine!

This habit continued, Spielberg daily slipping onto soundstages where films were being made, years later claiming to have been thrown out by legendary luminaries: "Hitchcock, Franklin Schaffner, I was bounced by the best."

Spielberg turned out three student films. The first two were personal and esoteric. (Most young would-be filmmakers were at that time attempting to imitate such European idols as Antonioni, Bergman, and Fellini.) For the third, he calculatedly decided to make a movie that would appeal to the commercially minded studio brass. He persuaded a would-be producer he had met, Dennis Hoffman, to hand over $15,000; in ten days, Spielberg expanded his five-page concept into a twenty-two-minute road-movie/romance, set in the Mojave Desert, about two hitchiking teens in love. The film was shot in 35 mm (for the necessary slick, professional look), without dialogue (but not, significantly, without sound), and he called it *Amblin'* (short for "rambling," later the inspiration for the eventual name of his own company formed in 1984).

17

Spielberg scoffs that it was nothing more than "a Pepsi commercial," a self-consciously artsy youth-grooving film. But it worked: When *Amblin'* won prizes at festivals in Atlanta and Venice in 1969, Spielberg immediately was perceived as being one of the bright young talents who might have a shot at the big time. Paramount paired *Amblin'* with *Love Story* for 1970 release. On the basis of the short film, Sidney J. Sheinberg, head of television operations at Universal, contacted Spielberg, offering the then 21-year-old an exclusive seven-year contract.

"But I have a year left to go in college," he replied.

"Kid," Sheinberg said, "do you want to go to college, or do you want to direct?"

Spielberg signed on the bottom line. Later, he reflected that in such a situation, "you sign your life away for one shot; it's really selling your soul to the devil." The five-foot six-inch boyish-looking director, with his tousled dark brown hair and brown eyes, described as "dreamy" and "far away" as they peered over aviator glasses, arrived to direct the Joan Crawford segment of the *Night Gallery* TV-movie pilot. The crew took one look and assumed it was a joke; the real director would arrive soon. So Spielberg set out to prove himself. On the TV set, he learned discipline by shooting a whopping ten pages a day. Insecure, he planned to film one shot through a bauble, achieving a take-your-breath-away look. Then he noticed crew members on the sidelines whispering about him, realizing he was being indulgent: The best way to do it was simple and straightforward.

Surprisingly, he was not at first interested in continuing on. Uncertain whether he could handle the pressure, Spielberg took nearly a year off, during which time he worked on three original scripts. Then he reapproached

KEY COLLABORATORS 1: Writer-conceptualizer-producer George Lucas and director Spielberg (*left*), gifted in different ways but sharing a singular vision, have happily collaborated on such films as *Raiders of the Lost Ark* (courtesy Paramount Pictures). A director of writers, cinematographers, and editors as well as actors, Spielberg rates as a total filmmaker (what the French call an *auteur*) involved with every element of the moviemaking process. Here he decides on the composition of a shot for *Empire of the Sun* (*right*) with cinematographer Allen Daviau (courtesy Warner Bros.).

18

Sheinberg and asked to be assigned to some shows, learning to his dismay that many at Universal considered him too avant-garde, owing to Spielberg's propensity to shoot scenes from bizarre angles, hoping to make threadbare material seem more interesting than it was. He persevered, eventually directing episodic TV *(Marcus Welby, M.D.; The Psychiatrist)* as well as a classic *Columbo* episode, "Murder by the Book." Sometimes his newfound resolve for simplicity went too far. When he realized he would have to knock out an entire eight-page, eight-minute segment for *Night Gallery* (the weekly series his film had spawned), he simply shot it all in one long, continuous take, allowing the camera to follow his characters without bothering to do any cutaways to closeups. The Universal brass was horrified; another director was brought in to augment the work with varied shots.

One story he developed during the year off was *Ace Eli and Rodger of the Skies,* containing several themes which would shortly be his hallmark. Set in the 1920s, it concerns a World War I veteran aviator (the Spielberg fascination with antique planes and the act of flying) who travels the country with his little boy (the recurring theme of wandering fathers and their responsibilities toward impressionable sons). Twentieth Century-Fox, however, reassigned the idea to an established writer, then turned it over to a mediocre director. Spielberg, trusting that the studio would allow him to both write and direct, was sickened. He did get to scout locations for a Burt Reynolds vehicle called *White Lightning* but after several months dropped out of that project when he become convinced it would be worthless junk.

Nonetheless, he became a regular at the Universal commissary, bringing his puckish sense of humor along with him. One day, Spielberg arranged to have Richard Nixon paged over the public-address system, then sat back and feigned innocence while watching an entire roomful of studio execs in suits craning their necks for a glimpse. Professionally speaking, the next logical step was the made-for-TV movie. The success of 1971's *Duel* assured Spielberg of a shot at directing a major feature, which he achieved with *The Sugarland Express.*

Paul D. Zimmerman of *Newsweek* hailed "the arrival of an extraordinarily talented new filmmaker," while Pauline Kael of the *New Yorker* went him one better, insisting that the movie was "one of the most phenomenal debut films in the history of movies." Such extreme statements had not been made about any director since 1941, when Orson Welles, at the identical age of Spielberg circa *The Sugarland Express,* turned out *Citizen Kane,* redefining the rules of filmmaking for an upcoming era.

KEY COLLABORATORS 2: Over the years, Spielberg has worked closely with behind-the-scenes personnel who have helped him realize his visions onscreen; Frank Marshall (*second from left,* in baseball cap) and Kathleen Kennedy (*third from right,* in sunglasses), here seen on the set of their own film, Disney's *Arachnophobia,* assumed many of the producing chores at Amblin, allowing Spielberg to concentrate on the artistic elements (photo by Ralph Nelson, courtesy Hollywood Pictures and Amblin Entertainment, Inc.).

Now, though, Welles's influence had spanned more than thirty years; the emerging youthful audience of the early seventies required its own film language. This would be created by Spielberg and such film-school graduates, recently entrenched in Hollywood, as Scorsese, Coppola, Lucas, John Milius, Peter Bogdanovich, Terrence Malick, and Brian De Palma.

Though *Easy Rider* had been a huge hit in 1969, moviegoers did not take to the follow-up "youth grooving" films. Nor could they sit still for threadbare traditional entertainment (John Wayne westerns, Doris Day comedies, elaborate but empty-headed costume spectacles). Needed now was some middle ground: young filmmakers who could revive the old craftsmanship, so central to the genius of the studio system, doing so in a hip, contemporary way. In 1971, Bogdanovich's *Last Picture Show* translated to the screen Larry McMurtry's novel about denizens of a small Texas town, circa 1948—a beautiful black-and-white evocation of forties films by Ford, Hawks, and Welles. But the strong language, sexuality, and psychology were all new to American movies. When the public responded positively, Hollywood sensed that the movie heralded the retro-wave of the future. The young writer-director-producers would come to be called movie brats; at the time, Spielberg was quite willing to acknowledge his brotherhood in this fraternity.

"We don't live near each other, but we talk to each other on the phone endlessly," a 1974 *Newsweek* interview quoted him as saying:

We often exchange scripts and ideas and offer to help each other out. We're interested in well-crafted, intelligent movies that can appeal to millions of people. We're not interested in making small critical successes nobody goes to see.

Spielberg would live to regret those last words, spoken with youthful bravado. An anti-Spielberg sentiment set in on the part of the intelligentsia that had, years earlier, turned against Spielberg's idols, particularly DeMille and Walt Disney. He appeared to understand this, making a fascinating distinction between "serious" artists, like Scorsese *(Raging Bull)* and Coppola *(The Godfather),* as compared to the popcorn and bubble gum crowd, including Lucas *(Star Wars)* and himself: "Marty would have to be the best *filmmaker* of our generation. George is the best *moviemaker.*"

In the midst of a rave review of *Close Encounters,* Jack Kroll paused to admit that "sophisticates will gaze upon Spielberg's wonders and cry 'Kitsch!' " That was only the beginning. By 1978, a humbled Spielberg had clearly changed his tune. "I'm very frustrated when I see movies like [Bernardo Bertolucci's] *The Conformist* and [François Truffaut's] *Small Change* and I haven't taken a position personally on how I feel about the world. I think my films will eventually get around to that." He hastened to add: "But I never want to stop entertaining!" He announced his intention to make *After School,* which would

treat the lives of neglected American kids in the same realistic manner that Truffaut's *Small Change* had explored those of French children. The project sounded worthy but never reached the screen. Twenty years later, though, Spielberg at last "got around" to that "personal position." While *Schindler's List* was hardly a movie "nobody went to see" (it has earned over $100 million in America alone), the commercial potential seemed so slight that had a director of Spielberg's by then phenomenal stature not insisted on doing it, the film would never have been made.

Why the change in attitude? To a degree, he had spent twenty years crying all the way to the bank. The perception of Spielberg was all but set in cement: "In terms of the pleasure that technical assurance gives an audience . . . Spielberg really has it," Kael remarked, "but he may be so full of it that he doesn't have much else." A friend like writer Lawrence Kasdan *(Raiders of the Lost Ark)* could give this a positive spin, insisting: "I don't think anyone in the world moves a camera better than Steven does. No one else has that kind of innate talent for what really works in terms of exciting the eye." The other extreme view was expressed, on the set of *Jaws,* by author Peter Benchley. Sensing that the people in his book and their adult (even adulterous) relationships were being simplified for the sake of cinematic razzle-dazzle, he cynically commented: "One day, Spielberg will be known as the greatest second-unit director in America."

In a *New York Times* attack, Stephen Farber lamented:

Spielberg (and other movie brats) have been weaned on old Hollywood movies, and they want to re-create the schlock that once mesmerized the masses. They have good memories, and a shrewd commercial instinct. These young film freaks have often been handling cameras since the age of three, and they know everything there is to know about lenses, filters, color stock, and solarization. Unfortunately, they are ignorant of everything else. They haven't had time to read a book; they are technical wizards with pea-sized brains.

His words may sound unnecessarily cruel. Yet Spielberg himself allowed the comment a certain viability: "I was not a reader, and I'm still not a reader. I don't like reading. I have not read for pleasure in many, many years. That's sort of a shame. I think I am really part of the Eisenhower generation of television."

In due time, Spielberg would become self-conscious about that admission, attempting to simultaneously expand his own range and answer critics via more substantial films, including ones based on serious works of literature: *The Color Purple; Schindler's List.* Meanwhile, there was always the pleasure to be had in watching his lighter films. *Time*'s Frank Rich, analyzing *Close Encounters of the Third Kind,* marveled at "the breathless wonder the director brings to every frame. . . . Spielberg seems to be looking at everything as if for the first time. . . . a celebration of innocence." Those same words could

OF ANIMATION AND DINOSAURS: Spielberg has often employed cartoons about prehistoric beasts to convey his recurring themes. In *The Land Before Time* (*left*, courtesy Universal Studios and Amblin Entertainment), brontosaurus parents attempt to maintain their family values, and care for their child despite changing natural phenomena. In *We're Back: A Dinosaur's Story* (*right*), a toned-down version of the Jurassic Park T-rex travels back to the future (courtesy Universal Studios and Amblin Entertainment, Inc.).

accurately describe *E.T.* and other early Spielberg vehicles, leading to a consensus that Spielberg possessed an overly benign view of life, tagged once and for all in 1977 by *Newsweek*'s Jack Kroll as "Spielberg's optimism." Spielberg acquiesced, once telling an interviewer: "I have a bubble-gum outlook on life." Kael complained about "an excess of kindness," while Andrew Sarris, writing favorably about *E.T.* and *Poltergeist* in 1981, admitted: "I cannot help feeling that Spielberg remains a somewhat regressive force in the American cinema . . . creating fairy tales that serve not so much as rites of passage as pleas for a permanent childhood." Kael put it even more bluntly: "It's not so much what Spielberg has done but what he has encouraged. Everyone else has imitated his fantasies, and the result is an infantilization of the culture."

Initially, none of this seemed to bother him. In 1979, when *Time* brought up the issue of "popcorn" pictures, Spielberg calmly replied: "It's what I've chosen to do. I like to see people jump out of their seats. In that sense, I'm as much of a whore as the vaudevillians were, and proud of it." Sometime thereafter, a *New York Times* interviewer asked if he were unable to make small, intimate pictures about human relationships. Spielberg reportedly grew "incensed," insisting: "If you look at my body of work on television, you will see that nearly all of my films dealt with people stories. I hope the next film I do is a comedy with no car chases and no special effects." In fact, he instead set to work on the *Indiana Jones* trilogy.

When *L.A. Weekly* inquired, in light of *Poltergeist*'s ghosts, what personally scared him the most, Spielberg momentarily thought about elevators (he has always been terrified about flying downward rather than up), then

abruptly stated: "Relationships." Intriguingly, what he saw as his problem in real life was precisely what critics perceived as the abiding weakness in his movies. Throughout the mid-1970s, Spielberg had seriously dated actress Amy Irving, though they suddenly split while in Japan, after flying off excitedly, planning to be married there. Spielberg, who would not explain what went wrong, didn't try to hide from his friends the fact that this had been a traumatic experience. In 1980, he began dating Kathleen Carey, a signer of songwriters at Warner Bros. Music. "I think Kathleen and I will have kids,"

Spielberg later said. "I made *E.T.* because I'm a frustrated parent. I want some of my own."

Those dreams would end, at least with Carey. As difficult as their parting would prove for the director, he nonetheless realized that all experiences, however painful, were useful to him as an artist, later admitting:

I cried for the first time in ages. The human being in me was pouring the tears out. But the doggone filmmaker in me ran to the other room, grabbed my instamatic, and took a picture of myself in the mirror. I had to have it on record. Actually, I can't imagine not being a filmmaker.

It became ever more difficult—impossible, even—for Spielberg to separate the moviemaker element of his self from his human side. "I often want to direct reality," he admitted, "to direct the [real-life] scene, to say, 'Stay in your frame. I'll deal with it, but stay there.' " He knew it was time to take on adult responsibilities. ("I want to stop having kids on the screen and have them in real life," he told interviewer Myra Forsberg.) He and Irving reconciled, and on June 12, 1985, she gave birth to their child,

Max. Once more, life and film had a strange way of intertwining. Irving went into labor as he was filming take three of Celie's birthing scene with which *The Color Purple* opens. Even as Spielberg finished shooting that sequence, his assistant director broke in to tell him Amy was on the phone and had, upon learning that filming was completed, said: "Okay, tell him to come home and deliver my baby now."

The story contains the seeds of why that relationship would not last: However wry and dry Irving's sense of humor, her statement suggests an implicit understanding that the filmmaking process would always come first, her needs as a woman, or as a person, second. "I ingest it while I make it," he admitted in 1982 of whatever project he might be working on. "That's all I think about." His words again bring to mind Charles Foster Kane running off to the newspaper office at all hours, smilingly assuring his wife that there's been no infidelity: "My dear, your only correspondent is the *Enquirer*." She sighs and says: "Sometimes I'd prefer a rival of flesh and blood." Shortly thereafter, the Kane marriage is a shambles, and they divorce: He had run off to the office once too often.

The place to which Spielberg ran off was described by journalist Bill Davidson as "a shabby one-story little bil-ious-green building nestled just outside the walls of the vast Burbank Studios—an ex-storage facility—housing Spielberg's 'A-Team Productions,'" an operation he ran from the confines of his tan-and-brown office "which matches, in decrepitude, the exterior of the A-Team building." Like Kane, Spielberg lived in an unfathomably luxurious home. Initially, he and Irving shared the pleasant, unpretentious Coldwater Canyon house he had purchased for $49,500; parked outside was his car, a bullet-riddled heap he had spent four hundred dollars to salvage from the *Sugarland Express* shoot. That humble abode had given way to a fourteen-room lumber-and-fieldstone

STEVEN SPIELBERG PRESENTS: In addition to writing and directing, Spielberg has (like idols Walt Disney and Alfred Hitchcock) emerged as a "producer" and "presenter" of numerous entertainments blessed with his seal of approval but that he is too busy to personally make. Spielberg relaxes with Barry Levinson (*left*, courtesy Paramount Pictures) on the set of *Young Sherlock Holmes*, and chats with Clint Eastwood (*right*, courtesy NBC-TV), who directed an *Amazing Stories* segment for Spielberg's 1985–87 series.

23

mansion in Beverly Hills, complete with a housekeeper who prepared tea for visitors. In the driveway outside, his green Porsche sat, waiting for the weekend when it would whisk the couple away to their Malibu beach house.

Their lifestyle seemed, for a while, perfect: Since Spielberg didn't smoke, drink, or do drugs, the couple avoided chic parties, remaining at home together, enjoying films, video games, and lots of junk food. They were so anti-chichi that even upscale pizza was a no-no: "I like pizza that curls at the edge like Aladdin's shoes," Spielberg said. Though they were married on Thanksgiving Eve of that year, rumors of discord began soon after. What went wrong? Close friend Richard Dreyfuss analyzed the director's personality this way: "He's a big kid who at twelve years old decided to make movies, and (on some level) he's still twelve years old—he's focused every one of his powers and capabilities on making movies and blocked everything else in the world out." Eventually, the marriage crumbled, causing him trauma, even anguish. But the hard times personally did not interfere with the creative process. "I do my best work when I'm in the pits emotionally. It's okay because my creative juices don't flow as well when I'm happy. The only time I feel totally happy is when I'm watching films or making them."

Making films had long since ceased to be synonymous with direction. Spielberg had—in part by conscious conception, in part by natural vent of his enormous talent—transformed into a virtual institution. *Saturday Review* marveled that he had long since become "the most convincing incarnation of the boy genius to hit Hollywood since Irving Thalberg." He served as executive producer not only for a wide array of movies but also TV shows—everything from expensive prime-time experiments *(Amazing Stories)* to afternoon cartoon shows *(Tiny Toons)*. He had always been highly committed to giving young talent a first shot, using American Film Institute apprentices as assistants, allowing his name to be attached, in some capacity, to projects by aspiring film-school grads, beginning with *I Wanna Hold Your Hand* in 1978. When he suggested that he'd be interested in preparing a TV-anthology show on the order of the ones his idols Rod Serling, Alfred Hitchcock, and Walt Disney had years ago presented, NBC was so overawed at the possibility that they immediately gave him a two-year, forty-four-show deal, offering him a budget of nearly $1 million per hour-long installment at a time when the norm would have been $350,000. He was not just an industry titan but *the* reigning industry titan.

The bilious-green building gave way to Amblin's new offices on the Universal lot: a Santa Fe adobe mission that Spielberg designed himself and Universal's parent company, MCA, paid more than $3.5 million to complete. When *Rolling Stone*'s Lynn Hirschberg visited, the reporter noted a game room, movie theater, and fishpond as well as full kitchen, gym, and vegetable garden. Spielberg admitted that he considered the place not just

an office but his true "home," the place that had "centered my life." "Amblin doesn't seem so much a building as a world unto itself," Hirschberg marveled.

The building struck some as a southwestern Xanadu; In *Citizen Kane,* the character Jed Leland said of his one-time friend, the title character, a control freak: "He didn't like the world, so he built one of his own, an absolute monarchy." Likewise, Hirschberg noted: "Spielberg is insulated here; there's something or someone to take care of his every need." The man who touched the masses had become something of a recluse despite a second, happier marriage to actress Kate Capshaw. He was a paradox: "A very enclosed person who makes open, impersonal movies" is how Spielberg described himself in 1978. The contrast between withdrawn person and easily accessible artist foreshadows another paradox, which Spielberg himself addressed in answer to a question about his supposed "innocence": "I think I'm an innocent. Well, I'm a cynical innocent. I can get to the purity of innocence when I really work at it. It's harder to remain an innocent—both in real life and the motion-picture industry—because things rob you every year of this kind of healthy naïveté. Actually, I think it's optimism more than innocence. This feeling positive about things, feeling that all's well that ends well. And I've always felt that."

The duality he suggests in his own personality would manifest itself in the heroes he created: Sheriff Brody, Indiana Jones, and Oskar Schindler each have an innocent, open side and a darker, Machiavellian one. Spielberg may appear remarkably childlike, but Hollywood has consistently gobbled up and spit out the remains of those truly innocent people who come there to work. Spielberg, on the other hand, not only survived but also flourished. He may have had an innocent element, yet there was always the archmanipulator as well. William Link, who with Richard Levinson created the *Columbo* series, later recalled of their then twenty-one-year-old boy director: "Even then, we knew we would all be working for him someday. He was a great politician."

One incident from that time reveals something of the cynic lurking just beneath the surface naïf. On his first job, directing Joan Crawford's *Night Gallery* segment, he appeared a bright, adoring, almost worshipful fan of the veteran star, bringing her flowers on the set, going so far as to put a rose in a Pepsi bottle, for she was that company's chairman. The elderly star, now somewhat insecure, was totally charmed, putting aside her concerns about his lack of experience. A scant five years later, Spielberg glibly admitted, during a seminar at the American Film Institute and Center for Advanced Film Studies: "I put the day of the week on the Pepsi bottle, and each day I'd give her one. She didn't know it was a countdown; I couldn't wait to get off the picture. Oh, yeah, I did a lot of that bullshit." No wonder, then, that in 1986 *TV Guide* argued that despite the widely held image of Spielberg as guileless, he was in fact "a consummate Hollywood operator."

On the bright side, Spielberg never forgot a friend.

Allen Daviau had agreed to do the cinematography on *Amblin',* though Spielberg could pay him little, insisting that if he ever made it big, he'd see to it that Daviau was eventually rewarded. *Amblin'* propelled Spielberg into the big leagues, but for his first theatrical features, the young director requested a highly experienced crew, realizing he would need all the professional support he could get. Daviau, assuming he had been left behind, drifted into the déclassé world of industrial films and TV commercials. Five features later, Spielberg sensed he now had enough command of his medium that he did not need to rely on famous craftsmen. Though twelve years had elapsed, Spielberg tracked down Daviau and offered him the job of photographing *E.T.,* immediately establishing Daviau as one of Hollywood's hottest cinematographers.

And why so generous with newcomers? Spielberg realized that in his current position of power it was only fair to give back some of what he had received. Recalling what Sheinberg and several others had done for him, he stated that his success "all boiled down to coming across a couple of people who were willing to give me a chance. It's always that way . . . you can't get the break unless somebody decides to be your godfather or godmother, and that's the problem." His approach to Daviau,

Zemeckis, and Chris Columbus (the writer of *Gremlins*) makes clear that it was a problem he wanted to help solve.

Moreover, in these people, Spielberg may have been attempting to re-create for himself the sense of family he had lost along the way. Ironically, moviemaking forced him to repeat, over and over again as an adult, the most despised ritual of his unhappy childhood: moving. "On a film," his sister Anne explained, "the people involved become his family. He loves them, and he hates for it to be done and to leave." From this perspective, his life sounds like a *Twilight Zone* episode with an ironic twist for the hero who sets out to avoid something painful, only to find himself in a situation that causes him to live it over and over again.

But if Spielberg's brighter half never lets him forget a friend, his dark side never allows him to forget an enemy—or a perceived one. While Frank Price was running Columbia, Spielberg submitted the *E.T.* concept, only to have Price rudely reject it as something that would appeal only to kids. Years later, Price was chairman of the movie division at Universal, the studio that had green-lighted *E.T.* Price would have happily let bygones be bygones. Spielberg instead insisted that a clause be inserted in his contract stating he would not ever have

THE ARTIST AS SHOWMAN: Like idol Alfred Hitchcock, seen here (*left*) shamelessly drumming up publicity for *The Birds,* (courtesy Universal Pictures) Spielberg has never minded doing publicity stunts that more serious-minded filmmakers, such as Martin Scorsese, wouldn't even consider. (*Below*) Spielberg poses with his creature from *Jaws.*

to negotiate with Price about anything or, for that matter, even speak to the man. That may not have been the only reason why Price eventually resigned, or even the main reason, but it was one of them.

Perhaps Spielberg's duality can best be seen in the different cases of two women who came to work for him in secretarial capacities. Kathy Switzer, who held that position for one year, later stated: "It was so easy to disappoint him. You could perform miracles, and it was never enough. There was never a 'good job.' Instead, it was: 'Couldn't you have gone just one step further and had me made God?' " Of course, it could be argued that such uncharitable comments derived from her bitterness. Spielberg simply demanded the extreme in excellence and total dedication from every team member. Kathleen Kennedy also began working for Spielberg in a secretarial capacity, but when she proved able to perform those required miracles, she was quickly promoted to producer and high-ranking executive at Amblin. In his defense, a former associate admitted: "His attitude is, this is the best job in Hollywood, and you'd better appreciate it."

Speaking to a former employee who had just resigned after finding she could not satisfy her boss's demands, Spielberg's own mother laughingly inquired of the young woman: "Have you ceased to exist yet?"

A Hollywood insider concurs: "People are scared of him, and he assumes a huge place in people's minds. They see him like a god." Which explains why Spielberg was again and again passed over for the Best Director Oscar. In the case of *E.T.,* that could be written off as one more example of Hollywood preferring to hand the award to someone who had made a "serious" film rather than an escapist one, the statuette going to Sir Richard Attenborough for *Gandhi*. Then came *The Color Purple* and the ultimate snub: Spielberg wasn't even nominated for Best Director, the only director whose film was up for Best Picture of the Year to be so ignored.

At that point, there was no denying a backlash not only from intellectual critics but also within the movie industry itself. While preparing a magazine feature on the filmmaker, Richard Turner noted: "I'd tell people I was doing a story on Spielberg; they'd say, 'I hate that guy,' but wouldn't be able to say quite why—maybe something about how he had fulfilled every fantasy and ambition but still looked like a kid at the Science Fair." That may have been base jealousy and resentment over Spielberg's remarkable commercial success. Or, as Turner put it: "No one questioned Spielberg's technical and visual genius as a director; they just complained because he was a vaguely unpleasant guy sometimes. It bugged them to see his press clippings portray some sort of friendly elf."

THE WINNER, AT LONG LAST: Slow but steady wins the race, as, after years of being ignored at Oscar time, in 1994 Spielberg won both the Golden Globe and the Academy Award for Best Director for *Schindler's List*, a film that most critics hailed as the beginning of his "mature" period as a filmmaker. Here, he receives the Irving Thalberg Award, an earlier compensation for not having been nominated in the Best Director category.

That duality could clearly be seen, by the mid-eighties, at his Universal office suite. Framed by the entrance was a plaque honoring the Boy Scouts and signed by Jimmy Stewart; a Norman Rockwell painting hung nearby. The paired items suggested an idealized memory of Middle American childhood, the romanticized image of a decent, spanking-clean, bygone small-town America that Disney earlier actualized in his theme park's Main Street, U.S.A. Yet deep within the office itself, nearly lost amid a myriad of toys (much like the Rosebud sled, stuck amid Charles Foster Kane's accumulated treasures), there sat a gross rubber heart with an exposed aorta that pulsed in and out. The "toy" resembled the exposed heart in *Indiana Jones and the Temple of Doom,* a movie which outraged parents who had brought their children expecting the modern Walt Disney, getting instead the equivalent of Hitchcock's shower scene. That pulsating heart—in the office, in the movie—represented the dark side of Spielberg.

A huge golden retriever stalked the halls of the office, adding to a sensation that inside, the Eagle Scout still stood proud: a boy and his dog. A former associate explained that he "lacked social graces" and rarely spoke with employees in the halls. "He never asks anybody about their personal lives. His only subject of conversation is the movies." Possibly, though, this average person failed to realize that a genius is often unaware of his surroundings, always fixating on the next work.

Still, there were hints that an attempt was being made to grow up: Assorted candies, once available everywhere in the office and allowing workers to indulge constantly like unbridled children, were by 1986 replaced with plates of fresh vegetables, which, as any parent can explain, are good for you. Also "good for him" was a project of considerable substance, one he had been considering, then consciously avoiding, for years: a movie about the Holocaust, a true story that would make demands on his talent.

In 1981, he had announced: "I'll probably never win an Oscar, but I'll sure have a lot of fun. I really believe that movies are the great escape." Twelve years later, he would not have made such a statement. He might never give up his playtime, personally or professionally, but one must become an adult, face responsibilities, even as his own personal variation on Peter Pan had done in *Hook.* A Holocaust film demanded that the "benign" director stare evil in the eye. So *Schindler's List* served as the necessary final testing of Spielberg's radical innocence: Would he retain his now legendary optimism while making a movie about such horror? Could he maintain a delicate balance between his own unique sensibility and the facts in the case? On some level, he sensed it was the movie he had to do, both as a Jew and a son who wanted to make his mother proud of him on more than a facile, show-offy, grandstanding level ("Look, Ma—I'm tracking!"), making it clear that he had learned from that strict upbringing the importance of taking his heritage and drawing on it for his work.

Still, it had to be a Spielberg film, more serious in intent than any he had previously presented, though at one with his body of work. The Schindler story may have seemed a far reach for someone long since typecast as a director of cars, sharks, and UFOs, though in truth that was only a superficial assessment of what he had been trying to get at for twenty years. Good film drama, he insisted, concerns "a protagonist who is no longer in control of his life, who loses control, and then has to somehow regain it." That statement did describe *Schindler's List,* though it is also an appropriate starting point for a deeper understanding of all the movies he made on the way to his Oscar.

THE FILMS

Duel

The debuting director: Steven Spielberg, sporting a cowboy hat not unlike those worn by so many golden-age Hollywood directors (courtesy Universal Pictures).

A UNIVERSAL RELEASE, 1971/1973/1983

CAST

Dennis Weaver *(David Mann);* Jacqueline Scott *(Mrs. Mann);* Eddie Firestone *(Cafe Owner);* Gene Dynarski *(Man in Cafe);* Tim Herbert *(Gas Station Attendant);* Charles Peel *(Elderly Man);* Alexander Lockwood *(Man in Car);* Amy Douglass *(Woman in Car);* Shirley O'Hara *(Waitress);* Lucille Benson *(Snakerama Lady);* Lou Frizzell *(Bus Driver);* Carey Loftin *(Truck Driver);* Dale Van Sickel *(Car Driver).*

CREDITS

Director, Steven Spielberg; writer, Richard Matheson; cinematography, Jack A. Marta; art direction, Robert S. Smith; sound, Edwin S. Hall; assistant director, Jim Fargo; editor, Frank Morriss; stunt coordinator, Carey Loftin; music, Billy Goldenberg; producer, George Eckstein; color, Technicolor; running time, 73 mins. (1971), 88 mins. (1973, Europe only), 90 mins. (U.S. theatrical); rating (1983): PG.

Duel was conceived of, filmed for, then broadcast as a made-for-TV movie in 1971, so its inclusion here may seem questionable. Still, two years after its American broadcast, *Duel* was widely seen as a feature in Europe; then, in 1983, it received an American theatrical release. Shot in sixteen days for a cost of $425,000 (unheard of for films other than cheap B-pictures, though the norm for TV movies at that time), *Duel* told a powerful story about a traveling businessman who finds himself drawn into an unwanted, inescapable, ever-escalating battle of wits with the menacing driver of an immense truck. Barely seen, the driver's shadowy presence transforms him into a symbol of motiveless evil. He first baits the hapless hero David Mann (Dennis Weaver) into passing him, then tries to force Mann off the road, adding to the growing sense that a relatively realistic tale is spilling over into allegory.

Spielberg's secretary discovered Richard Matheson's short story in *Playboy* and, sensing that this was something her boss might want to produce, passed it on to him. She was right: Learning that Universal already owned the rights to *Duel,* Spielberg attempted to interest the studio

In his first film, Spielberg made effective use of a rear-view mirror; he would eventually develop this concept into the greatest single visual gag in *Jurassic Park* (courtesy Universal Films/Universal TV).

in a theatrical feature, allowing him to direct. They agreed, but only if Gregory Peck would commit. When Peck said no, *Duel* was relegated to TV- movie fare, though Spielberg was given the go-ahead. He became involved during the time period when Matheson was writing the script, though Spielberg did not consult with him during the writing process. Methodically, he blocked out the entire film on IBM cards, the first time he tried what would become his regular approach. Each card contained the gist of the scene, the angle he would take on it, and how many camera setups he needed. While filming in Lancaster, he assembled those cards on a huge bulletin board in his motel room. Rather than opening the script to the day's page, he would instead take down several cards. They constituted the day's work, and when each scene was finished, he would tear the card up and throw it away, knowing every night, by glancing at the bulletin board, how much was left to complete.

In addition to cards, he had his art director sketch the entire film on one long mural that arced around the motel room, an aerial view portraying every moment in the movie, including chases. Never a great reader, Spielberg liked to avoid referring to his script and memorizing

Mann versus machine (courtesy Universal Pictures).

31

The monster truck (Dennis Weaver as the traveling salesman; courtesy Universal Pictures).

blocks of words, preferring to study this visual panorama, locking himself into it before filming any one day. The voice-overs by the hero were shot as Matheson had written them, though more than 50 percent were cut for the European version. So that they would match up with Dennis Weaver's facial expressions, Spielberg had the actor recite the voice-overs into a Nagra tape recorder each morning, then play them back, inside the car, while filming close-up shots of Weaver's reaction to what he had said. The original American TV print was without the scene involving the school bus and also did not include the early phone call home by David Mann to his wife. Though these scenes are highly characteristic of Spielberg's future work, he has insisted that he did not want them in the movie; they were edited in for the expanded version.

Essentially a two-character drama, *Duel* was ecstatically received by critics and fared so well in the ratings that Universal executives allowed young Spielberg to begin work on a theatrical film of his choosing, *The Sugarland Express*. Following a highly successful decade, Spielberg hit a career peak in 1982, when *E.T.* and *Poltergeist* were released simultaneously. Suddenly, he was the best-known filmmaker in America, the only film director of his time who, like his idols Walt Disney and Alfred Hitchcock, was immediately recognizable to the public, thanks to cover photos on *Time* and *Newsweek*. It isn't hard to grasp, then, why Universal would choose to buy back the television rights to *Duel,* which had for years been playing on TV stations around the country.

The company was betting that *Duel* would prove the old adage that absence makes the heart grow fonder, withholding it and thereby creating a public hunger. Though *Duel* ran a mere 73 minutes, Universal had in 1971 requested a longer version (88 minutes), released theatrically abroad. There was nothing particularly innovative about this; expanded American TV movies glutted movie-starved Third World countries without TV. Noteworthy, however, was the critical acclaim. *Duel* won the Grand Prix de Festival Award at the Festival de Cinema Fantastique in the trendy ski resort town of Avoriaz, France, in February 1973; Spielberg himself received the Cariddi D'Oro for his direction (the film was named Best Opera Prima) at the Taormina Film Festival in Rome in mid-July, a first ever for a TV movie. *Duel* also allowed Spielberg to learn firsthand how serious Europeans can be about movies and their own interpretations of them. After the screening in Rome, four highly politicized critics stormed out of the press conference when Spielberg refused to bow to their insistence that the only way to understand *Duel* was as a Communist-inspired portrait of the blue-collar class (the man in the truck) striking back against the white-collar class (the man in the car) that had oppressed them.

In February 1983, Universal's then president Bob

Rehme announced that America would finally get to see *Duel* on the big screen. Convinced a longer cut had "great potential as a theatrical release in this country," he decided to test-market *Duel* (now expanded from the European cut by two additional minutes) in the Midwest, closely monitoring its performance, then devise a strategy for national release. However, when the film opened in Cincinnati and Kansas City a few months later, business was disappointing, causing Universal to scuttle plans. William C. Soady, general sales manager and executive vice president at Universal, had to concede that in spite of unquestioned high quality, the public was not willing to pay to see a TV film.

Soady had become interested in releasing *Duel* theatrically when an exhibitor who regularly booked movies into New York City art houses inquired if it might be available, believing *Duel* had real potential on the upper East Side, where film-buff audiences regularly lined up for cult films. *Duel* did indeed play in April of that year at the Manhattan 1 on Fifty-ninth Street. Janet Maslin of the *New York Times* wrote that "it works as well on the wide screen as it did on the small one. Even without benefit of hindsight, *Duel* looks like the work of an unusually talented young director." Maslin also claimed that "*Duel* might almost have been a silent film, because it expresses so much through action and so little through the words." However, like the finest Hitchcock thrillers, *Duel* is as totally reliant on sound as it is nearly devoid of words. The contrasting engines of the sad, small car and the huge, threatening truck, as well as the strikingly authentic, highly expressive noises heard in each of the

hamlets both drivers pass through, are effectively blended with the evocative music. The film's edge-of-your-seat suspense derives as much from its sounds as its sights, which would likewise be true of the director's future films.

Maslin was correct in suggesting that the hero did not need externalized soliloquies, which "only awkwardly express Mann's anxiety." Mann mutters things like "Twenty, twenty-five minutes out of your whole life and then all the ropes that kept you hangin' in there are cut loose. And there you are, back in the jungle again." Such spoken words only make embarrassingly obvious what had been effectively suggested in facial expressions and body language; hearing the idea stated only hits us over the head with a storytelling sledgehammer. But that is a flaw in Richard Matheson's script.

Though it was screenwriter Matheson who chose to call the focal character "Mann," the connection to the director's then-forthcoming body of work cannot be dismissed. In film after film, Spielberg's leading character would be a modern Everyman, the ordinary guy (or girl) who rises to heroic proportions by choosing to fight back against seemingly unconquerable adversity. While the circumstances may be extraordinary, they are not contrived; the Spielberg hero confronts something basic and universal, a repressed nightmare that has been swimming around the edges of his waking hours ever since he can remember.

Spielberg has taken our universal fears and actualized them on-screen. Not surprisingly, then, J. Hoberman in 1983 chose to retrospectively view the truck in *Duel* as a

David Mann in a state of panic. Like so many Hitchcock heroes, Spielberg's protagonists are ordinary men who find themselves in extraordinary situations (courtesy Universal Films/Universal TV).

Hitchcock once confided that he'd like to make an entire movie in a telephone booth; for one unforgettable sequence in *Duel*, Spielberg partially realized that ambition (courtesy Universal Films/Universal TV).

precursor of things to come: "an ancient, exhaust-belching rig with a never-shown driver, that proves only slightly less malevolent than the aquatic villain of *Jaws*." Hoberman added that "auteurists will note Weaver's briefly glimpsed home is typical Spielberg—one harried hausfrau presiding over a living room cluttered with boys, toy helicopters, and windup robots." In fact, *Duel* is not merely an impersonal exercise in technical prowess that reveals talent in embryo; it is part and parcel of the filmmaker's emerging vision, a fitting starting point for in-depth analysis.

Duel begins with a totally blank screen, ending ninety minutes later with a daylight image so bright that all color appears washed out by harsh sunlight. As organized by Spielberg, Matheson's elements are visually transformed from an exciting, if essentially superficial, story of flight into a tale of biblical simplicity in which the main character undergoes a metamorphosis from darkness to light, understanding himself and his world in a way his glib, typical, narrow orientation did not previously allow. Our first sight is of a southwestern stretch of suburbia, the kind of neighborhood that will be revisited in *E.T., Poltergeist,* and a half-dozen other films. More importantly, in the opening we witness the desertion of such a home by the husband-father. Though he is ostensibly leaving on a brief business trip, we shortly learn

Dennis Weaver as David Mann ducks even as the unseen truck driver smashes into a phone booth, destroying the possibility of communication (courtesy Universal Pictures).

that there is turbulence between Mann and his wife. Implied, if not emphasized, is the possibility that the husband may run for the border and never return; he could, for all intents and purposes, be the missing husband in *E.T.,* now living "in Mexico with 'Sally.'" He is the nightmare image of the deserting father figure who haunts Spielberg's films.

We do not at first see the man, but view the house from his point of view; that he drives faster than necessary, barely slowing down for a stop sign at the street's end, adds to the immediate sensation that things are not as normal as they first appear. He turns on the car radio; the combination of music, advertising jingles, and voices—commingled with the sounds of other vehicles on the road around him—conspire to create the kind of "din" (the oppressive collective noise of everyday mechanical and natural reality) that will play a key role in Spielberg's work. When he settles on a radio talk show, it happens to be one in which dysfunctional modern marriages are discussed at length, specifically by distraught husbands.

"I'm not the head of the family," one particularly incensed male keeps repeating, "yet I am the man of the family." He states and restates this idea until what was initially a bit of realistic detail is transformed into an expression of what the film is all about: the fear of modern man (the radio caller, David Mann, any male viewer watching *Duel*) that he has lost a position of power in his home, is no longer masculine in ways men previously were expected to be. One wonders what the last words spoken by Spielberg's father before deserting the home may have been; it would not be surprising to learn that Steven recalls hearing, "I'm not the head of the family, yet I am the man of the family!" before his Dad walked out.

Then we briefly encounter the first of Spielberg's wife-mother figures as the camera cuts to the interior of the Mann home. Mrs. Mann (Jacqueline Scott) maintains an even tone while speaking on the phone from the typical living room, which precisely presages the many similar rooms to follow. "If we talk about it, we'll just get into a fight," she calmly explains, apparently having suffered through and survived many such arguments in the past. Mrs. Mann is surrounded by the kids, playing on the floor with robot toys that likewise presage the *Star Wars* figures future Spielberg kids will collect. Though the children must hear the subterfuge in Mom's voice, they ignore it, continuing their game with childish intensity; it isn't hard to imagine Spielberg drawing this image out of his own memory. When the conversation concludes, David appears devastated, literally stumbling away from the pay phone. It is clear now that the show he listened to on the radio was less an aural window into the world than a mirror of his own psyche; though a tall, masculine-looking fellow (star Weaver was best known for action-hero roles on TV shows like *Gunsmoke* and *McCloud*), David Mann is a little guy emotionally.

In this context, Maslin noted that "minor characters, at the various stops Mann makes along the highway, look uniformly freakish." This observation seems short-sighted, however. In fact, only the last—the Snakerama Lady—is a true eccentric, with her bizarre little front-yard zoo filled with assorted creatures. The first small community David drives through is the polar opposite of eccentricity; though located deep in the Southwest, it boasts white picket fences of the type we'd expect to see in the Midwest. David smashes into one, after which he is attended to by well-meaning, conventional people. The notion that David drives from one outlandish, isolated community to the next is, simply, wrong; more correctly, his journey takes him from the traditional through the marginal (a truck stop/diner) to a little circus that Dr. Lao would be proud to own.

Each of the stops mirrors the state of David's mind at that point. Indeed, the journey transforms into an odyssey, a physical trip symbolizing the central character's inner journey. David Mann has reached a different point in his life at the conclusion; essentially, he conquers something "out there" that represents the fear within and, having conquered that, finally becomes whole.

How effective, then, that Spielberg begins the film with tightly edited shots of David's face or other body parts (an arm, the torso, etc.), though by mid-movie we regularly see medium shots of David. At the end, the camera at last allows us to view him in full shot, standing alone. Other Spielberg themes are present, including those that connect him to both his key idols, Alfred Hitchcock and Walt Disney. In a notably Hitchcockian sequence, David sits at a booth in a diner, glancing at the lunch counter, where a line of nearly identical truckers sit; since the menacing diesel is parked outside, he knows one of these men must be the would-be killer. David looks for clues, noticing the black cowboy boots he spotted earlier when his antagonist stopped for gas; his moment of elation, certain he has at last isolated his enemy, is short-lived, for he then notices they all wear identical boots.

The sequence is psychological; David convinces himself it must be one, then another, of the men, owing to their looking askance at him, never realizing that their curiosity is due to the strange way in which he is acting. When he finally becomes hysterical and confronts a fellow he has decided must be the menacing driver, it turns out to be the wrong man; David is literally thrown out of the diner, like a Hitchcock hero who, in trying to point out a mad villain, himself appears mad. The sequence is practically wordless, though Spielberg's ability to edit not only images but also marry sound to images makes it memorable.

Later, there is a sequence involving children that foreshadows the important role kids will play in Spielberg's films via a Disneyesque interlude. Thinking the truck has passed him and gone up a winding mountain road, David stops to help when he encounters a stalled school bus in need of a push. The children swarm all over him, leaping up on the hood of his car, something he becomes particularly ornery about, concerned (still the typical suburban male despite the life-threatening horrors he has experienced) that it might be dented. When the monster truck appears, David shocks the bus driver and kids by desperately rushing away, though the truck driver will, before pursuing David, take time out to give the bus a push, much to the delight of the children.

Spielberg would, throughout his career, veer back and forth between the polar extremes of Hitchcock and Disney, occasionally fusing elements of the two in a single film.

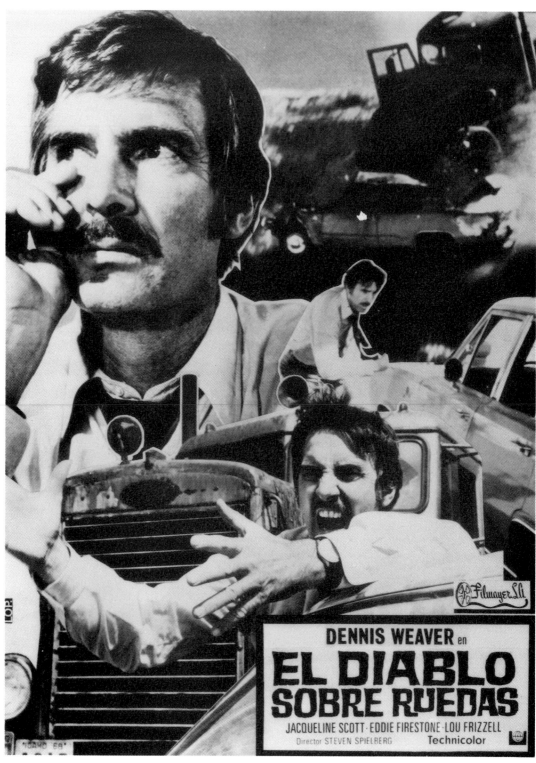

DENNIS WEAVER en
EL DIABLO SOBRE RUEDAS
JACQUELINE SCOTT · EDDIE FIRESTONE · LOU FRIZZELL
Director STEVEN SPIELBERG   Technicolor

A poster advertising the Spanish theatrical release; whereas overly talky American movies often have a hard time in rural European areas and Third World countries, a movie like *Duel* (which communicates almost without words, on the level of "pure cinema," all sound and action) was a huge hit (courtesy Universal Pictures).

The Sugarland Express

A UNIVERSAL RELEASE, 1974

CAST

Goldie Hawn *(Lou Jean Poplin);* Ben Johnson *(Captain Tanner);* Michael Sacks *(Slide);* William Atherton *(Clovis Poplin);* Louise Latham *(Mrs. Livvy).*

CREDITS

Director, Steven Spielberg; writers, Hal Barwood and Matthew Robbins, from a story by Barwood and Spielberg; cinematography, Vilmos Zsigmond; film editors, Verna Fields and Ward M. Abroms; music, John Williams; producers, Richard D. Zanuck and David Brown; running time, 109 mins; rating: PG.

The brass at Universal decided in 1973 that Spielberg ought to make his theatrical directing debut with *The Sugarland Express,* an idea for a fact-based film he had submitted several years earlier. Hoping to typecast their new boy genius, Universal—well aware of the phenomenal impact of *Duel*—noted the surface similarity between that film's concentration on cars in conflict and the parallel one in *The Sugarland Express.* Little did they realize that what had drawn Spielberg to this factual material was the theme of motherhood, the basis for most future Spielberg projects.

Fervently convinced of the talent of two young writer-friends, Hal Barwood and Matthew Robbins, Spielberg shared with them his concept: a pair of harmless criminals (real names, Ila Faye Dent and her husband, Bobby) and their doomed effort to retrieve their baby from a foster home. Basically, Spielberg hoped for a trade-off: He'd make the movie he wanted to make about motherhood at the price of providing the audience with a good car-crash show, balancing people with pyrotechnics; everyone would go home happy. Originally, the project was to be called *Carte Blanche,* then *American Express.* All three

Of life and movies: Following the completion of *The Sugarland Express,* Spielberg bought the film's bullet-ridden car for $700, then drove it around L.A. for several years (courtesy Tom Zito, *Washington Post*).

Goldie Hawn as Lou Jean Poplin: Spielberg considered it his key task to tone down Goldie's giggly-girlish image and draw from her a more complicated psychological portrait than people generally expected (courtesy Universal City Studios Inc.).

The dysfunctional family: As African-American families chat to their left and white families do the same on the right, Lou Jean and her estranged husband, Clovis (William Atherton), are caught between two worlds, outsiders who confront their personal problems on prison visiting day (courtesy Universal Pictures).

set up the movie's plot and characters on IBM cards, after which the two writers went off on their own and penned the script.

The studio wanted a hit, so even after all this work, Spielberg kept hearing: "If you don't get Goldie Hawn, we don't make the picture." Such a big name was a necessity; fortunately, the actress was interested in doing a straight dramatic role to counteract her typecasting as a giddy comedienne. Spielberg always felt that his greatest challenge would be to diminish her usual fluffy-cutesy image. Once Hawn signed on, Universal earmarked this as a $1.8 million Zanuck-Brown production with three months of preproduction and sixty days of on-location shooting.

For the sake of authenticity, the entire film was done in Texas. Production commenced on January 15, 1973, with ten days in and around the Houston area. Initial photography took place in Richmond, Clodine, and Sugar Land (not the fictional Sugarland of the title). The opening

prison sequence was shot at the Beauford Jester farm. The crew then moved to San Antonio for six and one-half weeks (the used-car-lot shoot-out sequence was filmed here); several sequences were subsequently shot in Texas's Universal City (not the film company's similarly named L.A. theme park). Then it was on to the border town of Del Rio for a final week, filming adjacent to the then new international Amistad Dam.

As the crew moved across the state, some five thousand extras were engaged in the small towns. More than 240 cars of every imaginable description were featured. Many extras were thrilled to loan their own vehicles to the company. Fifty cars were completely demolished during crash scenes, filmed by a Corvette camera car (constructed for the filming of *Bullitt*) and a helicopter following the action from on high.

Much of what occurs takes place inside a single car. Only scant years earlier, this would have had to be filmed in a studio, utilizing rearview projection. In the early

Captain Tanner (Ben Johnson, *right*), a throwback to the old-fashioned western lawman of the nineteenth century, is interviewed by a member of the modern media about the emerging folk heroes (courtesy Universal Pictures).

1970s, such a technique had become laughable to young, visually sophisticated audiences. At first, filmmakers who wanted to place the camera inside a car had only one option: Shoot the action, then have the actors lip-synch later. Audiences had already begun to spot and resent this technique. Fortunately, Spielberg's timing was just right: Panavision Inc. had recently developed the Panaflex, the first totally noiseless camera, compact enough to be handheld or shoulder-rested. Virtually the entire film was shot in sync dialogue, with only ten lines looped later. *The Sugarland Express* was one of the first films to be shot in this then revolutionary style, though shortly, all filmmaking would follow suit.

The person in control of the camera was Vilmos Zsigmond, a world-class cinematographer who had photographed several Robert Altman films, including *McCabe & Mrs. Miller, Images,* and *The Long Goodbye.* As a TV assembly-line veteran, Spielberg was wise enough to sense that he needed to work closely with someone who could support the debuting film director with knowledge of how a movie ought to be done. Happily, the two hit it off. They allowed themselves nearly three weeks to scout locations together before filming began. At that time, Spielberg realized the starkness of the terrain. Zsigmond then admitted that he believed Spielberg's concept was too lighthearted and convinced the director to give the movie a harder edge than planned.

From Zsigmond, Spielberg learned the importance of maintaining a point of view. It is not enough for a shot to be visually dazzling; it must also mean something. Spielberg had assigned Zsigmond to shoot a scene through the car's glass window.

39

"Who's point of view is this?" the cinematographer demanded, insisting he couldn't continue until told.

"It's *my* point of view, the *director's*," Spielberg replied.

"That's smart," Zsigmond answered, "but it's not valid."

Gradually, Spielberg realized that Zsigmond was right and began allowing function rather than flamboyance to dictate his use of camera. They then shot *The Sugarland Express* in perfect continuity, owing to the fact that the gradual buildup in the size of the pursuing fleet of cars—police, vigilantes, bystanders—made it financially impossible otherwise. Near the beginning, there are only a few cars; in mid-movie, about 150; at the finale, more than 300. Since cars had to be rented for the entire period of time they'd be on call, it would have been calamitous to hire the fleet for a day, not use them the following day, then use them again, paying for all three days. So Spielberg had the rare luxury of shooting from beginning to end, making it far easier for himself and the actors to keep in mind at which point in the story they were at any given time.

One of the few major problems was getting all those cars. Ordinarily, the police might have been cooperative. Only a short time before, however, Sam Peckinpah's *Getaway* crew had been in the area; there were endless barroom brawls initiated by crew members as well as missing police radios from vehicles generously loaned to them. The anger generated by Peckinpah's rangy group was misdirected at Spielberg's hapless company, necessitating the purchase of twenty-five cars at a police auction; the authorities refused to rent, much less loan, them any. The only other major problem was the latest round of flu to breeze in from Europe, this one the London flu. At one point, nearly half the crew was incapacitated. Spielberg was hit just before they were to begin two weeks of intensive night shooting. Production ceased for only two days when star Hawn was so sick she couldn't get out of bed. As for the director, he attempted to keep the others from realizing just how sick he was in order to maintain control. "Making a movie," Spielberg would later reflect, "is an endurance contest with yourself." Especially when one is far from home.

The opening sequence offers a perfect example of Spielberg's directorial approach—technique transformed into style when dictated by substance. We first see an extreme close shot of a typical highway sign; movie buffs can hardly help but recall that, in 1941, Orson Welles likewise began his formidable career by focusing on just a sign: No Trespassing. Now, though, as Spielberg's camera slowly pulls back, we note that this sign is only one of a number vying for attention. The cautious but unrelenting camera movement carries us from what initially seems a simple road direction to confusing (even contradictory) choices which will shortly confront the film's heroine. She is the first of many: Over a twenty-year period, assorted characters residing in varied universes will realize that the seemingly simple road of life is a confounding set of possible journeys.

In this film, the focal traveler is Lou Jean Poplin. As the camera pulls back to an extreme long shot, disclosing the desolation of the terrain, a bus slowly drives up to this humble crossroads, and she steps off, alone, first peering about awkwardly, getting her bearings, then turning toward the detention center to visit her incarcerated husband, Clovis. As Lou Jean resolutely walks, Spielberg's camera pulls back, keeping her in view on the left side of the frame while gradually revealing a junked car on the right. At first, this dilapidated auto seems nothing more than a realistic bit of litter on the contemporary landscape. Eventually, it becomes clear that Spielberg is up to something more than allowing us a vivid sense of place. As Lou Jean continues walking, the camera moves at a slightly faster pace, keeping her in the frame while descending from its heightened angle, settling in behind the junked car, where a nameless old cowboy fidgets with the wrecked motor.

Spielberg's camera has purposefully pulled back to a position which forces us to view Lou Jean over this wreck, momentarily giving the impression that she is walking directly toward it. In fact, we will shortly realize that Lou Jean is walking *past* the junked auto, as oblivious to it as the old cowboy attending this car is of her. In the unique visual language of the cinema, Spielberg has wordlessly set up the sensibility of his entire film. Though she cannot guess it, Lou Jean is moving steadily toward a confrontation with a wrecked car that will change her life, this sad old vehicle a precursor to all that will follow. Also, by here suggesting through a cinematic device that what is yet to come has already been predetermined, Spielberg sets into motion his abiding sense of fatalism.

His "way of looking" (and hearing) becomes evident in *The Sugarland Express*'s second sequence. Lou Jean is admitted to a visiting area where numerous prisoners are attended by relatives, the concept of dysfunctional family units trying their best to maintain a semblance of normalcy having already been established as a key theme in *Duel*. Reunited with her husband, Clovis (William Atherton), Lou Jean sits him down at one of the simple picnic-style tables to talk. She informs him of her sad plight. Their baby, Langston, has been taken away by authorities and turned over to a family in Sugarland; at the time, Lou Jean had been incarcerated for petty crimes. Absolutely refusing to accept separation from her child, Lou Jean—the first of endless Spielberg mothers to relentlessly search for her baby—is determined to get little Langston back. To do this, she needs Clovis's help, planning to spring him from the minimum-security prison, an easy task, since no one in his right mind would ever consider escaping. Lou Jean has it all planned. She wears men's clothing under her own. They will slip into a bathroom together; he'll replace prison garb with street clothing, and then they'll simply walk out.

Effervescent Goldie Hawn had already proven herself to be a delightful comedienne in the tradition of Carole Lombard and Judy Holliday, but Spielberg knew that it would be necessary to tone down her adorably kittenish screen image and draw from her a more subtle, complex, realistic performance for this fact-based film.

The car culture: Clovis, Lou Jean, and Slide (Michael Sacks) find themselves surrounded by a virtual caravan of police cars (courtesy Universal Pictures).

The outlaw Mom as pop celebrity: Lou Jean is stunned to discover her Warholian fifteen minutes have begun as she is cheered on by the common folk who support her claim to Baby Langston (courtesy Universal Pictures).

This expository material is fully spelled out in the Barwood-Robbins script. But Spielberg's playing of the scene reveals yet another example of "pure cinema." As Lou Jean explains her plan and Clovis, taken off guard, barely controls his oncoming sense of hysteria at the absurdity of her scenario, Spielberg purposefully cuts away from the establishing two-shot. From this point on, he focuses on one or the other, suggesting, though they are only a few feet apart, that they are in different worlds emotionally. Moreover, Spielberg effectively employs the scenery as something more than realistic backdrop. Lou Jean and Clovis are situated so that in the shots of his uncomprehending face we see behind him an endless array of vehicles—trucks, cars, tractors—that will shortly form his new reality on the road. Whenever Spielberg cuts back to Lou Jean, she is surrounded by people, the poor inmates and their families, suggesting her dream of the family that she, Clovis, and Langston will soon be.

Emotions always countermand reason in the world of Steven Spielberg. Clovis knows better than to try such a wild scheme, but Lou Jean insists that if he doesn't, their relationship is over. Dragging him into the men's room, she simultaneously hands over the escape clothing and hurriedly gives herself to him sexually. "If you don't (escape)," Lou Jean flatly states, "this is the last time." Spielberg's first attempt to create a believable female character is highly revealing. Her statements are as nonnegotiable as they are nondemanding; he can have his sex without committing to her cause, but if he doesn't join her, there will be no more sex ever again. His decision is to try and cohabit in her dream, try his best to turn her dream into a reality.

Essentially, he is a rube Prince Charming; she is the first Spielberg heroine to believe she can transform real life into a fairy tale. Lou Jean's plan, seemingly quite mad, in fact possesses an inner logic that cannot be denied; in that sense, it is the first of many such plans that will appear in Spielberg's films, culminating in Schindler's notion of how he can save his Jews. What will interfere with the plan (here, as in *Schindler*) is a series of unpredictable events, which could be perceived as accident or as destiny.

Lou Jean and Clovis make the mistake of talking the elderly parents of another prisoner into providing a ride back to town, where the couple plan to hop a bus toward Sugarland; Lou Jean already has the tickets. In the backseat, Lou Jean and Clovis bicker about where she got the sixty-five dollars to pay for them; it is obvious that she prostituted herself with an admiring male neighbor. While Clovis feels betrayed, Lou Jean refuses to hear him out. "I want my baby back," she insists, a refrain she will repeat throughout the film. At times, Lou Jean may seem simpleminded; in truth, she is single-minded. Like every Spielberg hero up to and including Schindler, she initially seems shallow, taking on epic stature after settling upon a seemingly idealistic, ultimately unrealistic notion, then sticking to it no matter what the cost.

Significantly, the backseat argument over Lou Jean's alleged infidelity appears likely to dominate the drama (this is at the heart of Peckinpah's *Getaway*), though it will barely be mentioned again. It is important to glance ahead, noting that in *Jaws*, Spielberg will likewise choose to drop the issue of Mrs. Brody's infidelity, so essential to Peter Benchley's novel. Some critics have suggested that Spielberg was incapable of dealing with such an adult issue. In fact, in his view, a woman's adultery is insignificant, only worth considering in passing. He then quickly moves on to what for him is the true drama at hand.

The drama unfolds when Lou Jean and Clovis realize they are in a precarious situation: The two cranky old people drive at ten miles an hour down a major highway, causing traffic to pile up. A young police officer, Slide (Michael Sacks), has already been glimpsed, via intercuts, transporting a prisoner. Slide will shortly pull the slow-moving car over and question the driver, inadvertently precipitating the horrific chain of events. Spielberg's characters obliviously cruise through life, though we consistently perceive the drama about to envelope them via intercutting. Louisiana highway patrolmen, who decide to help search for Lou Jean and Clovis, as well as several suburban rednecks, will be introduced in this manner. But the most important intercutting is to baby Langston and his well-to-do foster mother (Louise Latham), seen in front of and inside her stately home. We watch as the lady is informed of the mounting problem, then, later, as she and Langston are removed from the house to safety elsewhere.

The director's concept of predestination is expressed by allowing us to see more than the characters see. At various points, we become so involved in the Lou Jean/Clovis story that we momentarily forget what we know, likewise ignoring the encroaching sense of tragedy these intercuts imply. Still, Spielberg insistently cuts back to those outside forces that render the central story absurd in a way Lou Jean cannot possibly comprehend. In the essentially benevolent world of Steven Spielberg, there are few true villains, at least until we reach Amon Goeth. "The whole state mobilized and gunned them down," Spielberg said of the real-life situation in 1974, "and I really didn't want to make that kind of indictment." Many critics would complain that this ongoing sense of "the benign" has given his films a soft edge, kept them from being truly realistic. Perhaps, but they are quintessentially Spielbergian; they may be shot on location, but they take place in a universe of his own making. So likable Slide strolls toward the car to check the registration. Lou Jean panics and hops into the driver's seat, speeding away.

The irony, then, is that the adventure which turns into an epic comedy, which then breaks down into intimate tragedy, could have been avoided if she only knew as much as we do. However, Lou Jean operates from her limited field of perception, as will be the case with all Spielberg characters. So she does what she has to do. At this point, Spielberg provides an audience payoff: Slide pursues; their vehicle crashes in the woods; he attempts to apprehend them; Lou Jean, pretending to be hurt, grabs the officer's gun and tosses it to her husband; Clovis then takes the officer prisoner, forcing Slide to drive them toward Sugarland in his patrol car. Now that the exposition of act 1 is done, the characters enter act 2 not only as grand-theft-auto bandits but also as kidnappers.

The director infuses all of this with his characteristic touches. When Slide attempts to extricate Lou Jean from the car, we might expect the scene to be filmed in as tight a shot as possible, the obvious way to increase our emotional involvement. Instead, it is shot from a considerable distance, through the weeds, a visual reminder that however much we may come to care about the couple, we must observe what happens from an objective overview the participants in this pathetic event are incapable of. Also, when Slide and Clovis face off, Spielberg angles his camera so that the car—actually some distance behind them—appears directly between the two men. It is not the first time in a Spielberg film that cars will emotionally as well as physically come between people, nor will it be the last.

Paul D. Zimmerman of *Newsweek* hailed what he viewed as Spielberg's profound

vision, satiric but strangely beautiful, of an America on wheels. In this world the cars are as eloquent as the characters. The smashed-in police car in which the fugitive couple make their journey is a lonely, battered vehicle. The pursuing police cars are like four-wheeled robots, as remote as space capsules with their rotating red eyes. They hunt in packs and caravans, greedily sucking gas stations dry. Sometimes they crash into each other in acts of spectacular stupidity. Sometimes they trail the trio with a prudence that borders on cowardice. Like *American Graffiti*'s George Lucas, Spielberg creates a world in constant motion, with occasional pit stops.

However, even an enthusiastic supporter like Zimmerman felt the need to add: "Spielberg's forte is action, and generally his characterizations lack depth and consistency," noting that "Atherton vacillates between reluctant participant and willing accomplice as suits the demands of the film's big scenes." On closer examination, Spielberg is trying for a complexity of character. Clovis is not so much inconsistently drawn as he is an inconsistent character. His problem is that he alternately allows himself to live within Lou Jean's dream, under the spell of her hypnotic personality, and is occasionally shocked back into a comprehension that such activity is a denial of reality.

Spielberg has been compared to many classic filmmakers of the past—Howard Hawks's ability to play action as lighthearted comedy, William Wyler's striking tableau compositions, John Ford's sentimental portraits of the common man, Walt Disney's childlike wonder at the magical qualities of our universe, Preston Sturges's

ability to populate his seemingly normal world with engaging eccentrics. No one, though, has yet compared him with Jacques Tati, the French filmmaker widely acclaimed for his cinematic vision of modern life in which human enterprise is dwarfed and ultimately drowned out by mechanical noise. The machine-generated "din" is as constant here as in Tati's legendary film *Traffic,* likewise about people isolated from one another by the cars they drive—or, more correctly, live in.

In the police car, Slide immediately finds himself charmed by Lou Jean and touched by Clovis's fundamental decency; as so often happens in Spielberg's films, the decent characters instinctually form an unspoken community. This means, though, that their protagonist-antagonist situation is blunted; for the sake of drama, we now need another character. That is Captain Tanner (Ben Johnson), a tough old Texas Ranger (complete with high-reaching Stetson) in charge of the operation to capture and arrest. Tanner, drawn as much from collective memories of western movie lawmen as he is from real-life police officers, might well have been played by John Wayne; certainly, the fact that Johnson costarred with Wayne in numerous John Ford films (*Three Godfathers, She Wore a Yellow Ribbon*) and had recently incarnated the movie-myth cowboy in Bogdanovich's 1971 *Last Picture Show* had much to do with his being cast.

As Tanner drives up alongside the fugitives' captured police car, he furtively tries to communicate through the two-way. Throughout the film, humans will be isolated in their cars, making communication ever more difficult, finally impossible. There are marvelous moments: policemen, summoned to help in the capture attempt, darting out of car washes and away from fast-food highway restaurants; the entire caravan of slowly pursuing police cars waiting patiently in line as Clovis fills up his car with gas. Lou Jean gradually emerges as a media-created modern folk hero, something she never wanted but revels in. People line up along the sides of the road to watch her pass; hungry for a good human-interest story, TV news trucks drive alongside to shoot footage or attempt interviews. Bonnie and Clyde may have self-consciously immortalized themselves through doggerel, but Lou Jean and Clovis have the telecommunications industry to do it for them as they live out the Andy Warhol prediction and become famous; *The Sugarland Express* is about their fifteen minutes.

In the benevolent world of Steven Spielberg, however, villains are hard to come by. Captain Tanner is a fine and decent man who will not allow SWAT team members to execute Clovis when they have the chance. Knowing full well that the fugitives are harmless, touched by their mission, Tanner begrudgingly allows the circus atmosphere to continue, all the while hoping for some opportunity to stop them peaceably. One way to approach *The Sugarland Express* is as a film in search of a villain. Various characters pop up and briefly appear to fill that void, only to prove benign. Even Mrs. Livvy, adoptive

We three: Slide, Clovis, and Lou Jean are caught halfway between their outlaw–car-culture life on the open road and the Middle American suburban mainstream lifestyle surrounding them (courtesy Universal Pictures).

As in *Duel,* the characters find that their confrontations inevitably take place in between trucks and cars (courtesy Universal Pictures).

mother of Langston, has only the best interests of the child at heart.

Finally, the out-of-control situation itself becomes the villain. That is a profound notion, and *The Sugarland Express*—despite its endless entertaining qualities—is a more profound film than has been acknowledged. Clovis becomes at least dimly aware of their fate when the three spend the night at precisely the place where Spielberg car-culture characters should stop to sleep: a used-car lot. They slip inside an unlocked van, and for a few happy moments, Clovis and Lou Jean cuddle, chatting about how wonderful everything will be once they pick up baby Langston. We, of course, have seen enough to realize that this as an impossibility. Meanwhile, the two notice an outdoor movie playing across the way, watching as the Road Runner is pursued by Wile E. Coyote. They laugh at the cartoon antics, which for a moment provide temporary escape.

"Wish we had sound," Lou Jean says with a sigh.

"I'll be your sound," Clovis offers.

He then provides an improvisational sound track, much to Lou Jean's delight. As he does, though, an eerie look crosses Clovis's face. When the cartoon characters eventually explode and he makes accompanying noises, we can tell from his eyes that he knows—as a result of watching this seemingly unrelated film within a film—what is going to happen to them. Spielberg cuts to a shot in which, owing to the window through which they view the cartoon, the animated image is superimposed over the faces of Clovis and Lou Jean; visually, they and the cartoon are one.

45

Act 2 ends abruptly when Clovis grasps some vague precognition of his fate; act 3 begins the following morning as the doomed trio cover the final miles to Sugarland. To emphasize fatality, the camera now consistently precedes the characters into situations. At baby Langston's new home, armed policeman take up sniper positions. Captain Tanner tries to talk the kids out of going further, but when he cannot dissuade them, he does what he has to do: He lies, telling them their baby will be waiting for them and all will be fine. Essentially, he tells them a fairy tale, which they believe, he having long since become their adult father figure. But unlike mothers, who are pure and steadfast, fathers are far more fallible in Spielberg's films, so Captain Tanner serves as a precursor to similarly well intentioned but limited father figures until Oskar Schindler ultimately comes through and in so doing redeems all those others who have gone before.

Though technically a young adult, Lou Jean is spiritually a child, her way of viewing the world a combination of wonder, trust, and hope. "It's your baby, and don't let no one take him away from you," one well-meaning lady calls out, though in truth Lou Jean is a babe in the woods herself. Her open smile conveys her essentially innocent view on life; it is an innocence that will shortly be shattered when she realizes even as well meaning a father figure as Tanner can (indeed, must) disappoint, if only because that is the way of the world. Tanner casts his eyes downward at the end; he is not proud of what has to be done, he has attempted to avert such a conclusion, he has betrayed his own self as much as he has betrayed the "children" who trust him.

In a way, the film is ultimately his tragedy. Unlike Lou Jean, Tanner lives in the real world, and in the words of John Wayne, "A man's gotta do what a man's gotta do." This is the tragedy of father figures in Spielberg's films;

owing to traditional codes of male behavior, they cannot operate in the best of interests of the children, as Spielberg's mothers consistently do.

Clovis steps out of the car (at Lou Jean's insistence) and walks toward the house, realizing (since he, too, is a man) that the only thing waiting for him is a bullet, which he shortly takes in the chest. Lou Jean's situation is compounded by the sense of betrayal at Tanner's hands and the loss of both Clovis (whose death she has caused by forcing him to live inside her scenario until it came crashing against reality) and baby Langston (whom she at last realizes is not even nearby). The stunned, lost look on her face conveys the Spielbergian sense of innocence betrayed, shocking Lou Jean at the very last from her wonderful inner world into a cognition of the cold, hard reality everyone else—even slow-witted Clovis—has at one point or another sensed and, however reluctantly, accepted.

When Lou Jean cries at the very end, it is truly heartrending. Lou Jean cries not for Clovis but for her own lost innocence. The final shot of the movie—a police car obliviously running over baby Langston's discarded teddy bear—has been described as a maudlin, obvious symbol. In fact, though, it is the perfect image with which to end the first Spielberg film, symbolizing the childlike view that can never be fully recaptured. But if innocence dies, optimism survives. A written epilogue explains that Lou Jean spends only six months in jail. Then Lou Jean and her child are reunited. A real-life incident has been transformed into a Spielberg morality play: In his universe, nothing is more important than the reuniting of mother and child, even if it can only be achieved through the regretful but necessary death of the father.

Jaws

A UNIVERSAL FILM, 1975

CAST

Roy Scheider *(Brody);* Robert Shaw *(Quint);* Richard Dreyfuss *(Matt Hooper);* Lorraine Gary *(Ellen Brody);* Murray Hamilton *(Mayor Vaughn);* Jeffrey C. Kramer *(Hendricks);* Susan Backlinie *(Chrissie);* Carl Gottlieb *(Meadows);* Chris Rebello *(Michael Brody);* Jay Mello *(Sean Brody);* Lee Fierro *(Mrs. Kintner);* Peter Benchley *(TV Reporter).*

CREDITS

Director, Steven Spielberg; producers, Richard Zanuck and David Brown; editor, Verna Fields; music, John Williams; production designer, Joseph Alves Jr.; screenplay, Carl Gottlieb and Peter Benchley, from the novel by Benchley; cinematography, Bill Butler; special effects, Robert A. Mattey; process, Panavision/Technicolor; running time, 124 mins.; rating: PG.

When producers Richard Zanuck and David Brown viewed the dailies from *The Sugarland Express,* they were impressed enough to offer their young protégé another project without even waiting to learn if the current film would be a commercial hit. (It was not.) They wanted Spielberg to direct *MacArthur,* which they hoped would prove as popular as the Oscar-winning *Patton.* Spielberg declined on the grounds that he did not want to spend "two years working in ten different countries and getting dysentery in each one of them." When they inquired if there was anything around that did interest him,

All hands on deck: Spielberg, surrounded by crew members, prepares to direct a sequence with Robert Shaw *(far left)* and Roy Scheider *(far right,* courtesy Universal Pictures).

47

Spielberg dons a wet suit to oversee filming of a water-level sequence with a special camera (courtesy Universal Pictures).

The demise of hippiedom: Chrissie (Susan Backlinie) attempts to live out the ideals of the free-love era (courtesy Universal Pictures).

The traditional family unit: Brody (Roy Scheider) and wife Ellen (Lorraine Gary) do not pay proper attention to the rumored threat until it almost claims the life of their own son Michael (Chris Rebello; courtesy Universal Pictures).

The advertising poster that captured the film's essence and turned a superior modern
monster movie into an icon of popular culture.

Spielberg admitted he didn't have anything specific in mind. But on his way out of the office, he noticed a large stack of unpublished manuscripts piled high by the door. The one on the top had the words "JAWS" written in large block letters across its cover. This caught Spielberg's attention: In the age of *Deep Throat*, he wondered if it could be "about a pornographic dentist." So he turned to Dick Zanuck's secretary and said, "I'm going to borrow one of these, okay?"

He read it over the weekend, becoming ecstatic at the possibilities for a movie. The following Monday, he hurried to the office, admitted he had taken the manuscript without permission, and insisted this was what he wanted to do. They broke the bad news: *Jaws* had come to them with a director named Dick Richards attached. Spielberg was disappointed, but three weeks later, his agent called to tell him that Zanuck had phoned: Richards had dropped out of the project, and the producers wanted Spielberg. He agreed without hesitation.

Zanuck and Brown had picked up *Jaws* early on for the incredibly low price of $175,000 (the fee included an adaptation by author Benchley himself), long before the book became a surprise runaway bestseller (5 1/2 million copies in print). The origins of the novel were at best dubious: Benchley (semitalented grandson of esteemed writer Robert Benchley) had years before pitched the idea, via a one-page synopsis, at a meeting with a New York editor, who gave him the go-ahead and a $1,000 advance. *Jaws* might have been written by a computer programmed to turn out a story loaded with suburban sex (adulterous wife of small-town lawman attracted to intellectual newcomer) and intense violence. Understandably, Spielberg made clear that he was not interested in simply transferring the book, as written, to the screen. Instead, he would take its basic concept (shark-menaces-society) and transform *Jaws* into something different and decidedly Spielbergian: "I'd like to develop it from its raw state," he said. He would oversee the entire process, from scripting to editing, as well as doing the on-location direction. In the spring of 1974, Zanuck and Brown announced that *Jaws* would be shot that summer, over a thirteen-week period, at a cost of $2.3 million.

Benchley wrote the first script, trying to keep the upcoming film as close to his book as possible. It was quickly returned to him, and during the second and third drafts, he claimed to have "lost the ego problem," realizing his story would not be filmed. For the fourth and fifth drafts, *Jaws* was worked on by playwright Howard Sackler *(The Great White Hope)* and director-screenwriter John Milius *(Dillinger),* until the project—desperately in need of a sense of humor—was handed over to Carl Gottlieb. Previously, actor-writer Gottlieb had been a member of The Committee, a popular improvisational comedy troupe during the hippie era. He restructured and streamlined the plot while peppering the picture-to-be with comic relief. Ultimately, Gottlieb alone received screenplay credit with Benchley, though it is worth not-

ing that Spielberg improvised almost every scene the following summer in Martha's Vineyard.

Ultimately, the movie would be shot from the director's visual storyboards (comic-strip, shot-by-shot depictions of the story in visual terms) rather than the dialogue-heavy script. Spielberg's insistence on location shooting (to avoid the phony back-lot look that the emerging youthful audience would not tolerate) caused problems even before cast and crew arrived. Half the residents were convinced that a production company would despoil their paradise-like enclave and hurt their tourist season, much as the great white interferes with that moneymaking opportunity in the movie. Many old-timers were openly hostile not only to moviemakers but also to anyone who had not, like them, been born as well as bred on their little island. Spielberg, sensing this upon arrival, did precisely what any true artist would do: he integrated this fact into his film.

Finally, they were grudgingly accepted when local businesspeople realized that the 150 crew members, who would be living and eating there long before the arrival and after the departure of actors, would spend a great deal of money in the off seasons of spring and early fall. This hunger for money, even at the cost of violating long-held values, would likewise find its way into Spielberg's emerging, organic film. By May 2, Spielberg and his principal players had arrived. The movie would eventually take twenty weeks to complete, at a cost of over $8 million, now a mere pittance, though then an extravagance. Zanuck and Brown would, on a daily basis, bring themselves to the edge of ulcers trying to decide if they ought to shut down production and shoot the seagoing scenes in the big tank at Universal Studios or, horror of horrors, actually pull the plug on what seemed an out-of-control project.

Even as Spielberg set to work in Martha's Vineyard, special-effects artist Bob Mattey was still in Hollywood, attempting to complete the twenty-four-foot great-white-shark model, knowing full well that the degree to which this plastic one-and-a-half-ton contraption looked convincing on-screen would determine whether the costly film succeeded or failed. Though the dummy shark would eventually be christened "Bruce," Mattey had long since realized that he would need to build three separate models—at a cost of $250,000 per—for different functions: one for left-to-right surface movements, another for right-to-left, and the third for subsurface shots. Each Bruce would be operated by hydraulic pistons employing compressed air. As Mattey (aided by twenty assistants) hurriedly readied the trio of dummies for the seagoing shoot, Spielberg completed filming of the onshore social sequences.

The big day finally arrived: On July 1, a flotilla of boats set out to shoot the first Bruce sequence, which required that a twelve-ton steel platform be set in place on the ocean floor. From this base, a cable 100 feet long allowed Bruce extensive movement, even as a team of thir-

The intellect: Matt Hooper (Richard Dreyfuss), the polar opposite of Quint, is the man of the mind who employs his superior knowledge and reasoning powers to fight the shark (courtesy Universal Pictures).

Monster from the ID: As Quint, Robert Shaw perfectly embodied the raw animalistic side of human existence (courtesy Universal Pictures).

The man in the middle: Brody, halfway between the extremes of Quint and Hooper, comes to represent the average modern man, who early on gazes thoughtfully into the jaws of a long-deceased shark; those jaws line a window offering him a view of the sea on which he will eventually face his animal adversary as well as his own sense of self (courtesy Universal Pictures).

51

The *Orca* carries the primitive Quint, the intellectual Hooper, and the ordinary man Brody out to sea for a confrontation with a creature that embodies our worst collective nightmares.

teen technicians in scuba equipment ran the operation from below. Disaster ensued: Bruce immediately sank to the bottom. When the technical crew finally managed to make it move about, the hydraulic system exploded. After several further delays, Spielberg readied the crew to film, immediately noticing that the plastic skin was rapidly deteriorating (revealing it was a mechanical device rather than a real shark) due to salt water. This was solved by having a special-effects man regularly don scuba gear and dive in to touch up the problem areas.

So the daily regimen began, the crew setting out each day in boats, the Bruce of the day requiring an entire boat to himself. Bruce continued to be uncooperative—there were constant breakdowns, minor and major—and weather was often uncooperative. Members of the crew still shake their heads in amazement as they recall the many days when, after setting out with high energy, they would return despondent, failing to get even a single usable shot. "If any of us had any sense," Richard Dreyfuss recalls muttering to those around him, "we'd all bail out now." But sense implies logic, and they were going on emotions: their emotional trust that their director would somehow salvage things.

Now, though, there was another problem: They had waited so long to shoot the sea scenes that sailing season was in full swing. Whenever Spielberg tried to film a sequence involving the isolated trio of heroes, on the ocean and far from help, yachts and sailboats whizzed by in the background, entire families waving at the camera. The problem seemed so unsolvable that Spielberg desperately considered writing those other boats into the script, though he knew that would destroy the primal sense they were going for.

Finally the film was in the can. Spielberg, however, was far from finished: He now had to fly to the Pacific to oversee underwater work being done there, then return to Hollywood and collaborate with Verna Fields on the complicated editing, which would either make or break the movie. As a collection of locals and cast and crew members watched him sail to the mainland in a small boat, they recall that he mockingly pulled himself up tall like General MacArthur and announced, "I shall not return!"

Many months later, the editing finally completed, Zanuck and Brown took a look at the results, sighing with relief: Their trust had not been misplaced. They and Universal then launched an unprecedented promotional campaign, including an experimental use of $700,000 worth of saturation prime-time-TV advertising to hook the television generation, along with saturation booking that placed the film in over 490 theaters for its June 1975 opening weekend. *Jaws* soon broke box-office records and became the number-one moneymaker of all time, until eased off the top spot by yet another Spielberg pic-

The mayor (Murray Hamilton), wearing one of his expressively tacky suits, attempts to defend the town's economic base from any threat; the poster, idealizing what a young woman will find in Amity, strikingly contrasts with the real fate of an identical young woman in the opening sequence.

ture. No question that the film was the most successful piece of moviemaking commerce up to that point; less obvious was that it also succeeded as an artistic endeavor. Shot by shot, moment by moment, it displays not only the technical wizardry and crowd-satisfying craftsmanship of Spielberg but also his directorial personality.

Spielberg makes himself felt in the film's rightly famous opening sequence. As credits roll, the now-classic musical theme by John Williams is heard even before we can distinguish anything on-screen: The movie opens in blackness, suggesting the moral darkness from which the mindless eating-machine creature hails. This gradually gives way to an ever brighter image of an underwater world through which something relentlessly moves forward. It is, of course, the shark, and dimly, slowly, inexorably, we sense this. We do not *see* it because at this moment we *are* it. The camera's point of view forces us to share the way in which the film's "monster" (for this is, essentially, a realistic horror film, the monster not a supernatural being but a slightly exaggerated version of an actual creature) sees the world.

At the time, this approach was widely regarded as a remarkable novelty, one that would be repeated throughout the decade in considerably less artistic horror films. Here, though, form had function: Shortly, the shark would be identified verbally as the world's oldest eating machine, and in the opening, we share his search for food. Humans may be the most advanced form of the animal kingdom; sharks, one of the most basic. Still, if we can be made to see what he sees, we will understand on some level that a touch of this primal behavior remains within us. It should come as no surprise, then, that the two most significant conversations between the three heroes occur when they eat, first at Brody's house, later at Quint's.

The opening of *Jaws* is not only clever; but also it sets up the values of the movie to follow. As the simple but effective music (da-DA, da-DA, da-DA!) establishes the as yet unseen creature, these forward-thrusting movements alternate with a pan shot, moving from left to right on a nighttime beach, where teenagers party. They are early 1970s, late-hippie-era types, obvious from the length of their hair and their beaded clothing. We see one youth and then the next, others forming a hazy blur in the background. Spielberg's camera acts as an isolating device, implying that the "community" of young people (such an important notion at the time) is less a reality than they might want to believe. Our final impression is that they (and we) are all fundamentally individuals, out there on our own.

This idea, suggested here with impressive visual economy, will be developed later. Spielberg's adult characters likewise depend on an assumed sense of community (in their case, Establishment rather than counterculture) that will not, perhaps cannot, support members when they most need it, forcing them to rely on individuality instead.

What follows next is the initial shark attack. Chrissie (Susan Backlinie), an attractive blonde, makes eye contact with a likable, good-looking boy. She rises and leads him off toward the beach, where they strip away their clothes while heading for the water. Their casual attitude toward sex may seem shocking in the age of AIDS, though in the free-loving seventies, it was accepted as the norm. But even though both kids seem innocent and appealing, it is her naive flower-child promiscuity that leads to catastrophic results.

Just as *The Sugarland Express*, these briefly glimpsed kids are clearly dominating woman and ineffectual man. He asks her what they are going to do, and she tells him they will take a swim; she neatly strips out of her clothes and enters the water like some natural goddess, while he stumbles and falls, unable to get out of his pants, much less join her.

We hear the *Jaws* music as the unseen shark follows Chrissie from below, swimming back and forth beneath her, the camera movement suggesting that in the depths he imitates her surface movements. Spielberg relies on movie mythology, in this case the most memorable moment from the 1954 classic *Creature From the Black Lagoon* in which Gill-Man, upon seeing Julia Adams for the first time, slips into a bizarre underwater ballet, mimicking her every movement. At one point, Spielberg's young woman even extends her leg outward, like a dancer, then submerges, precisely as Adams did. This iconographic image is invoked, though, only to be quickly reinvented: In the old monster movie, the creature was a true romantic, obsessed with Julia's beauty, unwilling to harm her. In the modern version—and modern vision—the beast is an eating-killing machine. In Chrissie's specific death, we see the demise of the entire hippie generation, done in by the fact that such a sweet, idealistic viewpoint did not take into account the horrible realities out there. Spielberg's essentially conservative worldview has been established.

The following sequence introduces police chief Martin Brody (Roy Scheider) as he rises for what he believes will be a typical morning. He makes small talk about having a full day ahead of him, while his wife, Ellen (Lorraine Gary), busies herself with their two boys, one a teen, the other a toddler. Spielberg's vision of the Brody home is full of pop-culture, TV-generation echoes, evoking memories of *Ozzie and Harriet, Father Knows Best,* and a dozen other warmhearted 1950s sitcoms. There is no suggestion that the man we watch will turn out to be a cop. He never appears in full uniform, and when at one point we see him pull a gun and use it expertly, we are shocked. He is an average guy with an average family who approaches his police-chief position as a banker, teacher, or clergyman might their positions of responsibility within the community.

Important, too, is that in such an expository sequence, his wife is seen on-screen with him only for brief, fleeting moments; more often, they are physically near each other, though the camera isolates one or the other as they talk. This visually informs us that despite the calm sur-

Though the film would go on to be a classic, there were moments when producers David Brown (*left*) and Richard Zanuck (*right*) wondered if they should pull the plug on their young director (*center*) who was going way over budget (courtesy Universal Pictures).

Actors Dreyfuss and Scheider decided to stick with the film, owing to their trust in young Spielberg, who inspired a sense of faith that *Jaws* would not only reach completion but would emerge as something special (courtesy Universal Pictures).

face of a seemingly normal relationship, there is an emotional gap. Ellen half-jokingly refers to the fact that he is originally from New York, words which reverberate throughout the movie. Brody is (no pun intended) himself a fish out of water, a misplaced Manhattanite (presumably Jewish) in this Middle American community. (The Amity of Spielberg's imagination looks like Kansas with a seacoast.) For full acceptance, he must prove himself through some ultimate act, though he can hardly guess that the mechanics are already at work.

Shortly, we learn that Brody never goes near the water unless he has to; he doesn't or can't swim. Everything about him—attitude, demeanor, likes and dislikes—are alien to his community, much as Schindler's will be to his. Brody is, simply, the original Spielberg hero who has through some stroke of fate been placed in precisely the wrong social situation, steadfastly making the best of it, an average man who will shortly rise to heroic proportions, though seemingly the least likely person to do so. By implication, he is the alien Jew trying to assimilate into WASP society; he is essentially Steven Spielberg.

Spielberg then has Martin and Ellen share the screen at precisely that moment when they emotionally move in opposite directions. As they stand back-to-back and practically touch one another, Ellen speaks to her children, while Martin talks into the phone; the audience has trouble hearing either because their voices drown out one another as she takes on her domestic responsibilities and he assumes his professional ones. Though they move in seemingly separate directions throughout a typical day, they are joined by an invisible bond, one which will shortly carry them through frantic circumstances: their children.

As in *The Sugarland Express,* Spielberg's focus is on a modern marriage and the difficulties in making such a relationship work. Ellen follows Martin out of the house and toward his car, assuming a different, mock-serious voice: "Chief, be careful? Will you?" She consciously mimics all those movie wives of Hollywood police officers who know their husbands will stare death in the face. She kids, of course, because there are no threats in Amity; the irony is that there is indeed a threat, one which will force Brody to move from sitcom suburbanite to full-blown epic hero.

As Brody strolls toward his office building, he passes a mother with her child; they, in Spielberg's vision, are the members of the community who most need protection, though Brody will first be sidetracked into protecting the community's economy. This money base is also visually introduced as Brody continues walking, past a huge poster advertising Amity as a summer-resort attraction; the young, attractive woman depicted at play on the water is identical in appearance to Chrissie, the shark's first victim. The sign reappears throughout the film, staring down much as the highway billboard featuring the eyes of T. J. Eckleburg gazes down on the sad goings-on in F. Scott Fitzgerald's *Great Gatsby;* modern people are dwarfed by media misrepresentations. Meanwhile, the anecdotal details Brody has passed by—mother and child, advertising poster—neatly represent the extremes of Brody's upcoming moral choice.

Fleeting snippets of conversation, barely overheard in the din of daily life, reinforce the fact that there are islanders (longtime residents) and visitors (who will spill off the Woods Hole ferry to spend money and soak up the sun). Then there is Brody, neither islander nor visitor; rather, the resident outsider. When he visits the beach where Chrissie has met her fate, her companion appears frightfully blasé: "I'm sure she drowned," he says matter-of-factly. Spielberg plays against audience expectations: If we assume the boy will be hysterical, only to find him calm, we expect the policeman to be hard-boiled, though Brody is clearly broken up both about the girl's disappearance and the boy's (a representative of the new youth he can't comprehend) lack of involvement. Brody gazes out at the surf, a confused character, the sound of waves relentlessly pounding in clearly oppressive to him.

Returning to his office, Brody does not escape the din but is aurally bombarded, the Memorial Day parade rehearsal taking place just outside. As he passes the elderly secretary (who would appear more at home in a grade school than a police chief's office) and sits down to type his report, the camera shifts to Brody's point of view (for the first time) as he hits the keys, spelling out the significant two words "Shark Attack." Brody then engages in a flurry of activity, hurrying over to a general store, where he picks up materials to make signs, then to the beach he dutifully plans to shut down. He is photographed from an angle framing him with pink roses above and white picket fences below, isolating this near-frenzied outsider from the ultratraditional perspective of an idealized Thornton Wilder town. The visual clichés are evoked to lend what follows next a sharp edge of irony, as Brody is halted by the mayor, Larry Vaughn (Murray Hamilton), and the coroner, who coldly takes back his initial assessment of shark attack. "Amity is a summer town," the mayor (who, in each successive scene, sports an ever tackier sports jacket) reminds Brody, insisting that closing the beaches would turn tourists toward other, competing destinations.

Brody caves in—his authority only reaches so far—ordering extra security for the beaches, hoping the coroner's alternative explanation (now the official word is that Chrissie was cut by a boat propeller) may indeed be true. However desperately he wants to believe this, he knows better. Like Dr. Stockmann in Ibsen's classic 1879 play *An Enemy of the People,* Brody is a fine and decent sort who has always trusted in the essential goodness of his fellow man, until he makes the mistake of issuing a statement that could shut down his resort community. What he learns is that the people want to protect their capitalistic base. If he—Stockmann/Brody—endangers that, he will indeed be considered an enemy of the people.

Strangers are supposed to come, spend money, and leave; this one stayed and married one of the hometown girls. What to do with him? "If you're not born here, you're not an islander," one woman explains to another on the reopened beach. Though the words are not necessarily intended for Brody to hear, he does catch them through the din of noise as he sits, fully clothed, on the beach, where locals and a few early arriving tourists relax and frolic. Brody arrived because today's New York (that city as it will shortly be depicted in Scorsese's *Taxi Driver*) struck him as too nihilistic for a dedicated cop; he wanted to retreat to a simpler place where one man could still make a difference. Now his great fear is that such values are only illusory, even here.

What follows next borrows heavily from Sergei Eisenstein's 1925 classic *Potemkin,* in particular the Odessa steppes sequence: various comrades, introduced one by one, menaced by attacking Cossacks sent in to break up the early stages of the Russian Revolution. In Spielberg's variation, we see an overweight man in an inner tube, a cute little kid in red swimming trunks, a youthful fellow throwing sticks into the water for his big black dog to retrieve. Again and again, Spielberg cuts to Brody. We watch him apprehensively watching as a large, fin-shaped item rises out of the water and moves toward a swimmer, causing Brody to rise, trembling; it

A contrast in styles: Quint and Brody reveal their differing ways of dealing with their mutual problem through body language that had been carefully planned by the director.

Quint and Hooper bait the attacking great white shark.

turns out to be only an elderly man wearing a black rubber cap. Perhaps, Brody thinks to himself, the authorities were right, after all; perhaps all this fear of sharks is nothing more than mass hysteria, a foolhardy misreading of everyday elements invested with the horrible demons of our worst individual and collective nightmares.

The look on Brody's face gives us, in less than one second of screen time, the scad of information we need to understand what follows: his desire to do his job properly, countered by his vulnerability to threat from local bigwigs; his desperate hope, born of necessity, that if he just goes along, everything will somehow work out right, countered by his intense fear that his own individual perception was more correct than the truth which the community has agreed to agree upon.

Brody, gasping, leaps up as a young woman screams and flips through the air, reminding us of Chrissie's similar movements; we then see that the force moving her is a playful boyfriend and share Brody's relief. We, like him, are victimized by the distinction between appearance and reality; we, like him, fear the worst and hope for the best. Essentially, we *are* Brody: He is not only the film's central character but also the audience's surrogate; in his convictions and confusion he represents every one of us who would like to believe that under such circumstances we would do the right thing, though fearing we might, like him, feel intimidated by the power structure.

This feeling of intimidation strikes home for Brody when his wife wants to know if their kids can go in the water; when he says they can, his internal conflict is taken to the extreme, for he is risking the safety of his own children as a means of denying his basic fears that there may indeed be danger. Shortly, the theme music and the shark's point of view return as a child is yanked off his raft amid a spurt of blood while everyone swims wildly for the safety of the beach. Brody attempts to maintain some semblance of order while clearly sinking under the pressure of having known of the danger and not spoken up; this is emphasized by a quick cut to the mother of the lost child, unhappily searching for her boy, building on Goldie Hawn's mother, determined and distraught, in the previous film.

Spielberg quickly cuts through what, in the book, was emphasized: the process by which a $3,000 reward is announced for the killing of the shark and the reaction of townspeople to double threats—one to their lives and one to their livelihood. The local newspaperman (Carl Gottlieb) quickly makes clear (much as the editor in the old Ibsen play did) that he will side with the power structure, diminishing his coverage of what has happened to protect his community's finances: "I'll bury it as deep as I can," he assures authorities, "in the back with the grocery ads." (Groceries revive the film's food-eating theme.) But when put on the spot, asked if he is going to close the beaches, Brody answers affirmatively. Spielberg effectively has actor Scheider pause before saying, "Yes," again suggesting Brody's vulnerability and insecurity, a potential hero but all too human.

The mayor, meanwhile, insists that the ban will last only twenty-four hours, the ever-louder arguing voices in the meeting house then interrupted and silenced by a shrill, imposing, primal sound that cuts through the modern din: fingernails on a chalk board, as Peter Quint (Robert Shaw) relentlessly scratches downward, freezing everyone in mid-conversation. Noise—especially oppressive noise—was already introduced in *The Sugarland Express* as the chief means by which flurried activity of everyday people is cut short in Spielberg's world; Quint will throughout the film be the noisiest person on-screen, singing, whistling, and shouting as a means of diminishing the modern din and overcoming it. With his entrance, we enter act 2.

Spielberg's camera initially captures Quint in a long shot, through the crowd that has convened in city hall. But as this man now speaks to the hushed multitude, the relic from man's hunter past who can fight fire with fire and kill sharks with sharklike tactics, the camera slowly moves through the crowd toward him. As he finishes his speech, he is at last isolated visually. Earlier in the sequence, images of Brody began with close-ups of his face, isolating him from his supposed community, then pulling back to gradually reveal his presence among

them. The contrast of camera approaches to the two men visually states the contrast between them. Quint has always lived in this community, yet he is a man who ultimately stands alone; Brody is still considered an outsider by the populace, though in time they will have to accept that he is a member (rather than an enemy) of the people. They are the film's complements.

Spielberg then visually introduces another theme as the people—having refused to pay Quint's $10,000 demand for killing the beast—go out in their own small boats as makeshift vigilante/shark hunters, much like the rednecks in *The Sugarland Express* who grabbed rifles and tried to blow away the fugitives. A fear of the crowd, owing to its unpredictability and mercurial nature, is essential to Spielberg's ongoing vision; the ultimate will be the crowd in Nazi Poland in *Schindler's List*. Here the locals do manage to find and kill a shark, posing like gleeful morons in front of it for a picture. This all occurs even as ichthyologist Matt Hooper arrives on the island, trying without luck to make himself heard over the latest din of voices, boats, and local bands, shouting at people who do not listen that this could not possibly be the shark which killed Chrissie.

Hooper is the scientist from the Oceanographic

Institute who will complete the necessary triad of heroes, all of whom will shortly become a makeshift community and head out in the boat *Orca* to kill the great white shark. Hooper, with his grad-student beard and academic phrasing, is pure brain power; Quint, almost inarticulate, brute force; standing between them—morally, emotionally, intellectually, even physically in Spielberg's carefully constructed compositions—is Brody, a man of some brains and some brawn, dwarfed by Hooper in the former and Quint as to the latter. They are the extremes of mankind, the bookends that provide the proper foils on either side; Brody is average, the common-man hero who will eventually carry the day.

Brody will have to face the consequences of what he has done or, more correctly, failed to do. "I just found out that a girl was killed weeks ago," the mother of the recently deceased boy says, dressed in black as she returns from her child's funeral, "and you knew about it. There was a shark, dangerous, but you let people go swimming, anyway. My boy is dead. I wanted you to know."

She slaps him and walks away; "I wanted you to know. . . ." But Brody already knows, as his face makes clear; what the woman has done is force him into conscious awareness of the responsibility he failed to live up to. In Spielberg's films, there is no greater responsibility for a man than to protect a woman and her child. The impact is greater owing to Brody's intense love for his own boys, enhanced in the next sequence. Brody, despondent, sits at his dinner table, unaware he has brought his hands to his face in mute shame. The camera cuts to his small boy, watching, then imitating; becoming conscious of this, Brody brings his hands down but, again unaware, presses them against his mouth, a cut to the child revealing him again imitating his father's every action. Father Brody, now consciously indulging in this game, makes faces, and the child happily responds; they laugh together, and the camera finally captures them in a single shot rather than cutting back and forth. Not surprisingly, there is no source for this in Benchley's book.

The parent-child bond, and the responsibility of all adults to all children, will serve as a key theme to be played out in varied settings over the next two decades. Even the seemingly insensitive mayor is redeemed somewhat when, after insisting that the beaches be opened again in time for the Fourth of July holiday weekend, only to watch in horror as the shark attacks once more, he leans toward Brody and, voice quaking, reminds the lawman: "My children were on that beach, too." The ostensible villain of the piece, Vaughn is no mere caricature; conversely, Brody allows people to swim again in the supposedly shark-free water, only to instruct his own boys that they should sail their little skiff in the presumably safer pond. Villains aren't all bad, or heroes all good, in the world (a more complex world than has generally been acknowledged) of Steven Spielberg.

Now the near death of his own child will spark Brody on to the proper action he has hesitated to perform up to this point. As tourists arrive en masse, Spielberg cuts to

The mechanical shark (courtesy Universal Pictures).

Richard Dreyfuss, in granny glasses and hippie-era shirt, cools off between shots by hopping into the water (courtesy Universal Pictures).

trunks. This camera angle at first appears to be dishonest audience manipulation, a case of the director tricking us into believing that the shark is attacking. But Spielberg is not guilty as charged, for one reason: The famed *Jaws* theme music is notably missing. Since that music accompanied every previous shark-point-of-view shot, its absence foreshadows the fact that this time what will be misconstrued as a shark attack will in fact turn out to be a prank. Like Hitchcock, Spielberg manipulates, but not dishonestly, never tricking us but gleefully allowing us to trick ourselves.

When Brody and Hooper head for Quint's home to enlist him in the quest (the town has finally agreed to pay his price), the place is literally awash with sharks' jaws of varying sizes. At first, it appears only an eccentric, effective way of defining Quint as the ultimate shark hunter. Shortly, though, we sense it is this—and more: As Brody and Hooper bargain with Quint, the camera is placed at odd angles to frame the three of them, seemingly surrounded by sets of jaws, foreshadowing their impending danger. The first image of the boat *Orca,* as it embarks onto the open sea, is an over-the-shoulder shot of Ellen Brody, standing like one of those John Ford heroines who remain behind when their men head off to war. From this, Spielberg cuts to the confining framed image of the three men through giant jaws in Quint's window, visually suggesting they are menaced in a way they cannot guess.

Their tactic, in Act III, is to fire at the shark and puncture him with a projectile to which a rope is attached, a large yellow barrel hooked on the other side. This will allow them to identify, through the surface presence of the buoyant barrels, where the shark is at any moment. It also allows Spielberg to create some marvelous moments, which, like the best of Hitchcock, are effectively suspenseful for what they *don't* show. We sense and share the characters' menace as the yellow barrel circles them, first at a distance, then moving ever closer. That night, as Quint tells the frightful story of a World War II shark attack on the abandoned American seamen of the *Indianapolis,* the shaking lights are augmented by the great white's attempts to break the timbers of the *Orca,* drowning the trio. Their present plight is intensified by the amazing story from the past, the true tale enhanced, by Quint's spellbinding storytelling abilities (here he is a stand-in for Spielberg), into full-blown myth.

In combat the following day, each character operates according to his basic overriding personality trait. Hooper, the man of brains, tries using his metallic shark cage, though the great white breaks through; Quint, the man of pure muscle, fights the thing on its own brute terms. Significantly, he tears the phone out of the ship even as Brody calls for help, wanting the combat all to himself. In so doing, he knocks out the last vestige of that recurring Spielbergian motif, mechanical communication. Finally, Brody fights and defeats the beast while clinging to a mast on the sinking ship, falling into the water he so detests. His happy balance of physical prowess and brain power allows him to succeed where

images of kids playing the Shark Killer video game; reality and modern media entertainment become intertwined, the shape of things to come in Spielberg's films. Likewise, a reporter (author Peter Benchley) interviews people on the beach. They are afraid to step into the water, though helicopters whiz overhead, creating one more of those Spielbergian "dins" which drown out attempts at human communication with a mechanical buzz. Brody and Hooper communicate with one another via two-way radios, evoking the similar situation in *The Sugarland Express;* the difficulty they have in communicating is not merely a part of the plot but a recurring theme.

Spielberg shows swimmers who believe they are being menaced (in fact, they are the victims of a ruse by two children with a fake fin), employing underwater shots looking up from below, similar to the famed shot that preceded Chrissie's death and that of the boy in red the others failed; this is an indication of other Spielberg heroes to follow. Innocence died with that boy on the beach, but optimism survives.

In a pleasant Spielbergian touch, Hooper (killed in the book) is here allowed to live, bobbing up to the surface and rejoining Brody for the long swim home. The character's improbable survival is pure fairy tale, an admission to the audience that however realistic, even grim, the story may at moments have become, it is, after all, only a story and as such might just as well have a happy ending. As they swim together, the gulls circle overhead, drowning out their high-spirited conversation, one more Spielbergian din, this time a natural rather than mechanical one, reminding us of Hitchcock's *Birds*.

"I wanted to do *Jaws* for hostile reasons," Spielberg stated. "I read it and felt that I had been attacked. It terrified me, and I wanted to strike back." Also, Spielberg sounded playfully macabre, in the Hitchcock tradition, when explaining the lure of such lurid material: "After *Jaws,* I think a lot of people will rush into the water, not out of it. It's gambling with the unknown." Hollis Alpert of *Saturday Review* tagged the film "a perfect money machine," which is precisely what it proved to be. He meant the comment positively, yet there was a sense of condescension, however unconscious, which Spielberg would insistently try to overcome for the next two decades.

The triumvirate: physical Quint, brainy Hooper, and ordinary suburbanite Brody symbolize mankind itself on a collision course with those animal origins which frame our existence still, as this publicity shot well illustrates (courtesy Universal Pictures).

Close Encounters of the Third Kind

A COLUMBIA RELEASE, 1977

CAST

Richard Dreyfuss *(Roy Neary);* François Truffaut *(Claude Lacombe);* Teri Garr *(Ronnie Neary);* Bob Balaban *(David Laughlin);* Melinda Dillon *(Jilian Guiler);* Cary Guffey *(Barry Guiler);* Roberts Blossom *(Farmer);* Lance Henriksen *(Robert);* Warren Kemmerling *(Wild Bill);* Shawn Bishop, Adrienne Campbell, Justin Dreyfuss *(Neary Kids);* Dr. J. Allen Hynek *(Himself);* Howard K. Smith *(Newscaster);* Hal Barwood and Matthew Robbins *(Returnees).*

CREDITS

Writer/director, Steven Spielberg; special-effects photography, Douglas Trumbull; second-unit direction, Douglas Slocombe (India) and William Fraker (America); chief cinematographer Vilmos Zsigmond; Douglas Trumbull, William A. Fraker, Douglas Slocombe, John A. Alonzo, Laszlo Kovacs, Richard Yuricich, Dave Stewart, Robert Hall, Don Jarel, Dennis Muren; producers, Julia and Michael Phillips; associate producer, Clark Paylow; production designer, Joe Alves; editors, Michael Kahn and Charles Bornstein (assistant); art director, Dan Lomino; music, John Williams; technical adviser, Dr. J. Allen Hynek; film process, Panavision/MetroColor; running time, 135 mins. (original release) and 132 mins. (1980 "special edition" rerelease); rating: PG.

Spielberg left the fold of Zanuck/Brown, with their multipicture deal at Universal, to do a film for Julia and Michael Phillips at Columbia Pictures. The then husband

Steven Spielberg checks a key locale (courtesy Columbia Pictures).

A man and his mountain: The contemporary Everyman, Roy Neary (Richard Dreyfuss), ponders the metaphysical possibilities of ancient Devils Tower.

and wife team ran a highly successful independent production company, their hits including the 1973 Oscar-winning Best Picture of the Year, *The Sting.* Things would quickly fall apart: Julia would be forced to the sidelines before the release of *Close Encounters of the Third Kind,* her descent into cocaine eventually chronicled in her book *You'll Never Eat Lunch in This Town Again.* Meanwhile, she had had the foresight to back the first film to boast the credit "written and directed by Steven Spielberg."

Initially, though, Spielberg had planned to collaborate on the script. His first conception for the story was to focus on an air force officer named Van Owen, working for the government as a UFO debunker until he himself has a close encounter. Julia suggested that Spielberg tell the story to Paul Schrader, a writer who worked with Scorsese on *Taxi Driver.* Within several weeks, Schrader had knocked out a screenplay which added nothing new but had Van Owen delivering enormous monologues which in some cases ran on for a thousand words or more. Spielberg was so turned off by the results that he dumped not only Schrader but also the entire Van Owen

The ordinary man in extraordinary circumstances: Roy Neary (Richard Dreyfuss) has a "close encounter" with an alien spacecraft (courtesy Columbia Pictures).

François Truffaut as Claude Lacombe, the sensitive scientist who maintains a sense of childlike wonder when reacting to the world's abundant miracles. (courtesy Columbia Pictures).

to actors made suggestions, many of which Spielberg happily incorporated into the film.

Spielberg also drew on the writings of Dr. J. Allen Hynek, who appears in the film and served as technical adviser. Hynek's research identified three "kinds" of encounters: the first, sighting; the second, tangible proof of existence; the third, actual contact.

A seminal film for the twenty-year-old Spielberg was *2001: A Space Odyssey*. When the time came for his own work in this genre, Spielberg contacted the F/X people who had put together the special effects for that Stanley Kubrick classic, personally requesting that Doug Trumbull come on board. One of their most painstaking choices was the look of the aliens; after dozens of fanciful sketches were created, then discarded, the decision was made to rely on research from around the world that invariably described extraterrestrials as small.

The look of the mother ship (nicknamed "Big Mama")

approach. Spielberg took such an entirely different narrative angle that he was stunned when, two years later, Schrader appealed to the Writers Guild, insisting his name appear in the credits, though nothing of what he had turned in was included. The Writers Guild studied the scripts, then awarded Spielberg sole credit, based on the five drafts he had completed as well as his original treatment.

In reflection, Spielberg did not mellow on the incident: "It surprises me that Schrader would slink after someone else's success by vividly inflating his imagined contributions." Other writers did offer support and inspiration, however. John Hill worked on one of the drafts before Spielberg decided to go it entirely alone, drawing on memories of what he had tried, and failed, to achieve with *Firelight:* "*Close Encounters of the Third Kind* was really the remake of a film I wrote and directed when I was sixteen," he once told *Cosmopolitan.* One year later, Jerry Belson spent a week with Spielberg in New York, the comedy writer's bizarre sense of humor pumping whimsy into the Roy Neary character. Hal Barwood and Matthew Robbins, of *The Sugarland Express,* spent four days helping Spielberg design the sequence in which little Barry is kidnapped. Later, everyone from electricians presented a conceptual problem, since Spielberg was unsure of anything other than that it should be huge enough to blot out the starlight when it rolls over Devils Tower. In Bombay to prepare the film's India sequence, Spielberg drove past a power station unlike anything he had seen before: tens of thousand of 25-watt lightbulbs arranged on a steel mesh superstructure. He made a mental note, combining that with another notion: the mother ship ought to resemble a modern city as viewed from the air. He dictated these ideas to artists, who then conceptualized the look.

A huge space would be necessary to film the makeshift welcoming station, but it would be unwise to actually shoot outdoors, owing to natural factors (wind, rain) which could halt production and test their tight $18 million budget. He sent Joe Alves to find the largest indoor space in the country. Mobile, Alabama, boasted a defunct World War II dirigible hangar, bigger than two football fields and six times larger than Hollywood's most immense soundstage, but with none of the central support beams that would interfere with shooting an "outdoor" scene. Ironically, this refuge from weather contained a weather all its own, drizzle and mist regularly forming within.

Robert Swarthe, the animation supervisor, was in charge of the spectacular final effects involving colored lights dancing about on the mother ship. It proved easier to animate rather than use actual lighting. At the same time, John Williams was involved in coordinating these images with the score. "Steven's perception was always five notes," Williams would later explain, "though I believed it should be seven. I tried to persuade Steven to change, but he kept saying no; he felt it should be five. 'More of a signal than a melody,' he said." Williams played around with the possibilities until he came up with the now legendary arrangement. He and Spielberg were

The Spielberg signature shot: (*above*) the forces from beyond gather, projecting light and emitting a sense of spirituality; (*below*) the ancient rock formation known to Native Americans as Devils Tower hosts its own little circle of light, where visitors are to be welcomed (courtesy Columbia Pictures).

65

Though he is in the process of losing his own family, Neary becomes foster father to Jilian (Melinda Dillon) and her little boy (Cary Guffey).

fascinated by an idea they borrowed from the nineteenth-century Russian composer Scriabin, who argued that "every note has a color," leading to the coordination of sight and sound in the film.

Close Encounters of the Third Kind was shot during a five-month period in the early months of 1976. During much of the filming on western locations, Spielberg lived in a Winnebago, where he constantly screened *2001* during off hours for inspiration. Dreyfuss and other actors had to perform scenes in which they are overawed by what they observe while looking at nothing more than lighting points. The remarkable sights they react to were shot afterward and added a year following completion of live-action footage, as Trumbull was perfecting a technique called "motion control," in which a digital electronic camera system allowed for automatic control of all functions (pan, tilt, etc.). George Lucas's first *Star Wars* film had employed this system, but only for effects photography; in *Close Encounters of the Third Kind,* it would be used for sequences in which people reacted to the UFOs, allowing for a seamless meshing of separately shot footage.

In addition to groundbreaking technique, Spielberg also relied on time-tested approaches hailing back to the old Hollywood. To create nighttime country roads that would appear convincing yet heightened beyond everyday realism, miniatures were employed. Also, matte shots: essentially, painting elements of the scene rather than building them. Matte artist Matthew Yuricich, who

had painted castles in the background for such 1950s films as *Prince Valiant,* was hired to add the illusion of a Wyoming backdrop to live-action scenes shot at the Alabama hangar.

Columbia Pictures executives were so nervous about someone stealing and printing photos of the aliens (thereby giving away their expensive film's surprise) that they enlisted extra security guards around the clock. Once, Spielberg made the mistake of showing up without his ID badge and was unceremoniously evicted. On a happier note, there was the night when filmmaking was shut down because Spielberg became convinced he had seen a UFO. People grabbed binoculars and stretched out on the ground, looking up—only to discover that an Echo satellite was passing by.

The film begins with just such an appearance-reality theme. The opening shot offers a striking wide-screen vision of Mexico's Sonora Desert, swept by raging winds. An identifying card adds a documentary sense. Lights are perceived through the blowing dust; 1977 viewers assumed that the approaching object was a flying saucer, then were surprised to see a normal, everyday truck pull up. Various people hop out and scurry about; we barely hear what they are saying owing to a Spielbergian din. Then a bearded man in khaki jacket and glasses lunges toward the camera. This must be Richard Dreyfuss; it certainly looks and sounds like the fellow he played in *Jaws.* The audience soon feels confused again, realizing it is another actor, Bob Balaban.

66

In the first thirty seconds of film, then, Spielberg has twice allowed us to trick ourselves without in any way dishonestly manipulating our responses. The viewer watches a little differently from this point on, attempting to see what is there rather than quickly accept the surface as reality. The director's technique is perfectly aligned with his theme; he will do variations on this throughout *Close Encounters of the Third Kind.* One of its many ideas is that we, like the characters, need to adjust our way of seeing.

It is a perfect touch, then, that as Balaban's David Laughlin moves from the truck and across the screen, he joins another key character. A French scientist, Claude Lacombe, is played by François Truffaut (since deceased), noted French New Wave film director. More than a mere casting coup, Truffaut's presence brings with it the romantic notion of the child as a Rosseauian natural man, able to educate adults as to the joys and pleasures to be found in an unsophisticated appreciation of life's wonders. This theme was present in all of Truffaut's films, particularly 1969's *Wild Child,* about a doctor examining a boy raised in the woods, realizing he has more to learn from the child than he can ever teach him ("The child is father to the man," Wordsworth wrote), a theme developed in *Close Encounters of the Third Kind.*

Meanwhile, though, there is the sequence in which David, Lacombe, and other scientists marvel at their discovery: a fleet of World War II aircraft, perfectly preserved, sitting abandoned on the desert like nonmalevo-lent ghosts. Spielberg would further explore his own obsession with old planes—and the men who piloted them—in such diverse films as *1941, Always,* and *Empire of the Sun.* Spielberg's camera approaches them with tender respect, lovingly lingering on details of the control panel, revealing their structures with a nostalgia and sentiment not unlike that in John Ford's *Wings of Eagles.* The theme of communication, imperfectly achieved, has already been introduced in earlier movies, though here it will emerge as an overriding theme, as the characters find alternative systems to language and break through to one another.

Now Spielberg cuts to Muncie, Indiana, offering an atmospheric night scene of an isolated house set against a wondrous, star-filled sky. It is the sky as it looks in the opening sequence of Disney's *Pinocchio,* a film which will shortly play a key role in *Close Encounters of the Third Kind.* With that shot, filmmaker Spielberg established himself as the kind of person Wordsworth wrote about in 1802, the rare man who has managed to grow older without losing his sense of enchantment:

> My heart leaps up when I behold
> A rainbow in the sky;
> So was it when my life began;
> So is it now I am a man . . .

A major focus of Spielberg's art here and elsewhere (especially *E.T.*) is helping the rest of us reclaim that di-

The man-child and the child that is father to the man: The still uncertain Roy watches as innocent, open Barry readily accepts the image placed in his mind by aliens and attempts to actualize it, as Jilian looks on uncomprehendingly.

minished ability by reintroducing us to his special way of seeing. A little boy named Barry (Cary Guffey) is asleep in his room. One by one, his toys appear to come to life: A furry mechanical monkey clashes his cymbals; cars and trucks zip around in circles as Barry wakes and, spellbound, observes from the shadows. He is clearly fascinated but not afraid; his imagination is innocent.

Barry's single mother Jilian Guiler (Melinda Dillon) wakes in terror, not because what's "out there" is evil but because she has lost touch with that aforementioned innocent side of herself. As her child heads for the door, trying to let in what is out there, the mother screams and holds Barry close. In her mind, Barry is too ignorant to understand the threat she assumes is encroaching. The point of the film is that all such assumptions are what keep us from getting in touch with what is good in the world. Children have not yet been "educated" (in the negative sense) to the point of losing touch. Barry represents what Wordsworth would have called the Child as Swain: possessing inborn wisdom which most adults, through various civilizing processes, gradually lose.

There are, however, those rare adults who remain childlike. We are about to meet one. As the theme from Disney's *Pinocchio* ("When you wish upon a star . . .") appears on the sound track, we see Roy Neary (Richard Dreyfuss) playing with a toy train set. In sharp contrast, his kids' eyes are glued to the TV, miniature couch-potato adults. As the phone rings, Roy's wife (Teri Garr) exclaims: "Jiminy Cricket, it's Earl on the phone!" The Disney theme emanates from a Pinocchio doll (importantly, it belongs to Roy, not the children) near him; her everyday exclamation of surprise serves a double function as nickname for Roy, as much a companion to his doll as Jiminy Cricket was to Pinocchio. A non-Disney movie, just then playing on their TV, is also significant. Ronnie, dutiful middle-class mother, wants the kids to turn it off and go to bed; Roy, child-man that he is, argues that they should be allowed to finish watching.

"Its four and a half hours long," Ronnie complains about Cecil B. DeMille's 1956 version of *The Ten Commandments.* Spielberg was too subtle to cut to a close-up of Charlton Heston, waving his staff in the wind, rather allowing the identity of the televised film to be buried in his own film's texture. Still, one key element developed in *Close Encounters of the Third Kind* is religion, particularly in relationship to the soulless existence so many contemporary people lead. The Neary family is obviously a decent, hardworking, semifunctional American family, yet there is no vestige of any religious affiliation in their home, no suggestion they belong to a church and attend, if only on Sundays. Watching a religious film, then, is the nearest contact these kids will come to the Bible; indeed, televised DeMille is essentially the Bible for the TV generation. Significantly, Ronnie insists the kids don't need what is to be found here, even stating, "There's nothing in it for them." On the other hand, Roy argues that "it would be *good* for

them." However unconsciously, he is speaking for himself: What Roy wants, indeed needs, is some sort of center to his existence, which can only come from a spirituality missing in his daily routine. The "close encounter" Roy is about to experience will be with just such a potential force rather than a flying saucer in any conventional sense.

A massive power failure dims the area's lights, so the company Roy works for sends him out to remote Crystal Lake to try and get things going. This is where Jilian wanders about, searching for Barry with a flashlight; earlier, the child rushed out of the house and into the woods, laughing gleefully, pursued by a desperate Jilian, who failed to realize that in fearing the unknown, we ourselves make it malevolent, if only in our own minds. Roy will be noticeably more open and accessible. In his truck, parked near a train crossing, Roy considers a map, half-jokingly shrieking: "Help—I'm lost!" This connects him to David, by his own admission a mapmaker. David will serve as Roy's foil, the secret sharer who dramatically complements the protagonist, an idea already suggested by the fact that in the opening, we briefly believed it was Dreyfuss playing David.

Meanwhile, lights pull up behind Roy; he sees them in the rearview mirror and waves the vehicle around, though we wonder if perhaps it's a flying saucer. No, it's only another car, so our assumption is incorrect. When another set of lights appears and Roy likewise waves, we now conversely assume it's a car. This time, the lights go directly up instead of around. An audience-pleasing joke, yet one that extends the film's theme of appearance versus reality by again setting up the audience to make assumptions (tricking ourselves rather than being tricked) which will prove as untenable as those made by characters within the movie. We don't merely watch *Close Encounters of the Third Kind,* but experience it; we don't just view the on-screen characters' experiences but ourselves undergo a set of experiences that parallel theirs.

Important, too, is that Roy listens to a radio-communication device, precisely as key Spielberg characters have done (without any success at actually communicating) in *The Sugarland Express* and *Jaws.* Roy's feeble attempts to mechanically make contact with people is drowned out by an incessant din of voices as unseen characters try and make verbal contact with one another. The movie will lead directly to, then end with, a successful attempt at communicating on simple, nonverbal, if highly technological, levels; the characters will necessarily learn that modern systems must be abandoned in favor of a move back to the basics.

Meanwhile, the child Barry has darted down an open road, as if hoping to literally rise up into the seductive stars. He is halfway to the *E.T.* flight, also presaging *Hook.* At an isolated bend in the road, in the middle of nowhere, diverse people sit, waiting patiently. The singular look on their differing faces suggests a benign madness; they certainly are mad in the sense that they sud-

Spielberg's signature shot: Illumination pours into the room as little Barry, unafraid, opens a door to the magical but potentially dangerous possibilities of the universe.

denly comprehend reality in a radically alternative manner. They have unknowingly formed a cult, all "touched" by something that spiritually brushed by; they now "know" in ways that cannot be expressed in words. They resemble early Christians, expecting the imminent return of the Messiah; when, at film's end, we finally do see the star creatures, there is something saviorlike about them. As Pauline Kael would write in the *New Yorker*,

"They're sunburst Gods arriving through Blakean Old Testament clouds. This isn't nuts-and-bolts Popular Mechanics S.F.; it's beatific technology—machines from outer space deified."

"Ice cream," little Barry says while pointing heavenward, referring to the conelike shape of the UFO. Roy, joining them, watches as the rest of the "flock" rises. Roy is with them but not completely of them. As the others rise and stare heavenward, he does not, muttering: "This is nuts." Though Roy is more in tune than a typical suburbanite, he is normal enough to doubt in a way other observers do not. Which makes him an effective audience surrogate, also setting into motion the film's internal drama: Roy's spiritual journey from potential visionary to radical innocent who can accept the dazzling offer of a grand metaphysical adventure.

It also establishes Roy as a Spielbergian outsider, much like Brody in *Jaws*. It is in this mental state that Roy now enters the film's second act; the exposition is complete, the drama proper about to begin.

At the state line, comedy relief introduces the dozing tollbooth guard, who, sleepy-eyed, watches in amazement as the UFO whizzes by, with police cars (recyclings of the ones we saw in *The Sugarland Express*) in hot pursuit. One car even crashes, an obligatory touch for audiences expecting such payoff moments. Meanwhile, back at the flock, Roy now stands among the others, watching in awe as the triad of lights move apart, each heading in a separate direction. The moment they are gone, the area's own lighting power returns. But when Roy later tries to explain what he has seen to Ronnie, it is obvious she is as grounded in reality as he is poised for flights of fancy. Ronnie worries about his "sunburned" face, talks about his need to get to work, worries what the neighbors will think; he hungers to share his remarkable moment with her, giving up when he senses she can never see as he sees. They are not Spielberg's first husband and wife who married early, only to discover they are essentially incompatible, nor will they be the last.

Act 2 chronicles the inner conflict raging between Roy's two sides. He receives nonverbal information from above in a way everyday adults cannot, yet there is a conformist element that keeps Roy from easily becoming cognizant of this information, like the open-receptive Barry. For Roy, the Idea must slowly emerge into consciousness from behind layers of worthless social information that block spiritual salvation; it does so by assuming the form of a shape he becomes obsessed with. Everything he sees—shaving foam, the bed pillow, mashed potatoes on his dinner plate—begs to be moulded into a mountain. Understandably, then, when Roy returns to that epiphany spot the next night, Barry (in the company of his mother) likewise constructs just such a mountain while playing in the dirt. What is easy for the child to accept is difficult for the man; he has so much unlearning to accomplish first. Yet there remains within Roy a strong potential for childlike response:

> Though nothing can bring back the hour
>   of splendor in the grass, of glory in the flower;
> We will grieve not, rather find
> Strength in what remains behind;
> In the primal sympathy
> Which having been must ever be . . .

Roy possesses that "primal sympathy" described by Wordsworth in "Ode on Intimations of Immortality" (1802–4). To a lesser degree, so does Jilian. Understandably, then, he, Jilian, and Barry are (unbeknownst to them) becoming a makeshift alternate family; when Jilian recognizes Roy, it is clear some vague, unspoken understanding has begun, the very sort of bond missing in Roy's marriage.

Roy Neary can be interpreted as a (perhaps surprisingly) sympathetic portrait of Spielberg's own father, who left the family to find himself and something that had been lost in his conventional existence. When lights descend from the sky, the appearance-reality theme returns. The multitude (and we) realize (Roy now rising with the others in as open a manner as possible) that what is descending is a government helicopter. The mechanical din creates confusion, then chaos below, a replay of the helicopter hovering over the beach in *Jaws*. Spielberg has again allowed us to trick ourselves, believing we were watching the UFO return, only to realize it was an everyday object.

Eventually, government officials will tell the media that all supposed sightings are likewise explainable. The scene in which viewers realize that an apparent UFO may merely be a whirlybird lends validity to what they say. For the necessary contrast—the alternative way of seeing, spiritual acceptance as opposed to logical-intellectual—Spielberg cuts to Dharmsala, North India, as Lacombe and David arrive and find themselves surrounded by thousands of people. India was, at the time, perceived as a land where deeply held spiritual beliefs (however different from our own) remained firmly entrenched. When Lacombe asks one man from what direction the five notes these people repeatedly chant come from and his companion turns and repeats the question in his native language (Spielberg's theme of breaking down language barriers to communicate), they point fingers skyward en masse.

The moment conveys the filmmaker's vision of a simpler society where people can, as a community, still believe in the existence of something miraculous on high. This theme, as well as the recurring communication motif, reappears when Lacombe speaks in a large American auditorium. Significantly, only a few Western people bother to attend, spirituality being all but forgotten on our shores. Those who do create a simple sign language, based on that chant, for true believers to use when attempting to "break through" to whatever is out there. Lacombe and David then head for the Goldstone Radio Telescope, where they send out electronic signals based on the five notes. There, former mapmaker David realizes that the notes are translatable into geographic coordinates. We look not at them but with them as they grab a globe and point to the Devils Tower, Wyoming; we share their excitement as Spielberg's point of view induces us to become participants in these strange events rather than observers.

"There's still so much we don't know," Lacombe says, sighing. Overcoming fear by unlearning it is not easy:

Jilian will never fully arrive, foreshadowed by the image we see of her, an aspiring artist, tearing up her sketches of a mountain. Simultaneously, her son's openness is clear when he instinctually plays the five-note song on his xylophone. Barry's eyes light up as he realizes "they" are coming back for him. In the film's most memorable scene, he opens the door, allowing light to stream in and wash over him. It is the light of knowledge as well as the lights of a UFO. Still locked into contemporary adult perception, Jilian notices immense clouds rolling in, which appear menacing to her; how could they not when they visually echo the sinister cloud that enveloped Grant Williams in the classic 1957 sci-fi movie *The Incredible Shrinking Man?*

The next time we see Jilian, at U.S. Air Force headquarters, she is photographed from a new angle, emphasizing for the first time in the film actress Melinda Dillon's physical resemblance to Goldie Hawn. The theme of a mother attempting to recapture her lost child is revived, if in an entirely different genre. The military spokesmen look remarkably like the town elders in *Jaws,* insisting there is "nothing out there" (for the public good), though they know better. "There are all kinds of ideas that would be fun to believe in," a designated spokesman announces to the supposed UFO witnesses, mentioning everything from immortality to Santa Claus.

However hard, cold, even quasi-villainous this man may be, the bureaucrat does hit a nerve: It is nice to believe! Spielberg had already begun to divide mankind into two camps: the believers (those with faith in something beyond the here and now despite lack of proof) and the nonbelievers (the vast majority, who have become immune, through the grinding task of daily survival in an ever less pleasant world, to faith in anything other than what they can see, touch, or hear). Roy is in the process of discovering he is a believer: As the press conference ends, we see him sketching the mountain on his newspaper, an unconscious act of belief despite all the mounting evidence to the contrary.

Close Encounters of the Third Kind, then, is less a film about flying saucers than metaphysics. We watch as the military men, once rid of these pesky "witnesses," hop onto buses and head for the Devils Tower, making ready for the expected contact with aliens. They plan a massive evacuation (they will announce that deadly nerve gas has leaked in this part of Wyoming) while smuggling in equipment on trucks supposedly carrying food for chain stores. Spielberg ironically cuts to the dinner table where the Neary family—representatives of consumer culture—enjoys those very products. Roy has built a makeshift mountain near his train set and, joining the family for a meal, is clearly a man obsessed with an idea that is having difficulty in breaking through but which will not be denied. Spielberg and his cinematographer William Fraker effectively angle their camera around the table to visually isolate Roy; though there is no editing (it is one long, continuous shot) and Roy sits with his family, he is always perceived as alone rather than in their company, the camera carefully moving so as to reveal either him or them, visually affirming that he has become an outsider even in his own house.

When he builds the mashed-potato mountain and the kids join his wife in tears, he can only whisper: "This *means* something to me," reestablishing Roy's frenzied, obsessive search for something beyond the here and now. Unlike Barry, his own indoctrinated kids cannot comprehend; they are little adults now, and he is the child, a theme perfectly visualized as they remain in the house while Roy wanders out back and sits on their swing set. The following morning, as he wakes on the couch, Roy happens to see an old Warner Bros. cartoon on TV in which a little space invader perplexes Bugs Bunny; like the William Atherton character in *The Sugarland Express,* he is inspired by a seemingly insipid cartoon to comprehend his destiny.

The next sequence has Roy darting about the house, tossing all manner of things out the window, seized by a compulsion to build his own personal mountain, take the image from his mind and objectify it as an actuality. Perhaps Roy represents Spielberg himself envisioning a film project (mountain) perceived by others as too fanciful, willing to risk being labeled crazy by attempting to create it at the risk of alienating family and friends.

His wife shoves the kids into the car and (the camera inside with them) drives off to her sister's house. Importantly, Roy does not want them to leave; he would like to conform, has even tried to do so by pulling apart his mountain. But in so doing, he knocks off the peak and inadvertently completes his creation: The flat rather than pointed top at last completes his cognition.

Then, like other Spielberg heroes before and after him, Roy finds himself alone, possessing his vision but devoid of human contact. He is on the phone (the modern, mechanical, ineffectual way of attempting to communicate) with Ronnie, begging her to come back ("it was a joke!"), offering to do whatever she deems necessary. ("Anything you want, I'll do!") He is not a simplistically drawn nonconformist but, in many respects, an average guy, or at least a man who has tried hard to live as an average guy.

In one of the film's most striking images, Roy stands in the living room, his huge Devils Tower model to his left (his dark, unconventional side), the TV (his bright, conventional side) to his right, broadcasting soap operas and beer commercials. He not only stands between the two polar extremes physically, but also emotionally and mentally. Then the dualities merge, forming the oneness Roy has been searching for: He turns at precisely the right moment as an ABC news report shows the Devils Tower evacuated for supposed nerve-gas leaks. Roy glances to his left, then to his right; what he sees is one and the same. He hangs up on Ronnie (and, in so doing, on his past life), finally fully surrendering to his instincts. (There is no turning back now.) At this point, the film's third act begins: Roy heads for the Devils Tower and the inevitable resolution.

Jilian is also watching TV; in a touching gesture, she

71

The Spacecraft, a marvel of light and magical possibilities, captivates the child Barry.

Light, in Spielberg films, has many meanings: The light emitting from the mother ship represents the spirituality not only of these benign aliens but also of motherhood itself; it also represents the light of the movie projector that makes the viewing of films possible (courtesy Columbia Pictures).

leans forward, pressing her hand against the TV screen, as if through it she might feel the mountain and her missing boy as well: Think ahead to the mother in *Poltergeist* trying to retrieve her child from inside a TV! Hurrying out the door, Jilian glances back and forth from her painting of the Devils Tower to the TV image; before exiting, Roy glances back and forth from his model-mountain to the TV image. Though they are far apart, the rapid cutting between their parallel actions visually establishes the emotional marriage taking place. Shortly, he is in a car, driving rapidly while trying to read a map. ("I used to read maps," his alter ego, David, earlier told Lacombe.)

Cars are on the road everywhere as people try to leave the "condemned" area, likewise recalling the caravans of cars in *Sugarland*. Significantly, Roy drives in the opposite direction of the others, hoping to slip in as they desperately scramble to get out. The din—human and mechanical—is overwhelming; as Roy enters Moorcroft, Wyoming, he is surrounded by passenger cars and army trucks as well as screaming people as terrified as if they were on the shark-infested beach at Martha's Vineyard. Jilian, in a state of fear and confusion, is being herded aboard a train, a precursor of the *Schindler's List* victims. The two rush toward one another and embrace, something we accept (despite the fact that they have barely spoken) through the carefully established sense of a marriage of minds.

They drive away, over the prairie, up to a knoll where

Roy Neary, the child-man who maintains a potential for open and optimistic reactions (courtesy Columbia Pictures).

Newsweek: "If there's a presiding influence, it's Disney, with his metamorphic genius, sentimental idealism, and feeling for the technical magic of movies as a paradigm for a technological utopia." In truth, the key to Spielberg's unique appeal is the ability to combine what was best about those disparate, even polar (in sensibility), filmmakers.

Roy and Jilian are stopped by space-suited guards (who look so frightfully alien that for a moment we might believe they are the invaders) and brought to a headquarters. There, separated from Jilian, Roy at last confronts

an upward camera movement follows them to a barbed-wire fence, allowing us to see the Devils Tower at the moment they see it; essentially, we are the third member of their little party, the director having seduced us into becoming one of these open, believing, trusting people. In addition to its Native American spiritual significance, Devils Tower allowed for a Hitchcockian pursuit sequence, in the manner of *North by Northwest*'s Mt. Rushmore finale. It is worth noting that at this moment, John Williams's musical score suddenly turns Hitchcockian in general, reminiscent of *North by Northwest* in particular.

There is also much of Disney here (in the following sequence and previous ones), as Jack Kroll pointed out in

David Laughlin. As David softly cross-examines Roy, the camera crosscuts from one to the other, and they appear to be one man, looking into a mirror.

DAVID: You felt compelled to be here?
ROY: Yeah.
DAVID: What did you expect to find?
ROY: An answer.

Though the army wants to remove Roy, Jilian, and the dozen other civilian intruders, David (from his discussions with Lacombe, also present) knows better: He explains to the ranking officer that these people all received an "implanted vision" when they made "psychic connection." Hundreds of others doubtless did the same and tried to reach this point. In Kael's words, "it's a going-to-Bethlehem story. Only those with enough faith and luck make it." But the military will not listen: Roy is herded onto a waiting helicopter where Jilian and others sit, wearing gas masks. (The army still pretends there is a health danger.) These people consider one another knowingly, sensing they constitute a psychic clique. "A small group of people who have a shared vision," Lacombe says, noting their escape attempt.

"They were invited," David insists to the officer as Roy and Jilian make their way up the steep hill. The army drops sleeping gas to stop them. "They're just crop dusting," Roy tells Jilian, and we half-expect her to reply with that famous line from Hitchcock's *North by Northwest:* "They're dusting crops where there ain't no crops!" The others do indeed stagger and fall along the way, though Roy and Jilian continue on; at the summit, he can't quite reach the top, though she is already there. Spielberg reverses the roles from *North by Northwest;* now it's the strong woman who reaches down to the faltering man, grabbing his hand to save him. The inverse of the Cary Grant/Eva Marie Saint situation in Hitchcock's film, it is in keeping with the dominant-woman theme Spielberg set into motion in *Sugarland*'s Goldie Hawn/William Atherton relationship.

Eventually, Roy and Jilian do make it to the other side, where the meeting is already in progress. The assembled equipment continually broadcasts the five-note piece with an oboe solo, an attempt to communicate by returning to the basics. "Inter-gallactic Esperanto," one critic called it. When Lacombe steps out to greet the descending star craft, his arms wide open, Spielberg once more stirs moviegoing memory buds, this time echoing the image of the scientist in *The Thing,* produced by Howard Hawks, rewarded for such openness to an alien with a horrid death. Again, Spielberg revives the image, only to reverse it: His scientist's sincere greetings of friendship are returned. *The Shrinking Man* cloud then descends, containing within it the mother ship, which will shortly light up the sky like some great candelabra.

Here Roy and Jilian part company, he descending to join the scientists, while she chooses to remain behind.

JILIAN: I'm just not ready.
ROY: I can't stay. I've got to get down there.

He, not she, is the chosen one, the final existing member of that diverse cult, the only one who has passed all tests, persevering until his presence finally has to be acknowledged and accepted. Before he goes, they kiss—a kiss at once adulterous and innocent—before he descends to the area where the lights and music are all but dancing as initial communication is achieved.

"Oh, my God!" one scientist mutters as he glimpses the enormity of the mother ship. On the simplest level,

this is a commonplace utterance of amazement; on another, he has no idea how right he is, for the spiritual-religious quest Roy has embarked on is about to reach its happy conclusion. Feminists should rejoice at Spielberg films: In his view, God is indeed a woman (*mother* ship). As the mother ship's entranceway opens and a stream of light pours out, the missing World War II fliers exit, looking as young as the day they were abducted, offering a germ of an idea later expanded in 1989's *Always.* Barry emerges and is reunited with his mother (Jilian has at last come down from the mountain), recalling the epilogue to *The Sugarland Express.*

Then a spiderlike thing appears in the craft's doorway, frightening many onlookers; but it is the appearance, not the essence, that matters, allowing the film to conclude on the key theme introduced in the opening shot. While many onlookers turn and run (just as many moviegoers avert their eyes), those few who do not flinch at the sight—who have learned that beauty truly is in the eye of the beholder—form the "elect" that gets to go on board for the last, greatest adventure of all. Jilian will not be among them; she is seen snapping pictures, an observer rather than a doer. In contrast, Roy beamingly steps forward, but only after he and the other volunteers are blessed in prayer by a holy father ("Grant these pilgrims a happy journey, God"), making clear that Roy has indeed found in this physical journey the religious experience he has been searching for. He has at last made his innocent Disneyesque dreams come true; we know that from the reappearance of the melody "When you wish upon a star," heard again as he enters the craft. Then, in a rightfully famous finale, a diminutive alien (more child than midget) smiles sweetly at the onlookers before departing.

In the original cut, the film ended here. The director later insisted that the film, as released in 1977, was actually "a work in progress," hurried onto theater screens when Columbia decided to move up the distribution date from late December to mid-November so that *Close Encounters* would be around for more of the holiday moviegoing season. When the film more than met the studio's box-office expectations, Columbia responded by allowing Spielberg to shoot further footage, including an extended sequence within the mother ship. Several critics hailed this as an improvement on a fabulous but flawed film, since Spielberg also cut back on the manic mashed-potato-mountain sequence, generally considered "excessive" and "overdone." At any rate, in 1980, Spielberg turned out a "special edition" which ran three minutes shorter than the original while taking the story slightly further.

This writer has always preferred the original cut. Roy's apparent madness seems to me the very essence of what the film is about, a happy case of risk taking on the part of both the writer-director and actor Dreyfuss. On the other hand, the interior shots of the mother ship appear unnecessary. Though splendid to look at, they can't come close to the interiors that, in the original version, we were forced to mentally create, each of us in our own individual minds.

Apparently, Spielberg felt the same way. In an interview conducted for the laser-disc release of *Close Encounters of the Third Kind,* he states flatly: "I never wanted to show the inside of the mother ship." Columbia allowed him to film for seven additional weeks only if he guaranteed them this sequence. Notable among the moments Spielberg was anxious to complete is a shot of the *Cotopaxi,* an American cargo ship lost in the Bermuda Triangle. Spielberg envisioned it turning up (thanks to the aliens) in the middle of the Gobi Desert. Greg Jein and his staff built a replica, and this striking visual effect was at last created. It stands as a Spielberg equivalent to what critics refer to as "Hitchcock moments," those singular shots that haunt one's memory long after the overall movie has grown fuzzy. "I added more gestalt and took out some kitsch," the director later quipped.

Dr. J. Allen Hyneck, whose writings on UFOs provided key research for Spielberg, plays himself in the film (courtesy Columbia Pictures).

1941

Steven Spielberg (*center*) prepares to direct one of the elaborate Hollywood Boulevard sequences. Dan Aykroyd stands directly behind him (courtesy Universal City Studios).

A UNIVERSAL PICTURES/COLUMBIA PICTURES RELEASE, 1979

CAST

Dan Aykroyd *(Sergeant Tree);* Ned Beatty *(Ward Douglas);* John Belushi *("Wild Bill" Kelso);* Treat Williams *(Sitarski);* Nancy Allen *(Donna);* Robert Stack *(Gen. Joseph W. Stilwell);* Tim Matheson *(Birkhead);* Toshiro Mifune *(Commander Mitamura);* Christopher Lee *(Von Kleinschmidt);* Warren Oates *(Maddox);* Bobby DiCicco *(Wally);* Dianne Kay *(Betty Douglas);* Murray Hamilton *(Claude);* Lorraine Gary *(Mrs. Douglas);* Slim Pickens *(Hollis Wood);* Eddie Deezen *(Herbie);* Wendie Jo Sperber *(Maxine);* John Candy *(Foley);* Joe Flaherty *(USO MC);* Penny Marshall *(Miss Fitzroy);* Susan Backlinie *(Woman Swimmer);* also, Patti LuPone, Dub Taylor, Elisha Cook Jr., Lionel Stander, and Lucille Benson.

CREDITS

Director, Steven Spielberg; screenplay, Robert Zemeckis and Bob Gale, from a story by Zemeckis, Gale, and John Milius; executive producer, Milius; producer, Buzz Feitshans; cinematography, William Fraker; production design, Dean Edward Mitzner; editor, Michael Kahn; music, John Williams; special effects, A. D. Flowers; costumes, Deborah Nadoolman; art director, William F. O'Brien; associate to Mr. Milius, Kathleen Kennedy; running time, 118 mins.; rating: PG.

In 1975, University of Southern California (USC) students Robert Zemeckis and Bob Gale both attended a course taught by John Milius, bearded macho man of the movie brats, then penning the script for Francis Ford Coppola's *Apocalypse Now.* Spielberg took a liking to the enthusiastic, young would-be writers, encouraging them to collaborate.

Zemeckis and Gale, searching for a subject, poured over old newspapers at the USC library. They happened to notice a banner headline from thirty-five years earlier: "Battle Enemy Air Raiders Over L.A." Reading on, they learned that on February 23, 1942, a Japanese submarine had surfaced along the California coast, near Santa Barbara, lobbing some twenty-five shells at the Richfield Oil Refinery and inflicting minor damage. Observers

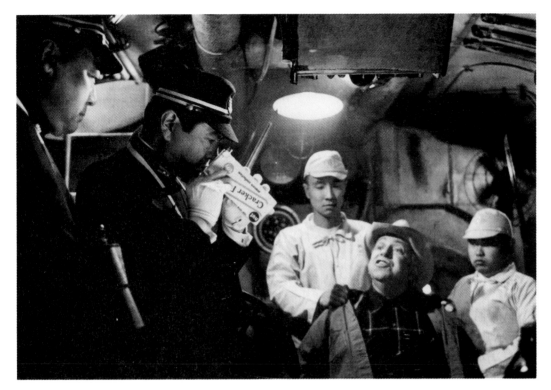

Lumberjack Hollis Wood
(Slim Pickens, *seated*) is
cross-examined aboard
the submarine by
Commander Mitamura
(Toshiro Mifune, *far left*)
(courtesy Universal City
Studios).

noted that the sub had an airplane hangar on deck, so several nights later, when the sound of a strange engine was heard in the skies above L.A., panic struck. Civil defense officials shot out porch lights and neon signs, while anti-aircraft batteries fired routinely into the sky. Street riots were reported, but after eight hours in which no enemy attack took place, things gradually calmed down, and the city returned to normal.

Zemeckis and Gale felt they were on to something and pitched their concept to Milius, who was intrigued enough to suggest they develop the idea further. Milius talked M-G-M into financing the script. In 1977, the writers handed their professor the untitled piece; it was Milius who, after reading it, coined the original title, *The Night the Japs Attacked.* This proved patently offensive to everyone at M-G-M. "I was practically accused of being a war criminal," Milius would later acknowledge. Studio executives rejected the script, in part because there were no good gags in what was supposed to be a comedy. Also, they estimated it would cost a (then) whopping $6 million to make.

Milius and Spielberg occasionally relaxed together by shooting skeet at the Oak Tree Gun Club. One day, Milius arranged for Zemeckis and Gale to show up and pitch the idea, supposedly to get another opinion, though in fact hoping to involve the world's most successful filmmaker. At that moment, Spielberg had been planning to at last put special effects and immense set pieces behind him, tackling a smaller, highly personal "people movie" based on his childhood experiences in Phoenix, tentatively to be titled either *Growing Up* or *After School,*

The typical (or, perhaps, idealized) American family meets Beetle Bailey and his boys: Sergeant Tree (Dan Aykroyd) asks permission to station an antiaircraft gun in the front yard of Ward (Ned Beatty) and Joan (Lorraine Gary) Douglas (courtesy Universal City Studios).

a Little Rascals–type movie. However, he had made the mistake of mentioning this in public, so the market was shortly glutted with just such films *(Stand by Me, The Goonies,* etc.). Besides, Spielberg found himself unable to bring such intensely personal material into focus.

"I hadn't grown up enough to make *Growing Up*," he admitted. So he allowed himself to be drawn into the emerging debacle. "It wasn't a film from my heart," he told *Rolling Stone* shortly after the film's release. "It wasn't a project I initiated, dreamed about for ten years, although I have shed blood over it as if it were my own. Rather than a bastard adoption, I like to think of it at times as if it were a project I was forced to take because of my own state of mind." Just what was that state of mind? Spielberg later told the *New York Times:* "They caught me at a weak moment." He was just then in the middle of grueling postproduction work on *Close Encounters of the Third Kind* and was desperately in need of being cheered up. "They cheered me up, all right," he declared in retrospect, noting that the script was not of high quality. "Reading the screenplay was about as tasteful an experience as reading *Mad* magazine. But the immediate spirit of heightened comic fantasy grabbed me. Besides, I always had wanted to do a comedy like *Hellzapoppin'.*"

It was Spielberg who gave the film its title, feeling *1941* would suggest an entire era of simplistic good feelings and American patriotic fervor. Spielberg also decided that the story should be moved from February 1942 to December 1941 to incorporate the Christmas season trappings into the texture. For reasons of his own, Spielberg did not want to work at M-G-M, so Milius—now with the role of "executive producer"—brought the script to Universal. They turned it down on the grounds that this high-concept comedy would cost close to $20 million, a hefty price tag for a project they rightly felt was, at best, a gamble. They might have taken it on the strength of Spielberg's name, but didn't really believe the preeminent Spielberg was serious about wanting to direct.

Milius then brought the project to Columbia, where it was given a green light. Immediately, Universal executives feared they may have made a major error by first passing on it, now insisting they be allowed to participate on the grounds that Spielberg still had obligations to fulfill at their studio, owing to clauses in a contract dating back to *Jaws.* Columbia agreed, partly because *1941* was looking more expensive by the minute (the budget eventually reached $40 million), so the resources of both studios would be required. A deal was worked out whereby Universal would release the film domestically, while Columbia would do so worldwide; everybody would make a whole lot of money.

But reality has a way of mercilessly intruding. "It was sorta like going in for X-ray treatments each day and you realize the cure is worse than the disease," he eventually recalled in an interview with Chris Hodenfield. "Every day I'd go onto the set, it would just get worse and worse. The utter pressure of having to deliver funny material. We had to come up with it privately or in a great crazed outcry of 'Make me laugh!' "

One way of trying to make the humor happen was by playing everything at a whirlwind pace, hoping such an accelerated approach might create a sense of slapstick speed. Spielberg employed what he called a "stopwatch method," imploring the actors to deliver dialogue in half the time it would normally take.

Much of the film was shot on vast interior sets at the Burbank Studios, including a carefully researched replica of Hollywood Boulevard circa 1941. At one point, Spielberg spent a week shooting a single sequence in which a street-corner Santa (played by Milius) runs down the street, firing a gun wildly, terrifying everyone; though it was necessary to keep the entire cast on hand for night shoots that lasted until 4:30 A.M., the sequence was eventually cut out, since it simply did not work. Other key scenes were shot at the Long Beach airport, where a dozen vintage World War II airplanes were leased, as well as inside a former theater, converted to look like the old USO, where Spielberg put more than a hundred dancers through their paces during an elaborate jitterbug contest. Over fifty stunt experts were employed, many of their immense undertakings filmed with the Louma Crane, a recently created technical innovation from France that employed a modular, hand-portable camera platform (Spielberg described it as looking like a *brontosaurus*), allowing for unprecedented flexibility in moving in and out of a scene, from close-up to long shot, creating a striking sensation of kinetic energy on-screen. Inventors Jean-Marie Lavalou and Alain Maseron were on hand to witness the Louma's first major Hollywood employment. Theirs was the only such crane in existence, and Spielberg's company rented it at a whopping cost of $8,000 per week.

Exteriors included an oceanside cliff near Malibu, where the crew constructed a two-story colonial house, eventually demolished for the spectacular finale. For the more difficult sequences in which planes soar down and strafe the city, miniature sets were constructed, including one of the largest ever, a precisely detailed replica of Hollywood Boulevard and the Ocean Park Amusement pier. Strangely enough, though, Spielberg—while employing such state-of-the-art techniques to make his period-piece setting ring true for modern, visually sophisticated audiences—told interviewers that what he was after was a retro-approach, adopting the filmmaking standards used when his story took place. "Everything here is done the way they did it then. I've had it with technology. I'm going to make this one as physical as possible. No more science-fiction films, either; the ones I want to do are more about sociology."

He would shortly eat those words, getting to work on *Raiders of the Lost Ark, E.T.,* and *Poltergeist.* Meanwhile, for the project at hand, Spielberg brought his talents as a visual-conceptual artist to bear, having originally been attracted to the gagless script's striking possibilities for vast panoramas. Before *Close Encounters of the Third Kind* even reached theaters, Spielberg was huddling with artist George Jensen. The director would, with his finger, indicate an imaginary line across the center of a tablet page, telling Jensen, "The horizon goes here."

Jensen quickly sketched it in. The city's streetlights followed, stars were added, with the tail section of an old airplane ultimately tucked into the corner. In no time at all, Jensen had, under Spielberg's direction, transformed a blank page into a fully realized aerial view of bygone Los Angeles. The process continued until every single camera setup for the movie had been sketched in vivid detail; these storyboard drawings were then tacked onto the wall of Spielberg's office.

This painstaking process worked when creating dramas like *Jaws* and *Close Encounters of the Third Kind*. But a comedy requires spontaneity, and the planning of each and every scene down to the tiniest detail automatically destroys an atmosphere in which spontaneity can be

achieved, especially during a production that takes up the better part of a year. As things grew ever more desperate, Spielberg called in Chuck Jones as a special consultant; the genius behind the greatest of the Bugs Bunny cartoons at Warner Bros., Jones attempted to help approximate the anarchic style of animation in hopes of energizing what was turning into a leaden mess. But what works in a seven-minute short—nonstop bang! bang! humor—grows exhausting and irritating when sustained for several hours.

The film was completed in mid-April, and the painstaking editing process began. Universal had hoped to open the film on November 15 in order to have the longest possible run during the upcoming Christmas sea-

The advertising poster that effectively captured Spielberg's zany vision for his epic-comedy film; if only the movie were half as much fun as this colorful panel promises.

A comic variation on the continuing Spielberg hero, an average guy who rises to heroic proportions under bizarre circumstances, dishwasher Wally Stephens (Bobby DiCicco) jitterbugs with Maxine Dexheimer (Wendie Jo Sperber) at the USO club; background singers resembling the Andrews Sisters attest to Spielberg's ongoing infatuation with the 1940s (courtesy Universal City Studios).

son. Theaters were booked, but as the date approached, distributors scrambled for some other feature to play for a month because *1941* was not ready. The film was previewed first in Dallas, then Denver, and the results of reaction cards handed in by computer-selected audiences were disastrous. Likewise, fifteen MCA executives, who had attended the Dallas screening, afterward made no secret of the fact that they were horrified at what they saw.

Worse still were the reviews. In *Variety,* Roger Angell wrote:

The movie is too childish and impatient to stay with most of its events and far-out turns of plot long enough for them to yield many laughs, and the basic humor is a sock in the jaw followed by a kick in the groin . . . the impression of the picture is of a very high-budget high-school variety show.

David Ansen of *Newsweek* complained:

Somewhere inside this bloated epic a slim movie is screaming to be heard. *1941* is like the most expensive Erector Set a kid has ever had to play with, and having put the pieces together, Spielberg takes a kid's relish in destroying them one by one.

The film's sub is piloted by a Japanese captain (Toshiro Mifune) and a German officer (Christopher Lee). The captain in this fictionalized version hopes to do damage to that most American of places, Hollywood, before departing. General Stilwell (Robert Stack) has been dispatched to protect the populace. His young aid, Larry

Warren Oates as Col. "Mad Man" Maddox (courtesy Universal City Studios).

Birkhead (Tim Matheson), is far more interested in scoring with Donna Stratton (Nancy Allen). Difficult to seduce on land, Donna has a deep, dark secret—she is a pushover when airborne, a problem for Larry, who flunked out of flight school. Other couples are having problems of their own: Wally (Bobby DiCicco) hopes to win a dance contest with pretty Betty Douglas (Dianne Kay), though serviceman Sitarski (Treat Williams) keeps trying to cut in. But Betty's plump best friend (Wendie Jo Sperber) considers Sitarski's arrogance a turn-on. As the film concludes, three young couples are arm in arm, a nod to ancient stage comedy from Plautus to Shakespeare.

The "big" special-effects sequences fall flat. Matheson's plane roars over Hollywood Boulevard amid a hail of antiaircraft fire from trigger-happy troops who suspect him of being the enemy, while he desperately attempts to conquer Miss Stratton. An immense roller coaster, shot off its hinges, rolls down the Santa Monica pier into the ocean, with Eddie Deezen, Murray Hamilton, and a dummy on board. These set pieces are as hollow in spirit as they are seamless in technique. Much of the film is downright annoying, including an early food-fight sequence, with various servicemen throwing eggs and other items in a diner. It is worth noting that staging food fights would never be Spielberg's forte; fifteen years later, the one in *Hook*'s lost boys' hideout is not a noticeable improvement.

Worse, the script takes a bad little boy's gleeful plea-

sure at looking up girls' dresses. It's childish (in the infantile sense) rather than childlike (in the innocent sense). Throughout the film, young women constantly fall over on their sides to reveal their 1940s garter belts and stockings or hike up their dresses to provide peekaboo pleasure for the male audience. Such sexist stunts constitute a modern young man's lewdest notion of the forties, based on Hollywood movie images glimpsed during his childhood. But there is an offensively leering quality here; intended as sophisticated, nostalgic scenes, they play as crass and vulgar in context.

Yet elements do attest to Spielberg's involvement, adding an aura of interest for any serious student of the director's body of work. At first, Wally seems the least likely character to emerge as a hero; he's a short order cook and, in his spare time, a lover, not a fighter. Like other Spielberg heroes, he tries to reason with his antagonists rather than fight them. Eventually, though, he does don one of those uniforms he claims to hate; before the film's end, he acts more courageously than any of the actual servicemen, taking over the command and chasing away invaders. In that sense, he is like Brody in *Jaws,* the outsider who moves in and saves the day.

Kelso, meanwhile, is at one point glimpsed flying around in circles, uncertain where he is, peering at a map and screaming, "Lost!" Though the context is different, this is a precise replay of the *Close Encounters* scene in which Neary became lost at the railroad crossing. Here, though, the character flies a World War II fighter plane; Spielberg has already demonstrated his great fascination for such warmly remembered aircraft.

The theme of a husband and wife who have grown apart reoccurs here: Lorraine Gary, the vaguely disaffected Mrs. Brody in *Jaws,* again plays a wife with little left in common with her gun-nut husband. Their impressionable boys imitate his every move and become so violence-prone that they set traps for the Japanese which instead ensnare their own sister Betty. Parent-child bonding may be only briefly suggested here, but it is present.

The film takes place under one of those Spielbergian dins as antiaircraft guns fire into the sky and people screech constantly. This incidental noise is always in danger of drowning out the feeble attempts at human communication. Also, a fearful view of the crowd that can change moods in a moment is present; the people panicking on Hollywood Boulevard resemble the crazed swimmers in *Jaws.* Again, the people in charge, screaming for order over loudspeakers, cannot communicate over the ever-escalating noise. Other characters likewise have trouble communicating through mechanical means; when Birkhead takes Donna up in the plane, he is terrified to realize that there is no two-way radio on board. Kelso also finds that his radio does not work at the moment when he needs it the most.

But the overriding theme is a love for old movies. Like so many other Spielberg films, *1941* is ultimately about films, based less on reality than *reel* life. It is hardly co-

incidental, for instance, that General Stilwell (the film's only historical character) spends almost the entire movie in a theater, watching a movie. Stilwell and the audience surrounding him mirrors the audience watching *1941;* the pleasure these on-screen people derive from the wonderful escapism (it's a film by Walt Disney, the Spielberg of the forties) represents the pleasure that modern audiences were supposed to derive from *1941.*

Also significant is that the particular movie the general watches is *Dumbo.* This is the single Disney film that most intensely focuses on the two overriding themes Spielberg would concentrate on throughout his own career: a mother separated from her child and after much adversity being reconciled with that child; ordinary characters who learn to believe and fly, eventually soaring in every sense of that term. Understandably, then, when on two occasions a character interrupts Stilwell with news from the real world, the scenes that the general is watching are among Spielberg's personal favorites: baby Dumbo briefly reunited with his jailed mother; baby Dumbo taking flight with the "magic" feather only after he learns to believe not in it but in himself.

The film is ripe with movie history. In the early diner sequence, character actors Elisha Cook Jr. and Dub Taylor bring to *1941* the richly textured tapestry of their long histories of film work. Shortly thereafter, another great character actor, Slim Pickens, plays a cowboyish handyman picked up by the Japanese; as they inspect the items in his pocket one by one, he reads the roll call of little objects, directly echoing that moment in Stanley Kubrick's *Dr. Strangelove or: How I Learned to Stop Worrying and Love the Bomb* when Pickens (on a fateful flying mission) reads off the items in every flier's personal survival kit.

Clearly, Spielberg had hoped to make his own *Dr. Strangelove.* The characters played by Robert Stack and Warren Oates are modeled after those played by George C. Scott and Sterling Hayden in Kubrick's 1963 classic. Movie mythology dating further back than that infuses *1941.* At one point, Oates's captain, who wears glasses, has a lens shattered, a direct homage to a similar moment in the famed Odessa Steps sequence of Eisenstein's 1925 Russian masterwork *Potemkin,* which earlier provided Spielberg with the editing patterns for *Jaws*'s beach hysteria. The fistfight that breaks out during the dance contest at the Crystal Ballroom (the first prize is, significantly, a seven-year contract with RKO Pictures, reestablishing the movie-about-movies motif) is timed to the same lilting music John Ford employed for his battle between John Wayne and Victor McLaglen in 1952's *The Quiet Man.* When Kelso fires the guns on his plane, he inadvertently knocks down the last four items on that huge HOLLYWOODLAND set of letters gracing the hills, providing a fanciful explanation for their disappearance and the changing of a venerable movieland icon.

Ultimately, though, the most significant homage is the film's first: Spielberg plays off the already substantial

Miss Fitzroy (Penny Marshall) lectures her girls at the USO club on proper behavior; listening intently are Betty Douglas (Dianne Kay) and Maxine (Wendie Jo Sperber) (courtesy Columbia Pictures).

"Wild Bill" staggers away from the remnants of his plane after landing on Hollywood Boulevard (courtesy Universal City Studios).

mythology of his own earlier work. The opening shot features a young, vaguely familiar blonde driving up to the beach. She slips out of her Polar Bear Club terry-cloth robe and, nude, darts down the shore as John Williams's score segues into an echo of his own *Jaws* theme. At that moment, we realize where we've seen the blonde before: Susan Backlinie is the actress who played the menaced swimmer. Now she stretches out a leg in a precise replication of her moment in *Jaws* as we hear the shark theme grow ever louder. The gag is that a periscope, rather than a set of teeth, lift her (harmlessly, this time around) out of the water.

This is one of the film's more effective gags. From that point on, *1941* moves steadily downhill. No critic has ever phrased its failure quite so honestly as Spielberg himself, who admitted to interviewer Bill Davidson just one week before the picture opened: "I'll spend the rest of my life disowning this movie."

The typical American housewife, Joan Douglas (Lorraine Gary), is stunned by a phallic-looking antiaircraft gun (courtesy Universal City Studios).

Raiders of the Lost Ark

A PARAMOUNT PICTURE, 1981

CAST

Harrison Ford *(Indiana Jones);* Karen Allen *(Marion Ravenwood);* Paul Freeman *(Belloq);* Ronald Lacey *(Toht);* John Rhys-Davies *(Sallah);* Denholm Elliott *(Brody);* Alfred Molina *(Satipo);* Wolf Kahler *(Dietrich);* Vic Tablian *(Barranca);* Terry Richards *(Arab Swordsman);* Anthony Higgins *(Gobler);* Jack Dearlove *(Ford's Stand-in).*

CREDITS

Director, Steven Spielberg; producer, Frank Marshall; executive producers, George Lucas and Howard Kazanjian; screenplay, Lawrence Kasdan, from a story by Lucas and Philip Kaufman; production design, Norman Reynolds; cinematography, Douglas Slocombe; editor, Michael Kahn; music, John Williams; second-unit director, Michael Moore; stunt coordinator, Glenn Randall; costume design, Deborah Nadoolman; visual-effects supervisor, Richard Edlund; mechanical-effects supervisor, Kit West; associate to Mr. Spielberg, Kathleen Kennedy; art director, Leslie Dilley; special effects, Industrial Light and Magic; music performed by the London Symphony Orchestra; Panavision, Metrocolor, Dolby Stereo; running time, 115 mins.; rating: PG.

Following the thud of *1941,* Spielberg would either continue to self-destruct or quickly rebound. Fortunately,

The director at work: Spielberg, wearing a baseball cap that acknowledges the work of his friend and collaborator George Lucas, carefully sets up a jungle shot (courtesy Paramount Pictures).

his next film returned him to the top of his form: *Raiders of the Lost Ark* immediately joined *Jaws* and *Close Encounters of the Third Kind* as one of the great crowd pleasers in movie history. If there was any downside, it was that the film firmly reestablished Spielberg in the public imagination as a creator of theme-park movies. In fact, *Raiders of the Lost Ark* is, like Spielberg's previous work, deceptively entertaining; beneath its surface of razzle-dazzle fun, there beats a serious sensibility struggling to get out. Above all, from the hindsight position of *Schindler's List,* we can note a Jewish filmmaker's growing preoccupation with the Holocaust. In 1981, he must have sensed his own lack of maturity to successfully confront such an issue head-on.

Initially, it is worth pausing to consider *Raiders of the Lost Ark* in terms of the politics, as well as pop culture, of its day. By the mid-1970s audiences sated with realism began to grow wistful for the bygone world of escapist films. The timing was perfect when, in 1977, George Lucas created the first *Star Wars* feature, combining elements of the beloved 1930s Flash Gordon–Buck Rogers serials with bits and pieces of other genres: westerns, war epics, samurai stories. The movie re-created in a grand fashion, through the magic of modern technology, the kind of old-fashioned adventures that had in the past been tackily thrown together.

The film's remarkable box-office success made clear that as the eighties approached, the upcoming approach to moviemaking would be neoconservativism: Everything old was new again. This perfectly paralleled the pendulum swing in American politics. The complexity of the 1970s had simply been too much for most Americans; they needed to once more believe that a rugged individualist could face off against evil empires and defeat them. The public found such a hero in the political arena when, at the dawn of a new decade, they elected former B-movie actor Ronald Reagan to the presidency; not coincidentally, they likewise wanted to go back to the basics in popular entertainment, watching Harrison Ford do a variation of roles Reagan had played in *Hong Kong* and *Tropic Zone.*

It is doubtful that either Spielberg or Lucas were conscious of any of this when they began collaborating. Between projects, the two regularly vacationed in Hawaii together. They were there during the summer of 1977, one week before *Star Wars* opened. Lucas was initially depressed, fearing the film would fail. Then reports of an international phenomenon in the making reached them, so Lucas began laughing again, opening up and talking about future projects. Over dinner one night, he described an idea he had had back in 1973 for a series of archaeology-based adventure films. He and Philip Kaufman *(Invasion of the Body Snatchers)* had worked for two weeks on a script that never jelled. Spielberg excitedly suggested that elements of the Masked Marvel, Tailspin Tommy, and Spy Smasher might be added. Lucas admitted that he hoped to make the movie primar-

ily because it was "a film I had always wanted to see." In fact, it was a film he had been watching over and over again for years, not on theater or TV screens but in the screening room of his mind, where an inveterate movie lover can take the memory of tacky movies and idealize them into something quite magnificent, transforming humble pictures into the grand, glorious film they could and should have been. Now the writer-producer was going to actualize his dream movie, share it with the world, making what Stanley Kauffmann would later call "the Saturday-afternoon serial in excelsis."

Lucas, who did not enjoy the daily grind of directing and would turn that chore over to others on future *Star Wars* projects, sensed that Spielberg shared his vision. Six months later, Lucas formally offered Spielberg the project. They agreed to begin production in 1980, since Spielberg first had to complete postproduction on *Close Encounters of the Third Kind* and had already committed to direct *1941.* While Spielberg attended to these chores, Lucas developed the story line, setting it in 1936, the date when so many of his favorite serials had been made. He had discovered a fascinating fact: Hitler had been obsessed with the occult, so that became the starting point for the story he, Spielberg, and Lawrence Kasdan (several years away from *The Big Chill*) developed together.

For five consecutive nine-hour days, the trio engaged in shouting, arguing, agreeing, and acting out scenes until the story structure had been established and the central character created. Kasdan recalls that Spielberg and Lucas wanted their hero to be a straitlaced cardboard cutout, though he insisted on giving the man some darker edges. They named the hero after Lucas's malamute dog.

Spielberg filmed *1941* while Kasdan wrote. "When I first read the screenplay, I almost wept," Spielberg later admitted, owing to the endless array of incredibly complicated shots he would need to successfully bring it to life on-screen. He and Lucas embarked on a worldwide search to find the perfect locations. They decided on the French coastal city of La Rochelle, the EMI-Elstree Studios outside London, the Tunisian desert, and their beloved Hawaii. The first stop was La Rochelle, located some 100 miles north of Bordeaux. Spielberg and Lucas had discovered that a German U-boat rested there in a submarine pen (huge caverns built to house six submarines apiece), left over from the war years, perfect for the scene in which the tramp steamer is ambushed by a German sub.

For a clear skyline, it was necessary to film three miles out at sea. However, the owners of the U-boat insisted they would not allow their precious relic to be used on days when waves were higher than three feet. Spielberg had to get all the shots he needed in five days, since he would then be due at the next location. But when he arrived, it was raining. Somehow, though, the required shots were completed, and they pushed on to London's EMI-Elstree, where five of the huge soundstages had been reserved for two immense sets which had consumed

Spielberg coaches Harrison Ford, as Indiana Jones, as to how he should respond at the sight of a skeleton in the hidden tomb (courtesy Paramount Pictures).

three months of construction. Working from a conceptualization by Lucas, Norman Reynolds, Academy Award–winning art director of *Star Wars*, had created the Well of the Souls (site of the lost ark) and the Temple of the Chachapoyon Warriors (the prologue sequence).

So that the snakes protecting the ark in the well would appear convincing, Spielberg insisted on the presence of

Spielberg explains to Karen Allen how, as a modern embodiment of the Hawksian woman, she should smack her man around just a bit (courtesy Paramount Pictures).

Spielberg makes certain that the couple is properly bound in what appears to be a hopeless situation, a throwback to so many charmingly corny cliff-hangers of the 1930s and 1940s (courtesy Paramount Pictures).

Spielberg finally takes a moment to relax with actress Allen and her nasty little pet monkey (courtesy Paramount Pictures).

more than six thousand live reptiles: pythons, cobras, and boa constrictors, handled by snake expert Mike Culling and five assistants. Though most of the cobras were six feet long, there was a twelve-foot one that took four snake experts to control. For safety during the shooting of this sequence, every unit member was required to wear protective clothing consisting of high rubber boots and strengthened canvas trousers and jackets. Doctors stood around nervously, holding serum ready.

For the prologue, Spielberg again was determined to make the fantastic concept come believably alive through vivid details, insisting on actual tarantulas in the dark, dingy cave that Indy and a companion enter. Then Spielberg packed up his company and departed for the Sahara Desert at Tozeur, Tunisia, where, in 130-degree blistering heat, they shot the scenes involving the Nazis' archaeological excavation. If the area struck moviegoers as vaguely familiar, there was a reason: Lucas had shot the *Star Wars* canyon sequence here.

The now-famous pursuit sequence was filmed by action director Mickey Moore (which represented the first time Spielberg ever allowed a second-unit director to complete a key sequence for one of his films) while Spielberg was still filming at Elstree; still, Spielberg exerted an element of control, owing to the two hundred storyboard sketches he provided and which Moore adhered to, essentially serving as a surrogate director.

The cooperativeness of his British crew allowed Spielberg to actually bring the immense project in twelve days ahead of schedule by averaging forty setups a day on location and, for exteriors (under excessively difficult lighting conditions), an average of fifteen shots per day. Spielberg and Lucas had always hoped to make a movie that would cost $20 million but appear as if it had cost $40 million. They accomplished that goal: Though the budget was considerable, the movie looks expensive, as every penny spent is up there on-screen. In order to keep within that range, however, Spielberg did something he would never have considered in his pre-*1941* days: renting stock footage to save money rather than re-creating everything out of his own imagination. The DC-3 flying over the Himalayas is lifted from 1973's *Lost Horizon,* while a 1930s street scene was borrowed from *The Hindenburg.*

It is important to grasp that the former boy genius had been humbled by his *1941* experience. Spielberg was at a low ebb, as his price tag proved: $1.5 million to direct, as compared to Lucas's $4 million to produce; Lucas also received four times greater a share of the profits than Spielberg. Spielberg not only wanted to make a good movie but also to film it with great discipline. Whereas in *1941* he had often averaged a whopping forty "takes" for each individual shot, here he did no more than four per shot. Lucas persuaded him to "not shoot for a masterpiece," insisting it was enough to make the film good. It is worth noting, too, that Lucas—not Spielberg—had the much-sought-after final cut.

The combination of talents clicked. In *Time,* Richard Schickel hailed *Raiders of the Lost Ark* as "an exemplary film, an object lesson in how to blend the art of storytelling with the highest levels of technical know-how, planning, cost control and commercial acumen," while Vincent Canby of the *New York Times* lauded it as "one of the most deliriously funny, ingenious and stylish American adventure movies ever made." A few contemplative critics, however, admired the polish but resented the approach. Kauffmann complained in the *New Republic:*

The future is the past—spiffed up with the latest technology (and the) seeping belief that the best has already been. . . . None of this is as much regard for the past as it is a refuge from the present. Nostalgia used to be characteristic of older people; now, there are probably more youthful nostalgia addicts than ever before in history.

In fact, the public—including the young—had decided it did not like the present, which had been emerging in the seventies, so they attempted to step back to a romanticized, bygone world that had never existed anywhere except in the movies. Spielberg and Lucas had a finger on the pulse of the public at that precise moment.

That this is a movie about movies is clear from the opening shot: the famed Paramount mountain logo, the opening of all their films, transforming, before the viewer's eyes, into an actual Andean mountain. The transition is perfect and gave the 1981 audience its first chuckle, but it is also an illustration of Spielberg's theme: We are entering a universe in which reality and fantasy are inseparable.

Like Lucas's first *Star Wars* film, *Raiders of the Lost Ark* thrusts us into an adventure in progress, a title card informing us that the jungle we see is somewhere in South America. Only after an explorer steps into a booby trap and is spiked to death by spears do we see the group leader, who steps forward to investigate, his leather bomber jacket and natty, if battered, brown felt fedora first glimpsed from behind. Finally, a change in camera angle reveals him to be Indiana Jones (Harrison Ford).

Indy's ability with a whip is established when he employs it to scare members of his little group who have turned traitor. His quick wit and dexterity serves him and sidekick Satipo well as they step deeper into the cavern. The fast-thinking Indy is always one step ahead, outguessing where the next threat will come from as the two move on toward their goal: a golden idol, perched atop a tablelike rock, seemingly unprotected, though of course surrounded by the most deadly weight-sensitive triggering mechanisms. Importantly, the idol is a religious icon. At film's end, Indy will encounter the title object representing more familiar spiritual values. It is important to recall, then, that despite the romance and adventure, each Indy film follows the hero's search for an item that offers tacit proof that there is something beyond the here and

In the film's much-admired opening sequence, Indy hurries away with the religious artifact, only to be pursued by an immense bouncing ball (courtesy Paramount Pictures).

now. Indy—like Spielberg's heroes before and since—searches for these objects at least in part because, as a modern postexistential man, he needs some source of meaning, proof positive that life is not *nada*.

Indy manages to grasp the idol, deftly dropping a sandbag in its place. However, the machinery of the booby trap is too clever even for him, so a series of potentially deadly traps is kicked off, domino style. Indy's companion is killed (not to worry, since he has betrayed the hero out of greed); in what became the film's signature shot, Indy rushes down the hillside, pursued by a huge ball about to squash him at any moment. He darts out of its way and, outside, is confronted by a semicircle of

Flavidos natives, holding him at bay. They are in the service of Belloq, French soldier of fortune competing with Indy to secure the valuable antiquity. "Dr. Jones," Belloq smirkingly says, "again we see there is nothing you can possess which I cannot take away," making clear their competition is long-standing.

In addition to Lucas's recycled pulp plot, something Spielbergian is happening. Indy suggests that the natives would not be so quick to obey Belloq if only they knew the fate he has in store for their artifact; Belloq grins, insisting he is glad that Indy can't speak the natives' language. The theme of communication, the importance of overriding specific languages that interfere with rather

Harrison Ford as Indy, at a key juncture in the plot that reveals his split personality as both serious-minded college professor and free-spirited man of adventure.

than facilitate our universal interests, is introduced in the opening and will be marbled throughout.

Indy makes a break for freedom and is pursued by the natives as he runs toward an aquaplane sitting on a nearby lake, the pilot blithely fishing. Spielberg borrows from a great Disney film: Kirk Douglas, running down the beach of a jungle island, pursued by spear-waving natives, trying to reach Peter Lorre in his little rowboat so they can escape in *20,000 Leagues Under the Sea.* Of course, Spielberg gives the scene his own special touch: The archaic charm of this little biplane establishes it as one more of those old-time aviation relics the director so cherishes. Another key element is introduced here. Strapped into his seat, Indy looks down and spots a snake near his feet. At this point, the previously unflappable hero squirms; when he speaks, it is actually a whine, though his pilot assures Indy that the snake is a pet. Nonetheless, Indy cries out: "I hate snakes." This admission is significant. Without it, we might assume that the seemingly unflappable Indy would stoically face the Well's snakes; instead, we know of his vulnerability.

On a traditional college campus, the elderly Brody (Denholm Elliott) approaches a classroom where Dr. Jones teaches. We barely recognize Harrison Ford now: It is as if, in the earlier scene, he had been playing Superman and here, he is Clark Kent. The Indy we now see sports college-professor tweeds and glasses; his voice and body language are entirely different, suggesting a softspoken, nervous man, unsure of himself, rather than the earlier, commanding presence. This is the inner reality of Dr. Jones; previously we viewed the outer appearance of "Indiana." The Spielberg notion of the hero is based on duality; no man is a hero all the time, though anyone and everyone can become a hero if, when circumstances demand, he rises to the occasion.

Indy's fear of snakes, so beautifully set up earlier in the film, reaches a moment of audience payoff.

92

In the *Humanist,* Harry M. Geduld connected this to Spielberg's ongoing religious element:

The superhero is essentially an updating of the religious fantasy of the meek and mild individual who becomes the saviour of humankind: a "gentle Jesus" who never married, who insisted that his mission was not to bring peace but a sword. . . . The fantasy is updated in significant ways. The miracles and spiritual triumphs of Jesus are transformed into the miraculous physical exploits of the superhero, and the forces of evil in the biblical narrative are transformed into concrete familiar villains—the Nazis. The superhero's cause becomes the equivalent of the saviour's message, and his dual identity—apparent weakness concealing vast strength—can be interpreted as a simplistic analogue for the Christian conviction that the kingdom of God is within each and every man. The superhero is frequently "resurrected" by escaping at the last moment from a seemingly endless succession of deadly dangers.

Brody, we learn, has arrived with several government officials who want to speak with Dr. Jones about Prof. Abner Ravenwood, with whom Jones studied at the University of Chicago. American agents in Europe have intercepted German communications between Cairo and Berlin, which mention Ravenwood. Our government fears he may be a collaborator, though Jones insists that is unlikely. He speaks with quiet respect about his mentor, though he implies that a falling out occurred between them.

In fact, the Nazis were after Ravenwood because he was rumored to possess the headpiece to the staff of Rah; if placed on a staff of the proper length, it could be used

While Marion (offscreen) plans their eventual escape, Indy fights a huge Nazi even as the moving plane constantly circles (courtesy Paramount Pictures).

Though actually an insecure man named Dr. Jones, "Indiana" rises to heroic proportions at moments of dire need.

93

to direct sunlight onto a model of the ancient city of Tannis, located in Cairo, revealing the location in the actual buried city of the lost ark of the covenant. The ark was stolen from the Hebrews by an ancient pharaoh and hidden in Tannis, a year later buried by desert sandstorms. The Nazis are already mounting an archaeological dig, though that headpiece would simplify things. The ark, rumored to have leveled mountains and razed entire armies in biblical times, would render anyone who possesses it invincible, an idea that Hitler finds attractive.

American agents want Jones to reach the ark first. He must first locate Ravenwood, now lost somewhere in the wild, unmapped Asian provinces beyond Tibet. Jones asks Brody if it's possible that "she'll still be with him?" sounding less the reckless adventurer or serious professor, more a normal male who has never gotten over some remarkable woman. He also sounds surprisingly "everyday" when he and Brody discuss the upcoming trek.

BRODY (*fearfully*):   For three thousand years, man has been searching for the lost ark.

INDY: I don't believe in magic, hocus-pocus. I'm going after an object of historic significance. You're talking about the bogeyman.

The Indy we encounter at film's end will have realized, through terrifying contact with the ark, that there is magic, even metaphysics, in the cosmos; all is not here and now. Indy will break through; he will encounter forces from the beyond, a recurring Spielberg theme which he here brings more into line with his own traditional Jewish thinking. No wonder, then, that the Commentary review noted that "when the Lord goes into action He produces effects suspiciously like those produced by the extraterrestrials in Close Encounters of the Third Kind." Or, for that matter, like those in The Ten Commandments, already alluded to in Close Encounters of the Third Kind and a seminal film in Spielberg's youthful moviegoing experiences. Aliens, poltergeists, or the spirits inhabiting the ancient ark are all variations on his recurring theme.

Indy boards a plane, apparently unaware that a dangerous man in glasses (Ronald Lacey) peers over his *Life* magazine (one more nostalgic touch), considering him menacingly. Then there is the self-consciously outdated technique of an animated map, with a constantly moving line of light indicating Indy's progress, superimposed over the image of his antique plane flying halfway around the world. Characterizations, like such technical conventions, are also drenched in nostalgia: Marion Ravenwood (Karen Allen) is introduced as a Hawksian woman, in charge and tough talking. In her déclassé bar, Marion goes drink for drink with men.

Importantly, she speaks their language: Unlike Indy, she can communicate with the locals, thereby surviving among them. When Indy enters, she looks up and sighs the oldest line in movies: "I always knew someday you'd come walking back through my door." It echoes what Bogart said Bergman in *Casablanca*. ("Of all the gin joints in the world, she had to walk into mine!"). This time, it is the woman who, in a classic case of role reversal, utters the line. Then, like a true tender-tough woman of movie mythology, she slugs him; it's Angie Dickinson knocking over John Wayne himself in Howard Hawks's *Rio Bravo*.

What follows, though, is an interchange that is contemporary, believable, even disturbing, keeping the film from turning into one of Mel Brooks's broad burlesques of old movie genres. We finally learn why the two parted company:

MARION: I was a child—in love.
INDY: You knew what you were doing.

Their confrontation is a classic case of an adult male engaging in sexual activity with an underage young woman, then claiming he isn't responsible because he saw a flicker of desire in her eyes. Perhaps surprisingly (considering the film's supposed light-entertainment tone), Spielberg will not relent:

MARION: Do you know what you did to me? To my life?

Indy will never answer that question; instead, he babbles on about the need to find Abner's medallion (Professor Ravenwood is long since deceased) before the Nazis do. But the question, and his avoidance of it, are very much with us. It hardly seems coincidental when, later in the film, Indy has to choose between loyalty to Marion and loyalty to a cause, once more betraying her. Spielberg's portrait of the American male value system is more complex and critical than has generally been acknowledged.

"Trust me," Indy says to Marion as he leaves. He has requested (practically demanded) the headpiece-medallion and has been told to return the next day. His line is rife with nastiness; although he appears to be the idealized 1940s hero, Indy is in fact something else entirely. he revels in the hard feelings Marion harbors; we think back to the university sequence and recall that one precocious coed constantly made eyes at him, causing Dr. Jones to lose his train of thought. Possibly, if Brody and the agents hadn't intruded, Indy would have shortly bedded her. There is evidence, then, that the situation with Marion was anything but an embarrassing onetime fling; his interest in younger women—his virtual pedophilia—has not diminished over the years.

Simply, Indy is child rather than a man: The supposedly mature Dr. Jones is a front for a fellow who cannot accept his virtuous but dull pose as a teacher. He creates another pose, an alter ego—a child's vision of the idealized male hero—allowing himself to escape from the grind of daily reality by immersion into fantasy-like ad-

Indiana Jones is lowered onto a clear space on the floor of the Well of Souls, past gigantic statues and surrounded by a sea of hissing snakes (courtesy Paramount Pictures).

ventures. As such, he is incapable of behaving like a hero unless he is in a life or death situation, precisely what occurs momentarily. The team of Nazis (led by the Peter Lorre look-alike in glasses) enter Marion's bar, threatening to take the medallion by force. She responds appropriately for a Hawksian heroine: "Nobody tells me what to do in my place!" But when Toht is about to shove a hot poker in her face, Indy appears, whip in hand, to save the day. This he can understand: a woman is being menaced, so a male hero's gotta do what a male hero's gotta do.

In one of the film's effectively staged fight sequences, he defeats the Nazis with Marion's active-participant help. She is clearly an equal, insisting he now has a partner on his hands, so they head for Cairo with her medallion in hand. Though there's the matter of $5,000 he promises her, we sense Marion is in this for more than money. There's a love-hate chemistry between them: She detests what he did years earlier, but the fact is, the deed is done, the two bound together by intense, confusing emotions. He is, simply, the man in her life, so the upcoming adventure may at last allow them to make some sort of commitment.

In Cairo, they meet Sallah (John Rhys-Davies), the plump, trustworthy Arab who informs Indy that none other than Belloq is in charge of the Nazi dig. Sallah now assumes Brody's role as voice of reason as well as hu-

mility in the face of larger questions. Upon seeing Marion's medallion, he shudders: "If it is true, it is something that man was not meant to disturb." Though Indy doesn't reply, the wise-guy look in his eyes indicates that he still thinks such talk is nothing but superstition. Before the film is over, he will be humbled, forced to meet the bogeyman face-to-face—though, wisely, with both eyes closed.

In the marketplace, Marion picks up on the betrayal-of-trust theme while adding an entirely new dimension: the parent-child bond so basic to the previous Spielberg theatrical films:

MARION: Father loved you like a son. It took a lot for you to alienate him.
INDY: Not much. Just you.

Throughout the trilogy, he will emerge as a man in search of a proper father figure, coming to terms with this need in the final movie. He feels so betrayed by the father who was not there during childhood that he suffers a compulsion to misdirect anger by betraying all other father figures, however worthy. There is also hostility toward the female in his crude remark; if you hadn't been there, it implies, I wouldn't have been compelled to seduce you. It's all your fault.

Villains attempt to kidnap Marion, who hides in a basket, though her pesky pet monkey gives her location away. Indy, meanwhile, faces off with a huge Arab swordsman in what became one of the film's most oft-cited scenes. The two initially appear men of honor, in the tradition of knights or samurai; we assume they will enter into chivalrous one-on-one combat. The Arab swings his sword about skillfully; Indiana considers his own little bullwhip, and his heroic demeanor dissipates. Instead, he pulls out his pistol and blows the man away. This action appeared in a 1979 exploitation film called *Seven;* whether or not Spielberg or one of his collaborators saw that Andy Sidaris flick is not known, but the bit is too precisely repeated to be written off as coincidence.

Still, Spielberg redeems the gag, through meaningful context. We are meant to see the Indiana Jones image as just that, a self-conscious caricature, mounted by a man who needs just such bravado to cover his own deep insecurities. Harrison Ford is playing Dr. Jones, while Dr. Jones is playing at being Indiana. There are times when the role-playing must give way to imperatives of reality. It is dangerous to accept Indy at face value: later, when a threatened Marion asks him how he'll save her (trusting in his self-styled heroic image), he nervously replies: "I'm just making this up as I go along!" She appears shocked: She actually believed his hype about being in control. We share her shock; we should know better.

Another grand action sequence follows in which the villains, having kidnapped Marion, crash their truck, seemingly killing her in the explosion. Indy then drinks himself into a stupor, in the company of Marion's monkey. Belloq joins him, here speaking the lines that make clear they are Spielberg's secret sharers:

BELLOQ: You and I are very much alike. Archaeology is my religion, yet we have both fallen from our religion. I am a shadowy reflection of you.

The notion that Indy initially viewed his profession as a source of spiritual guidance, though he has recently lost touch with this aspect, again raises the film above genre. Belloq speaks the truth; Indy will need to redeem himself.

Yet it is Belloq who tags the ark a "transmitter," taking Spielberg's long-standing theme of communication (often some form of radio communication) and combining it with the metaphysical theme. Belloq refers to the ark as "a radio for speaking to God." What Belloq fails to understand is that man's proper role is at the receiving end. We then see a hint as to why Indy will survive when he is rescued from the Nazis by Sallah's children. In the Spielberg world, any man who is at one with little children has the potential to achieve salvation.

Indy discovers that Belloq's calculations are wrong; he and the Nazis are digging in the wrong place. Disguised as natives, Indy and Sallah pass through an earthen hole and into the map room, where they use the medallion to discover the ark's actual location.

"Indy, why does the floor move?" Sallah asks as they slip inside the hiding place. Of course, the answer is that it is covered with snakes, carefully established as this Superman's kryptonite. A snake of a different sort threatens Marion: Belloq, who offers her food and clothing, attempting to turn the tent into a sheikh's den of romance. Fortunately, her ability to drink—as clearly established as Indy's fear of snakes—allows her to outlast Belloq when he tries to get her inebriated.

Belloq would like to keep Marion alive, though the Nazis insist she be dropped down with Indy into the pit. She darts about in fear, colliding with mummified bodies, even as the Nazis attempt to fly the ark out. But Indy and Marion break loose, exploding the planes, together fighting their way toward the ark. The Nazis instead load the ark onto a truck and head for Cairo; Indy, riding a white horse and (again, rising to the occasion) now appearing truly heroic (John Williams's famed theme playing patri-

otically), pursues. What follows is an elaborate chase sequence modeled on the one in John Ford's *Stagecoach*. Indy leaps onto the truck and takes over the wheel from the Nazi driver, who is thrust out; pursued by other Nazis, he slips under a moving truck (hanging on to a rope) in an elaborate attempt to wrestle the ark from them. It is a valiant battle, certainly adding to Indy's questionable stature as a hero.

That stature is soon dubious once more as, aboard a

Spielberg and Lucas peppered the film with action sequences so that it would resemble an oldtime serial, with all twelve episodes strung together.

tramp steamer contracted by the ever-reliable Sallah, Marion attends to Indy's wounds; as she dabs them with antiseptic, he whines like a child. Reunited with the woman, he is something of a wuss. She, meanwhile, wears a sleek satin dress that the pirate crew "just happened to have lying around," a takeoff on an old movie cliché, dating back to silent days, in which leading ladies managed to appear incredibly glamorous even in the least likely situations.

The boat is captured by Nazis, though Indy once more becomes a true hero and escapes. He is there, on the hidden Nazi island, when they bring the ark to be opened. Though Indy threatens to blow the ark up with a bazooka, Belloq, his alter ego, reminds him that, as archaeologists, they have a greater duty than to either country—their shared "religion" demanding they sustain the ark's existence at any cost: "We are simply passing through history; (the ark) *is* history!" Unable to argue with this, Indy surrenders; he and Marion are tied together as the Nazis open the ark while ancient Hebrew incantations are read. What appears first seems beautiful, then turns grotesque; spirits of the past whip through the cavern, though Indy recalls a bit of biblical apocrypha. If he and Marion are to survive, they must accept it as absolute truth. He who looks on the face of God is doomed. "Don't look at it," he insists, "no matter what, shut your eyes, keep them shut."

She does, and so does he; they do survive. The others do not: What we see, in their destruction, is the inverse of the *Close Encounters* ending, here turned negative owing to the negativity of the people on the receiving end. Only by rejecting his own earlier, hubrislike belief that the ark was merely a historical object, and all supernatural beliefs mere mumbo jumbo, does Indiana survive.

The final irony is that the American government has no inkling as to the potential power unearthed. Over Indy's objections, it is crated up and sent to a top-secret area for eventual analysis by scientists. As the camera slowly pulls back, like Orson Welles's at the end of *Citizen Kane* from the Rosebud sled, we see the enormity of the cavernous building and sense, without the need for words, that the ark is as safe from human contact here as it was when lying at the bottom of a building buried in the desert sands; ages will have passed before anyone gets past all the other crates to open this one. The ultimate treasure—the one that could unlock all the secrets—is lost once more amid piles of junk and gems.

Strong-willed, independently minded, tough-talking, but endearingly feminine Marion makes her way through the piles of ancient mummies in the catacombs (courtesy Paramount Pictures).

Poltergeist

A METRO-GOLDWYN-MAYER FILM, M-G-M/UNITED ARTISTS RELEASE, 1982

CAST

Craig T. Nelson *(Steve Freeling);* JoBeth Williams *(Diane Freeling);* Beatrice Straight *(Dr. Lesh);* Dominique Dunne *(Dana);* Oliver Robins *(Robbie);* Heather O'Rourke *(Carol Anne);* Zelda Rubinstein *(Tangina);* Martin Cassella *(Marty);* Richard Lawson *(Ryan);* James Karen *(Teague);* Virginia Kiser *(Mrs. Tuthill);* Michael McManus *(Ben Tuthill);* Dirk Blocker *(Jeff Shaw).*

CREDITS

Producers, Steven Spielberg and Frank Marshall; screenplay, Spielberg, Michael Grais, and Mark Victor; director, Tobe Hooper; associate producer, Kathleen Kennedy; photography, Matthew F. Leonetti; editor, Michael Kahn; music, Jerry Goldsmith; production manager, Dennis E. Jones; visual-effects supervisor, Richard Edlund; set designers, Bill Matthews and Martha Johnson; costume supervisor, Ann Gray Lambert; special-effects makeup, Craig Reardon; mechanical-effects supervisor, Michael Wood; wide screen, Metrocolor, Dolby Stereo; running time, 114 mins.; rating: PG.

An open letter, typed on personal stationery, was published in its entirety as a paid full-page advertisement in the *Hollywood Reporter* on June 8, 1982; dated June 2 and addressed to Tobe Hooper, it read:

Regrettably, some of the press has misunderstood the rather unique, creative relationship which you and I shared throughout the making of "Poltergeist."

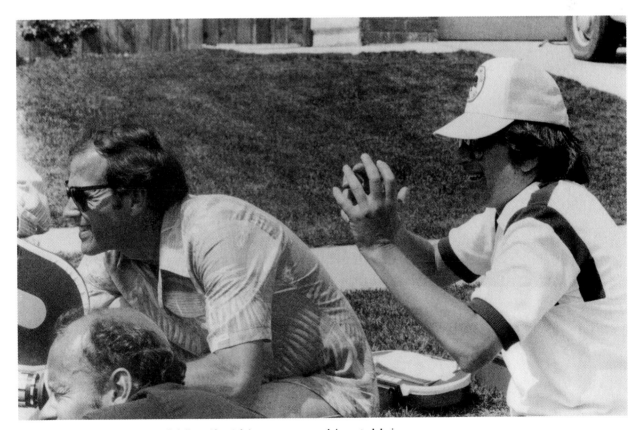

Though ostensibly not the director, Spielberg *(far right)* appears very much in control during the shooting of this scene; coproducer Frank Marshall is to his left (courtesy M-G-M/United Artists).

I enjoyed your openness in allowing me, as a producer and a writer, a wide berth for creative involvement, just as I know you were happy with the freedom you had to direct "Poltergeist" so wonderfully.

Through the screenplay you accepted a vision of this very intense movie from the start, and as the director, you delivered the goods. You performed responsibly and professionally throughout, and I want to wish you great success on your next project.

Let's hope that "Poltergeist" brings as much pleasure to the general public as we experienced in our mutual effort.

Sincerely,

Steven Spielberg

Spielberg's deeply felt but politically phrased letter attests to the brief significance in Hollywood of a controversy which surrounded the film's opening in mid-1982, a moviegoing season tagged "The Spielberg Summer" by *Time* and *Newsweek*. The press and film community sensed, from advance screenings, that *E.T.* would become a gigantic success. This realization was accompanied by the fact that Spielberg's name also appeared on the credits of another movie opening a week earlier. The double-barrel inpact of the near simultaneous releases allowed for an easy angle: If *E.T.* represented Spielberg's softer Disney side, then *Poltergeist* could be hyped as the movie that revealed his darker Hitchcock side.

Spielberg himself contributed to this building notion, stating to reporters: "It's nice that I can release two sides of my personality in 1982 so close to each other. *Poltergeist* is what I fear, and *E.T.* is what I love. One is about suburban evil and the other is about suburban good. One is a scream, and one is a whisper." The major problem involving "the scream" was that despite Spielberg's name in the credits as coscreenwriter and co-producer (as well as the formidable "A Steven Spielberg Production"), he was not the ostensible director. That was Tobe Hooper, who had made a cult reputation for himself with 1974's ultra-low-budget (and effectively horrific) *The Texas Chainsaw Massacre*. Like John Landis *(Schlock),* Joe Dante *(Piranha),* and George Romero *(Night of the Living Dead),* Hooper was perceived as an

Carol Anne Freeling (Heather O'Rourke) screams out to her parents for help when ancient ghosts enter their home through the television set (courtesy M-G-M/United Artists).

A variation on a recurring Spielberg pose: The Freeling family members, Dominique Dunne, JoBeth Williams, Craig T. Nelson, and Oliver Robins, accompanied by Beatrice Straight as a parapsychology expert, gather together and stare at inexplicable phenomenon invading their little corner of Middle America (courtesy M-G-M/United Artists).

out-of-the-mainstream boy genius. As such, he was invited to Hollywood, where he could exercise his offbeat artistry with considerably greater means at his command.

So in the early summer of 1982, the question of whether Hooper or Spielberg had really "made" *Poltergeist* was debated in hushed but serious tones, so much so that the Directors Guild opened an investigation into the question of whether or not Hooper's official credit was being denigrated by statements Spielberg had made, apparently claiming authorship. Coproducer Frank Marshall stepped into the fray, telling Dale Pollock of the *L.A. Times:*

The creative force on the movie was Steven. Tobe was the director and was on the set every day. But Steven did the design for every storyboard and he was on the set every day except for three days when he was in Hawaii with Lucas.

The word "design" is significant. Ordinarily, the director is perceived as the primary creative artist, the "auteur" who oversees everything from preproduction writing to final editing, as well as the expected on-set creative elements. The movie is, simply, "his" film.

But when questioned, Spielberg admitted that as writer-producer (and, more important still, conceptual artist who originated the project) he had "approved" camera setups and the "designing" of specific shots. Afterward, he "supervised" postproduction, including addition of special effects and the all-important editing, sound recording, looping, and musical scoring that took place between late October 1981 and the first public screening on April 17, 1982. Hooper had not been directly involved since turning over his "director's cut" back in October. Apparently, Spielberg would have directed the film himself except that a restrictive clause in his contract with Universal forbade his directing any other film while still preparing for *E.T.*

Now, though, a threatened Hooper publicly challenged Spielberg's statements: "I did fully half of the storyboards. I don't understand why any of these questions have to be raised." He was literally fighting to hang on to his career, which he must have believed would soar after this major film opened; though the movie was indeed a huge hit, it nonetheless set into motion the decline of

Robbie Freeling (Oliver Robins) finds his worst nightmare coming true when the old oak tree outside his window crashes through and pulls him out (courtesy M-G-M/United Artists).

Hooper's briefly luminous Hollywood period. Spielberg, meanwhile, responded with uncharacteristic harshness: "Tobe isn't what you'd call a take-charge sort of guy. He's just not a strong presence on a movie set. If a question was asked and an answer wasn't immediately forthcoming, I'd jump up and say what we could do. Tobe would nod agreement, and that became the process of collaboration."

The two first met in 1978, shortly after Spielberg first saw *The Texas Chainsaw Massacre,* claiming it was "one of the most truly visceral movies ever made. Essentially, it starts inside the stomach and ends in the heart." That was precisely the kind of impact he needed for *Poltergeist,* which would provide a typical Spielbergian situation: ordinary people who, without warning, find themselves in an extraordinary situation. Hooper would bring to this blueprint his own ability to set up, then sustain, an acute sense of terror and tension.

Spielberg wrote his first draft in five days, turning out twenty pages a day, stream of consciousness style. His original treatment had been prepared some time earlier, so he knew where he was going and simply sat down and wrote, as he would later reflect, as if "telling the story around a campfire at night to a bunch of frightened chil-

Diane Freeling attempts to keep her son from being sucked away by supernatural forces terrorizing their home (courtesy M-G-M/United Artists).

102

dren." He began at the beginning and ended at the end, not necessarily the way most scripts are written. He then read the pages out loud to Kathleen Kennedy, Frank Marshall, and Tobe Hooper. He did this on a daily basis—twenty pages a day, "like telling them a serial," as he later put it, then went back to work from eight at night to four in the morning (the only time he is able to focus and write), after which he'd meet with them again, continuing with the next "chapter." Afterward, he turned over what he had written to Michael Grais and Mark Victor, who then completed their own draft; they handed it to Spielberg, who completely rewrote it.

The film had been set for a twelve-week shooting schedule, with an approved budget of $9.5 million, though it eventually cost $10.8 million to make, and was completed in fifty-seven days, two less than it later took to shoot *E.T.* Necessary for such controlled shooting were three elaborate, intricate sets, built on soundstages at M-G-M Studios. The key "house" set created unique problems: It had to be built fifteen feet above the ground, since they couldn't dig through the concrete floor and had to construct the set with a removable floor, allowing for the installment of a swimming pool and needed crawl space for manipulation of special effects.

Though the press hungered for intriguing stories that might play up the possibility of ghostly visitors, Spielberg had to disappoint interviewers, insisting that other than a few minor accidents (people bumping into one another on dimly lit soundstages), nothing of a supernatural order occurred. However, a sense of the macabre did come to surround the film: actress Dominique Dunne, who played the teenage sister, was killed shortly after filming was completed by a jealous ex-boyfriend; Heather O'Rourke, who played the child Carol Anne, died suddenly a few years later, just before the release of the third *Poltergeist* film.

There were close calls involving the child actors. O'Rourke and Oliver Robins were not frightened by the monstrous creatures, added afterward in postproduction. But in one sequence, O'Rourke had to dangle at an uncomfortable angle from her bed's headboard while the wind machine blew her into what appears to be an abyss, with only fifty feet of air between the harness that kept her in place and the hard ground below. O'Rourke be-

Striking lighting effects and bizarre camera angles add to the impact of many scenes, including this one featuring Steve (Craig T. Nelson) rescuing his wife and the spiritualist Tangina (Zelda Rubinstein) (courtesy M-G-M/United Artists).

"My revenge on TV" is how Spielberg described this film, which depicts the monstrous things that can happen to a child who becomes a couch potato, much to the dismay of her parents.

came so fearful that Spielberg had to replace her with a stunt child in a blond wig. There is a certain irony here: To make his sensitive films about the abuse children suffer at the hands of adults, Spielberg had, to a degree, to become one of those adults. But when O'Rourke began crying, he ran up to her, embraced the child, dried her tears, and told her that they would not do another take. And they didn't.

Little Robins came close to death while shooting the climactic scare scene in which his clown doll grabs him from behind, dragging the boy under the bed. The arms clasping him somehow became too tight, cutting off circulation. He started screaming, "I can't breathe," but Spielberg and Hooper assumed the boy's frantic call for help was merely great acting; as in so many Spielberg movies, life and art became all but inseparable. Spielberg was calling out, "Great, Oliver, look toward the camera!" when he noticed that the boy's face was turning crimson. He leaped up and tore away the clown arms just in time.

For better or worse, the film was completed and special effects added at Industrial Light and Magic. Happily, Lucas's technicians had just developed a system for adding special effects to existing images, which eliminated the old problem of a grainy aura inadvertently

being added as well. This had become a dead giveaway for young, visually sophisticated audiences that craved seamless special effects. Spielberg, however, wanted a film of substance as well as a special-effects extravaganza. In 1982, he explained to interviewer Michael Verona that *Poltergeist* was a variation on a theme basic to all his pictures: "I think people lead lives where their deepest wish is that something would interrupt the mundane everyday routine. And someone (or something) comes into their lives that disturbs everything, disrupts everything, makes them suddenly have to work at life, and live it [to the fullest], to survive."

Spielberg also insisted on the autobiographical element. Just as there is a tiny crack in the wall of the Freeling home, gradually widening to allow us a vision of another society living within that house, but in another dimension, so, too, did Spielberg the child peer into a similar crack in one of the houses where he and his family lived: "I remember lying there, trying to go to sleep, and I used to always imagine little Hieronymous Bosch–like creatures inside, peeking out and whispering to me to come into the playground of the crack and be drawn into the unknown there, inside the walls of my home in New Jersey."

Though this, and his other films, take wild flights of fancy, they connect to the audience because they are firmly grounded in reality: Spielberg's own personal reality as well as the greater reality of "normal" suburban life. An important element of that lifestyle is television; *Poltergeist* is *about* TV, particularly its impact on the young. "*Poltergeist* is my way of getting back at television for what it did to me as a kid," he has said.

In the opening, as the screen remains black, we hear the strains of our national anthem. When the image finally fades in, we find ourselves staring at a grainy TV screen as a southwestern station signs off for the night. Gradually, the camera pulls back to reveal a typical American family, having fallen asleep in various spots, the ever-buzzing TV central to their experience. It makes sense, then, that the creatures choose to enter everyday reality through this device. Here television is a window on the world in ways even Edward R. Murrow could never have imagined. *Poltergeist* is less horror film than black comedy, illustrating what so many parents have warned their children about: "Don't watch so much TV; it will rot your brain." That generalization is made frightfully specific here, little Carol Anne emerging as the ultimate symbol of American children turned into zombies by staring endlessly at a TV set. *Poltergeist* functions as a cautionary fable: the nightmare scenario of what could happen to any one of us if we totally lose touch with the real world, allowing ourselves to be transfixed.

Poltergeist also predicts what, in the early nineties, has come to be called "interactive TV." Little Carol Anne doesn't only watch; she talks back to the set. Something inside it—or inside her house, connecting to her through this medium—responds. Communication, another recurring Spielberg theme, is present. Carol Anne speaks, but at first the creatures are unable to respond. It is clear they can't understand her; if they attempt to answer, she can't understand them. Then she and "they" gradually learn how to communicate, just as the earthlings eventually manage to break through to the extraterrestrials in *Close Encounters of the Third Kind* and *E.T.*

This is Spielbergland: southwestern suburbia, portrayed in a relatively realistic fashion but with just enough of an edge of caricature, cartoonishness, even a touch of condescension to allow his portrait a slightly surreal ring. "Cuesta Verde" is a place where, on sunny afternoons, children play outside while their dads gather together to guzzle beer and watch baseball on TV, even as their moms do the washing for the week. It is the suburbia of Spielberg's own boyhood as filtered through the glass darkly of Rod Serling's *Twilight Zone*, in which such seemingly "normal" locations proved frightfully vulnerable to unexpected intrusions by forces from the outside—sometimes dangerous, sometimes benign.

Into this heightened suburbia the filmmaker inserts a quick bit of self-satire. The opening sequence, straining toward the tone of a 1950s TV sitcom, but with contemporary-looking characters, features an overweight suburbanite heading home from the local 7-Eleven, via bicycle, with a six-pack of beer. But mischievous neighborhood kids have other ideas; they aim their remote-control toy cars directly into his pathway, sending the man sprawling. As he falls, the cars crash into one another; the Spielberg motif of car crashes is here played out in miniature, making it clear that the filmmaker could poke fun at himself and the sort of scene which, if the critics were to be believed, had become his stock-in-trade.

Into this happy valley Spielberg immediately imposes the idea of death. It is this dark subject, along with the brightening promise of everlasting life through death, that the film is primarily about. Diane Freeling discovers the family's pet canary dead on the floor of its cage and decides to flush it down the toilet before the kids can see. She is interrupted by little Carol Anne, intruding just before the act can be completed and quite aghast at the scene. It is that universal, initial confrontation with the reality of death when a pet is disposed of in just such a manner by an adult who knows not what she does to the impressionable child's imagination.

Being a dutiful parent, Diane participates in a ritualistic cigar-box burial (her husband, a real estate agent, is in the next room, obliviously watching a game) in which little Tweety is buried in the backyard. Spielberg takes haunting memories from his own childhood, which touch upon the collective memories of everyone, then re-creates them so vividly that the moments strike us as archetypal rather than stereotypical, thanks to his enchanting ability to redeem "ordinary" moments by making them brim with cognition. When the sequence is about to turn maudlin, sad-faced Carol Anne turns to her mother and, suddenly smiling, asks: "Can I have a goldfish now?" Her quick recovery from grief, typical of childhood mourning, adds a comic kicker, rescuing the scene from sentimentality.

Shortly thereafter, a bulldozer (scraping ground away for the Freelings' new swimming pool) accidentally uncovers Tweety's grave. At that moment, the incident may seem nothing more than a mildly sad fact of everyday suburban life; before the movie is over, we will realize that this brief shot prepares us for everything to come, the movie's plot motored by other graves uncovered during the building of that swimming pool. Spielberg is also at work setting up a visual scheme which borrows from ideas already established in earlier movies. In *Close Encounters of the Third Kind,* Spielberg effectively visualized the suburban community in which the Neary family lived, showing their neighborhood from a distance as ominous clouds (right out of a 1950s monster movie) rolled in overhead. There are several such shots early in *Poltergeist;* the key to their meaning is the filmmaker's organization of his frame. Above, there is the unknown, the magical, the metaphysical, glorious if potentially dangerous; below, there is the ordinary, the normal, the everyday, mundane though safe. The great problem for

The modern American family, blithely going about its daily business, finds itself threatened by metaphysical forces it cannot comprehend, at least not without help.

those inhabiting the lower half of the screen is that they fail to acknowledge, much less appreciate, what is taking place on the top half until it forcefully presses down into their lives. This, like the earlier films, is a moral fable about moderns who live intently in the here and now, a world in which old-fashioned notions of faith in the forces beyond our line of vision have been all but forgotten.

In one key shot, Steve and other suburbanites return to their homes following a hard day's work without even noticing scary-looking clouds rolling in. One key element in Spielberg films, *Poltergeist* included, is the notion of seeing: People, accustomed to seeing certain things, do not notice other objects, creatures, experiences, which fail to fit into the expected visual agenda. Children, though, can sometimes see farther and deeper, if not necessarily able to communicate their experience;

little Robbie notices the clouds overhead, and they clearly strike terror in his heart, though he dares not tell his parents, fearing they would insist he was "seeing things."

Spielberg's point is that a childish imagination allows one to see what is there rather than be blinded to it through endless "education" and everyday life. The process of adults "unlearning" is important. When Diane notices the kitchen chairs are rearranging themselves, she suddenly looks ten years younger. Acting like an ecstatic child, she tells her husband upon his return home: "Reach back into our past, when you used to have an open mind." In Spielberg, children play an essential role in teaching their parents to see. Here Robbie and Carol Anne are as frightened of the toys in their room (especially a maniacally grinning clown doll) as little Barry was enamored of his in *Close Encounters of the Third Kind*. In a marvelous bit of business, Robbie realizes he cannot stare, in the semidarkness, at the clown face any longer and tosses his red jacket over the thing's head. When he returns to bed, he realizes that a picture of the Wolfman, embossed on the back of his jacket, now peers at him, suggesting that horror cannot be shut out, no matter what he does.

During a thunder-and-lightning storm, Robbie reads horrible faces into the disfigurations of the old tree just outside his window. It resembles one of those trees that haunt the heroine of Disney's *Snow White* when she darts through the woods at night or the living trees that frighten Dorothy in *The Wizard of Oz*. In fact, that 1939 M-G-M classic is essential to understanding *Poltergeist*. As a storm rises, and Steve runs outside to make sure Carol Anne has not been blown into the muddy excavation for the swimming pool, we see behind him an approaching twister which looks remarkably like the one that spirited Dorothy Gale off to Oz. One way of interpreting Spielberg's film is as a variation on Frank Baum's book;

In a scene that horrifically resembles one from an old Fred Astaire musical, Mrs. Freeling (Jobeth Williams) finds herself all but dancing on the ceiling.

in fact, *Poltergeist* suffers by focusing on the distraught parents while keeping the child offscreen. One legitimate complaint is that it is akin to watching Aunt Em and the farm people fret over a comatose Dorothy rather than taking us down the yellow brick road.

Though Steve and Diane are hardly simple farm people, they are as much the typical American couple of today as those heartland folks were in their time. Steve is seen reading a book about Ronald Reagan, while Diane casually smokes a joint; the two bits of business are perfect in their incongruity, establishing the Freelings as a representative couple of the early 1980s. Doubtless, they

Diane finds herself dancing across the wall, though in her case, unwillingly (courtesy M-G-M/United Artists).

107

were pot-smoking hippie types in the seventies, but after moving into suburbia, a conservative streak set in. They now incorporate pot into their conventional suburban lifestyle without a thought as to the onetime supposed "political" implications of that drug of choice.

In short, Diane and Steve have become everything they once hated; they are their parents, though in small, strange, unconscious ways (most notably lighting up or their strongly suggested sexual attraction for one another) they carry with them the trappings of the long-gone summer of love and peace. As such, they serve as sobering representations for the young-adult audience.

Carol Anne is clearly *Poltergeist*'s Dorothy. The film even makes us conscious of the child's moving directly into a "movie situation," approaching the haunted TV while everyone else sleeps. As she crawls toward the flickering light, there is a strobe effect, appearing less like a television tube than the flickering light of an old silent movie. Though Carol Anne may be physically moving ever closer toward a TV, she is also entering a motion-picture world.

"They're here!"

Her oft-quoted line, as the child gleefully accepts these creatures, is followed by the phrase Carol Anne uses to identify the intruders: "The TV people." Earlier, in a satiric bit, Spielberg has Carol Anne stare at the blank TV—making contact with the forces inside—even as her mother walks by and, noticing there's nothing on, switches the channel to, of all things, a violent war movie. The desire of parents to do good and the way in which such positive intentions can instead expose children to ugliness are essential to Spielberg's vision. Also

brought into play is another recurring motif, the limitations of sight. When Diane realizes that something is present, she nervously turns to her daughter.

DIANE: *THE TV PEOPLE?*
CAROL ANNE: Uh-huh (yes).
DIANE: Do you . . . see them?
CAROL ANNE: Uh-uh (no).

Diane wants to believe but has a hard time trusting in what she can't see; the old adage that "seeing is believing" is constantly tested in Spielberg's films. Adult characters must learn to imitate children and trust—have faith in—what they cannot see. In Spielberg, believing is seeing.

More than anything else, they will have to believe that their daughter is still alive somewhere after suddenly disappearing that terrible night. (Again, like Dorothy, Carol Anne is on her bed when transported.) As blindingly bright blue-white light streams into the house, Robbie is attacked by limbs of the "monster tree," and Carol Anne is gone, though her frightened voice emanates from inside the TV. Carol Anne, lost in the netherworld, also has to continue believing that her mother is out there, though the child screams: "Mommy . . . I can't *see* you, Mommy . . . where are you?" At this juncture, Steve (Spielberg's projection of himself as a well-intentioned but far from perfect father figure) initially takes the major physical risks when prying Robbie loose from the tree's limbs or searching through the swimming pool for Carol Anne.

When the final conflict comes, it is the mother who risks everything to try and pull her daughter back into the world of the living (courtesy M-G-M/United Artists).

In the films Spielberg made during his first working decade, it is always the mother who must overcome all odds to save her children.

Still, Spielberg focuses on Diane as the key parental figure. The plot of *Poltergeist* is the plot of *The Sugarland Express,* here presented in the context of a ghost story rather than a relatively realistic tale. Moreover, it is the essential Spielberg story: a mother who will go to any length necessary to recover her child. One thing Diane does not do is call the police; nor do the police ever stop by the house to inquire why their little girl is not attending school. This can be viewed as a nar-

rative flaw. It violates all sense of reality; though the film is a ghost story, Spielberg chose to ground it in suburban reality and now violates that reality. *Variety*'s review complained:

The story is truly stupid. The houses are so close that [people] can't even watch television without interference from the next-door remote control tuner. But nobody in the neighborhood ever seems to notice [anything that goes wrong]. Here you have a

POLTERGEIST: In addition to the mother with her parental love and the scientist with her intellectual approach, the film's triad of strong women included Tangina (Zelda Rubinstein, seen here in *Poltergeist III*), who represented the spiritual and metaphysical element so necessary for the saving of that lost child (photo by Dean Williams, courtesy Metro-Goldwyn-Mayer).

house in the middle of the street going berserk in Dolby Stereo and nobody ever calls the cops.

To accept any of this, the viewer has to take *Poltergeist* less as a ghost story than a fairy tale set in modern times; common sense does not prevail here any more than it does in a story by the Brothers Grimm. Spielberg himself explained: "In *Poltergeist,* I wanted to terrify, and I also wanted to amuse. I tried to mix the laughs and screams together."

An interesting approach, also taken by John Landis in *An American Werewolf in London* and Joe Dante in *Gremlins.* Still, an approach which does not jell here, perhaps because of an awkward sense of tension (rather than happy collaboration) clearly existing between Spielberg and Hooper. Yet despite the patently absurd lines of dialogue, delivered in the most matter-of-fact manner possible, leaving the viewer to wonder if the filmmakers were serious, kidding, or just uncertain, there is nonetheless something significant going on at the heart of this flawed film. Peter Rainer of the *L.A. Herald Examiner,* wrote:

Buried within the [weak] plot of *Poltergeist* is a basic, splendid fairy-tale scheme: the story of a little girl who puts her parents through the most outrageous tribulation to prove their love for her. Underlying most fairy tales is a common theme: the comforts of family. Virtually all fairy tales begin with a disrupting of the family order, and their conclusion is usually a return to order.

Though *Poltergeist* was made a decade before the Bush-Quayle reelection campaign of 1992, the concept of "family values" is one Spielberg has, in his neoconservative treatises, hammered away at since his first theatrical release. As Andrew Sarris wrote in the *Village Voice:*

When they lose their youngest child to dark ghosts the two parents and the two older children come together in blood-kin empathy to form a larger-than-life family that will reach down to the gates of hell to save its loved ones.

Poltergeist's first act ends with the abduction of Carol Anne; act 2 begins when the Freeling family calls in a team of professional parapsychologists headed up by Dr. Lesh (Beatrice Straight). As Diane talks to the spirit of Carol Anne through the medium of TV, Dr. Lesh backs her up with advice: "Stay away from the light!" she insists, as it's the portal through which the afterlife is entered. *The Wizard of Oz* theme is further developed: Diane desperately calls out: "Can you find your way home?" As Dorothy Gale put it, there's no place like home; however, this house is haunted by angry spirits which keep objects flying through the air and household appliances always running at full speed.

This allows for already established themes to be further developed, including Spielberg's attempt to understand death and his insistence on the importance of believing without seeing. Earlier, Steve was seen sleeping, though the film playing on TV was something he really ought not to have missed: *A Guy Named Joe,* the seminal scene in which Spencer Tracy realizes he is dead, then grasps that it is not the end of existence, only the beginning. Then, shortly before Robbie and the family dog are taxied off to safety, the boy admits he has never gotten over his grandfather's death. "I didn't see his soul go up," Robbie tearfully says.

When Robbie's mother is unable to come up with a suitable answer to his question, Dr. Lesh—acting as a surrogate mother and armed with quasi-scientific research—explains forcefully: "When people die, a wonderful light (appears and beckons them). All the answers to all the questions you ever wanted to know are inside that light. And when you walk toward it, you become a part of it. Forever." Death, then, is not the end-all; Dr. Lesh articulates Spielberg's own abiding optimism.

Dr. Lesh is also the character who explains the nature of poltergeists: "People who have not walked into [the light], they resist [and] hang around [the everyday world], unhappy and jealous [of the living]. Some people get lost on the way to the light, need someone to guide them." Those are the spirits that haunt this house, so frightening the scientist Marty with horrible hallucinations (a steak turns to worms, his own face appears to disintegrate) that he eventually runs away. He is frightened because he trusts too much in sight. But Dr. Lesh and her other assistant, Ryan, remain. The two are overjoyed when, using a video camera, they actually record an identifiable image of "the thing" when it appears, continuing the film's seeing-is-believing theme.

Spielberg then belatedly introduces the film's villain, Mr. Teague, Steve's boss at the real estate company. A variation on the Murray Hamilton character in *Jaws,* he is the Middle American hypocrite who has power and authority but corrupts everything with money-based thinking. He and Steve meet and talk on a bluff overlooking the development, allowing for a brief, much-needed respite from the goings-on inside; it is refreshing for viewers to get a visual perspective on the neighborhood, noting how normal everything appears from a stone's throw away. From casual conversation, we learn that Cuesta Verde was built in 1976. This being the bicentennial year hardly seems coincidental, considering "The Star-Spangled Banner" music with which the film opened or the fact that the central characters in this "land of the free" are named Freeling. It was built on a graveyard, which Teague insists was relocated. We now have a vague hint as to the reason for the haunting but no notion as to why such creatures are still there or why they have chosen the Freelings, rather than another family to menace.

The Freelings are so decent that the haunting seems arbitrary, unfair. On this note, Spielberg moves on to act 3, in which what seemed inexplicable will be made com-

Tobe Hooper, who directed *Poltergeist* from a concept by Spielberg, seen here on the set of his next film, *Lifeforce* (courtesy Tri-Star Films).

prehensible. Dr. Lesh admits the limits of science by bringing in yet another expert. This is Tangina (Zelda Rubinstein), a diminutive spiritualist; she will assume total control, allowing Spielberg to express the need to fully embrace old-fashioned beliefs and go with emotions as a means of breaking through to the other side. Significantly, all three key characters—suburbanite mother, scientific expert, spiritualist—are women; each is notably older than the last as well as more matronly in appearance. When, in another context, Spielberg was asked by *People* magazine why there were so many women on his staff, the filmmaker answered: "I grew up in a family of women, with three sisters. I claim no profound understanding of women, but I have *faith* in them." His movies attest to that faith. A key theme is the need for male characters like Steve to have faith that the women can, and will, solve everything.

In Spielberg's films, women are earth mothers who understand and accept in ways men are unable to grasp: "I can do almost nothing without your *faith*," Tangina immediately tells the distraught family members; Diane and Dr. Lesh deliver what she needs. To rescue Carol Anne, she will take them beyond normal limits. Tangina talks a great deal about "life force" (intriguingly, the name of Hooper's next movie), noting that this is what attracted the spirits to Carol Anne: Unaware that they are dead, they exist in "a perpetual dream state, a nightmare from which they cannot wake. Inside the light is salvation.

Carol Anne must help them cross over." The child, then, will serve as a savior to the sad, lost spirits, aiding them to begin their souls' necessary journey.

Yet there is the beast, the terrible presence also inhabiting the netherworld, existing in a state of primal (male) rage and all-encompassing anger. To Carol Anne, this presence appears to be another child, though it is the Dark One; to help Carol Anne escape it, Tangina instructs Steve to scold his child harshly, reducing the unseen girl to tears by threatening to spank her if she does not do as told. Steve recoils, insisting he has never hit any of his children; he is the enlightened contemporary suburbanite. Still, Tangina insists that such fear tactics are necessary. Finally, it is the mother who must go where no man has gone before, entering the netherworld, pulling her baby back to the real world, since it is not yet her time to enter into the light. When she does, the Spielberg morality play is completed; the ritualistic action, reoccurring in his movies ever since Goldie Hawn defied all odds to reclaim her child, has been played out.

Act 3 may be over, but there remains the need for an epilogue; Carol Anne is back, but much remains unexplained. They are together again (even the dog is there), the family unit having been happily restored. But as a result of her other worldly experience, Diane now has premature touches of gray hair; she looks bewitchingly like Elsa Lanchester in *The Bride of Frankenstein.* Their reality has begun to resemble a movie, so she has come to resemble a movie icon. They prepare for their move away but decide to spend the last night in the house. An unwise decision: The head on Carol Anne's doll falls off and rolls across the floor; Robbie's frightful clown doll is not where he left it, suddenly attacking the boy from behind. Mom finds herself, like Fred Astaire in an old M-G-M musical, crawling antlike up from the bed, onto the walls, over the ceiling. When she finally gets her breath and speaks, her words are those of the prototypical Spielbergian mother: "Don't touch my babies!"

When Diane falls into the backyard swimming pool, the molding bodies of the dead rise up and grab her. It is then that Steve realizes the reason for all that has happened: His boss moved the headstones but not the graves themselves, causing the cadavers to be disturbed. The Freelings unfortunately were the first in the neighborhood to put in a pool, the excavation unleashing the spirits. As Diane struggles to hang on to her children, fearing she cannot continue to keep both from being sucked into the abyss, she resembles Meryl Streep in *Sophie's Choice. Poltergeist* is a *Sophie's Choice* in which Sophie refuses to make the choice; she will not give either child up and hangs on precariously to both, overcoming all odds, symbolizing Spielberg's bountiful faith in mothers.

A suburban apocalypse takes place around them as they drive away, resembling the dysfunctional family in Hitchcock's *The Birds,* having finally pulled together, becoming a true family for the first time, thereby managing to escape. It makes sense, then, that the film ends with a

Hitchcockian twist: Having checked into the Holiday Inn for the night, Steve unceremoniously shoves the TV set out of the room. It is a rejection of television that comes from the filmmaker's heart: "Most TV shows figure the audience isn't very smart," he has said. "That's why TV stinks."

Before the film could be released, yet another controversy arose. The Los Angeles–based Classification and Rating Board of the Motion Picture Association tagged *Poltergeist* with an R. The decision, which would have restricted the film from being seen by anyone under seventeen not accompanied by an adult, horrified executives at M-G-M, the studio near bankruptcy at the time, their last hopes riding on this film. So in early May, Spielberg and M-G-M chairman Frank Rosenfelt flew to New York to argue for a PG. Rosenfelt insisted that *Poltergeist* was devoid of sex, profanity, or overt violence; CARA, represented by chairman Richard D. Heffner, initially argued that the "cumulative effect" of cadavers and the "intensity" of the images necessitated an R rating. Quickly, though, they reversed themselves, allowing the film a mild PG. "I don't make R movies," Spielberg angrily insisted. (*Schindler's List* would be the first.)

E.T. The Extra-Terrestrial

A UNIVERSAL RELEASE, 1982

CAST

Dee Wallace *(Mary);* Henry Thomas *(Elliott)*; Peter Coyote *(Keys)*; Robert MacNaughton *(Michael)*; Drew Barrymore *(Gertie)*; K. C. Martel *(Greg)*; Sean Frye *(Steve)*; Tom (C. Thomas) Howell *(Tyler)*; Erika Eleniak *(Pretty Girl)*; Richard Swingler *(Teacher)*; Debra Winger and others *(Voice of E.T.)*.

CREDITS

Director, Steven Spielberg; producers, Spielberg and Kathleen Kennedy; writer, Melissa Mathison; production supervisor, Frank Marshall; cinematography, Allen Daviau; production design, James D. Bissell; editor, Carol Littleton; music, John Williams; costume design, Deborah Scott; E.T. creator, Carlo Rambaldi; visual-special-effects supervisor, Dennis Muren; special-effects coordinator, Dale Martin; spaceship design, Ralph McQuarrie; matte painting supervisor, Michael Pangrazio; animation supervisor, Samuel Comstock; Technicolor, Dolby Stereo, running time, 115 mins.; rating: PG.

It all began with an item in daily *Variety* on February 28, 1978, mentioning that even as preparations continued for *1941,* Spielberg was planning a small film, tentatively to be titled *Growing Up.* Spielberg claimed he wanted to shoot it on an ultratight $1.5 million budget, setting the story in his onetime hometown, Phoenix. His original

Steven Spielberg directs *E.T.*, which would quickly become the most popular motion picture of all time, until eventually replaced by another Spielberg film, *Jurassic Park* (courtesy Universal City Studios).

Spielberg, who already had proven his unique abilities at directing a child-actor in *Close Encounters of the Third Kind,* here outdid himself working with young Henry Thomas as Elliott (courtesy Universal City Studios).

concept was to have Robert Zemeckis and Bob Gale pen the script. Spielberg planned to shoot the movie beginning on May 15 of that year, before work began on *1941,* completing this quickie in a mere twenty-eight days.

Spielberg also stated publicly that the film would be "a personal story of [my] own growing up." Needless to say, it was not shot in 1978, but was set aside as work on *1941* grew all-encompassing. Over the years, though, the concept continued to take (and change) shape. For a while, it was to be called *A Boy's Life,* then *E.T. and Me.* Spielberg, of course, had already done a classic UFO film, *Close Encounters of the Third Kind,* and over the last several years had been toying with an idea for a sequel. Yet he was never able to come up with a concept he felt would live up to the original and had too much respect for his audience to even consider a movie that would exploit them without properly entertaining them.

Then, while filming *Raiders of the Lost Ark* on exotic locations around the world, far from family and friends, he grew terribly lonely. In his tent at night, Spielberg lapsed into a child's loneliness-denial device, creating an imaginary friend who was there with him. As that friend gradually took shape in his imagination, it began to resemble one of the benign aliens from *Close Encounters of the Third Kind.* Rather than an obvious sequel, Spielberg began to wonder if perhaps he ought to create a companion piece instead, a film that would compliment *Close Encounters of the Third Kind* by showing a similar situation but from the alien's point of view.

About that emerging film, Spielberg announced: "It's a 'personal' movie for me, and closer to my heart than any movie I've ever made before." Though *E.T.* would contain the story of an alien abandoned on earth when his fellows flee in their spacecraft ("A movie about that little guy who was left behind," Spielberg said), it would also be grounded in reality. Focusing on a ten-year-old whose parents consider divorce, the film would ring true, since Spielberg had been about that age when his own parents split.

"Elliott's a normal, everyday kid, growing up in arcades, playing Asteroids and Galaxy and PacMan," Spielberg surmised, making clear that even if the character was in part based on himself, Elliott's experiences would be those of a 1980s child. Video games aside, some things never change: "He's at that stage where he's just bored with everything around him. He watches a lot of television, doesn't read, is starting to look at girls. Older girls, eleven or twelve. And he's starting to have those feelings like I had when I was ten or eleven. Elliott's not me, but he's the closest thing to my experiences in my life, growing up in [southwestern] suburbia."

Even as Spielberg was shooting *Raiders,* he found time to mentally develop this personal project, talking it over with producer Kathleen Kennedy. Kennedy had recently become friendly with Melissa Mathison, girlfriend of Harrison Ford (explaining why she was around for the *Raiders of the Lost Ark* shoot) and, before that, cowriter on *The Black Stallion* with Carroll Ballard. Mathison had recently grown so frustrated with her own writer's block while living in England that she vowed to abandon screenwriting entirely. Since *Black Stallion* was one of Kennedy's all-time favorite films, the idea occurred to her that Mathison's proven ability to depict an innocent child locked in a nontraditional friendship with an "other" creature might qualify her to tell the story of Elliott and E.T.

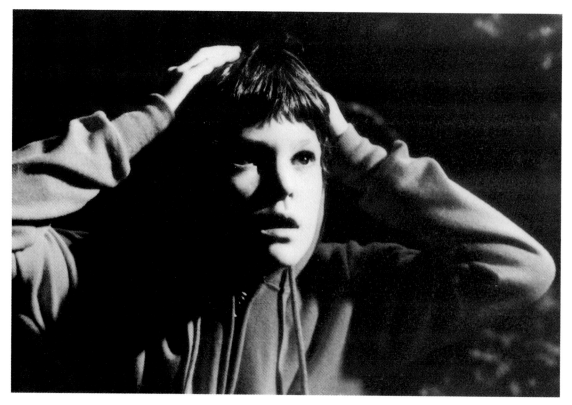

Elliott, the open and innocent child, encounters E.T. for the first time (courtesy Universal City Studios).

Spielberg mulled the idea over for a while. Then, during dinner one night, he approached Mathison and literally "pitched" the story to her, asking if she was interested. Mathison, weakened from a bout with dysentery, turned him down cold with the words "Thank you very much, but I've decided never to write again." Immediately, she regretted that decision, but was now too embarrassed to say anything. The *Raiders* crew then moved on to Tunisia; one day, while Melissa and Steven were out in the wilds, turning over rocks in search of scorpions for an upcoming scene, he happened to mention the script idea again. Mathison this time jumped at the offer.

Upon their return to the states, Mathison immediately began writing. After each week's work was completed, she met Steven at the marina (his location for the complex editing of *Raiders*) to discuss what she had come up with so far. This went on for eight weeks, at which time the first draft was completed. All in all, Mathison wrote three drafts. To simplify the story, she and Spielberg entirely eliminated the character of Elliott's best friend–worst enemy, a kind of Eddie Haskell figure. On the other hand, they decided to build up the final confrontation with adults as the kind of grand set piece Spielberg, working in the Hitchcock tradition, preferred as an audience payoff ending. Spielberg himself suggested that she add the scene in which E.T. gets drunk.

By this point, it was clear that the minuscule budget would not work. The film would cost $10.5 million to make, still fiscally responsible compared to the more

Elliott and his brother Michael (Robert MacNaughton) cover E.T. in order to sneak him outside the house at sunset (courtesy Universal City Studios).

Drew Barrymore nuzzles E.T.: Note that Spielberg places a flower in the foreground as a visual metaphor, representing the emotion that the two characters are experiencing.

than $30 million then being spent on "prestige" pictures like *Annie* and *Blade Runner.* The movie was expanded to a sixty-five day shoot, most of it to be completed in Los Angeles at the Laird International Studios, with some additional locations in and around L.A. and several more days of location work in northern California. Everyone agreed that *E.T.* would be shot in such a way that the setting did not appear to be trendy L.A. but rather a medium-sized southwestern city. Indeed, what we see on-screen looks far more like Phoenix than Los Angeles.

A key decision was picking the right child to play Elliott. Spielberg and Kennedy auditioned hundreds of boys before they came across a San Antonio ten-year-old named Henry Thomas. Though he had no previous acting experience, the filmmakers intended to cast a child less for acting ability than looks, wanting a boy with an innocent but believable presence. Another key decision was to shoot the film without reliance on intricate storyboards. Previously, everything had been drawn out in vivid detail prior to the commencement of principal photography. Now, though, Spielberg's gut instinct told him not to work this way. He later admitted: "I sketched about forty percent of this movie on paper and decided that I was being penciled into a corner. I always think five shots ahead. On this picture, I couldn't." He would, at each step along the way, think only as far as the next shot, which would be "better for this movie, which has so much emotion in it." Despite a fantastic premise and some special effects, *E.T.* was always meant to be a "people movie."

117

Ralph McQuarrie, who had been employed as the design consultant and conceptual artist for Lucas's *Star Wars* as well as Spielberg's *Close Encounters of the Third Kind*, was hired to design the spaceship. As for E.T. himself, Spielberg made all sorts of verbal suggestions to production illustrator Ed Verreaux, who incorporated these ideas into his drawings. The director talked a great deal about "old people, young people" until it finally registered on Verreaux that what Spielberg actually wanted for E.T. was a unique combination of the innocence of youth and the wisdom of age. He would draw pictures, Spielberg approving of certain aspects of each, rejecting other elements. "We put the final drawing together much the same as a police composite-sketch artist would," Verreaux later explained. Spielberg hadn't known precisely what he believed E.T. should look like, but he knew he'd know when he saw it. "I wanted a creature that only a mother could love," he later reflected, bringing up a subject so significant in this movie and his other films as well.

At last happy with the results, Spielberg then turned the sketches over to the person he had picked to do the actual design. It didn't work out; $700,000 went out the window on an E.T. prototype deemed useless. Spielberg then turned to fifty-seven-year-old Carlo Rambaldi, an Italian immigrant who had won two Academy Awards for his work on *King Kong* and *Alien*, also having created the extraterrestrial for *Close Encounters of the Third Kind*. When he listened to Spielberg's descriptions, Rambaldi told the director it would take a full nine months to complete; Spielberg granted him six. A sculptor, builder, and artist, Rambaldi spent between fifteen and twenty hours a day working; he and his four-member team put in more than five thousand hours.

Originally, Rambaldi wanted to streamline the building of E.T. by creating a single model of a creature that would do everything necessary. He and his team soon realized that this was impossible. Instead, they set about creating three separate E.T.s, each designed for maximum effectiveness at some special function: a mechanical model operated by cables, an electronic one for the close shots of precise facial movements, and a "walking E.T." for movement sequences, operated from the inside by several dwarfs and a little boy who had been born without legs. Each E.T. was constructed with a skeleton of aluminum and steel, padded with a musculature of fiberglass, polyurethane, and foam rubber. Firmly grounding the fanciful character in reality, Spielberg insisted that when E.T. moved, it had to be clear "he's slow, not surefooted; he's much more conditioned to a heavier atmosphere, a heavier gravity. He's a little clumsy on earth, always stumbling, getting knocked into by refrigerators, hitting walls."

Spielberg contributed advice at every stage. It was his idea to give E.T. eyes like Albert Einstein as well as a derriere resembling Donald Duck's when he waddles, once more evoking a Disney favorite. At last, Spielberg had the three-foot six-inch creature he wanted, able to maneuver through 150 varied movements, manipulated by a dozen men who stood at separate control boxes, each connected to E.T. through twenty-foot-long cables. The creature's realistic breathing and pulsation were simulated by having thin tubes, connected to plastic bags, which the controllers then slowly squeezed air into and out of. E.T. was created at a total cost of $1.5 million (the original estimated budget of the entire film back in 1978); seventeen assistants and specialists eventually assisted Rambaldi.

This mechanical approach was fine for the torso, but E.T.'s ultraexpressive hands demanded something more specific still. Rambaldi hired Caprice Rothe, a thirty-four-year-old professional mime, to don E.T. gloves and perform the expressive movements when E.T. reaches for candies and treats or stretches his arm into the refrigerator for another beer. One marvelous quality here was purely accidental; nervous about working on a Spielberg movie, Rothe drank a great deal of coffee, then realized her hands were shaking uncontrollably as she tried to execute her moves. Fearful that Spielberg would dismiss her, Rothe was stunned to discover that he considered this a wonderful addition. "Things are new to E.T., so he's cautious," the director insisted. "He uses his fingers to explore."

Getting E.T.'s voice just right was also tricky. Actress Debra Winger contributed some vocal effects, but the bulk of E.T.'s speaking was provided by an unknown sixty-fiveish Marin County housewife named Pat Welsh. She happened to be talking to a salesperson at a local camera store when Ben Burtt, Lucas's then thirty-four-year-old sound designer, walked by. Burtt approached the now-retired elocution teacher, convincing her to remove her dentures and speak toothlessly for him. Convinced that her appealing screechy voice (addicted to cigarettes, Welsh smoked two packs a day) was what he wanted, Burtt paid her $380 to spend nine and a half hours speaking E.T.'s lines off the set. Burtt recorded Welsh's line readings, later fitting them in to precisely match the movements of E.T.'s mouth.

Finally, permission was needed from the M & M people to allow their product to be used in the film. Mathison had specified the popular treat in her script, but when approached, executives at M & M/Mars chose not to bankroll the formidable publicity drive which Universal insisted run concurrently with the film's release. Meanwhile, Jack Dowd, a sixty-year-old vice president at Hershey's Chocolate, had been assigned to create a greater public profile for their relatively new product, Reese's Pieces. He responded positively to an offer from Spielberg/Universal. Within two weeks of *E.T.*'s release, Reese's sales tripled, bolstered by posters showing E.T. eating the tidbits, underscored by the words "E.T.'s Favorite Candy."

Filming commenced on September 8, 1981, with Allen Daviau as a cinematographer. Daviau understood that

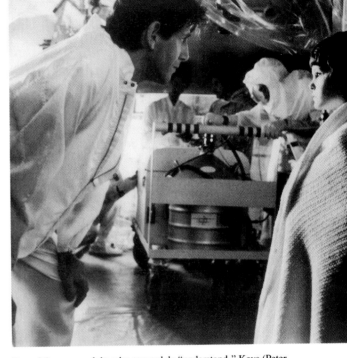

E.T. enjoys his first meal on earth, though his special treat will always be Reese's Pieces (courtesy Universal City Studios).

One of those rare adults who can and do "understand," Keys (Peter Coyote) tries to explain to Elliott that E.T. must be isolated for his own good (courtesy Universal City Studios).

The Touch 1: In Spielberg films, the ultimate communication comes through human contact rather than words (courtesy Universal City Studios).

The Touch 2: Another angle on the moment of contact (and complete communication) between Elliott and E.T. (courtesy Universal City Studios).

The search for a true friend: fanciful as the film may seem, it served as an emotional autobiography for Spielberg, who as a little boy never stayed in one place long enough to have a soul-mate.

Spielberg needed "such a feeling of [everyday] reality to" the setting "that you can accept the fantastic thing" that happens. Likewise, costume designer Deborah Scott created clothing that would at once be believable but would ever so slightly satirize suburbanites.

The first two days were given over to interior scenes at a Culver City high school, after which the production company moved back and forth between Northridge and Tujunga for eleven days of exteriors. A full forty-two days were spent on the three soundstages which production designer Jim Bissell created at Laird to represent the upper floor of the home, the ground floor, and the redwood forest outside. The final six days of exterior shooting were done on location near Crescent City, a small coastal town near the Oregon border. There had only been one major mishap: An E.T. costume caught fire with dwarf Pat Bilon inside. Bilon later recalled: "Everyone panicked except Steven; He just yanked the wires out of the battery," and the trauma was over.

The happy shoot was actually completed four days ahead of schedule. That, however, was when the real work began, for the ultracomplicated postproduction schedule included tricky special-effects sequences by Lucas's Industrial Light and Magic as well as the addition of John Williams's musical score. He wisely chose to create distinct theme music for Elliott and E.T. rather than a single overriding theme for the picture. This required that Spielberg and Kennedy constantly commute, over the next several months, between Los Angeles and the Bay Area, supervising such technical aspects as mixing, editing, and looping to be certain the final film looked precisely as originally conceived.

Perfectionist tinkering with myriad details continued up until a first public showing at the 1982 Cannes Film Festival. Raves there were followed by an ecstatic reaction from the public at a May sneak preview in Houston. Word spread that a phenomenon was about to happen; Universal, at last grasping what they had, scrapped their initial distribution strategy. They had planned to throw the film away by opening it in a mere five hundred theaters, owing to early lack of exhibitor interest. Now they wanted to go wide with eighteen hundred playdates, though Spielberg felt this was overdoing it for what he still considered an essentially intimate movie. He and Universal compromised at eleven hundred screens nationwide.

Shortly after the film's opening day (June 11, 1982), *E.T.* was on its way to becoming the all-time box-office champ, a status it would hold until replaced by another Spielberg film, *Jurassic Park*. During its first year of release, *E.T.* grossed a record-breaking $359,687,000 in the United States and Canada alone; before long, the film had been seen by more than 200 million people worldwide.

The reason for the unparalleled success? *E.T.* boasts an enchantingly simple surface which covers a rich lode of complex ideas and emotions. Mathison's script neatly divides the story into three easily identifiable acts. In the first, E.T. is left behind when his fellow space travelers, surprised by U.S. scientists, are forced to fly off and leave him behind. E.T. is discovered by Elliott, who hides the alien in his room and eventually shares this secret with his overbearing teenage brother, Michael (Robert MacNaughton), and smaller, ever-sniveling sister, Gertie (Drew Barrymore), who rise to the occasion and help Elliott hide E.T. from encroaching adults. Act 2 begins when E.T. persuades the three kids to help him use parts of their portable computers and other electronic equipment to create a makeshift radar system by which the ever more homesick creature can "phone home." All the while, though, government security agents are monitoring, then moving in, on the house where they suspect an alien is living. The third act begins with E.T. near death, after a nightlong exposure to the elements while trying to contact his fellow aliens. He is captured by the scientists, who try to save him. The act concludes with Elliott, his brother and sister, and other neighborhood bike-riding kids forming a rebellious but positive youth cult, aiding E.T. in his escape from adult authorities (however well meaning) to return home via the small spacecraft that has

A recurring image: In Spielberg films, the positive characters learn to move beyond the everyday business of life around them and once again "look upward," spiritually as well as physically.

arrived. The film concludes with the bittersweet parting of E.T. and Elliott.

The ending is reminiscent of several classic Disney films. Whether it is Snow White saying goodbye to the seven dwarfs or Cinderella waving farewell to the mice, Disney movies consistently end on a bittersweet rather than simplistically happy note, the sweet sorrow of parting as necessary as it is difficult. Spielberg has referred to this as "an up cry," and *E.T.* is clearly designed with just such an effect in mind. Understandably, more than one critic tagged *E.T.* as "the best Disney movie not made by Disney."

Still, the unique quality of Spielberg's work derives from the combination of Disney and Hitchcock. Just as Hitchcock's films are filled with what have come to be called "the Hitchcock moments," so, too, have Spielberg fans learned to expect just such unforgettable images from this emerging master of cinematic storytelling. In *E.T.,* those moments include:

- E.T. wolfing down his favorite food on earth, Reese's Pieces.
- Elliott's mom, positive she has heard a noise in her boy's supposedly empty room, peering in but not noticing E.T. crouched among the stuffed toys in the closet.
- E.T. staggering about the empty house in a bathrobe, getting drunk on beer from the fridge.
- Elliott and E.T. riding the boy's bicycle up across the sky and past a hauntingly beautiful moon.
- E.T. dressed in a wig and girl's clothing from the doll collection of Elliott's younger sister.
- E.T.'s magical finger lighting up and miraculously curing Elliott's cut hand.
- E.T.'s "phone home" scene in which he raises a finger skyward, its long, thin shadow falling across Elliott's face.
- All the neighborhood children on bikes following E.T. up into the sky like so many modern "lost boys" flying along behind Peter Pan.

In fact, the legend of Peter Pan—one of Spielberg's personal favorite stories about normal people taking flight and the source of his eventual film *Hook*—plays a key role here. At one point, the overworked Mary actually finds a few quiet moments to read to her smallest child; the book is James Barrie's *Peter and Wendy.* We watch as mother and daughter share that scene in which Tinker Bell is on the verge of death. The mom gets into the story (her own potential for childlike wonder revealed) as she emotionally reads the lines "Clap if you believe in fairies." Both she and the child clap together even as the camera cuts away to another room where E.T.'s finger is just then lighting up magically, resem-

bling the ball of light so often used to represent Tinker Bell in stage productions of *Peter Pan.* E.T. is, then, as much fairy as alien, a supernatural creature one either does or does not believe in. Near the film's end, the fairy tale ceases to be a make-believe story read by a mother, instead spilling over into the "real" world. As E.T. lies dying (much like Tinker Bell in the old tale), mother and daughter are together again. "I wish . . ." the child says, and a moment later, E.T. comes back to life. The little girl's words might just as easily have been, *I believe. . . .*

For like so many other Spielberg projects, *E.T.* is based on the notion that children possess a wealth of natural knowledge which adults, inhabiting the gray workaday world, have largely forgotten. E.T.'s spaceship lands in the forest, presented as an enchanted place compared to stultifying suburbia. E.T. even passes by a rabbit that somehow senses the little alien means him no harm; later in the film, a gentle deer likewise recognizes and responds to E.T.'s goodness when he returns to the forest primeval. Not once do we see a snake or some other menacing creature, those readily available symbols of nature as a place to be feared. In the film's context, nature is a sanctuary, especially for those good characters who are themselves "natural" in their responses.

A key moment involves Elliott and his siblings following E.T. into the woods, where they all become nicer as a result of their contact with the magic found there. Everything they experience in the civilized, adult suburban world is soulless, represented by the nameless, faceless soldier-scientists who search for E.T. In Elliott's own range of daily experiences, there is the equally faceless schoolteacher, never seen as a whole person, purposefully photographed as a series of fragments, the camera dehumanizing him. This adult coldly instructs the kids to kill frogs so they can then dissect them. When Elliott is seized with an inspiration to free all the frogs and shepherd them back to the woods, he is inspired by E.T.'s innate goodness. Elliott suddenly "unlearns" what he's being taught, allowing him to follow his own decent instincts.

Elliott, of course, always possessed good instincts, which were what led him to E.T. in the first place. "Elliott, you're crazy," he mutters to himself when, after hearing something "out there," the child is moved to step out into the unknown. Older than little Barry in *Close Encounters of the Third Kind,* Elliott has learned enough about fear from his suburban society to be more hesitant. Still, he has not become so indoctrinated that, like an adult, he now sees the unknown as totally threatening. At ten, Elliott contains elements of each, and it is his emotional journey back to a full embrace of childlike wonder that the film chronicles.

When Elliott first discovers E.T., the child screams, and so does the alien. The effect, achieved through a rapid crosscutting from one face to the other, provides the viewer with one of the film's first great gags. In fact, it is one more example of Spielberg and his collaborators creating an audience-pleasing effect that is a part of the film's artistic subtext. Shortly thereafter, Elliott grows tired, and E.T. also begins to yawn. One concept is that E.T. and Elliott are emotionally in tune with one another. This is set up through the rapid editing, which makes it appear as if each of the screamers is peering into a mirror; it is also inherent in their names, as E.T. could easily be a shortening of Elliott's name.

Though he may not look like Brody from *Jaws,* E.T. is indeed one of Spielberg's representative heroes. In the tradition of that lawman who felt at home nowhere, equally out of place in the New York city streets and a small town, E.T. is a lost soul. He sees the world differently from his fellow aliens, who stayed close together during their earthly sojourn, while he wandered off. Yet even after he is given a loving "home" by Elliott, E.T. feels lost and lonely. Likewise, Elliott—the title character's alter ego—feels something of a stranger in a strange land.

The Spielberg signature shot: Friendship and flight, artistically wrought into an unforgettable screen image.

Four teenagers watch E.T. ascend; Tom Howell, (*left*) later achieved some notoriety as an actor (courtesy Universal City Studios).

Mary (Dee Wallace) listens intently as Keys explains the government's seemingly frightening, though in fact benign, designs on E.T. as Elliott listens; considering the religious implications of the film, Mary's name is clearly symbolic (courtesy Universal City Studios).

Significantly, we never once see Elliott with a friend his own age. Like E.T., he is alone, this being one more film about characters attempting to overcome loneliness by breaking through to one another. Which qualifies it as a film about communication. Significantly, when Elliott is first seen in the company of his brother's friends, he speaks to the older boys, but they do not respond; it's as if they don't hear him, though he's present. Shortly thereafter, Elliott encounters E.T., and they do communicate, but without words; as the boy unconsciously raises his fingers to his face, E.T. imitates the action. They make their "breakthrough," creating a sign language much as the earthlings and aliens did in *Close Encounters of the Third Kind.* Here, though, Elliott is able to communicate with E.T. in words as well; Elliott's younger sister—closer still to basic wisdom and natural wonder—proudly teaches E.T. the ABCs from her schoolbook.

In Spielberg films, what the positive characters communicate is emotional rather than intellectual. Indeed, there's a certain anti-intellectualism at work in all the director's films, a belief that complex ideas are of a lesser order than simple feelings. The primacy of feelings is driven home in a dialogue exchange as doctors rush about, trying to keep E.T. alive. One uniformed man tries to draw information from Mary, who explains that her child and the alien are physically connected.

SCIENTIST: Elliott thinks his thoughts?
MARY: No. Elliott feels his feelings.

The interchange not only makes clear the director's priorities but also the fact that Mary has at last come to understand the situation as well as her own son. Earlier in the movie, that was not the case.

"Dad would believe me," Elliott sadly announces at the dinner table on the night he first spots E.T. His realistically inclined mother rejects this as nothing more than a lonely child's attempt to get attention. The image of a boy trying to reach maturity without a proper father figure is nothing new in the Spielberg canon. The home seen in the film's exteriors was discovered by production designer Jim Bissell, who later recalled: "It was like a tract house, but removed and isolated somehow. It wasn't quite like all the rest surrounding it." It is, then, a house that sits squarely in suburbia (like Roy Neary's), yet strikes the viewer as being off on its own (like Jilian's).

As such, it is, then, the perfect house for the film's central conception. Though Dee Wallace effectively manages to make Elliott's mom a believable and singular character, there is no question she is drawn in the mold of Spielberg's early-middle-aged, youthfully blond mothers from previous pictures. Mary can be as silly as Goldie Hawn in *Sugarland,* then as frantic (when she believes her child has run away) as Melinda Dillon in *Close Encounters of the Third Kind.* Like Jilian, she is so locked into her suburban lifestyle that she literally cannot see the magic around her. At one point, Elliott insists he

wants to introduce her to someone, and E.T. stands on the sidelines, waiting to make her acquaintance. Talking frantically, she brushes by him, not even noticing that there's an alien in her home. She has eyes, but she cannot see, at least not anything she isn't prepared to see. Still, she will prove to have more of a potential for childlike innocence within her than Jilian; when, in this film's final act, her children force her to consider the now-sickly E.T., Mary has enough of the child's spirit in her to, like Roy Neary, become a true believer and join their little clique.

No wonder, then, that her name is Mary and there is no husband sleeping by her side. Since we never see the "dad" in question (there are vague references to his living in Mexico with someone named Sally), it is easy to accept the film as a religious allegory. E.T. descends from on high (much like the savior-aliens in *Close Encounters of the Third Kind*), providing the boy with the wise, otherworldly father figure he so desperately needs. Certainly, none of the human males we see on-screen will suffice. While E.T. is photographed in long enough shots to make him always appear whole (spiritually as well as physically), we see his antagonists as fragmented body parts—arms or legs.

However, Spielberg's essentially "benign" attitude also comes into play. As the scientists struggle to keep E.T. alive, the camera gradually pulls back, at last humanizing them by allowing us to see them as whole people. Then, in a striking image, Spielberg focuses on one individual: Though he still wears his space helmet with plastic face guard, we are able to catch his sympathetic face peering through the transparent shield. Superimposed horizontally over his face, owing to a reflection in the helmet's window, is little Elliott, stretched out alongside E.T.

As this man (whose name, though never mentioned in the film itself, is intriguingly listed in the credits as "Keys") speaks, it quickly becomes apparent that he is an equivalent to the benign scientist Lacombe from *Close Encounters of the Third Kind.* Or, to look at the situation in another light, he is an older version of little Elliott. "I've been waiting for this since I was ten years old [the same age Elliott is now]," he says sweetly, sincerely. "I don't want him to die." He and Elliott are, essentially, one and the same, justifying the striking shot of Elliott over Keys's face as something more substantial than show-off pictorialism. Keys is one of those adults who hangs on to a childlike way of seeing, able to recognize the spiritual quality of not only E.T. but also the boy Elliott.

Earlier in the film, though, even Elliott's spirituality is in danger of being diluted. E.T. arrives just in time to help him hang on to his spirituality, an idea conveyed not through dialogue (which would be mawkish) but the way in which Elliott's room is lit. Our first view of it reveals an effectively realistic portrait of a normal little boy's typical room. But from the moment E.T. begins hiding

The pursuit: It was Spielberg's idea to add a Hitchcock-like chase sequence for the film's finale.

out here, the room changes. As the film progresses, Spielberg lights the room in an ever more stylized manner; the same objects we earlier saw in harshly realistic source lighting gradually take on a charmingly eerie quality as warmer choices add a magical glow to what transpires here.

Indeed, from the very first image, in which a series of white lights cut through the night sky, *E.T.* is organized around patterns of light. There are the lights of the house that draw E.T., initially revealing him to us through a dazzling backlight technique. There are the flashlights of the authorities as they comb the woods for little aliens, contrasted with the single flashlight Elliott carries when he sets about searching for E.T. himself, oftentimes shining the light directly at the camera—essentially, toward "us." There are endless backlighting effects as E.T. and Elliott, frolicking in his room, are lit via natural light pouring in through the window. Most notably, there is the classic image of Elliott and E.T. soaring up into the sky on the boy's bicycle, thanks to E.T.'s magical properties which allow them to fly (another key Spielberg theme), as they pass the full round whiteness of the moon. For a moment, it almost appears as if they are an image projected upon the moon rather than characters illuminated by it from behind.

Which makes sense, since light in Spielberg films is more than just a technique masterfully employed. On the one hand, it is light in the sense that light has always represented wisdom, not accumulated factual knowledge but wisdom as a true deep grasp of the universe. The mother ship in *Close Encounters of the Third Kind* was covered

with actual lights in part to suggest that inside that ship was the "light" (wisdom) Roy Neary so desperately searched for; here E.T.'s finger "lights up" as an indication that he is sage, a creature who understands.

On another level entirely, light is also a reminder of the fact that we are watching a movie, the screening of any film made possible by the projection of light carefully filtered through photographed images. As *Newsweek*'s Jack Kroll wrote in 1977, citing the *Close Encounters of the Third Kind* finale in which Big Mama descended like some remarkable candelabra: "Never has a movie produced such an overwhelming, ever-changing rhapsody of light—so much so that you realize that a movie is, in fact, nothing but light projected onto a surface." Spielberg's films contain the visual motif of projected light because they are, essentially, movies about movies.

So at a key moment in *E.T.,* the title character hides out in Elliott's house (everyone else is gone for the day) while Elliott sits in school. E.T. watches TV, and after sitcoms, cartoons, and assorted old movies (including an ironic glimpse of a malevolent flying saucer sucking up the main characters in 1954's *This Island Earth*), he eventually ceases channel surfing, entranced by John Ford's *Quiet Man*. E.T. watches that scene in which John Wayne, the ultimate symbol of American masculinity, stalks through the Gallic cottage he has just bought. Discovering Maureen O'Hara there, he watches as she attempts to rush out the door, grabs her by the hand even as a tumultuous wind tears through the place, spins her around, and kisses her. Elliott, psychically linked to E.T., magically receives that image in his mind; Spielberg intercuts the televised movie E.T. is watching with an image of Elliott doing precisely the same thing at school with a pretty blond coed (Erika Eleniak).

In a comic variation on the original, diminutive Elliott must stand on a friend's back to kiss the girl of his dreams. Still, kiss her he does, as the film suggests that what every one of us wants most is to live out the idealized fantasy moments from classic movies. More recent movies are evoked, too, in particular those of Spielberg's sometime collaborator George Lucas. Elliott, introducing E.T. to his room (essentially, his own little world), parades out all his *Star Wars* figures, so popular with real-life kids of precisely his age during the early eighties. Later, as Elliott and his siblings take E.T. Halloweening (the alien, sporting a sheet, is dressed as a ghost), he passes a child wearing a Yoda costume. Of all the *Star Wars* characters, Yoda was the one E.T. most resembles. The two stare at each other, long and hard, as they pass in the early-evening twilight, providing a neat commentary on contemporary movies; in a way, it is as if Spielberg and Lucas (through their representative aliens) were passing one another and communicating telepathically.

Near the very end, Elliott and his siblings, trying to escape with E.T. from the authorities, run into the other biking kids.

ELLIOTT: He's a man from space. We're taking him to his spaceship.

BOY: Can't he just beam up?

ELLIOTT: This is reality, Greg!

Of course, it isn't reality; it's the world of Spielberg's movie *E.T.* The point is, the world Spielberg has here created is consistent and believable enough that we accept it as reality.

In addition to critical raves, box-office success, and major merchandising, *E.T.* inspired something else: interpretation. Though conceived and created as a work of mass entertainment, the movie quickly proved to be something other than mere escapism. Something significant was going on here, though the filmmaker himself may have been less than totally conscious of what he was creating. Depending on how one approached it, its central character could be perceived as representing a staggering number of concepts. For Andrew Sarris, "E.T. is the teddy bear we crush forever to our bleeding hearts. E.T. is every childish fantasy we never outgrew. E.T. is the eternal child in all of us." Not just working critics offered their insights; in *McCall's*, Marta Tarbell quoted the editor of a national magazine as saying:

The movie is really about fatherhood. These three kids have been abandoned by their father—and what do they find? Someone who knows what they're thinking and feeling, who can heal them when they've been hurt and make them laugh. E.T. is the father that we all wish we'd had or would like to be.

But there were less earthbound ways to consider the movie. Ted Koppel, host of ABC's *Nightline,* insisted that E.T. was not a father but a son—or, more correctly, the Son, announcing: "It's essentially the Christ story. Christ was the ultimate extraterrestrial." More than one religious leader agreed wholeheartedly. Rabbi Harold S. Kushner, author of several inspirational books, explained: "Like religion, E.T. is real, even though it is not history. Real, because it tells us something that's true about the human spirit. It gives us a mythology that offers hope and comfort." At a time when many people had grown to feel disassociated from their society, unable to return to the old religious truths and the spirituality they so desperately needed, E.T. provided an alternative to conventional religion, conveying the same hopeful message one would experience at a traditional synagogue or church.

Essentially, Spielberg addressed our collective, ongoing need for spiritual reassurance, but did so in the context of seemingly secular entertainment. Tarbell reported, "Like Christ, E.T. can heal the sick and perform miracles; he also dies, is resurrected, and finally leaves earth for home (somewhere above). It is a familiar story, one we have all grown up hearing and one we are bound to respond to, however new the form in which it is told."

Importantly, this relates to an idea discussed earlier, in the chapter on *Close Encounters of the Third Kind:* Spielberg's conception of the Neary family as believably specific people, yet at the same time clearly representing spiritually starved Americans. Dr. Phil Lineberger, pastor at the Metropolitan Baptist Church in Wichita, Kansas, wrote:

I went to see the movie with my kids. As I sat watching it, I noticed E.T.'s telepathic sympathy and I thought, That's an interesting sort of parallel to the gospel. But it wasn't until E.T. was dying, when the little boy gains strength as E.T. comes closer to death, that I thought, My goodness, that sounds like the atonement. In the gospel, Christ died for our sins so that we might live, just as E.T. was doing. When E.T. was resurrected, and then at the end when he was ascending, being watched by all the kids who had become his disciples, it all started lining up for me.

Yet people can't help but ask: Did Spielberg actually intend any of this? In 1982, he told *L.A. Weekly:*

I've been too busy making movies to stop and analyze how or why I make 'em. Lucas was the most surprised kid on the block when *Star Wars* became a megahit. He had tapped a nerve that not only went deep but global. George has theories now, about five years later, but at the time there was no explaining. I think George realized the meaning of what he had done as much from the critiques he read, and the psychological analysis they pinned to *Star Wars,* as from his own introspection. I'm the same way.

In other words, it's all there, whether Spielberg consciously intended it or not.

Twilight Zone—The Movie

A WARNER BROS. RELEASE, 1983

CAST ("KICK THE CAN")

Scatman Crothers *(Mr. Bloom);* Bill Quinn *(Mr. Conroy);* Martin Garner *(Mr. Weinstein);* Selma Diamond *(Mrs. Weinstein);* Helen Shaw *(Mrs. Dempsey);* Murray Matheson *(Mr. Agee);* Peter Brocco *(Mr. Mute);* Priscilla Pointer *(Miss Cox).*

CREDITS

Producers, Steven Spielberg and John Landis; executive producer, Frank Marshall; music, Jerry Goldsmith; production design, James D. Bissell; "Kick the Can": director, Spielberg; screenplay, George Clayton Johnson, Richard Matheson, and Josh Rogan, from a story by Johnson; associate producer, Kathleen Kennedy; editor, Michael Kahn; cinematography, Allen Daviau; Technicolor, Dolby Stereo; running time (total film), 102 mins.; rating: PG.

Spielberg first met John Landis while in Martha's Vineyard shooting *Jaws.* Realizing that the script desperately needed to be peppered with comic moments, Spielberg had various people flown in to interview for the job. Landis had written and directed a tongue-in-cheek horror film, *Schlock,* at age twenty-one. Landis did not get the job. However, after Landis hit the big time with *National Lampoon's Animal House* in 1978, it was Spielberg who contacted the now-hot younger filmmaker, inviting Landis to his house for dinner, signifying that the door was open: Landis was invited to join "the club" of Hollywood's movie brats.

A now-bearded and obviously maturing Spielberg sets up a shot for his "Kick the Can" segment (courtesy Warner Bros.).

The two realized they shared many interests, most notably a great love of old movies, though each had also been extremely influenced by television. No one show made more of an impact on either than *The Twilight Zone* (1959–64), writer-producer-conceptualist Rod Serling's seminal sci-fi series. Serling had successfully transferred the high quality previously associated with his work for dramatic anthologies like *Playhouse 90* to the more commercial medium of fantastic fiction. Spielberg already had two close connections to *The Twilight Zone:* His first directing job had been the Joan Crawford segment of *Night Gallery,* Serling's follow-up to *The Twilight Zone;* Spielberg's first major hit, *Duel,* had been written by Richard Matheson, a regular *Twilight Zone* contributor.

The Twilight Zone had been at best a modest ratings success during its initial run. Serling, never guessing what a long shelf life the series would enjoy via syndication, had sold his interest in it back to CBS, though he did maintain the right to make a motion-picture version. Following Serling's death in 1975 at age fifty during open heart surgery, those rights were passed on to his wife, Carol. Eventually, she sold them to Ted Ashley when he became chairman of the board at Warner Bros. films. Ashley, who had been Serling's agent back in the late fifties, still harbored warm feelings for both the man and his series. As Steven Farber and Marc Green explain in *Outrageous Conduct: Art, Ego, and the 'Twilight Zone' Case* (Arbor House: Morrow), Ashley noted that TV's other great cult sci-fi series, *Star Trek,* had recently been turned into a commercially successful film, *Star Trek—The Motion Picture.* So why not *Twilight Zone— The Movie?*

But *Star Trek* had been a continuing series; *The*

Scatman Crothers as Mr. Bloom, who carries the miracle of youthful hope to the elderly (courtesy Warner Bros.).

Mr. Bloom allows the elderly to rediscover the child still existing inside each of them by learning how to play again; (from left to right) Helen Shaw, Selma Diamond, Martin Garner, Bill Quinn, Peter Brocco, and Murray Matheson (courtesy Warner Bros.).

Twilight Zone, an anthology. The question of whether the film should tell a single story or maintain the anthology format was so intensely debated by Ashley and Mark Rosenberg, a Warner Bros. vice president who had been put in charge of this project, that the film was endlessly postponed. It might have been shelved entirely were it not for the fact that Terry Semel, following his promotion to company president, decided to draw as many of the wunderkind directors as possible into the Warner Bros. fold. During a meeting with Spielberg, Semel bounced around a great many concepts that were then in development at the studio, hoping Spielberg would pick up on one. When Semel mentioned *The Twilight Zone,* Spielberg suddenly became all ears.

Quickly, he signed on as producer. He and Landis had already discussed and rejected several ideas for collaboration as coproducers, but *The Twilight Zone* was the first project they became equally ecstatic about. They gleefully swapped favorite *Twilight Zone* stories, just as so many members of their generation enjoy doing; Dan Aykroyd and Albert Brooks, similarly retelling *Twilight Zone* tales as they drive together, late at night, in the eventual film's prologue, can be taken as stand-ins for Spielberg and Landis, or for that matter symbols of TV-bred young adults in general. At any rate, it was finally decided that (in order for Spielberg and Landis to maintain total creative control) the film would be shot as an independent project, financially backed and then released

Bill Quinn, Helen Shaw, and Martin Garner as rest-home residents who discover the ultimate miracle of youth is that it is merely a state of mind (courtesy Warner Bros.).

The elderly play, they appear to be children once more; for kids in a Spielberg film, believing is seeing. The child actors (from left to right): Laura Mooney, Chris Eisenman, Scott Nemes, Tanya Fenmore, Evan Richards (courtesy Warner Bros.).

by Warner Bros.; the budget would be $10 million. Both filmmakers were big fans of classic horror anthology films such as the British *Dead of Night,* so there was no question in either man's mind that their film would be composed of four separate stories plus the prologue, with approximately $2.5 million allotted to each of the episodes. Spielberg and Landis would each direct a segment, the others to be handled by Joe Dante *(The Howling)* and George Miller *(Mad Max).*

Spielberg would remake one of his favorites, "The Monsters Are Due on Maple Street," which seemed just right for him: Like *Poltergeist,* "Monsters" concerned a normal neighborhood that suddenly, inexplicably experiences a strange phenomenon; like *Jaws,* it vividly portrayed everyday people lapsing into hysteria; like *Close Encounters of the Third Kind,* it involved an invasion from another world. Frank Marshall, then a recent arrival at Spielberg's company and already a highly trusted team member, would be executive producer, in charge of coordinating the entire project.

The idea was to "redeem" the *Twilight Zone* concept by doing all those great old stories with state-of-the-art technology. Carol Serling mused: "Rod's stories were about people. The movie, on the other hand, placed an emphasis on special effects. How could it be otherwise with Spielberg? But that was antithetical to Rod's original intentions." In her eventual *New Yorker* review, Pauline Kael likewise insisted that the film's conception was all wrong, doing damage to the stories that were supposed to be enshrined:

It's a naive (and dubious) sort of tribute that sets out to do essentially the same thing with the implicit expectation of doing it better; the original shows were ingenious partly because of how economically they got their effects . . . the [film's] production is overscaled for its dinky idea.

Yet Matheson agreed to come on board as chief scriptwriter, creating new versions of three popular episodes. Landis would write, as well as direct, the fourth, an original story, conceived and executed in the *Twilight Zone* tradition. His tale concerns a bigot (Vic Morrow) who sneers at all minority groups, only to inadvertently step into the "zone," finding the tables turned as he is transformed into a Jew in Nazi Germany, a black pursued by Klansmen in the South, and a Vietnamese hounded by an American helicopter in Vietnam. On July 23, 1982, while filming that sequence in the Indian Dunes Park north of Los Angeles, the helicopter suddenly went out of control and crashed, killing Morrow and two Asian-born children, leading to one of the most costly and controversial trials in contemporary Hollywood history. What transpired has been carefully researched and thoroughly documented in Farber and Green's 1988 book.

Spielberg was not on the set that night. He refused to speak publicly about the accident at all except in a single interview in which he told the *L.A. Times*'s Dale Pollock:

"No movie is worth dying for." Though Spielberg and Landis, still coproducers, necessarily met to discuss postproduction and plans for distribution, their relationship rapidly disintegrated. For a while, Warner Bros. execs seriously considered shutting down the project altogether, though they eventually reversed themselves on that one; Spielberg apparently would have liked to see the project canceled and move on with his life and career. That this happened on a film he was producing must have been particularly anguishing (and somewhat ironic) for a man whose movies so consistently concern themselves with the needs of adults to treat children responsibly and safely.

Still, Warner Bros. insisted he go through with his obligation. Not wanting to deal with material as macabre as "Monsters," Spielberg instead picked the most mellow of all *Twilight Zone* episodes: "Kick the Can," about a sad group of elderly residents in a rest home who suddenly revert to childlike states of behavior, finally turning into happy children. Spielberg agreed to a six-day shoot, beginning on November 26, the Friday after Thanksgiving. Ordinarily almost obsessive in his desire to maintain careful control over every element in a film, he reportedly did not attend preproduction meetings, allowed script supervisor Katherine Wooten to block part of the scene for him, and had Melissa Mathison (who pseudonymously rewrote the old story) work with the actors on interpretations of dialogue. The shoot began with a single night's filming at an actual senior citizen's home, the episode then completed on a Warner Bros. soundstage. There were child actors in the episode, but as Farber and Green duly note, they were employed "in strict accordance with child labor laws," which had not been the case in the Landis episode.

Though George Clayton Johnson collaborated with Richard Matheson and "Josh Rogan" in the adaptation of his own 1962 TV show, the short work has clearly been Spielbergized, filtered through the director's own value system to express his personal point of view. Whereas the original concentrated on the elderly people, who more or less discover the truth of the old adage "You're only as young as you feel" on their own, Spielberg has them learn it through one of his typical heroes: a common man who rises to the occasion at hand and performs something of a miracle. He is Bloom, presumably written as a Jewish character but here played by an African-American blues musician turned actor, Scatman Crothers. The opening narration (spoken by Burgess Meredith) introducing the segment likewise sounds more like Spielberg than Serling: "Where there is no hope, there is no life," the old quote goes, but in the Sunnyvale rest home, the elderly live without hope until Bloom arrives. When he does, "hope just checked in" in the form of "an elderly optimist who carries his hope in a tin can."

That tin can is magical, so with it Bloom also carries along Spielberg's metaphysical theme. The absorption-by-TV theme is suggested, since the old people do nothing but sit around and watch *Jeopardy,* which appears to

John Landis, coproducer with Spielberg of the film and director of the now-notorious Vic Morrow sequence; their friendship did not survive the accident on Landis's set that took the life of actor Morrow and two children (courtesy Warner Bros.).

be on all day long. The desire to be in the movies—not an actor in the movies but a character in the movies—is here symbolized by Mr. Agee (possibly a reference to legendary screenwriter and film critic James Agee), who dreams of being a swashbuckling hero in the tradition of Douglas Fairbanks. That tradition includes Errol Flynn as well: "Welcome to Sherwood, my lady!" Agee announces after being transformed into a child. In the original TV show, the old folks wanted to be children; in Spielberg's, they want to be children who live out favorite movie roles, and the distinction is significant.

The original "Kick the Can" ended with the characters going outside to play and miraculously becoming children again. Spielberg extends that situation, at this point adding ideas of his own. The precocious-child version of Mr. Agee briefly introduces the theme of a little boy who refuses to grow up, the Peter Pan concept that will eventually be dealt with directly in *Hook*. Spielberg's Agee even flies off like Peter Pan, adding the notion of flight, that great Spielbergian symbol of escape from the everyday. The seeing-is-believing theme is here, too, when Mr. Conroy, the one elderly person who did not join the others in childlike play, is unable to take what happens on faith, only able to convince himself and the nurse when they actually see the children.

Brief as this segment is, and however little time Spielberg spent working on it, he did take the preexisting story and make it his own. That did not win over many critics, however, who considered it only slightly more successful than the universally panned Landis sequence. (The Miller and Dante scenes gradually rated higher, and most everyone liked Landis's prologue.) Of "Kick the Can," Farber and Green wrote: "Drenched in sentimentality, the story reveals Spielberg's gushing, cockeyed op-

Dan Aykroyd and Albert Brooks in the Prologue as two nostalgia buffs who swap old *Twilight Zone* stories while driving at night; many critics considered this to be the best part of the movie (courtesy Warner Bros.).

timism . . . an insipid fantasy about old people." Kael called it a

lump of ironclad whimsy . . . the tone here is sentimental-comic, and horribly slick. It's as if Steven Spielberg had sat down and thought out what he could do that would make his detractors happiest.

In *Newsweek,* David Ansen wrote:

The theme is *echt*-Spielberg, and his technique is as stylish as ever, but here it's pushed dangerously close to self-parody. What was innocent, wondrous and charming in *E.T.* here looks like an advertisement for innocence, wonder and charm. Alas, hardsell whimsy is a contradiction in terms.

Ansen did offer one of the few attempts at serious interpretation, however, seeing the character of Bloom (not present in the original story) as representing Spielberg himself. "Spielberg's segment means to demonstrate his familiar compact with the movie audience: 'If you believe, I can make you all feel like children.' " Extending this concept, the magic that Bloom brings in his little can stands for the magic that Spielberg offers to his audiences. (Movies are traditionally delivered to theaters in "cans.") Certainly, Spielberg's films—his other, more successful enchantment films like *Close Encounters of the Third Kind* and *E.T.*—have succeeded in making older viewers feel young again while watching and at least for a little while after leaving the theater and reentering the real world.

Indiana Jones and the Temple of Doom

A PARAMOUNT PICTURE, 1984

CAST

Harrison Ford *(Indiana Jones);* Kate Capshaw *(Willie Scott);* Ke Huy Quan *(Short Round);* Amrish Puri *(Mola Ram);* Roshan Seth *(Chattar Lal);* Philip Stone *(Captain Blumburtt);* Roy Chiao *(Lao Che);* Dan Aykroyd *(Weber);* Raj Singh *(Little Maharajah);* Nizwar Karanj *(Sacrifice Victim);* Maureen Bacchus *(Temple Dancer).*

CREDITS

Director, Steven Spielberg; producer, Robert Watts; screenplay, Willard Huyck and Gloria Katz, from a story by George Lucas; executive producers, Lucas and Frank Marshall; cinematography, Douglas Slocombe; editor, Michael Kahn; music, John Williams; visual-effects supervisor, Dennis Muren; production design, Elliot Scott; Costumes, Anthony Powell; second-unit director, Michael Moore; Panavision, Deluxe Color, Dolby Stereo; running time, 118 mins.; rating: PG.

A sequel to the remarkably popular *Raiders of the Lost Ark* was a foregone conclusion; at the dinner in Hawaii during which Lucas first pitched the "Indy" idea to Spielberg, he explained that he already had two other stories in mind. So when Lucas eventually shared a concept for a prequel involving black magic and unspeakable rites in an underground temple of devil worshipers, Spielberg's mind raced ahead to what he felt would be necessary to balance all this darkness: a strong sense of humor. Once again, the final results grow out of a collaboration between the differing perceptions of producer and

Steven Spielberg sets up a complex shot for the second installment in the Indiana Jones trilogy (courtesy Paramount Pictures).

director; this time, the general consensus was that their two visions clashed, creating an uncomfortable hodge-podge rather than the happy compromise achieved with *Raiders of the Lost Ark.*

Spielberg, who described himself as a "hired hand" on producer Lucas's trilogy (as compared to a total film-maker on projects derived from his own ideas) relied on a method that worked before: preplanning every shot through numerous (in this case, more than four thousand) storyboards. Each shot was designed in advance, elimi-nating the costly situation of arriving on a set, then hav-ing cast and crew stand around while the director decides how a scene ought to be shot. Spielberg actually brought the storyboards, drawn like Sunday funnies (by Ed Verreaux, Joe Honston, and Elliot Scott, under his own tutelage), to the set with him instead of the script most di-rectors carry. Storyboards had been cut up and placed in looseleaf books. Under each sketch was a description of the action, accompanied by all the dialogue.

In addition to drawings, Spielberg this time went a step further. Production designer Scott had built elaborate miniatures of the crusher room, quarry cavern, and mine-tunnel train. Spielberg then photographed these seven-teen-inch cardboard sets, populated by half-inch cutout characters, with his Nikon, studying the various angles from which he could eventually photograph his live-ac-tion scenes. Four months were lavished on such meticu-lous preparation, even as locations were being scouted. Spielberg was also busy supervising the building of the life-size sets.

This process, Spielberg admitted to interviewer Merry Elkins, "exhausts me. It makes me tired and a little bored with the sequence. In a way, I've already shot that se-quence by sketching it." That statement is similar to one made by Hitchcock, who often claimed: "I wish I didn't have to shoot the movie." For Hitch, the creative process took place during preplanning; he improvised endlessly until finally deciding on shots he would religiously fol-low during filming. Critics of Hitchcock have always complained that this caused his films to be technical in nature, lacking in spontaneity, while the actors suffered, walking through their paces, solid professionals not al-lowed (much less encouraged) to try anything new.

Was this also Spielberg's approach? In an *American Cinematographer* interview, he admitted: "The actors learned to paint their emotions by the numbers [and] fell into step with the storyboards. *Indiana Jones and the Temple of Doom* is a very technical movie, and the actors had to be technical without losing their own believabil-ity," though in truth many critics felt the actors did in-deed lose precisely that quality.

Most of the original crew was reunited, though the Marion Ravenwood character had to be eliminated, as *Indiana Jones and the Temple of Doom* takes place a year before the first film. Kate Capshaw, shortly to become Mrs. Steven Spielberg, joined the cast. While Capshaw may be the equal of Karen Allen as an actress, the sub-

Harrison Ford returns to the role of Indiana Jones, man of adventure (courtesy Paramount Pictures).

stitution (character, not performer) proved unfortunate. Whereas *Raiders of the Lost Ark*'s Marion Ravenwood was a variation on the tough-talking Hawksian women of yore, Willie is a variation on an alternative 1930s type: the "gold digger," a sleek, self-serving blonde who cares about nothing except money. The Hawksian woman will consider marriage only if she meets a man clearly her equal; the gold digger views matrimony in a cold, calcu-lated way, a means to an end, financial security.

"The biggest trouble with her is the NOISE!" Indy con-fides. He's right: alternately a shrill screecher and insuf-ferable whiner, Willie is less a true Spielbergian heroine than a one-woman Spielbergian din: incessant, unpleas-ant, exhausting. She can't ride an elephant without facing the wrong direction; her superficiality and selfishness are grating rather than funny.

What everyone failed to take into account was that the Hawksian heroine is the most durable of golden-age Hollywood women, a precursor of today's liberated fe-male. The gold digger, on the other hand, is entirely retro, such a Material Girl that she might just as well have been

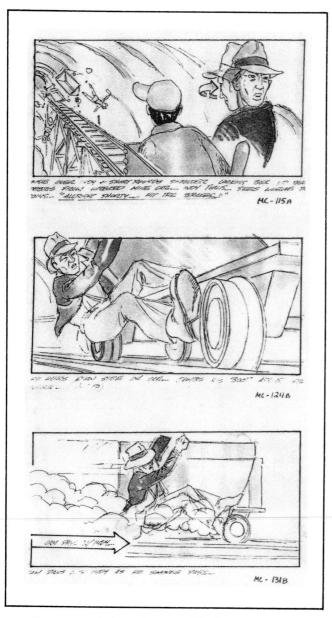

Every sequence in the movie was carefully planned out in advance via detailed storyboard sketches, including the roller-coaster mine-train ride (courtesy Amblin Entertainment).

Indy, Willie, and Short Round (Ke Huy Quan) escape the Thuggees by hopping aboard a mine car and heading down the shaft. So often accused of being a maker of theme-park movies, Spielberg here actually built a workable ride!

played by Madonna. If the film only offered a thoughtful consideration of such a type from today's point of view, the concept might have worked. Nowhere in the film is there any sense of such a sophisticated approach. Also missing were two other key players: Sallah, beloved Arab companion, and Brody, genteel elderly professor. There was no reason why they couldn't have been included; their absence diminished the movie.

As in the first film, we are plunged into an adventure already in progress (taking place in Shanghai, 1935), a prologue virtually unrelated to what follows. Indy, in conflict with several Oriental gangsters, meets cabaret

For the exterior sequences involving the physical journey that mirrors the characters' inner journey toward self-knowledge, Spielberg brought his actors to actual jungle locations.

Indy, Short Round (Ke Huy Quan), and Willie Scott (Kate Capshaw) make their way through an Indian village (courtesy Paramount Pictures).

singer Willie Scott and is joined by a diminutive Asian sidekick, Short Round. They narrowly escape together. There is no sojourn back to America (another serious omission); they instead drop (without benefit of a parachute, employing a rubber raft to break their fall) down to a river, gradually drifting into India. There they encounter a pestilence-ravaged village, then set out on a mission to restore both the missing sacred stone and kidnapped children, held prisoner in the palace at Bangkok.

In order that the palace look like something out of an old fairy tale (or from a 1940s film set in some exotic land), Spielberg decided that its exterior should be a combination of miniatures and matte paintings. For the journey to the palace, however, it was necessary to go on location. Principal photography commenced on April 18, 1983, on the island of Sri Lanka. Here three weeks of exteriors were completed, making use of the country's jungles, mountains, lush valleys, and striking rock formations. In the provincial hinterland, production designer Elliot Scott (new to the team) created an entire Indian village from scratch. While Spielberg was at work here, the second unit was in Macao, filming the opening car chase. The last sequence to be filmed in Sri Lanka was the rope-bridge battle between Indy and his Thuggee enemies. A British engineering company, building a large dam near a gorge, helped construct the rope bridge with steel and cable, ensuring that it would prove considerably safer than the bridge appears in the film.

Spielberg then moved cast and crew to the EMI-Elstree Studios in Borehamwood, on the outskirts of London, where indoor sets had been completed under the supervision of Scott, a veteran of early Hitchcock

thrillers. Literally, every soundstage in the vast studio complex was put to use. For the complicated mine-shaft pursuit, Spielberg decided on a tricky combination of an actual set (built at Elstree) and miniatures (done months later). As for the set itself, Spielberg later explained that "what we actually did was build a roller-coaster ride on the soundstage. And it really worked. It was safe, electrically driven. You could take rides in it." He had his actors whiz around in the cart at ten miles an hour, undercranking his camera so that they appeared to be going twice as fast. Though they completed each circular ride in twenty-five seconds (which, in fast motion, would yield twelve seconds of film), Spielberg knew his sequence must be seven minutes long. So he shot each rotation from a different angle, while cinematographer Doug Slocombe lit it varyingly, a red gel over the light for one go-around, another color for the next, creating the illusion that each turn took place in a different section of the shaft. What would have been too dangerous to actually film (the mine car leaping through the air over missing sections of track) was accomplished with miniatures and carefully edited in afterward for a virtually seamless effect.

Three months were spent in Elstree, after which "blue screen" (back projection) sequences were shot in the United States at Lucasfilm's Marin County facility. Also, additional sequences were at this time completed at other northern California locations. The shoot ended on September 8 (five days under schedule), though the creation of optical and special effects continued at Lucas's Industrial Light and Magic through March 1984 for a final cost of $28 million, precisely as planned.

Despite Spielberg's description of himself as a "hired

hand," there is certainly much in the film that attests to his ongoing sensibility. The movie-about-movies theme is evident from the first shot, a variation on the opening of *Raiders of the Lost Ark.* Once again, we see the famous Paramount mountain logo; now it dissolves not into an actual mountain but a painting of a mountain on a huge gong as the camera pulls back to reveal an Asian servant striking that gong, his motions comical in nature. The image provides a visual echo of the opening se-

quence of 1939's *Gunga Din,* in its own time a parody of the J. Arthur Rank films, which portentously opened with a serious image of a gong being struck; in *Gunga Din,* the man wielding the mallet grows more exhausted with each individual swing. What we see in *Indiana Jones and the Temple of Doom,* then, is a parody of a parody, a movie image that kids a movie image that kidded a movie image.

By stirring moviegoing memories of *Gunga Din,* the

Spielberg and George Lucas always conceived of Indy as the legitimate cinematic son of James Bond; in the second film's opening sequence, Harrison Ford does resemble the suave Bond who, in so many 007 films, is initially glimpsed at an elegant gambling casino in the company of a gorgeous woman (here, the future Mrs. Spielberg).

Indy, preparing for a romantic interlude with Willie, is unaware that a Thuggee is about to strangle him (courtesy Paramount Pictures).

opening also serves to set up what follows. Like *Gunga Din, Indiana Jones and the Temple of Doom* will set its trio of heroes against India's Thuggee insurgents, likewise taking place in a forbidden temple where the devil-god Kali is worshiped. Not only the plot but also the tone of *Gunga Din* served as inspiration, since Spielberg attempts an approximation of George Stevens's remarkable juggling act between exciting action, screwball romance, slapstick comedy, and deeply felt emotions. Unfortunately, the mixture does not jell here.

The movie mythology extends from Stevens's classic to more recent films, including those by Lucas and Spielberg. The nightclub in the opening is called Obi Won, after the Alec Guinness character in *Star Wars.* Toward the end, Indy finds himself face-to-face with two immense sword-wielding enemies. In *Raiders of the Lost Ark,* he surprised us by foregoing his whip, instead pulling out his pistol and blithely shooting down the single big man. Here he grins self-consciously (all but winking at the audience) and reaches for that pistol, shocked to discover it has dropped out of the holster. His double take provides a double laugh for the audience, funny in and of itself but also building on our sensation of being a part of the moviegoing-elect. As with the *Jaws* parody that opened *1941,* the humor clicks owing to our familiarity with the body of the filmmaker's work, our acquiescence (however unconscious) to the fact that what we're watching is an ever-building cinematic artifice.

Spielberg's fascination with this approach—calling attention to the artificiality of his construct rather than attempting to make his make-believe world appear "real"—is announced immediately. The camera moves

Short Round warns Indy of a clear and present danger above them in the temple; as always in Spielberg films, the child is father to the man (courtesy Paramount Pictures).

Like Peter in *Hook,* Grant in *Jurassic Park,* and Oskar in *Schindler's List,* Indiana Jones is here the typical hero of Spielberg's second decade as a filmmaker (courtesy Paramount Pictures).

from the gong toward what appears to be a cave (a patently phony looking cave), then descends into it, smoke and fire billowing forth. Suddenly, Willie leaps out and dances in a gaudy costume, the camera pulling back to reveal a vast stage in a nightclub in which Asian girls perform a Busby Berkeley–type routine. What we mistook for reality—or a phony movie-set reproduction of a fantastic reality—is the set for a show; we're watching a show (film) about a (stage) show.

As the camera pulls back further still, we notice Indy, at a stageside table, dealing with adversaries who demand the artifact he holds but are less than willing to turn over the diamond they've promised him in exchange. This is "reality": that is, the film's fabricated reality, based on old (unreal) 1930s movie situations, with a touch of suave, tuxedoed James Bond in the casino opening of so many 007 films thrown in for good measure. Willie finishes her song and dance and joins them, even as the men fight. At first, people in the club are unsure whether the battle is part of the floor show (since Willie is involved) or actuality, a broad comic variation on Spielberg's theater-as-life/life-as-theater theme.

His appearance-and-reality motif is also revived. Willie—herself going after the diamond—realizes it is mixed up with ice cubes, knocked onto the floor. Diamonds have always been referred to, in slang, as "ice," and Willie can't discern between the actual ice and the gem. Other themes are immediately present, including communication. Willie and her Asian backup singers perform Cole Porter's "Anything Goes!" (the song's title setting up the attitude of the entire film), singing some lyrics in American English, others in Chinese. Their blending of two languages gives way to the film's first line of dialogue spoken in English: "You never told me you spoke my language, Doctor," one gangster informs Indy.

Indy is a typical Spielberg hero in many respects, one being his ability to cut across those language boundaries which separate us. If Indy looks suspiciously like so many movie heroes played by Ronald Reagan, he, like the actor-turned-president, can be tagged the Great Communicator. Indy is also a Spielbergian male hero whose main problem has to do with separation from his mother. Surprised that such a striking-looking man could be a college professor, Willie notes upon meeting him: "I always thought archaeologists were funny little men, searching for their mommies/mummies!" Indy's pained expression makes it clear that she has struck a chord.

Indeed, one major weakness of the film is that Spielberg fails to make use of the marvelous contrast between "Indy" and his alter ego, Dr. Jones. Though *Time*'s Richard Corliss unaccountably claimed that "again you will savor the Indiana Jones schizophrenia; by day a bow-tied, bespectacled archaeologist; by night a resourceful swaggerer," the fact is, we never see Dr. Jones here, so his duality is missing. Which makes the experience of watching *Indiana Jones and the Temple of Doom* akin to seeing a Superman movie in which Clark Kent never appears.

Spielberg does revive his metaphysical theme and the corresponding concept of the protagonist as a self-interested man who, when the situation demands, rises to heroic stature by becoming a religious savior. When Indy, Willie, and Short Round arrive in India, it is clear from the look on the priest's face that he was awaiting them. The village natives greet the trio as they would religious figures descending from on high; their reaction stirs echoes of the Devils Tower scientists greeting the extraterrestrials in *Close Encounters of the Third Kind.*

Spielberg incorporates his notion of fate: the spirituality of an experience exists more in how one considers an event than the event itself.

WISE MAN: Fate brought you here [to help us].
INDY: We weren't brought here. Our plane crashed.

The film chronicles Indy's growing realization that what he (the modern realist) perceives as accident is, if one chooses to view it from another angle (old-fashioned religion), an act of fate, preordained by some force of goodness. Perception is all, though in Spielberg, successful perception is based on believing, not seeing.

That "force" is akin to the Force in Lucas's *Star Wars* trilogy. There is an alternative force (the dark side) at work in *Star Wars* symbolized by Darth Vader, just as Obi Won represents goodness. On the other hand, the priest of Kali, Mola Ram, is the film's Darth Vader, symbol of evil incarnate, the dark side of spiritualism. He scoffs at Christians and Jews: "The Hebrew god will fall. The Christian God will be cast down." And he has stolen the good Hindu god for his own base purposes.

Jones, a less than religious Christian, will oppose him for the sake of the Hindus. Indy leaves the village, heading for Bangkok; the old priest is glimpsed praying, knowing full well it will take help from on high to make things come out right. When Indy, a reverse Pied Piper, at last leads his flock of children back to the village, the old priest and other villagers raise their voices in thanks to the forces that guided Indy along.

"You don't believe me, Mr. Jones?" the evil priest grinningly tells the hero. "You will become a true be-

liever," he adds menacingly. In fact, Indy will become just that, but a true believer in Shika, one more variation on the good god (and, in Spielberg's all-inclusive view, the equal of Jehovah or Jesus), rather than Kali, as much the evil one as Beelzebub or Lucifer. "Just ghost stories," Indy whispers to Short Round after the good village priest insists that fate delivered the trio to him; by film's end, Indy will have surrendered to the priest's vision.

PRIEST: Now you can see the magic of the rock.
INDY: I understand its power now.

It's worth noting, though, that Indy is in this film initially more mercurial and mercenary than at the beginning of *Raiders of the Lost Ark.* Whereas the Indy of that

Indy and Willie Scott (Kate Capshaw) believe they've fallen out of the sky and into an Indian village by accident, though the residents accept them as saviors, precisely what they will become.

of fathers who wander off in search of adventure and the children who need them. Short Round, along with Willie, quickly bonds with Indy as a makeshift family unit, however dysfunctional. After being thrown together (by fate or accident), they squabble endlessly but gradually come to the conclusion that they can only survive if they cooperate as a family, which by film's end they have become, the adventure itself the catalyst that brings them together as a unit.

Also, Short Round is the diminutive hero who understands more than the adult hero does, another example of Spielberg's variations on Wordsworth's "The child is father to the man." At the key moment when Indy has been drugged with black blood, surrendering to his own dark side, Willie tries to pull him out of the spell but can't. However, when the child cries out, "I love you, Indy," the foster father is able to snap out of his catatonic state. In the world according to Spielberg, the parent-child bond is more basic, potent, positive than the man-woman bond. Like Sheriff Brody, Roy Neary, and a half-dozen other Spielberg heroes, Indy discovers that there is more he can learn from the child than he can ever teach him.

Critics were not kind. Tom O'Brien of *Commonweal* wrote that *Indiana Jones and the Temple of Doom* "has no hint of interiority; there is never a pause to Indiana's escapades; it's as if we're supposed to be on the edge of our seats before we're even in them." The pacing was the element most attacked. Whereas *Raiders of the Lost Ark* offered an action sequence every ten to fifteen minutes (with dramatic, romantic, and comic moments, many subdued in nature, in between), *Indiana Jones and the Temple of Doom* was all chase. Lawrence O'Toole wrote in *MacLean*'s that *Indiana Jones and the Temple of Doom*

hurtles from one climax to the next without pause. *Raiders of the Lost Ark* boasted wit and crackling rhythm as it hopped all over the globe; *Indiana Jones and the Temple of Doom* is merely dull-minded and pushy, and stays put in India . . . the character becomes a prop (and) after more than two hours of climaxes, they lose their meaning and become wearying.

film searches for ancient artifacts for his university's museum, here he is more self-interested, apparently planning to keep some for himself. "Fortune and glory," he repeats regularly during the first half of this film.

That Indy's companion is Short Round, a child, serves as an effective way of emotionally involving child viewers, who identify with this surrogate, each kid fantasizing he is Short Round, accompanying the hero on a grand adventure. But Short Round is this and more. He allows Spielberg an opportunity to rework his recurring theme

Spielberg previously announced that his greatest single fear as a filmmaker was of someday boring somebody. Only a director with such a fear could make a movie like *Indiana Jones and the Temple of Doom,* and the general cry of disappointment was, perhaps, an antidote to that fear. Whatever their limitations, upcoming films like *The Color Purple* and *Empire of the Sun* display a worthy desire to slow down and pay attention to the niceties of character, plot, and setting. While making *Empire of the Sun,* Spielberg even stated: "For the first time, I'm making a movie to satisfy me, not the audience." With *Indiana Jones and the Temple of Doom,* he had commited the cardinal sin of playing to what he mistakenly believed to be the audience's expectations. It's as if he and Lucas convinced themselves that most people

143

would have enjoyed *Raiders of the Lost Ark* far more if all the human interludes had been left out.

Far worse, though, was the endless violence. David Denby of *New York* magazine, who had loudly championed *Raiders of the Lost Ark,* wrote that the prequel was

heavy-spirited and grating. The frivolous treatment of child slavery makes you slightly sick. This lurid and gloomy trash goes on and on, without a joke anywhere, and it's not only sadistic and dumb, it's oppressively ugly. That Spielberg should devote himself to anything so debased in imagination is unbearably depressing.

The most significant impact of the film, then, was in creating a new rating. *Poltergeist* had been the center of a ratings war, clearly deserving a designation midway between the family-film PG and adults-only R. Spielberg would have happily acquiesced, but Jack Valenti refused to budge. Then came *Indiana Jones and the Temple of Doom,* with people eating jellied monkey brains and a human heart torn from an innocent victim's body, after which he is lowered into an inferno and burned alive.

Though Spielberg openly admitted he didn't believe the film should be seen by children under the age of ten, *Indiana Jones and the Temple of Doom* was blessed with a mild PG to ensure that Paramount recouped its investment; money, not morality, dictated the rating. Parents were outraged: They had brought little children to what they believed would be the modern equivalent of a Disney film, instead exposing their kids to a virtual chamber of horrors. Spielberg, who initially defended his film, would eventually admit he had gone way over the top. Valenti was so barraged by angry parents that, within a week, he acquiesced to a new rating, PG-13.

The team (from left to right): executive producers Frank Marshall and George Lucas, Spielberg, cinematographer Douglas Slocombe (courtesy Paramount Pictures).

The Color Purple

A WARNER BROS. RELEASE, 1985

CAST

Whoopi Goldberg *(Celie);* Danny Glover *(Albert);* Margaret Avery *(Shug Avery);* Oprah Winfrey *(Sofia);* Willard Pugh *(Harpo);* Akosua Busia *(Nettie);* Desreta Jackson *(Young Celie);* Adolph Caesar *(Old Mr.);* Rae Dawn Chong *(Squeak);* Dana Ivey *(Miss Millie);* Leonard Jackson *(Pa);* Larry Fishburne *(Swain);* John Patton Jr. *(Preacher);* Bennet Guillory *(Grady);* Carl Anderson *(Reverend Samuel);* Phillip Strong *(Mayor).*

CREDITS

Director, Steven Spielberg; producers, Spielberg and Kathleen Kennedy; executive producers, Jon Peters and Peter Guber; co-producer, Quincy Jones; music, Jones; screenplay, Menno Meyjes, from the novel by Alice Walker; cinematography, Allen Daviau; production designer, J. Michael Riva; editor, Michael Kahn; costume design, Aggie Guerard Rodgers; second-unit director (Kenya), Frank Marshall; color: DeLuxe; cameras, Panavision; running time, 152 mins.; rating: PG-13.

"The biggest risk," Spielberg admitted on the eve of *The Color Purple*'s release in December 1985, "for me is doing a film about people for the first time in my career—and failing. The risk that (audiences) will not respond. It's the risk of being judged—and accused of not having the sensibility to do character studies." In fact, that was precisely the accusation hurled at him for most of his career. Spielberg, edging ever closer to that formidable age of forty, was no longer able to ignore such crit-

On location, Spielberg directs Whoopi Goldberg, then a cult comedienne making her film debut as Celie, heroine of *The Color Purple* (courtesy Warner Bros.).

icism. Like the well-paid star of a TV sitcom who seethes inside because some unknown actor receives rave reviews playing Hamlet in the park for scale, Spielberg wanted (needed?) to show everyone he could be a heavyweight artist like Scorsese or Coppola. Searching for just the right property, he came across *The Color Purple* one day when collaborator Kennedy handed him a copy of Alice Walker's 1983 Pulitzer Prize–winning novel about a poor young southern black woman's experiences spanning a forty-year period.

The book concerns quiet, withdrawn Celie, who escapes her humble existence as an abused child (she has two children by the man she believes to be her biological father, discovering years later he was actually her mother's second husband), only to find herself equally abused by her own husband, Mr. Albert. Celie somehow survives, eventually even overcomes, owing to her positive relationships with other women, most notably Shug Avery, Albert's beautiful blues-singing mistress. Also a key player is Nettie, the younger sister torn from Celie's side at an early age, who attempts to keep in contact through a series of letters, mailed from Africa, where she works as a missionary. Another female friend who makes the tough times bearable is strong-willed Sofia, wife of Celie's son-in-law Harpo. Eventually, Sofia is beaten and jailed after refusing to pay proper respect to Georgia's white ruling class.

Such material may sound like the makings for precisely the sort of film our African-American community would greet with open arms. In fact, that was not the case. Objections had less to do with the fact that this film about the black American experience was to be directed by a white filmmaker (though that was indeed a legitimate issue) than with the book itself. In Los Angeles, a media-monitoring group calling itself the Coalition Against Black Exploitation announced its objections through their chairperson, attorney Legrand H. Clegg II: "The elevation of Alice Walker's book to the status of a movie will be devastating to the black community. The book's degradation of the black male and its subtle promotion of lesbianism as an alternative to failed heterosexual relationships conveys a negative message that is potentially destructive to the black family."

That the moviemaker who consistently hammered home the need for family values would be attacked for making a movie that might possibly undermine those very values his films promoted seems ironic. In fact, his version of *The Color Purple* (as adapted by Dutch-born screenwriter Menno Meyjes) leads inevitably to Celie's realization that she must establish a solid home, if without her alcoholic, abusive husband; having gradually grown as a person, learning self-respect through the influence of other women, she becomes a dark-skinned sister of E.T.'s white heroine. In the film's final shot, Celie is seen as warmly ruling over her roost, where family members (including both of her long-lost children as well as the sister she has not seen in some twenty-five years)

are all reunited. Though the basic story line does derive from Walker, what we see here is a Spielbergian image in every sense of the term.

Once again, Spielberg managed to be highly personal without becoming overtly autobiographical. While ostensibly retelling Walker's tale, Spielberg invests in this project his emotion-charged memories about his own mother and her difficult but ultimately successful task of maintaining a household after her husband is gone. In addition to a conservative's belief in family values, combined with a liberal's admiration for the responsibilities of a strong single mother, there is Spielberg's recurring theme of a woman separated from her children and fighting to regain them, so essential to *The Sugarland Express* and *Poltergeist.* Celie communicates with her children psychically (she sees a baby in a general store and rightly knows it is her own), much like Elliott and E.T. There is Spielberg's metaphysical theme, in that Celie's entire monologue is directed to God. And the theme of blocked communication as Celie and Nettie write back and forth, their efforts interfered with by Albert. Finally, there is the theme of sight, so basic to all Spielberg films, here the very element that lends this story its title: "God gets pissed off if you walk past the color purple in a field," Shug tells Celie, "and don't see it."

This is all well and good for Spielberg. Yet attorney Clegg's comments cannot be summarily dismissed. Not only does a motion picture reach a far larger audience than a book; but also it transforms the story from a highly personal reading experience into a shared public experience. Instead of telling one unique family's story, the film version would be universally perceived as the representative story of a typical black family of that time and place; however unintentionally, the film becomes the public's central experience with this subject, refining and defining the way people (black and white) will henceforth view the African-American experience during this period of history.

When Clegg's group demanded a prescreening of the film and was turned down, several dozen people demonstrated outside the Beverly Boulevard offices of Quincy Jones, musical supervisor and coproducer, claiming that the film he and Spielberg were about to release promoted "negative black images" which would be disheartening to black audiences while misinforming whites. Also, it cannot be discounted that a white man had brought a black story to the screen. Spielberg admitted that he originally had reservations about directing *The Color Purple* for just that reason. Jones was, like Spielberg, a great fan of the novel, having taken it along with him on vacation for a quick read. Jones, who had never produced a film before, learned that Jon Peters and Peter Guber held the rights and approached them about joining the project. They were delighted that the Oscar-winning composer and scorer of more than thirty major films wanted to work on their upcoming project. Jones perceived this as an opportunity to bring a golden age of black music to

(Facing page) The Spielberg signature shot: A silhouette captures his warm, romantic feel for the era, so very different from the bleak and embittered portrait in Alice Walker's novel.

Margaret Avery as Shug, mistress to Celie's abusive husband, Mr. (Danny Glover). Shug eventually becomes Celie's best friend and confidante; in the highly politicized novel by Alice Walker, the two women embrace lesbianism, though Spielberg purposefully muted this element for his mainstream motion picture (courtesy Warner Bros.).

vivid life on-screen, forever immortalizing and preserving that period when gospel spilled over into juke-joint jazz. They were surprised, though, when Jones all but begged them for a coproducer credit, insisting he wanted to help shape and actualize the work.

They agreed, largely to ensure Jones's musical collaboration. Rather than picking an African-American director, either old-hand Gordon Parks or newcomer Spike Lee, Jones immediately set his sights on Spielberg. Steven recalls telling Jones, upon being approached: "I don't know that I'm the filmmaker for this. Don't you want to find a black director or a woman?" Jones reportedly replied that if this line of reasoning were to be followed, *E.T.* should have been directed by a Martian; in his mind, *The Color Purple* ought to be directed by the person who loved it the most in order that the broader human issues would be emphasized. Listening to Spielberg's thoughts on the novel ("All Celie has is God, memory, love for her sister, and the eternal wisdom dormant inside her!"), there was no question who that person was.

After completing the film, the director took a defensive position: "The issue was not the color of my skin but whether I'd make a good movie out of the book." In all honesty, one reason he was so sought after is that Spielberg's name ensured that a film without big box-office potential would be made. Warner Bros. agreed to a budget of $12 million. (The film eventually cost nearly $15 million.) Ultimately, it proved possible to complete this period piece on so tight a budget because Spielberg agreed to take no salary except for the $40,000 Directors Guild contractual minimum, quickly spent on "overages." Whenever Spielberg wanted a touch that would

Oprah Winfrey (*right*) is Sofia, wife of Harpo (Willard Pugh) and mother of his child (courtesy Warner Bros.).

add to the authenticity or the aesthetics, producer Kennedy made clear how much that would cost. Each time, Spielberg instructed her to take the expense out of his minimum fee.

He also had to go through what can be the humiliating process of interviewing for the job. Not with Peters and Guber, thrilled to have him on board, but with Walker. Jones, believing it would be best for the two to meet (and, hopefully, see eye to eye), flew with Spielberg to San Francisco. Together, they visited the writer, a virtual recluse and incessant gardener. The three went to dinner, during which time Spielberg pitched his idea for the film much as a novice director might to a studio boss. Walker was impressed enough to give Spielberg her blessing, ultimately signing on as a consultant for the production's design and also making casting suggestions.

One was Whoopi Goldberg, the cult comedienne who had read the book and contacted Walker, insisting if a

Whoopi Goldberg, stand-up comedienne who achieved instant movie stardom as Celie.

Mr. overhears the conversations of young Celie (Desreta Jackson) and her sister Nettie (Akosua Busia), determining to seduce the younger woman (courtesy Warner Bros.).

town, but it had become so modernized over the years (he feared low-flying airplanes would ruin the period flavor) that it was necessary to move out of the novel's designated state. After considerable searching, he happened on a pre–Civil War plantation in the countryside near a small village named Marshville. There production designer Michael Riva made use of authentic preexisting buildings, which could be dressed up to look like a turn-of-the-century town, also moving other old buildings (including a church) onto this land and constructing some new facades. He and everyone else involved were inspired by Spielberg's insistence on absolute authenticity: two planeloads of red Georgia clay were flown in so that the dirt in the streets would be precisely right.

Spielberg brought a hundred professionals (many from the Bay Area rather than Hollywood per se) with him, then hired more than two hundred residents as extras, laborers, and security people. During the eight-week shoot-

movie were ever made, she would love to read for the part of Celie. Attracted by the politics of Goldberg's comedy, Walker caught her act, was impressed by what she saw, and became convinced that Goldberg would be ideal. Walker argued in favor of unknowns to keep the movie intimate rather than a commercialized all-star extravaganza. Margaret Avery was cast as Shug, though only after Tina Turner—the producers' original choice—turned it down. Herself a victim of abuse, Turner was not psychologically ready to become involved in a movie that contained such scenes. Then Quincy Jones, in Chicago on business, happened to flip on the TV in his hotel room. One look at the outspoken then-local talk-show host Oprah Winfrey and he knew he had found the perfect Sofia.

Filming began in mid-July of 1985 in North Carolina. The location manager was Kokayi Ampah, one of the many black craftspeople working on the project. Walker's contract stipulated that aside from the nearly all-black cast, a full half of the working crew must be black, female, or "Third World." Ampah had initially scouted locations in Eatonton, Georgia, Walker's home-ing schedule, Spielberg's crew ranged as far away as Union and Anson counties (southeast of Charlotte). Monroe was the key shooting site, most of the cast and crew staying at the local Holiday Inn, where they escaped oppressive heat (often hitting 100 degrees), along with unbearable humidity, before and after working hours, thanks to contemporary creature comforts (air-conditioning, swimming pool) which the earlier generation they were re-creating could not have dreamed of. During the long, sweltering days, cast members also had to deal with a strong odor of frankincense, since Spielberg relied on the old Hollywood technique of having smoke in the shot to enhance the visual definition of a crowd scene, making his image appear like the actual past in an old photograph rather than a group of costumed actors standing around and pretending to be denizens of an earlier time; frankincense proved an effective source for such smoke.

Spielberg, wearing his ever-present baseball cap, kept a close eye on every detail. Journalist Elena Featherston, who covered the shooting for *San Francisco Focus,* reported:

Spielberg was a moving bundle of energy and intensity. He seemed to be everywhere at once—checking camera angles,

Oprah Winfrey (photographed by Gordon Parks) as Sofia, whose pride leads to a tragic fall after she stands up to the condescending whites in the community (courtesy Warner Bros.).

The relationships of women are as significant in Spielberg's film as in Walker's novel, though it was his nature to play down Walker's lesbian theme, instead emphasizing deep friendship and spiritual sisterhood.

151

talking with actors, joking with the crew, introducing his baby son, Max, to his first movie camera, showering affection on Max's mother, actress Amy Irving—all the while letting nothing go unnoticed. Nothing was insignificant: Spielberg directed the action of each extra or the placement of a farm animal with the same meticulous attention he gave the principal actors.

Also on hand was Walker, who remained with the company for half the shooting schedule. She was a consultant not only in name: Spielberg later recalled that "a couple of times, we'd go over to her and say, 'We're adding something here, and could you help us?' She'd add a line or two." On particularly sweltering afternoons, Walker would sit in the shade of a tree where (to Spielberg's delight) she took on an unofficial role as voice coach, teaching the cast proper phrasing of black

folk English. She also helped set designer Riva achieve total authenticity by preparing a list of vegetables and flowers Celie would actually have had in her garden, making endless suggestions about everything from articles of clothing to hair color.

Though these talented craftspeople gave the project their all, there was never any question that success or failure would rest on the shoulders of the director. One of Spielberg's key decisions was a change in the relationship between Celie and Shug. In the book, it is emphatically physical: Celie finds the sexual satisfaction in the arms of another woman that she never knew with a man. Though the two kiss briefly in the film, it isn't quite clear whether they are in fact lovers or merely two women who deeply love and respect each other as friends, expressing their warm feelings through occasional embraces. Those

In Spielberg's benign and essentially optimistic film, the denizens of the juke joint sing and dance their way over to the church, where jazz and gospel happily blend into one; in Walker's dark, downbeat, and considerably less hopeful book, no such reconciliation between the two groups ever takes place (courtesy Warner Bros.).

Only when close to nature do the women escape the constricting influence of the men in their lives.

Whoopi Goldberg as Celie, whose child has been taken away from her in the film's first sequence (courtesy Warner Bros.).

Mr. takes the frightened young Celie (Desreta Jackson) away from her home . . .

. . . and off to his own farm, where he immediately begins abusing her (courtesy Warner Bros.).

who objected to this approach charged that Spielberg, to make the movie more commercial by keeping it within PG-13 family-film boundaries, had excised one of the key points Walker had been making. In *L.A. Weekly,* John Powers insisted that

Spielberg is afraid of the dark. But the bogeymen who haunt him aren't supernatural monsters (like those in his earlier films)—they're the stuff of real life. He can't stand to look at sexual heat. . . . He dreads psychology with its hidden depths . . . and he despises ambiguity, those dark corners of meaning where anything might lurk . . . he seems constitutionally incapable of depicting real-life sexual love, especially the lesbianism that underlies Walker's political stance. He all but eliminates the novel's sexual boldness, and gets cold feet when forced to show it.

Defenders insisted that Spielberg's approach merely made the scene more subtle while clearly implying (rather than overemphasizing) the physicality of this relationship. Certainly, his approach allowed the work to be seen and experienced by millions more people (including children) than would ever have attended an R-rated movie. Spielberg defended his choice, saying: "I didn't categorize (the Celie-Shug relationship) as a lesbian relationship so much as a love relationship of great need. No one had ever loved Celie other than God and her sister. And here Celie is being introduced to the human race by a person full of love. I didn't think a full-out love scene would say it any better."

The key issue here is how one defines "it." If by "it" you can accept the fact that Spielberg is talking about his own interpretation of the story (the story as

Many African American organizations, expected to applaud the film, complained that its popularity would do great damage to the image of black men in America.

Spielbergized, much as preexisting stories had been Disneyized), then what he did was precisely right. His decision was not only tasteful but also the perfect expression of his own attitudes and values. If, on the other hand, one feels that "it" means the relationship between Celie and Shug as envisioned by Walker and that a film ought to remain true to the concept of the novelist, then what we see on-screen is an outrage.

Another major change proved less controversial The novel is told entirely in the form of letters: written by Celie to God and to her sister as well as letters Nettie mails to Celie but which over the years are purloined by Albert. An epistolary novel is a literary conceit and, as such, essentially unfilmable. Spielberg sensed this: "Finally I realized that the book left me with a residue of emotion, and I decided to deal with that" on film. What he shot, then, was not Walker's novel but his own emotional response to her novel. Which helps explain why his film is not merely a recording of various actors (how-

ever talented) reciting lines of dialogue, lifted from the printed page, to one another, but original scenes he and collaborator Meyjes conceived of in cinematic terms.

One notable example is a simple early scene in which Albert excitedly prepares to run off and see Shug, his mistress. Though Celie knows where Albert is going, she is too shy and frightened to stand in his way; instead, she helps him make ready. Albert rushes for the stairs, then realizes he doesn't have the right socks and heads back to the bedroom, where Celie stands, holding them out for him. Albert again hesitates, aware he's got the wrong tie, running back once more, only to find Celie sheepishly smiling as she holds it out for him. He looks slightly embarrassed; though she says nothing, we see in Celie's face a desire to please, a happiness (Celie knows Albert will not beat her after enjoying sex with Shug), coupled with a sadness (Celie knows that, no matter how hard she may try, she can never make him happy). These emotions, marbled throughout the book in words, are here conveyed wordlessly, through body language and eye contact. The scene is funny and tender, a perfect movie sequence that translates the book's idea into visual language.

In addition to the Celie-Albert relationship, other key relationships are also conveyed visually. Most notable is the Celie-Nettie sister love, which we come to understand in Walker's book through Celie's words: She literally tells us, again and again, how close the two are and always will be. Knowing it was necessary to seize on some simple bit of business that would effectively translate such passages into visuals, Spielberg and Meyjes came up with the idea of a little hand-clapping game, which they introduce early on. At first, it is nothing more than one more charming Spielbergian rendering of innocent children at play, just before darkness descends, which we have seen in so many of his previous pictures. But Spielberg takes it further; when the film's "monster" (Albert, as much a male monster to these women as the poltergeists and dinosaurs are to other Spielberg protagonists) forces the two to part, the now-mature women communicate through their hand-clapping game as they say goodbye for a period that will last twenty-five years. That they both still play the game clearly indicates that they exist in the tradition of those Spielbergian heroes and heroines who do not lose the sense of childhood wonderment.

Walker tells us directly that Harpo is clumsy; Spielberg and Meyjes create a series of sight gags in which Harpo constantly finds himself on the roofs of buildings and falls through, landing splat in the middle of some social gathering. Essentially, the novel takes place inside Celie's mind: a collection of thoughts, emotions, reactions to events. Such internal material is perfect for a novel, but a movie must be external, showing us the events. Understandably, Spielberg and Meyjes created their own visual movie metaphors for Walker's verbalized plot points.

One striking example is the introduction of Shug Avery. The book gradually reveals, through Celie's comments, that Shug is her husband's mistress and a blues singer and may someday arrive at the house. To hear Whoopi Goldberg literally read all this on the soundtrack while we watch Celie walk around the kitchen with a nervous look on her face would be book-to-film adaptation at its worst. Instead, Spielberg concocts a chillingly evocative image, one of those sudden, scary dark-sky windstorms of the type that haunted his characters in *Poltergeist*. He allows us to glimpse a handbill for Shug's performance being blown out of the mailbox. Then his camera follows that piece of paper as it whirls around in the air, finally landing (seemingly by accident, though this action is all carefully planned out) hard against the door of the house. The wordless sequence serves as a visual metaphor for everything Walker had to explain; in a matter of seconds, we know who Shug is, what she does, and that she is heading directly for this place.

A piece of paper is also employed to show us, rather than tell us, that Celie never stops thinking about Nettie. Before Nettie is thrown off the farm by Albert, the more educated younger sister teaches Celie to read. In Spielberg's version, she does this by placing little slips of paper all over Celie's kitchen; a pot is accompanied by a slip on which she has written "pot," and so on. One piece of paper, inscribed with the word "sky," is placed by the window. After Nettie is gone and Albert has trashed the papers, we continually see the one that says "sky," which Celie has kept hidden. As it gradually fades and grows wrinkled, we note time's passing; every time Celie fondles it lovingly, we know she is thinking of Nettie. Nothing would be more obvious (or less artistic) than hearing Goldberg's voice claim, as she paced around the house, "I was thinking about Nettie again today." Nothing reveals the filmmaker's command of his medium more effectively than his seizing upon the scrap of paper—a visual addition of his own—to take the place of words.

The director also understands that "pure cinema" can be based on what one chooses not to show. One striking example occurs early, when Nettie leaves her abusive father and comes to live with Celie and Albert. As the child is on her way to school, walking down a path that takes her through a virtual wall of trees, she notices Albert riding along parallel to her, smiling lasciviously. He keeps appearing, then disappearing from sight, as he rides by trees; the effect of this is to momentarily make him look like a menacing character in an old flickering silent movie. Spielberg cuts to Nettie's ever more frightened face, then back to Albert, though he isn't there: The horse now trots along riderless. Then there is a long shot of Nettie, terrified, reaching the end of the wall of trees. This is a striking sequence because it is so cinematically rendered. When Albert then approaches Nettie, attempting to drag her off into the woods, Spielberg only chooses to follow them so far; he stops his camera the moment they are in the bushes as we hear her scream for help. A moment later, there is a thud; then it is Albert who screams. Nettie comes running out of the woods, with Albert—holding his crotch in horrible pain—staggering after her. There is an incredible sense of relief as Nettie rushes out, unscathed, then a wonderful laugh as Albert comes crawling back into sight. To have shown the actual moment of conflict may have been more obviously "realistic," but Spielberg's approach is more creative, artistic, and suggestive, making the viewer an active participant in the film rather than a passive observer of events.

An even more impressive example of this technique occurs when strong-willed Sofia, standing in the town's streets surrounded by her children, is confronted by the white mayor, angry because Sofia has spoken sharply to his wife. We see Sofia in a relatively close shot, realizing she is going to hit the man and, in the racist climate of those times, seal her own fate. Rather than take the obvious tract—show the blow in extreme close-up to empha-

Rae Dawn Chong as Squeak, the juke-joint waitress who wants to become a singer, meets Grady (Bennet Guillory), the dapper fellow Shug brings home (courtesy Warner Bros.).

size its importance—Spielberg tries something more subtle and satisfying. As Sofia pulls back her arm, Spielberg cuts to a long shot, making us feel as if we're watching from a great distance and, like Sofia's gathered friends, helpless to stop her. Then, as her clenched fist moves forward, we are spellbound, steeling ourselves as we wait to see the moment of impact. We don't see it: As her fist comes toward the man's face, a huge yellow truck pulls across our line of vision; we hear its roar instead of the fist-on-face impact. As the truck pulls out of view, we watch as the mayor falls to the ground. Spielberg's technique is the cinematic equivalent of a human's blinking or covering his eyes at the sight of something horrifying; his camera is not a mere recorder of the event but a surrogate for the audience's own emotional reaction to such a scene.

However, not everyone found the take-your-breath-away mastery of technique satisfying. Julie Salamon of the *Wall St. Journal* was mildly annoyed by what she perceived as "the overreaching for artiness," arguing that the striking technical prowess, however impressive, did a disservice to Walker's writing. Despite the director's stated desire to share Walker's novel with the world,

what Spielberg apparently didn't want us to "share" was the pain, the bitterness and the anger that gave Ms. Walker's book

Celie and Shug are proud, strong women who learn to survive without men (courtesy Warner Bros.).

Danny Glover as Mr. (courtesy Warner Bros.).

and gospel are not so far apart; the two groups become one group, the two musical styles happily melding together. Shug and her father at last embrace and are happily reunited; if secular and sacred music can come comfortably together, then so can the characters. It's the kind of highly charged, visceral moment that a filmed drama needs at precisely this point. And it is pure Spielberg: the ongoing optimism, the parent-child reunion, the merging of seemingly irreconcilable groups.

Still, it inverts rather than expresses Walker's ideas. In her embittered view, Shug and her father are never reunited, nor are the extremes of gospel and blues. The church does not embrace the new form of music but is sadly out of touch with the reality of these people's lives. There is no question that Spielberg's sequence is marvelously mounted, was so masterfully shot and edited that audiences, white and black, wanted to rise, sing, and clap along with the characters. There is a question, though, whether a book that is bleak in outlook ought to be subverted and turned into what is commonly referred to as a "feel good" film.

No wonder that Janet Maslin wrote in the *New York Times:*

The combination of his sensibilities and Miss Walker's amounts to a colossal mismatch. . . . Realism and grit, the signal qualities of Miss Walker's story, are all but absent here, being largely irrelevant to what Mr. Spielberg has in mind. His film is

its power. From the moment this movie opens, with the pretty picture of young black women frolicking in a sunlit field of purple flowers, you get the sense that we are in for *The Sound of Music* approach of making it through hard times. Suffer a little, sing a little.

John Powers of *L.A. Weekly* wrote:

Spielberg has so little faith in his human drama that he tarts up every shot and pumps up every scene . . . bathes everything in the Spielberg-esque light that comes bursting through every window that isn't coated with lead. His zippity-doo-dah outlook reaffirms the very values Walker challenges.

In particular, Powers complained about one sequence added for the film that has no precedent in the book. Spielberg followed Walker's plot involving the creation of a juke joint which Harpo runs and where Shug sings bawdy songs. Not far away is the church where Shug's estranged father leads his congregation in gospel music; the old-fashioned religious music and the new, alternative secular (and highly sexual) music vie for dominance in the emerging twentieth-century lifestyle of this minority culture. Spielberg diverges from Walker when he has his jazzy characters rush across the fields and into the church. In his version, we realize that the singing of blues

Adolph Caesar as Mr.'s prosperous father (courtesy Warner Bros.).

Rae Dawn Chong, daughter of comic actor Tommy Chong, as Squeak, the waitress who represses visions of a grander life (courtesy Warner Bros.).

an upbeat, affirmative fable in which optimism, patience, and family loyalty emerge as cardinal virtues. . . . Spielberg has looked on the sunny side of Miss Walker's novel, fashioning a grand, multi-hanky entertainment that is as pretty and lavish as the book is plain. If the book is set in the harsh, impoverished atmosphere of rural Georgia, the movie unfolds in a cozy, comfortable, flower-filled wonderland.

Maslin and other critics cited the fact that we never once see Celie, Albert, or anyone else actually working their large farm; even a few brief transition shots of the family's everyday life would have added a sense of believability.

It is worth noting, though, that Spielberg is working in a respected tradition here. Many of our acclaimed Hollywood film classics are richly colored, highly romanticized movies derived from novels written in shades of gray. One great example is the gorgeously colorful film George Stevens fashioned in 1953 from Jack Schaefer's somber novel of farm life in the old West, *Shane*. Spielberg's approach is similar to that of Stevens, a filmmaker he has admired: That story's child narrator, Little Joey Starrett, the Celie of his film, maintains a childlike innocence, even in the face of adversity. Once again, Spielberg has less in common with contemporaries like Scorsese and Coppola than with the great ones from

the past; he might be considered the last golden-age director, the popularity of his films due to the public's nostalgia for the kind of movies "they" (everyone but Spielberg) don't make anymore.

Though the comparison to Stevens is fair, a more significant influence is John Ford, whose work Spielberg cited so charmingly in *E.T.* The key recurring image in *The Color Purple* is of the family, gathered together in groups on the front porch of a home: first Celie's house, later Albert's, finally Celie's again. The shots strikingly resemble those of the Edwards and Jorgenson families in *The Searchers,* generally regarded as not only Ford's masterwork but also the single most influential film on Spielberg's generation. The final scene of *The Color Purple,* in which Celie looks out the window of the house, then opens the door and passes through the doorway with the camera following her, eventually staring out over her shoulder at the fields beyond is a precise redux of *The Searchers'* opening. At the end, when the entire family gathers on Celie's porch—at last reunited despite years of separation—it is not only akin to, but also identical (emotionally as well as visually) with, the final moment in *The Searchers* when Little Debbie (Natalie Wood), stolen away years ago by the Comanches, is restored to the household. In Ford's view, the disruptively machismo male Ethan Edwards (John Wayne), whose intruding presence is what upset the normal workings of the household, cannot be readmitted because of past sins. Likewise, Albert staggers across the field and out of sight, a lost Flying Dutchman. In Walker's book, however, Albert is last glimpsed sewing in the tailor shop Celie opened. Simply, there is more of John Ford here than there is Alice Walker.

To be fair, though, other critics concentrated on the film's abundant positive qualities. In *Newsweek,* David Ansen wrote:

Early on I had the disorienting sensation I was watching the first Disney movie about incest. When Spielberg's images don't dazzle, they can fall into Hallmark-card banality. . . . Yet *The Color Purple* triumphs over its own over-eagerness to please . . . the joy of the work, which rises out of the ashes of Celie's anger and oppression, shines through and overcomes the suspicion that one is watching the coloring-book version of Walker's book. When the women, all gathered around the dinner table, finally rise in rebellion against their men, it's hard not to cheer their declaration of independence as one's own.

Or, for anyone interested in the film as an expression of the filmmaker, as Spielberg's. He has often commented on what it was like to be raised in a house filled with women, in which he and his dog were (after his father's departure) the only males. Still, no one missed the fact that at thirty-eight, now a husband and father, Spielberg clearly felt the need to move in new directions. When asked if *The Color Purple* represented his attempt to "grow up," he made it clear that he resented the idea that he was some sort of arrested adolescent. "I've always been a grown-up," he replied to interviewer Glenn Collins. "I've been playing in the sandbox for years—as a grown-up." *The Color Purple* was his first attempt to leave the sandbox.

So there were no F/X pyrotechnics in *The Color Purple*. Still, it's worth recounting what happened when that long, hot summer of shooting finally drew to a close and Spielberg assembled his cast and crew for a champagne celebration. As the evening wore on, the assembled multitude gathered on Albert's back porch to watch a fireworks display. As everyone quietly stared at the darkening sky with delight at the breathtaking explosions occurring there, the man in the baseball cap who stood at their center wryly remarked: "At last—special effects!"

Empire of the Sun

A WARNER BROS. RELEASE, 1987

CAST

Christian Bale *(Jim);* John Malkovich *(Basie);* Miranda Richardson *(Mrs. Victor);* Joe Pantoliano *(Frank);* Rupert Frazer *(Jim's Father);* Emily Richard *(Jim's Mother);* Leslie Phillips *(Mr. Maxton);* Masato Ibu *(Sergeant Nagata);* Peter Gale *(Mr. Victor);* Takatoro Kataoka *(Kamikaze Boy Pilot);* Ben Stiller *(Dainty);* Zhai Nai She *(Yang);* Burt Kwouk *(Mr. Chen),* Nigel Havers *(Dr. Rawlins).*

CREDITS

Director, Steven Spielberg; producers, Spielberg, Kathleen Kennedy, and Frank Marshall; second-unit director, Marshall; executive producer, Robert Shapiro; screenplay, Tom Stoppard (and Menno Meyjes, uncredited), from the novel by J. G. Ballard; cinematography, Allen Daviau; editor, Michael Kahn; music, John Williams; production designer, Norman Reynolds; costume designer, Bob Ringwood; Technicolor, Dolby Stereo; running time, 152 mins.; rating: PG.

Spielberg's movies are filled with characters who learn, during the course of the story, that what at first appears to be accident is, in fact, the inevitable working out of fate. It is not surprising, then, that the filmmaker views his own life and career as being largely predestined. So in describing the way in which *Empire of the Sun* occurred at a particular juncture, his phrasing is revealing: "This movie [happening] and [my] turning forty at al-

A total filmmaker, Spielberg does not merely direct the actors but shapes every element of the film, beginning with the writing and on through to the editing and musical scoring; here he and cinematographer Allen Daviau *(left of camera)* collaborate on a shot so that the final result will be precisely what Spielberg originally envisioned (courtesy Warner Bros.).

most the same time was no coincidence." In the world according to Steven Spielberg, it happened because it was meant to.

British director David Lean, a filmmaker Spielberg has always admired, contacted him, requesting that Spielberg acquire the rights to J. G. Ballard's autobiographical novel. Lean hoped Spielberg would produce and that he himself would direct. But by the time the rights became available, Lean had so immersed himself in another project, *Nostromo,* that he could not consider collaborating. Spielberg had to either scuttle the project or direct; he chose the latter route.

"From the moment I read the novel, I secretly wanted to do it myself," he said of this tale about a British boy, Jim Graham, living in Shanghai and, at the outset of World War II, interned in a Japanese prison camp. Spielberg was fascinated that the book dealt with an issue which he found intriguing. "A child saw things through a man's eyes as opposed to a man discovering things through the child in him. It was just the reverse of what I felt was [in previous pictures] my credo." Characters like Roy Neary in *Close Encounters of the Third Kind* rediscover a childlike view of the world; little Jim in *Empire of the Sun* embarks on an opposing, if complementary, journey, quite appropriate for the work of a filmmaker who himself had just reached a crucial turning point in his own life. It was time to consciously pursue a more mature type of filmmaking, though one that grew naturally from what had come before.

He had long since hoped to do a film in the style of Truffaut, who, in *Small Change* and *The Wild Child,* dramatized the very theme Spielberg discovered in this material. "I was attracted to the idea that this was [about] a death of innocence, not an attenuation of childhood, which by my own admission and everybody's impression of me is what my life has been." Critics loudly demanded to know if the boy genius would ever become a mature filmmaker or forever remain Peter Pan with a movie camera. Perhaps the best way to prove he was indeed a grown-up would be by telling the tale of a child (who serves as surrogate for the filmmaker) and the traumatic experience of coming to terms with the real world that intrudes on Never-Never Land.

With this in mind, Spielberg noted the comparisons between Ballard's book and Charles Dickens's *Oliver Twist:* to survive, Jim becomes a pint-sized thief, working for a Fagin-like American (John Malkovich) called Basie. Jim's childish view of the world is shattered when, shortly after becoming a prisoner, he unwisely asks for "More!" at dinnertime and receives a whack from one of his captors. Understandably, Lean had been attracted to the book: the sheer scope resembled his *Lawrence of Arabia,* the prison camp recalled the one in *Bridge on the River Kwai,* and he had directed the classic 1948 English version of *Oliver Twist.* Spielberg also has a strong feeling for that book. When, in *The Color Purple,* he decided to add a scene in which Celie learns to read, the book he chose for this special moment was *Oliver Twist.* When we first meet Jim, he is a total innocent, indeed morally ignorant of the world and its workings. During the course of the story, his innocence will be tested, then die; the key question for Spielberg is always whether optimism can outlive the death of innocence.

Playwright Tom Stoppard *(Rosencrantz and Guildenstern Are Dead),* hardly a Spielberg regular, proved an effective choice for screenplay duties. Like Ballard, the Czechoslovakian-born writer had been living in Asia (Singapore) with his parents since age three and as a child had witnessed the Japanese invasion. Stoppard expressed interest in doing a screenplay to Robert Shapiro, at the time in control of the rights to the book, eventually serving as executive producer. Spielberg became aware

After setting up the shot, Spielberg joins cast members Christian Bale, Emily Richard, and Rupert Frazer for the crucial Spielberg signature sequence in which the child is separated from his parents (courtesy Warner Bros.).

of the project and the fact that Stoppard was already penning an adaptation. Though they were notably different types of creative artists (Stoppard's writing tends to be dark, obscure, and intellectualized), they "danced around each other for a while" (as Stoppard later put it), "then became good friends," working on subsequent drafts together.

Stoppard's concept had been modest, though he acquiesced to Spielberg's desire for big, spectacular sequences, such as the evacuation of Shanghai near the beginning of the film and the bombing of the airstrip toward the end. An even more significant difference of opinion had to do with the conclusion. "I'm quite unsentimental, but Steven knows how to let the emotions out," Stoppard later said. "My ending was cool. His was warm."

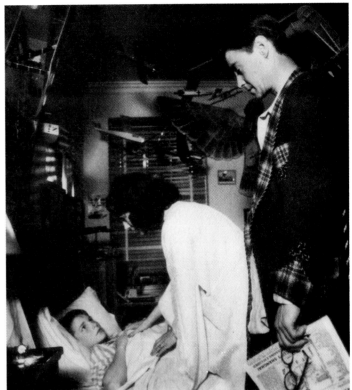

In his bedroom—a miniature world in which aviation and the promise of flight form the boy's romanticized dreams of adventure—Jim awakens to an all-too-real nightmare as his parents inform him they must evacuate the city immediately; shortly, the family unit will be shattered when Jim fails to listen to his mother's instructions (courtesy Warner Bros.).

Stoppard's concept was that following the death of innocence, the child's life could never be pleasant again, even after reunification with his parents. Spielberg could not shoot such a scene: It was one thing to mature, quite another to create a work that went counter to everything he has consistently believed. So he persuaded Stoppard to make the ending more Spielbergian.

From the beginning, Spielberg wanted authenticity; his production was scheduled to be the first major Hollywood film ever shot in the People's Republic of China. To his dismay, he learned that obtaining permission could require a three-to-four-year period of negotiation. Since this was restrictive, Kennedy and Marshall traveled around the world, searching for an appropriate city: Buenos Aires, Vienna, Liverpool, Stockholm, Hong Kong, and Lisbon were all considered, then rejected. Desperate, the Amblin execs flew to Beijing for face-to-face negotiations with bureaucrats from the Shanghai Film Studios and the China Film Co-Production Corporation, winning cooperation through perseverance and shortening the negotiation period to a year.

Upon arrival for a March 1, 1987, shooting start, Spielberg realized that Shanghai had virtually stood still for the past forty years. The crew only had to alter modern, simplified signs and billboards, restoring traditional Mandarin lettering. Few viewers outside Shanghai would know the difference, but Spielberg would know, so more than a thousand were changed. Then they waited for equipment to arrive, dealing with labyrinthine nightmares at customs as the necessary equipment—everything from Japanese tanks to 1939 Packards, in addition to the usual cranes, lights, generators, and cables—arrived two days before filming commenced.

Since they were strictly limited to twenty-one days, it was decided that only those scenes which absolutely had to be shot in Shanghai would be. On the first day, certain key streets had to be shut down so daily commerce and traffic would not spill onto Spielberg's chosen locations. Such a street closing had only been agreed to by the gov-

ernment one previous time, in 1959, for a Chinese moviemaker. Thousands of policemen were needed to keep the city's 12 million residents from descending on the location; thirty-five Japanese and Chinese translators conveyed Spielberg's comments to those around him. Meanwhile, Amblin execs had hired five thousand costumed extras to play street vendors, students, peasants, sailors, and bar girls, with Spielberg guiding them around "The Bund," the city's main waterfront highway. For the mass flight sequence from Shanghai, five thousand more extras were recruited from factories and offices. Rickshas were absolutely needed, but they had long since been abolished by the Communist government, so elderly Chinese craftsmen who could recall the precise construction were hired to create fifty replicas.

Jim Graham (Christian Bale, *center*) nervously inches his way through the streets of Shanghai (courtesy Warner Bros.).

Spielberg guides young Christian Bale through a difficult scene in the prison camp (courtesy Warner Bros.).

The film contrasts a child's trusting view of the world with the cynical vision of some adults: Jim crawls outside the prison camp, believing his mission is to trap a wild pheasant for the prisoners' Thanksgiving dinner, though in fact Basie (John Malkovich) is using the boy to test for deadly land mines (courtesy Warner Bros.).

Even when working under such intense time constraints, Spielberg knew what he wanted for each shot and was determined to get it. As the crowd riots in the Shanghai streets, Spielberg envisioned a take-your-breath-away shot in which the camera would at first be trained on several thousand people, darting about in panic at a key intersection. The camera would then slowly pull back until at last our view is from the top of a building, behind the shoulders of the Kuomintang rebels firing down into the crowd. In addition to the striking effect, the shot would also function thematically: We first see the chaos, then gradually learn its cause. But the shot was so complex that few believed it could be achieved. Undaunted, Spielberg had a newly built device, the Multicrane, installed on top of a ten-story office building. It consisted of a standard camera car with an arm, though this arm could come off and move onto a pipe track dolly, allowing for remarkable flexibility by which Spielberg did achieve his dream shot, with only a slight modification of his original concept.

For exterior shots of the lovely Tudor homes on Amherst Avenue, where members of Shanghai's then prominent European community lived, Spielberg found he could use the street with little alteration. However, Chinese families now lived in all those homes. It was deemed unwise to disrupt them, so interior shots were later completed in Sunningdale, England. Even as Spielberg was shooting exteriors in Shanghai, construction was under way in England and Spain for filming the bulk of the movie. Three hundred people—from highly skilled craftsmen to day laborers—constructed an approximation of the prison camp on the banks of the Gualalquiver River near Jerez. They needed to vividly recreate a pagoda, prison bunkers, railway line, and a turntable, plus a totally operational thousand-foot runway, complete with hangars for the World War II–era planes. Shortly after setting to work, their efforts came to a sudden halt when five weeks of constant, unexpected rain decimated their three-and-one-half month schedule.

When the torrents at last subsided, they went back to work, barely finishing before Spielberg arrived. For the film's spectacular air-raid sequence, Spielberg employed three U.S. P-51 Mustang fighter planes, each a collector's item valued at $500,000, guided through their paces in the film by Roy Hanna, former leader of Britain's Red Arrows aerobatic team. Tom Danaher, the former marine officer generally credited with having shot down the last Japanese plane during the war, was ironically put in charge of flying the Japanese zeroes through their paces. In addition to the antiques, Spielberg also used a dozen one-third-scale versions of the planes (six Mustangs, six Zeroes) for riskier scenes so as not to take any chance of damaging irreplaceable originals. Though the fabled American B-29 was a key element, Spielberg had to content himself with replicas of the superbomber, since only one capable of flying still exists.

In retrospect, it is difficult to believe that Spielberg could have read Ballard's novel and not filmed it. The privileged ten-year-old Jim, fleeing with his parents after Pearl Harbor, finds himself torn for a split second between his two great loves. One is a toy plane, which he holds in his right hand, representing the concept of flight this boy (like the filmmaker) is obsessed with. The other love is his mother, symbolizing here-and-now security. In the confusion and chaos, Jim drops his toy plane and must either lose it or release his mother's hand to retrieve it.

"Do whatever your mother says," Jim's father strictly informed him the night before in their hotel room.

"Just don't let go!" his mother insisted moments before.

But Jim does let go, certain he can grab the toy plane, then regrasp her. He is wrong about that; he has made a choice that will change his entire life. Previous Spielberg films dealt with either separation anxiety or seductive flight, but Ballard's literary conception provided the filmmaker with a perfect opportunity to combine the two. The child-hero of the film in some ways resembles Ballard, whose initials stand for Jim Graham. But Jim was transformed, during the filmmaking process, into one more variation of Spielberg's own recurring hero. Later, while in the Soochow prison camp, Jim attempts to maintain a delicate balance, doing what he has to do to stay alive, including amoral acts, such as stealing from the dead. But he also becomes a makeshift saint, looking after the dying simply because no one else bothers to. When the camp's doctor realizes that Jim is working even harder than himself, bringing boiled water to the elderly and children, he warns: "Don't exhaust yourself, Jim. You can't save everyone."

If Jim is a diminutive precursor of Schindler, the film also features its own Amon Goeth: Sergeant Nagata, who randomly takes his anger out on the camp's internees. When Nagata beats some helpless victim, the well-intentioned doctor stands up to him, though such courage accomplishes little. He may be a hero, but he is not a Spielbergian hero, rather serving as a foil for Jim. Jim willingly bows down before Nagata, humbling himself before his enemy, paying this cruel tyrant the respect he demands. Jim's manipulative, self-debasing tactic works: Nagata forgets the beating and wanders away. This is how Schindler will charm Goeth into backing off his Jews; it's how Spielberg survived when, as a child, he cast a bully in an amateur movie to defuse hostility.

The communication theme is present. Jim is at first locked into conventional language, with which he tries to establish a meaningful father-son relationship with scavenger Basie. "I learned another word today," he proudly announces, though Jim's already-advanced prowess with language initially caught Basie's attention. As in other Spielberg films, conventional language does not have its desired effect: Despite a (verbal) promise to take Jim along when he escapes, Basie deserts the boy. Spielberg warns that we should be cautious of false father figures,

166

who identify themselves through dishonest words. At the end, Jim rejects Basie, even as the man ceaselessly talks (his language is cynical and corrupt) to the nonresponsive child.

Jim has come to realize, like the characters in *Close Encounters of the Third Kind* and *E.T.,* the limitations of spoken language, as compared to the enormous possibilities of nonverbal communication, directly from the heart and soul. Just such communication occurs between Jim and the Japanese fliers; he salutes them proudly, and they sense the sincerity of his gesture (the mutually appreciated mystique of flight), respectfully returning his salute. This culminates in Jim's wordless relationship with the unnamed Japanese boy who shares his obsessive love of planes. The boy is first glimpsed playing with a model outside the compound's barbed-wire fence. Secret sharers, he and Jim constantly make eye contact; their first great communication happens when the boy glides his

A boy reaches toward the light and simultaneously salutes magical World War II planes. The image, so visually characteristic of Spielberg, is also a perfect rendering of the filmmaker's personal philosophy.

Basie (John Malkovich) gives Jim his first lesson in survival, warding off starvation; early on, Jim incurs the wrath of the guards by passing his plate and asking for "More!" much like Oliver Twist (courtesy Warner Bros.).

Spielberg relaxes with Bale and Malkovich between shots (courtesy Warner Bros.).

While others run and hide during the attack of American P-51s on Soochow Creek Airbase adjoining the prison camp, Jim celebrates the event (courtesy Warner Bros.).

plane over to Jim, who smilingly sends it back. They make a separate peace: though divided by race and war, their special bond overrides their opposing countries, with their divisive languages.

Which explains why, when a guard is about to capture Jim, the Japanese boy purposefully distracts the man so that Jim can escape; they are like Elliott and E.T. Basie cannot comprehend this, and so he sets into motion the film's tragic finale. Watching as the boy lifts a sword above Jim's head, Basie mistakenly thinks Jim is in danger; we know Jim's Japanese companion is about to open a can of food. But Basie fires, killing him. Spielberg's appearance-versus-reality theme stems, as always, from the limitation of human perceptions. Seeing may be believing, but it can also be misleading.

The abandoned house allows Spielberg to take his mother-love theme in more serious, disturbing directions. When Jim first enters and finds his house empty, he slips into his mother's private room, only to discover that the floor is covered with talcum powder. Then, like Robinson Crusoe noticing Friday's footprints on the beach, a wide-eyed Jim spots a single footprint in the talc. Fascinated, he steps closer. Then Jim's innocence is sorely tested when he finds more footprints and jagged lines, suggesting a struggle, even rape. As he stares at the evidence, Jim becomes aware of something horrific in the house—and in the universe. To keep that cognition from coming into being, Jim rushes to the window and throws it open, allowing the wind to blow away the talc and its implications. Jim negates reality so that he can continue living in his dream world.

But some realities cannot be denied. Spielberg offers yet another variation of his appearance-reality theme when Jim later returns to the house, seeing what he believes to be his mother approaching. For a moment, the director sets up his shot so that we see what Jim sees: an Oedipal fantasy of the mother as reassuring parent and seductive woman in a flimsy nightgown. Then the approaching figure steps into the light, to Jim's (and our) shock revealed as an angry Japanese male. The world as Jim wants to see it crashes up against the world as it really is.

That was what happened to Lou Jean Poplin in *The Sugarland Express* and, to a degree, to every Spielberg protagonist since. *Empire of the Sun* offers yet another meditation on this idea, beginning with an early shot of Jim playing with his toy plane, holding it up in the air, even as a real fighter plane roars by. For a moment, the fantasy plane and the real one lock into a single image on-screen, the toy overshadowed by reality. The key moment occurs later, when Jim is playing Arabian Nights, dressed in an Aladdin costume for a masquerade party. A typical child, he becomes lost in a fantasy of adventure in which he wields his sword and defeats imaginary enemies. He crawls up onto a ridge, at which point he—and we—are startled to see hundreds of Japanese solders, readying for an attack. Jim freezes in his tracks, his innocent game shattered by harsh reality.

The earlier chauffeured drive to that party is equally telling. Jim's parents wear gaudy costumes; they pass through the teeming streets of Shanghai, where the poor and hungry gaze at them through locked windows. War, political upheaval, and ugly actuality are on display everywhere. But the family, as if in a time or space craft (looking surreal in their costumes), glides through, seemingly inhabitants of a different dimension. Still, hints abound that reality cannot be denied forever: one man waves the chicken he is holding too close to the car, and it splatters against the window, the blood foreshadowing a war that will demolish their hermetically sealed lives.

A little later, when the shooting starts and Jim finds himself alone, he walks through the deadly street combat as if still inhabiting a dream, virtually immune to the brutal reality on every side. Then, caught in the crossfire between warring factions, Jim experiences combat as grim reality rather than the *Two Fisted Tales* comic-book fantasy he previously enjoyed. *Empire of the Sun* "grows out of [Spielberg's] early films," David Denby wrote in *New York* magazine, "which all felt like boys' dreams of adventure blown up to gigantic proportions."

Spielberg transforms Ballard's recollections into yet another religious allegory. Spielberg's Jim is searching for some sign from up above. Jim is first encountered in a cathedral, singing (his voice is perfection) a religious song. Importantly, he performs in a technically proficient but soulless manner, coldly and calculatedly, clearly indicating that he does not consider the deeper meaning of the words. Though only a child, the film's Jim is a miniexistential hero.

JIM: I was dreaming about God.
JIM'S MOTHER: What did he say?
JIM: Nothing.

Then, for the first time, Spielberg at last allows us some insight into his own ongoing obsession with flying and its connection—previously undeveloped—to his religious theme. "If God is above us," Jim asks his mother, "does it mean 'up'—like flying?" Flying, then, is the physical manifestation of the Spielberg hero's desire to reach God, to undergo a metaphysical experience, to see and therefore believe in something beyond the here and now. As always, the Spielberg hero lives out the dream of Spielberg himself.

For a time, though, Jim remains earthbound, physically and spiritually. "I have become an atheist," he announces early on. That may be, but he's an atheist who constantly dreams of God, at one point seeing the Lord playing tennis. Later, he will tell a companion at the prison camp: "You should play tennis with my Dad. He's really good!" His father and Our Father become intertwined; Jim is the Spielbergian child, desperate for a dad who approaches divinity. At this point, God appears to be a make-believe character, religion a form of fairy tale with which adults comfort children. When one of the

Despite nonstop action audiences watch on-screen, the process of making movies is largely about standing around and waiting for the next shot; here Spielberg and Bale pass the time together (courtesy Warner Bros.).

Jim hopes and trusts that Basie will prove to be a fitting alternative father for the real dad the child has lost along the way (courtesy Warner Bros.).

ladies dies, Jim watches as her husband comforts his kids, saying: "Come on, children. She's with God now."

Near the end, Jim unwittingly witnesses the atomic bombing of Hiroshima from a distance. Half delirious with hunger, he thinks he's watching fellow prisoner Mrs. Victor's soul leave her body, heading for heaven. A scientific achievement appears, to someone lacking the information to understand it on a realistic level, to be a metaphysical act. Seeing is believing, and Jim, after seeing the burst on the horizon, discards his atheism and believes. The white light of the bomb, in this context, recalls the Spielbergian light of truth pouring into the doorway which the little boy opens in *Close Encounters of the Third Kind.* But we know more than Jim, and so we have an ironic edge on his conception. The atomic bombing brought to an end the era of the 1930s and early forties that, for Spielberg, has always been romantically portrayed as far more innocent than our own. The bomb blast, then, ends the child Jim's innocence at the same moment that, on a grander scale, it ends the world's innocence. With it, we enter the atomic age; life will never be so glorious again.

Janet Maslin of the *New York Times* wrote that scenes like this were

set forth so spectacularly that the film seems to speak a language all its own. In fact it does, for it's clear Spielberg works in a purely cinematic idiom that is quite singular. Art and artifice play equal parts in the telling of this tale. And the latter, even though intrusive at times, is part and parcel of the film's overriding style.

That *Empire of the Sun* is actually one more Spielberg movie about movies is apparent from the opening sequence, in which various pieces of flotsam and jetsam drift by a boat. The sequence is borrowed from Hitchcock's patriotic wartime effort *Lifeboat.* Two and a half hours later, our final image will be of Jim's discarded suitcase bobbing up and down in the water as he (at last reunited with his parents) zips by in a boat. The film is in part about Jim's ridding himself of "baggage" (in a symbolic as well as physical sense) during the course of the story. His piece of lost luggage is this film's Rosebud sled, a conceit drawn from Welles's *Citizen Kane.*

Denby noted that during the climactic bombing scene "the planes become darting streaks in a larger-than-life wide-screen movie playing in front of Jim's face." Continuing his movie-about-movies theme, Spielberg emphasizes the presence of movie cameras during the fall of Shanghai. These are journalists recording the incident for a documentary film. The impact of the sequence is that all life is to a degree raw material for motion pictures. But as Jim strolls past that newsreel camera, which captures him against a backdrop of reality, Spielberg's camera follows Jim as he wanders farther, past an immense advertisement for *Gone With the Wind.* Now Jim is framed in such a manner that we cannot see the "real" world surrounding the poster: Jim has virtually stepped out of reality and into a Hollywood movie fantasy. Significantly, the shot also features a city—Civil War–era Atlanta—which, like Shanghai, has fallen into chaos. In the romanticized vision of David O. Selznick, it all seems exciting and glorious, far preferable to the real chaos Jim experiences.

Hollywood movies can make anything (even anarchy) appear romantic. Spielberg's movie is a Hollywood movie about the impact of such Hollywood movies. In *Newsweek,* David Ansen complained that "this is a secondhand film, the war filtered through the sensibility— and astonishing technique—of Hollywood's greatest virtuoso. And that may account for both its greatness and its failings." By secondhand, Ansen infers that *Empire of the Sun* is obviously a movie about World War II made by an artist who had not even been born then. In fact, the director appears aware of that situation, making it his subject. As a stand-in for the filmmaker, Jim's stepping out of everyday reality and into the world of movies is Spielberg's visual statement of his point of view. Spielberg made the only film a member of his generation could create about this war, a movie by and for those who know it through film.

Even the references in the credits to Jim's parents as nameless (Jim's father and Jim's mother) attests to movie influences. Few films had as great an impact on Spielberg's generation as 1955's *Rebel Without a Cause,* also about a lost boy named Jim (whose parents are referred to only as Jim's father and Jim's mother) who, after likewise being separated from his parents by circumstances, attempts to create an alternative family while also searching (however unconsciously) for a source of belief in something greater.

Natalie Wood costarred in that film as well as in John Ford's *Searchers* one year later, another Spielberg favorite. The *Empire of the Sun* scene in which parents and children are reunited but have difficulty recognizing one another has precedents in both *The Searchers* and Ford's *Two Rode Together* (1961).

One possible reading of *Empire of the Sun* is as a compendium of the greatest moments from films of the fifties. Jim becomes a voyeur, spying on Mr. and Mrs. Victor as they engage in furtive sex in an adjoining room. As they make love, a bombing mission takes place outside, lighting up the night sky; it is Spielberg's variation on Hitchcock's *To Catch a Thief,* with its famous crosscutting back and forth between Cary Grant and Grace Kelly kissing to the fireworks display occurring outside their window. Hitchcock is, in fact, a major influence here. The two-tone black-and-white shoes Jim wears resemble those worn by Robert Walker in *Strangers on a Train;* often Spielberg will begin a sequence just as Hitchcock shot that film's opening, with the camera trained on the shoes, hinting at the personality of the fellow wearing them, himself "two-toned," alternately selfless and selfish. Like James Stewart in *Rear Window,* Jim uses binoculars to spy on people across the way.

Beyond Hitchcock, though, Spielberg's film (like so many of his other movies) contains varied homages. When Basie and others plan their escape, they resemble the prisoners in Billy Wilder's *Stalag 17;* when forced to build an airplane runway, a few (Jim included) envision the attacking Allies as the enemy that will destroy their determined effort. They lose sight of which side they are on, making the same mistake as Captain Nicholson (Alec Guinness) in *The Bridge on the River Kwai.* Later, during a mass exodus from camp, the prisoners appear identical to the fleeing Hebrews in DeMille's *Ten Commandments.*

Finally, they reach an area where their onetime household valuables have been placed in a pile, priceless treasures turning into junk through exposure to the elements. They appear to have wandered into an outdoor version of the storage house with which Orson Welles ended *Citizen Kane.* One scene in mid-movie particularly stands out: Jim, Basie, and others arrive at the internment camp. The camera, initially tight on the small group, gradually pulls back to reveal the enormity of the place. As Jim steps over a hill, the camera concurrently moves upward to keep him in the shot and allows us to see first hundreds, then thousands, of British and American prisoners, all working at carrying rocks for the Japanese construction. It is a take-your-breath-away moment, even if, to a degree, the sense of spectacle is undercut by echoes of familiarity: This is modeled (consciously or otherwise) after the *Gone With the Wind* shot of Vivien Leigh stepping into the open-air hospital.

Tom O'Brien, writing in *Commonweal,* argued

171

Empire is a curious case of arrested development: Spielberg wants to depict maturity but is too close to the childish. The trouble comes with treatment of character . . . Spielberg's weakness in handling a mature character, or rather handling character maturely.

O'Brien admitted that he had been charmed, like everyone else, by the fairy-tale qualities of *Close Encounters of the Third Kind* and *E.T.* but insisted that the director's approach was essentially the same here, which didn't jibe with Ballard's story: "In *Empire,* Spielberg has tackled tragic material unsuitable for his special gifts." Essentially, the same critics who had earlier attacked Spielberg for not attempting a more mature film now criticized him for doing just that. Badly burned, Spielberg would back off, returning to fairy tales for adults *(Always)* and kids *(Hook).* In time, though, he would have to swallow hard and once more attempt to overcome his own limiting reputation, with *Schindler's List.*

Indiana Jones and the Last Crusade

A PARAMOUNT PICTURE, 1989

CAST

Harrison Ford *(Indiana Jones);* Sean Connery *(Prof. Henry Jones);* Denholm Elliott *(Marcus Brody);* Alison Doody *(Dr. Elsa Schneider);* John Rhys-Davies *(Sallah);* Julian Glover *(Donovan);* River Phoenix *(Young Indy);* Michael Byrne *(Vogel)*; Alex Hyde-White *(Young Henry)*; Kevork Malikyan *(Kazim)*; Richard Young *(Fedora)*.

CREDITS

Director, Steven Spielberg; executive producers, George Lucas and Frank Marshall; screenplay, Jeffrey Boam, from a story by George Lucas and Menno Meyjes; cinematography, Douglas Slocombe; editor, Michael Kahn; music, John Williams; production designer, Elliot Scott; producer, Robert Watts; Panavision, DeLuxe Color and Dolby Stereo; running time, 127 mins.; rating: PG-13.

On May 30, 1977, during the dinner meeting at which the Indiana trilogy was born, Spielberg inadvertently broke the ice, explaining that he dreamed of someday doing a James Bond movie, though only if he could get Sean Connery. That caused Lucas to share his own idea for "a modern James Bond film" featuring the eighties equivalent of 007. Spielberg quickly acquiesced, storing his Connery concept away. Then, nearly twelve years later, the two decided that in the final installment, Indy

Spielberg *(left)* directs Harrison Ford *(center)* and Sean Connery *(right)* (photo by Murray Close, courtesy Paramount Pictures).

River Phoenix as young Indiana Jones (photo by Bruce Talamon, courtesy Paramount Pictures).

Christianity. *Raiders of the Lost Ark* provided the first; *Indiana Jones and the Temple of Doom,* the second. Needed now was the Christian variation on this theme. Indy, then, must go back one last time, traveling the hero's journey from initial skeptic to ultimate believer. If there is a flaw in the trilogy's conception, it is that at the end of each film, Indy appears to fully accept spirituality, only to have regressed again at the beginning of the next movie, needing to learn the same precious lesson all over again.

Jeffrey Boam, who previously impressed Spielberg while working on the script for *Innerspace* (which Steven produced), won the coveted writing job this time. According to Boam, his most difficult function was serving as a bridge between the vastly different talents of Spielberg and Lucas: "George would paint in broad strokes [whereas] Steven was great in coming up with how to embellish them." Once again, Spielberg chose to work from storyboards rather than the traditional script; sketch artists took his initial drawings and turned them into an elaborate comic strip.

"Paying off the audience" with a grand action scene, Spielberg stages an elaborate fight and chase through the canals of Venice, recalling similar incidents in James Bond movies; here Indy struggles with Kazim (Kevork Malikyan) (photo by Murray Close, courtesy Paramount Pictures).

should come to terms with his own oft-mentioned father. Lucas envisioned a fussy, supercilious professor: Oscar winners John Houseman *(The Paper Chase)* and Henry Fonda *(On Golden Pond)* came to mind. Spielberg suggested Connery, an idea Lucas initially rejected. Spielberg persisted, believing that Connery could stir echoes of the Bond role; by having him play Jones Senior, the filmmakers would acknowledge that Indiana Jones was indeed Bond's cinematic son.

There was another reason why the third film provided a necessary addition to the series. Spielberg continually expresses the need for twentieth-century man to unlearn modern nihilism by rediscovering old-fashioned faith, jaded sophistication giving way to enlightening simplicity. Spielberg is decidedly all-inclusive, rejecting the idea that any one positive religion has a lock on the truth. So it was obligatory that there be one Indy movie for three of the world's leading faiths: Judaism, Hinduism,

One key decision was to film the stunt sequences, whenever possible, without use of the blue-screen process or traveling mattes, lending the film a more realistic appearance. Since *Indiana Jones and the Last Crusade* (budgeted at $35 million) was intended as the biggest (and hopefully best) of the series, a production office was established early in the process so that gargantuan organizational demands could be met; though *Raiders of the Lost Ark* had been considered an immense undertaking, *Indiana Jones and the Last Crusade* would dwarf it. Production supervisor Patricia Carr later recalled the work as akin to "an army maneuver," as carefully planned and coordinated as the D-day invasion.

Principal photography commenced on May 16, 1988, in Almeria, Spain, where literally every type of transportation available in 1938 had been assembled, from horses and camels to trains, planes, and automobiles, as well as a zeppelin. The first sequence shot was Indy's climactic horseback battle with a Nazi tank. From there, the filmmakers moved to Majorca, where, on a long-abandoned airfield, scenes involving the Nazi fighter planes

were completed. Then it was on to Granada, where the railway sequences were shot at Gaudix Station, transformed into a replica of the Middle Eastern town of Iskenderun, complete with marketplace and scores of livestock. A mosque had been built in the background for additional atmosphere rather than added later as a matte-painting-effect shot.

Following three weeks in Spain, Spielberg moved his crew to England for an additional ten weeks on the soundstages at Elstree, where various interiors (Donovan's Central Park apartment, the catacombs of Venice, inside the zeppelin) were completed. For the catacombs sequence, Spielberg used mechanical rats (a thousand were manufactured), making the situation less tense for actors (rats literally crawl over their bodies) while appeasing animal-rights activists. Even the wildest interiors look more real than the sets in *Indiana Jones and the Temple of Doom;* the sensation of artifice was jettisoned here for a sense that this one took place in the real world, perhaps because the story directly involves Adolph Hitler, necessitating that the tone be less that of a fairy tale, more serious, paving the way for *Schindler's List.*

While in the United Kingdom, Spielberg also shot sequences on the Tilbury Docks in Essex and the Stowe School in Buckinghamshire. On August 7, Spielberg packed up his company and moved to Venice for exteriors in St. Mark's Square and at the Doges Palace. Later that week, they flew to Jordan and shot scenes in the ancient city of Petra, which served as the long-lost secret temple, filming in a building over three thousand years old.

For consistency, the film (which opened in a whopping 2,327 movie houses across the United States and Canada) had to begin with some clever variation on Paramount's mountain logo fading into an actual mountain. As the dissolve from painting to actuality takes place, we view John Ford country: that fabled "four corners" of the American Southwest, the Monument Valley location for so many classic westerns which impacted on the young Spielberg's imagination. The opening links the two filmmakers, Spielberg as much the cinematic son of John Ford as Indiana Jones is of James Bond.

A title card informs us that this is Utah, 1912, though what we see—a uniformed troop of riders disappearing into the rock formations—at first seems drawn from Ford's cavalry trilogy set in the late 1800s. As the camera moves closer, we realize these are not adult soldiers on patrol but Boy Scouts on a camping trip. Young Indy and a friend slip off from the main group and discover villains looting the legendary cross of Coronado. Like objects in other Indy films, the cross is at once a religious artifact, valuable antique, and museum piece, causing each and every "raider" to come face-to-face with his own motivations: spiritual, mercenary, or social. The villains are motivated by base greed; Indy, by social concern: "That cross belongs in a museum," the child says,

Indy and a duplicitious blonde worthy of Hitchcock's classic World War II thrillers precariously enter the domain of the long-dead.

this being that point when he solidifies his worldview. During the course of the story, his attitude will transform from social to spiritual.

The leader wears a fedora hat and leather bomber jacket; he looks remarkably like the adult Indy we already know. Moments before spotting these looters, young Indy says with a sigh, "Everybody's lost but me," an echo of earlier Spielberg heroes. When Indy grabs the cross and runs from the villains, he enters into the realm of movie cliché. Standing on a bluff, he whistles to his trusty horse; it trots up. As we expect, Indy leaps down toward the saddle; Spielberg invokes movie mythology, only to undermine it. This is, after all, "reality" (or what we accept as reality while watching), so something happens here that would never happen in an old western. The horse moseys away just as Indy jumps, and he thuds down onto the ground. That appealing gag sets up the film to follow: a revival of beloved golden-age movie clichés tempered by a gentle, understated spoof of them.

Next comes the first extended-action sequence. Indy escapes by climbing up onto a train, pursued by looters. Importantly, it's a circus train. This allows for wonderful episodes in individual cars, one involving a lion, during which Indy grabs a nearby whip, establishing his primal connection with this weapon. In another, snakes crawl all over Indy's body, helping us grasp his fear in *Raiders of the Lost Ark.* More importantly, the circus train is a personal touch: the first film Spielberg ever attended was *The Greatest Show on Earth,* featuring a memorable circus-train sequence. Finally, in the "magic caboose," Indy escapes by slipping into a box, appearing to vanish. That is precisely the approach taken by the title character in Alfred Hitchcock's *Lady Vanishes.* Also, by having Indy escape his adversaries through magic, Spielberg slips in a key theme. Later, adult Indy realizes only by employing magic, religion, and spiritualism can he defeat the forces of evil.

What follows is of even more significance. Indy rushes into his house, calling out: "Dad!" Whereas most Spielberg films focus on the positive relationship of a

The generation gap: Spielberg took time out from high adventure to allow for serious father-son confrontations between Senior and Junior: since Indy was conceived as the cinematic son of James Bond, the casting of Connery took on an additional level of meaning (photo by Murray Close, courtesy Paramount Pictures).

Professor Brody (Denholm Elliott, *center*) is not only reintroduced (his absence from the second film was a major mistake) but allowed to actively take part in the great adventure, serving as an ideal father figure and foil for Indy's own fallible father (photo by Murray Close, courtesy Paramount Pictures).

177

Senior and Junior are taken captive by the Nazis; whatever their personal differences, they are united by their desire to fight this force of evil (photo by Murray Close, courtesy Paramount Pictures).

The treacherous Elsa ties the two heroes together; the mildly kinky bondage sequence is reminiscent of those in James Bond films (photo by Murray Close, courtesy Paramount Pictures).

boy and his mother after Dad has deserted, *Indiana Jones and the Last Crusade* complements those by concerning a son and father, without the mother present.

YOUNG INDY: It's important!
FATHER: It can wait.

The father browses through old books, leaving no time for the present reality of his son, recalling Spielberg's own father's preference for his stack of *Analog* magazines. Though Indy's father is physically present in the house, Spielberg refuses to reveal the man's face. This may have been done for technical reasons (Connery could not be made up to look young enough for this sequence), though it functions thematically as well: ostensibly there, the father is on some level already gone.

The communication-through-language theme is brought into play. While Young Indy desperately tries to enlist Dad's aid, the older man insists that the boy translate back and forth between ancient Greek and modern English, allowing us to understand the source of Indy's multilingual abilities. Then the man in the hat enters and (with local law-enforcement officials supporting him) removes the cross. "You lost today, kid," he laughingly says, placing his hat on the boy's head. "Doesn't mean you have to like it." The bad man's good-natured way of talking to a child sharply contrasts with Indy's own father, a good man who is extremely bad (rather, awkward) around kids.

Indy's dad reads from his ancient book:

PROFESSOR JONES: May he who illuminated this, illuminate me.

The tone is ironic: Though Professor Jones is well-read, he lacks wisdom, the spiritual savvy that should be derived from such works. There is another level to the line: "Illumination" invokes light (physical and spiritual). Spielberg consistently employs the "light" that physically projects images onto a screen to suggest his thematic "light," the knowledge passed on through his films that faith is the only source of salvation.

At this moment, Indy is clearly torn between the two men, accounting for his own eventual dual personality. On some level, he senses the essential social goodness of his father, so the scholarly side of him—Prof. Henry Jones Jr.—represents his attempt to emulate that. Yet

INDIANA JONES AND THE LAST CRUSADE: Whereas the films of Spielberg's first decade (1973–83) dealt largely with the sacrifices of idealized mothers after the father has left, movies from Spielberg's second decade (1984–94) portray reconciliations between a less-than-perfect, oft-absent father (here, Sean Connery) and the now mature son (Harrison Ford) who forgives after realizing he's capable of the same sort of failures himself. As always, Spielberg's seeming "light entertainments" reflected the serious experiences of his life, unobtrusively expressing an autobiographical element (photo by Eva Sereny, courtesy Lucasfilm Ltd./Paramount Pictures).

Indy to the rescue: Under extreme pressure, the ordinary man Henry Jones, Jr., really does rise to the occasion and transform into the superhero. While writing the third film, George Lucas was highly influenced by Joseph Campbell's *Power of Myth,* including the notion of the hero's journey (spiritual as well as physical) from ordinary man to mythical figure, in touch with both his father and Our Father (photo by Murray Close, courtesy Paramount Pictures).

In one of the film's marvelous stunt sequences, Indy single-handedly takes on a German tank in which his father is held prisoner (photo by Murray Close, courtesy Paramount Pictures).

young Indy senses the appeal of this dangerous, dark intruder; his Indy identity constitutes an emulation of this man as alternative father figure. Throughout his life (and the three films), Indy will be torn between the desire to be like one and/or the other (wearing the raider's hat while on adventures, shifting to his father's conservative suits when in the classroom). In the last moments of this, the final film, Indy will have to finally choose between the two.

The raider turns the cross over to a villainous man in a white suit. Spielberg cuts over the decades, tossing us (along with Indy) onto a storm-swept tramp steamer on the Portuguese coast, circa 1938, where Indy finally wrests the cross away from the man in the white suit, in-

sisting: "That belongs in a museum." The kind of a boy he was, the kind of a man he has become. His duality is beautifully conveyed when, a moment later, the button-down university professor Jones (Jr.) informs spellbound students that archaeology is not about adventure (the kind we've just seen him enjoying) but scholarly research. Having made the transition, he rejects the recent guise, the other side of himself.

"X never marks the spot," he tells the class, dashing their hopes. Moments later, embarked on another outlandish adventure, he will proclaim: "X marks the spot!" This is not an inconsistently drawn character but an inconsistent character in deep conflict with his two sides: Each man—Professor Jones, Indiana Jones—means precisely what he says. When operating in either guise, he rejects the values of the other, which makes him a very sick man and far more fascinating than the cardboard-hero cliché he's often regarded to be.

Museum curator Marcus Brody then arrives. The film's third father figure, Brody represents an idealized version of Indy's own father, with the same scholarly bent but none of the off-putting smugness or self-importance. If Senior had been more like Brody, Junior would have had nothing to rebel against, would have had no need to create and become Indiana. Brody—though a modern intellectual—possesses the kind of wisdom Jones Sr. lacks: "We cannot afford to take mythology at face value," Brody warns, making it clear that there is more than mumbo jumbo in this artifact. Marcus Brody's attitude toward ancient mythology is precisely the same as Spielberg's toward movie mythology: Though he adores it, the filmmaker always gives each movie myth some fresh twist.

When Brody explains that they must search for the Holy Grail, that chalice in which Christ's blood was contained after the crucifixion and which now possesses great power, Junior replies: "We'll discuss my honorarium over dinner." By film's end, he will once more complete his ritualistically repeated hero's journey by rejecting both greed (the man in the fedora) and glory (the professor) for something of ultimate significance: enlightenment, or as Senior would put it, "illumination." His father has, in fact, disappeared (much like foster-father Ravenwood in *Raiders of the Lost Ark*) while pursuing his lifelong quest, a search for the grail. Now Nazis are (as in the first film) closing in on this artifact that might provide frightful power to armies of darkness. Brody and Junior must head for Venice, where Senior is closing in on the grail's location; Junior proves to be, in his Professor Jones guise, as feeble a father figure as his own father, leaping out the window rather than meeting with students (his "children") who need time and attention.

Psychiatrists can testify to the truth of this: Abused children almost always become abusers, having no other role model. Yet Junior does have another model—the man in the fedora—a role he sublimates into, departing by plane. When Indy eventually encounters his own father, the ideal father figure, Brody, will be there, too, serving as a foil. In fact, the only narrative flaw is that Indy's dark foster-father figure fails to reappear. It might

have been fascinating to have the original man in the hat in on the final confrontation for a total sense of closure.

Before he departs, Indy first meets with Donovan, who provides the film's next Hitchcockian touch. He is Hitchcock's upper-crust villain: classy, charming, cold-blooded. First, we view him in his immense apartment overlooking Central Park; it is the scene from *Vertigo* in which the seemingly friendly Gavin Elster (whose own office overlooks San Francisco's docks) hires James Stewart's Scottie Ferguson, only to later betray him. Then Donovan's well-dressed wife barges in from the adjoining room, asking him to rejoin their chic party. In both *The 39 Steps* and *Saboteur*, Hitchcock's working-class hero finds himself in just such a situation, pitted against above-suspicion pillars of society who prove to be corrupt.

Before he leaves, Indy makes clear that he's after an artifact, not existential truth:

INDY: The Arthur legend. I've heard this bedtime story before.
DONOVAN: It's every man's dream. Your father's!

Perhaps one reason Indy continually rejects the spirituality of such objects is that the father he feels compelled to

Despite its entertainment qualities, the film serves as a precursor to *Schindler's List* by introducing Adolf Hitler as a symbol of evil, an image of the cynical politician as modern celebrity all too willing to sign autographs.

Indy fights a Nazi in a sequence reminiscent of so many propagandistic Hollywood movies of the 1940s, an era that has always been tinged with nostalgia for Spielberg (photo by Murray Close, courtesy Paramount Pictures).

Sallah (John Rhys-Davies; *left*), Indy, and Senior all gaze down at what is presumably the remains of Indiana Jones; the father-son reunion, begun here, will be developed further in future Spielberg films (photo by Murray Close, courtesy Paramount Pictures).

reject *believes.* But the villain also believes, and that's a problem; as the poet Yeats wrote in "The Second Coming" about life in our time:

> The best lack all conviction, while the worst
> Are full of passionate intensity. (1919)

Donovan, the worst, is full of passionate intensity; Jones, far from perfect but the best of a bad lot, at this point lacks all religious conviction.

Yeats continued, noting that in our century, innocent faith is ever harder to come by; he feared that in such a climate, an Antichrist could be born:

> The ceremony of innocence is drowned [and so]
> what rough beast, its hour come round at last,
> Slouches toward Bethlehem to be born?

Critics have noted that Hitler can be perceived as the "rough beast" Yeats warned the world of. Indy will come face-to-face with that beast in Berlin, even as he watches the book burnings, the fiery equivalent of Yeats's drowning of innocence. Yet Spielberg knows in retrospect what Yeats could not: The Allied crusade in Europe would crush the rough beast. Such knowledge allows Spielberg a guarded but fervent optimism in the face of unspeakable horror.

"Find the man," Donovan says, referring to the fellow (now disappeared) on the verge of discovering the hiding place. "You'll find the grail." Donovan says more than he knows. For Indy, the search for Our Father and his father become different aspects of a single search. At film's end, Junior's realistic reconciliation with Senior occurs simultaneously with his gaining religious faith. Only by believing in the Father can Indy save his own father.

In the meantime, there are matter-of-fact things to be dealt with, including the Austrian art historian who was working closely with Senior. Indy assumes that such a learned person will be an elderly male; his chauvinism is tested when Dr. Schneider turns out to be a striking young blonde. Using the lifelong diary of his grail quest that Senior mailed (fearful Nazis might get it), Junior, Brody, and Elsa enter St. Mark's Cathedral and locate the burial place of Sir Richard, one of three crusader-brothers who dedicated their lives to defending the grail. They are menaced by rats in the catacombs, then engage in an exciting boat chase across the canals. Such action is (as in *Raiders of the Lost Ark*) effectively sandwiched between comic and dramatic sequences in which characters, their relationships, and themes are developed; burned badly by aghast reactions to *Indiana Jones and the Temple of Doom,* Spielberg and Lucas had no intention of repeating their mistakes. While *Indiana Jones and the Last Crusade* was, ironically, rated PG-13, it is actu-

In one of the film's many action sequences, Junior and Senior escape from the Nazis via motorcycle.

Heroes triumphant: Brody, Indy, Sallah, and Senior become the Four Musketeers as they leave the Grail in its proper resting place (photo by Murray Close, courtesy Paramount Pictures).

Alison Doody as Dr. Elsa Schneider, who, like the deliciously duplicitous women in so many early James Bond films, is not to be trusted (photo by Murray Close, courtesy Paramount Pictures).

ally mild enough to have received the PG so wrongfully awarded to *Indiana Jones and the Temple of Doom.*

The charge of sexism—leveled against *Indiana Jones and the Temple of Doom*—is not an issue here. During the boat chase, Elsa—extremely intelligent, highly educated, a clear-cut equal of Indy—shares the adventure of the canal chase with him, steering the boat even as he fends off attackers. Spielberg's communication theme is in evidence, especially the inadequacy of language: When Indy tells her not to go between two large vessels, the surrounding din drowns out the key word, so she mistakenly believes he has instructed her to drive between them. Also, Spielberg's theme of death, as a beginning rather than end, resurfaces when Kazim tells Indy: "My soul is prepared. How about yours?"

Kazim challenges Indy further. "Ask yourself," he says, a voice of conscience, "why do you seek the cup of Christ—his glory or yours?" Though Kazim is clearly not Christian, he belongs to another good faith; his defense of the grail parallels Indy's own defense of the good Arabic religious artifact in *Indiana Jones and the Temple of Doom.* In answering Kazim's question, Indy takes an important first step: "I didn't come for the cup of Christ; I came to find my father." The honorarium he spoke of in his earlier, mercenary stage is forgotten; though he still exists in the here and now, his intentions are noble. Kazim, sensing what Indy does not yet grasp, is enlightened enough to realize that such a selfless undertaking, however reality-based, will inevitably lead to spiritual salvation: "In that case, may God be with you on your quest."

From Kazim, Indy learns that his father is being held prisoner in an Austrian castle. Before departing, there is a romantic interlude with Elsa, the most mature man-woman romantic scene to appear in a Spielberg film thus far. Indy grabs Elsa and kisses her—hard. "How dare you kiss me!" she hisses; then she grabs him and returns the kiss, equally hard. There is the hint of sadomasochism in their embrace (just as there always was in the great Hitchcock romances), but if their emotions are hardly politically correct (they insult each other nastily between lustful embraces), their equality certainly is. Elsa is every bit as formidable (if psychologically flawed) as Indy. Instead of the coitus interruptus of the previous Indy film, it is clear here that Indy and Elsa make love, like grown-ups.

Then it is act 2, and off to that castle, where Indy spots a Nazi Bund in the basement ("I hate these guys!") and crashes into the room where his father is captive.

PROFESSOR JONES: Junior!

INDY: Yes, sir.

With one word, Professor Jones reduces Indy—leather-jacketed (and self-conscious) symbol of raw masculinity—to the level of little boy; the inner child that Junior's been attempting to repress surfaces the moment he is with Senior. Indy still wears fedora and jacket, an action-adventure hero reduced to stammering child. At this point, Junior and Senior finally realize that despite years of bitter estrangement, they are Spielberg's secret sharers. Junior tells Senior that he now knows the location of the grail (the lost city of Alexandretia), the single element missing from Senior's map.

PROFESSOR JONES: Junior, you did it!

INDY: No, Dad. You did it!

In fact, they did it together, though it will take some time before they acknowledge they are, despite all the bad years, a team. When a Nazi enters and cryptically asks, "Dr. Jones?" the two heroes respond, "Yes?" simultaneously, an audience-satisfying gag but, beyond that, a suggestion of their growing sense of interdependence.

Indy will make the mistake of trusting Elsa, handing over his weapon to the Nazis. "You should have listened to your father," she smirkingly says, revealing that she's a Nazi and introducing the appearance-reality theme. "She talks in her sleep," Senior says, revealing not only his means of knowing her politics but also that they were sexually involved. This element, added to the script after Connery accepted the role, works because he is indeed one of the screen's sexiest elder statesmen. It also adds a complexity Spielberg has layered onto his mother-love motif since *Empire of the Sun:* the suggestion of an Oedipal theme. In the *Village Voice,* Georgia Brown wrote that Elsa is "the woman who screws both Pop and Junior, so who can she be but Mom?"

The map the Nazis need has been torn from the book and handed over to Brody, briefly seen (in a crosscut) wandering about the Middle East, comically reintroducing two key themes. First, he is lost (like every Spielberg hero from Roy Neary to Wild Bill Kelso). Second, he can't communicate through language. ("Does anyone here speak English?") Fortunately, old friend Sallah is there to save him, though the Nazis are soon on his trail, hungry to get their hands on the map leading to the canyon of the Crescent Moon. As Nazis leave Junior and Senior tied together in the castle, Elsa—similar to one of the beautiful betrayers in a James Bond film—pauses to kiss him goodbye. The manner of that kiss is significant: not a fantasy kiss but real, lustful, and cruel, ending with Elsa's teeth tugging at Indy's lower lip in painfully tantalizingly close-up. This is a far cry from so many nonsexual Spielbergian kisses, including the Celie-Shug "friendly" (rather than lesbian) kiss in *The Color Purple.*

Junior and Senior escape the castle, stealing an armored jeep, pursued by Nazis on motorcycles. One more satisfying action chase, the sequence also makes clear the film's symbolic implications. To fight the Nazis, Junior grabs a flag, employing it as a makeshift lance. Junior is well on his way to becoming a true "knight," like those three crusader brothers who vowed to protect the grail.

"Jesus Christ," Junior mindlessly proclaims, realizing that his father has forgotten key details. He is stunned when Senior slaps him across the face, the most shocking moment in the movie. It is like watching a *Mad* magazine "Scenes We'd Like to See" comic panel in which the unthinkable is actualized. Senior's act is too extreme: A verbal reprimand might have done the trick. Still, Senior's justification has some merit: "That's for blasphemy!" Whereas the words "Jesus Christ" are, to Junior, nothing more than an everyday expression, to Senior they signify a religious code he takes seriously: "The quest for the grail is not about archaeology," he explains. "It's a race against evil."

Junior backs down, though he does express the resentment he (and his unseen mother) felt when Senior left them to pursue his obsession: his quest for the grail. For a moment, though, their differences become minor when in Berlin they witness book burnings. "We're pilgrims in an unholy land," Senior confides as the ultimate Spielbergian "din" (the chanting of several thousand Nazis) threatens to drown them out. Elsa is reencountered, clearly less than pleased with what she sees; though Austrian-born, she is anything but a fervent party member, intellectual enough to recoil in horror at the sight. At this point, Spielberg at last presents Hitler, the great evil he has often alluded to. Fascinatingly, Hitler is portrayed less as political dictator than modern celebrity, mistaking the magical volume Junior holds for an autograph book.

Characteristically, Spielberg heroes look toward the source of spiritual illumination; here, Indy Junior and Senior do just that.

Junior and Senior escape by zeppelin, allowing for a picturesque sequence. Father and son sit across from one another, enjoying a drink, the problem of communication through language immediately surfacing as they discuss their dysfunctional relationship:

JUNIOR: The last time we had a quiet drink, I had a milk shake.
SENIOR: What did we talk about?
JUNIOR: We didn't talk. We never talked.

When Indy expresses his childhood loneliness, raised without the presence of a strong father figure, escapist entertainment again gives way to personal expression.

SENIOR: I'm here now. What do you want to talk about?
JUNIOR: I can't think of anything.
SENIOR: Then what are you complaining about?

Significantly, Senior presents his point of view, making it clear that there is a positive way to perceive his absence: he wasn't around scolding all the time, like most fathers.

Though he is less than thoroughly won over, Junior's reactions suggest he does buy some of what he hears. *Indiana Jones and the Last Crusade* was made at a time when Spielberg, himself an absentee father owing to his divorce, was beginning to portray such characters in an ever more sympathetic light.

Then two classic Hitchcock moments are combined into one uniquely Spielbergian sequence. A Nazi fighter pilot, bearing down as the heroes run along a deserted beach, rekindles memories of the unforgettable crop-dusting pursuit in *North by Northwest*. Senior brings down the enemy by squawking so much that gulls fly up wildly, as in *The Birds*. On the desert, real father and ideal father are reunited when Senior and Brody are held captive in a German tank; "in the belly of that mechanical beast," as Sallah puts it. Indy rises to heroic proportions in a spectacular chase.

When it appears that Junior has fallen over the cliff with the Nazis, Senior stares down sadly. "I never *told* him anything. I just wasn't ready, Marcus." When Junior then steps up behind them and glances down, too, the gag/audience payoff is also thematically linked to the theme of communication without language. The look that now passes between father and son makes clear they are at last communicating, without need of the talk Junior once wanted but Senior was incapable of providing.

"I thought I lost you, boy," Senior says with a sigh, embracing his son. Throughout the film, they have been physically together; this line heralds the transition to act 3. Everything has changed: now they are together emotionally as well as physically. By film's end, they will also come together spiritually as a direct result of what happens. In the hidden cave, Nazis shoot Senior as a means of inducing Junior to hurriedly follow the risky path on which numerous villains have perished. It's the villainous but believing Donovan who reminds the heroic, skeptical Junior: "The healing power of the grail is the only thing that can save your father now; it's time to ask yourself what you believe." As in previous pictures, Indy will do precisely that.

"The penitent man will pass [safely]," Senior keeps repeating, lying near death; "The penitent man will pass," Junior mutters as he bravely walks the deadly trail. At last, father and son have become secret sharers; Junior has that "conversation" he so desperately wanted with Senior, though the two men are out of earshot. Junior has become the "radio receiver" to his father's "broadcasts" and will shortly receive his Father's broadcasts as well. It is one of those psychic connections, dating back to E.T. and Elliott, so basic to Spielberg's stories.

When Junior (thanks to Senior's intense concentration) realizes the implications of that phrase and bends down a moment before a pendulum scythe can behead him, his action exists both on the level of physical reality and the metaphysical: he has at last begun to kneel before the forces he once dismissed as fairy tales. "The word" of God is what Junior must accept next as he makes a "leap of faith": stepping across an invisible bridge that spans a chasm. Spielberg's perception theme is upon us. The bridge is there, though it cannot be perceived with the eyes alone and will not support anyone who, because of its invisibility, is unable to believe in it. Junior surrenders fully to spirituality, so the bridge is there for him. As always in Spielberg, believing is seeing.

"You must believe," his father keeps repeating. Junior receives that "radio message" and, sharing it, does as he's told. When he encounters the last ancient knight, still guarding the grail (surrounded by false grails to mislead the wicked), after seven centuries, the knight recognizes Indy as heir apparent. "You're strangely dressed, for a knight," the elderly man says.

"I'm not a knight," Indy insists, unaware he has in fact become just that.

Elsa aids Indy by purposefully pointing Donovan to a shiny, silver false grail; drinking from it, he decomposes before their eyes. Indy and Elsa know that Christ's cup would be a humble carpenter's mug, carved from wood. When Indy risks all by taking a chance and drinking, he reaches full heroic height; when he pours liquid from the grail onto his father's wound and it is miraculously cured, he completely connects his father to Our Father. "The grail is a crucible for male bonding," Brian D. Johnson noted in Macleans, "bridging the father-son abyss." Elsa, consumed by greed, attempts to reach the grail, in a crevice, plunging to her death. Imperfect Indy almost makes the same mistake, though he is able to overcome the mercenary side and listen to his father, who now clearly speaks for Our Father: "Let go."

Just as the boy in Empire of the Sun had to choose between the dropped prize and the parent's hand (making the wrong choice, for which he paid dearly), so, too, does Indy have to make such a choice. And what did Senior find? For the sense of closure, he replies with the only word that serves the purpose: "Illumination." As the four heroes ride away, there is one last tag line, a gag in which Indy admits he took his name from the family dog; indeed, the name Indiana did come from Lucas's dog. If the name served as the starting point for these collaborative films, this admission to the moviegoing audience fittingly served as an ending.

In her New York Times review, Caryn James summarized the reaction of most critics and audiences: "Though it cannot regain the brash originality of Raiders of the Lost Ark, in its own way, Indiana Jones and the Last Crusade is nearly as good, matching its audience's wildest hopes" and dispelling fears of another disappointment on the order of Indiana Jones and the Temple of Doom. In Newsweek, David Ansen proclaimed: "This thrice-told tale gives you your money's worth. Now it's time to hang up the bullwhip and move on." Indeed, with the trilogy complete and reputations redeemed, Spielberg could leave the Lucas fold, pursuing several highly personal and long-planned projects.

Always

A UNIVERSAL/UNITED ARTISTS
PICTURE, 1989

CAST

Richard Dreyfuss *(Pete Sandich);* Holly Hunter *(Dorinda Durston);* Brad Johnson *(Ted Baker);* John Goodman *(Al Yackey);* Audrey Hepburn *('Hap');* Marg Helgenberger *(Rachel);* Roberts Blossom *(Dave);* Keith David *(Powerhouse).*

CREDITS

Director, Steven Spielberg; producers, Spielberg, Frank Marshall and Kathleen Kennedy; coproducer, Richard Vane; screenplay, Jerry Belson and Diane Thomas (uncredited), based on *A Guy Named Joe* by Dalton Trumbo; cinematography, Mikael Salomon; editor, Michael Kahn; music, John Williams; production design, James Bissell; costumes, Ellen Mirojnick; visual-effects supervisor, Bruce Nicholson; Technicolor and Dolby Stereo; running time, 125 mins.; rating: PG.

Every true movie lover has some special film, caught by accident on TV. Not a film of the movie lover's era, but from several years earlier, already shrouded with nostalgia when first seen, conveying to the impressionable a glowing feel for that entire period, which the viewer just missed. For Spielberg, that era would be World War II, magical for him from that moment when his father told bedtime stories about the war, conveying the sense of community which pervaded the country at a time when we were embarked on a literal crusade in Europe: a Holy

Steven Spielberg, in a notably jovial mood, directing *Always* (photo by John Shannon, courtesy Amblin Entertainment and Universal City Studios).

War in which we were heroically pure, opposing not only an enemy but also evil incarnate. Also, for Spielberg, it would have to be a film about flying, another key element of his father's wartime experiences, already something of an obsession for young Steven. Considering his metaphysical bent, it could not be one of those airborne movies which, their titles notwithstanding *(A Wing and a Prayer, Only Angels Have Wings, Air Force)* were relatively realistic; it had to touch on something spiritual in nature.

That film was Victor Fleming's 1943 paean to patriotism, *A Guy Named Joe.* In it, a flier (Spencer Tracy), killed in action, guides his replacement (Van Johnson) through training and into aerial combat, even as a romance kindles between the young flier and the former girlfriend (Irene Dunne) of his guardian angel. It is altogether possible that some other young movie fanatic (say, John Landis or Martin Scorsese) might have found this too sentimental, preferring other, tougher films from that era. But *A Guy Named Joe* was made to order for the young Spielberg's already active imagination.

In truth, *A Guy Named Joe* was never a great film of its era, on a level with *A Walk in the Sun* or *The Story of G.I. Joe.* Only an extremely tolerant viewer can stick with its obvious emotions today (emotions which, it's important to note, were in vogue a half century ago). Yet it is only fair to mention that those emotions were effectively played thanks to the guidance of veteran director Victor Fleming *(Gone With the Wind, The Wizard of Oz).* At any

Pete (Richard Dreyfuss) is an unseen presence as he watches the woman he loves, Dorinda (Holly Hunter), gradually fall in love with pilot Ted (Brad Johnson) (photo by John Shannon, courtesy Amblin Entertainment and Universal City Studios).

rate, Spielberg was obsessed with remaking *A Guy Named Joe* from early on in his career. Essential for success was a hip, modern twist on the material, provided by the writer. Initially, Diane Thomas worked on Spielberg's project. She seemed a happy choice: Her *Romancing the Stone* had taken old-fashioned romantic adventure and kept what was best about such formula films while effectively updating the clichés. When Thomas died in an automobile accident, *Joe* was turned over to Jerry Belson, who failed to provide the combination of forties whimsy and eighties wit, updating the situation from World War II fighter pilots to contemporary firefighters.

The movie was shot on locations in Montana and Washington State, with additional work completed on soundstages at Universal and Lorimar studios. Sequences at the firefighting air attack base, including the elaborate opening action sequence, were completed in Libby, Montana. Production designer Jim Bissell felt that the remoteness of that location and the breathtaking mountain backdrop would give Spielberg the needed sense of a self-contained world in which people living in our time still follow codes of conduct that were widespread forty years before.

Spielberg decided to push for this *Twilight Zone*–like quality, in which everything appears to be out of time al-

John Goodman as Al, fellow pilot and best friend to both Pete and Dorinda (photo by John Shannon, courtesy Amblin Entertainment and Universal City Studios).

together, allowing him to use vintage planes he adored. "A lot of the old World War II bomber pilots have kept their old airplanes, or at least restored, bought, and used parts and turned them into firefighting equipment," he explained while publicizing the film. "I thought that would give a timeless feeling. It's a contemporary movie. It feels like it's set in the forties, but in fact it is set today." Among the many planes employed were vintage A-26s, tanker bombers the U.S. Forest Service contracts from Denny Lynch of Lynch Flying Service of Billings, Montana.

Radiant Audrey Hepburn, star of so many golden-age Hollywood classics, came out of retirement specifically at the request of Steven Spielberg, who in movies like *Always* attempted to recapture the bygone glories of such innocent entertainments; her role is Hap, the spiritual guide who sends the deceased Pete back to earth (photo by John Shannon, courtesy Amblin Entertainment and Universal City Studios).

In addition to the proper planes, the film's producers had to create forest fires so that Spielberg could then film them, a more difficult task than it might seem. Coproducer Richard Vane later reflected: "Because forest fires aren't always cooperative and set up at angles that the camera is ready to shoot, we had the tremendous task of trying to create forest-fire scenes that were safe and shootable. With the expertise and research of special-effects coordinator Mike Wood, we created our own trees that could burn on cue; we did not burn trees that were still alive." The company did, however, record the devastating 1988 Yellowstone Park fires and featured some of that footage in their film.

The material allowed Spielberg to treat two of his most personal themes, death and the metaphysical experience, developing their relationship in a way he had not done before. Numerous Spielberg movies suggested that death can be a beginning, not an end; here, though, we watch a character embark on his spiritual life. Pete becomes a vivid example of one of those vaguely glimpsed ghosts in *Poltergeist,* the deceased who have not yet squared themselves with the world and, confused, can not find their way to the "light."

Also, by mounting a remake of a World War II–era film, Spielberg acknowledged his great, abiding love for that era, the last age of American innocence which came crashing to an end with the atomic bombing of Hiroshima, an incident he had already chronicled in *Empire of the Sun.* Strange, then, that he rejected the idea of doing *Always* as a period piece, for that would have allowed him to re-create the forties in all their glory: the planes, the clothing. Perhaps the failure of *1941* had been too much for him. At any rate, Spielberg tried to cover the updating with a single line of dialogue, when Pete's best buddy, Al, says of their airport: "What this place reminds me of is the war in Europe. B-26s: It's England, everything but Glenn Miller." In fact, the problem is that we, watching the movie, don't accept that; his words are forced onto the situation in cookie-cutter fashion, though the dough does not cut neatly, owing to a dull edge of dialogue.

Most critics felt that the decision to update doomed the film to failure. As Vincent Canby wrote in the *New York Times,* "The shift from 1943 to 1989 means the difference between Pete's dying in battle and his dying to save a friend while fighting a forest fire, and the difference is enormous; everything about the story's emphasis on sacrifice and its stirring, inspirational tone presupposes a wartime mentality." Ralph Novak of *People* added:

Spielberg's miscalculation was to forget that *A Guy Named Joe* responded to a most particular need. Coming in WWII, when young lives were so palpably precarious and the need for comforting illusions so great, it had a ready audience. These were Americans who, if not more naive than we, were at least more willing to suspend their cynicism.

Peter Travers of *Rolling Stone* insisted that the time shift

In a lovely field suggesting the happier possibilities of the afterlife, a radiant Hap (Audrey Hepburn) informs
Pete (Richard Dreyfuss) that his work on earth is not yet complete.

As Dorinda, Holly Hunter is the typical Spielberg woman (photos by
John Shannon, courtesy Amblin Entertainment and Universal City
Studios).

as if Spielberg can't decide whether he wants to make an honest movie about today's flying firefighters, whom he could easily observe firsthand at any Northwest outpost, or a sentimental film about the wartime pilots he knows only from old movies and stories told him. Either approach would probably have been fine, but the combination in a single film is uncertain and all wrong.

However, *Always* did allow Spielberg to continue his work as an essentially religious filmmaker, one who made such moral fables palatable to modern audiences by presenting them within the context of seemingly secular entertainment. Pete is one more example of the here-and-now hero who becomes aware of the spirit world, also discovering his own potential for saintly behavior. While Spielberg has always mouthed the politically correct and ingenuously liberal platitudes required of today's hip young Hollywood types, *Always* (like the films which preceded it) reveals him to be essentially traditionalist, his movies serving as propaganda pieces for old-fashioned values. In *America,* Richard Blake noted

Pete learns that he will return to earth, having failed in his lifetime to tell Dorinda that he loves her (photo by John Shannon, courtesy Amblin Entertainment and Universal City Studios).

was nothing short of "calamitous—Joe spoke to a nation's sorrow; Always lacks a similar sense of scope or urgency."

At one point, the still-living Pete and other fliers treat Dorinda like a goddess, standing in line just to get a dance with her, saying things like "Gosh!" and "Swell!" when she makes a grand entrance wearing the "girl clothes" Pete bought for her birthday. They are acting like fliers in a forties film by John Ford; since Spielberg is Ford's legitimate heir, it might have been nice to watch as he revived and reconsidered such clichés. Instead, he unwisely plays them at face value. As David Denby noted in *New York* magazine, Dorinda's grand entrance is "the most purely sexless moment in Spielberg's long, long career as a boy, and it made me realize to what extent sex in his movies is a matter of dreams and idealization." However, when Pete and Dorinda retire for the night, they do what a pair of lovers would do today: Get in bed together, though they're not married, something the couple in a forties film would never do.

Their frank attitude about sex only makes the earlier idealistic attitude toward Dorinda seem all the sillier; it's

Pete plays a joke on Al, smearing his friend's face with oil; though the story line was updated for today, the male camaraderie hearkens back to old World War II–era films (photo by John Shannon, courtesy Amblin Entertainment and Universal City Studios).

Pete is displeased to realize that his young protégé/foster son (Brad Johnson) is falling in love with Pete's girlfriend, Dorinda (Holly Hunter); Oedipal themes began to creep into Spielberg's movies as his work matured.

that "conservative Catholic theologians will enjoy Spielberg's *Always,* but not many other people will. The story presents an updated version of the traditional Catholic notion of Purgatory." Like the *Poltergeist* spirits, Pete "cannot let go of his life. His love for Dorinda is still 'eros,' the love of desire, rather than 'agape,' the pure, selfless love of benevolence. The story is quite successful as a parable, less so as a film." *Always* follows Pete's journey from selfish to selfless love as he learns how to set Dorinda free. That is a pilgrim's journey, essentially, to Christ, a journey this ostensibly Jewish filmmaker has been doing variations on (though never quite so clearly as here) since the beginning of his career.

But he did not make *Always* at the beginning of his career; he made it in 1988–89. As is always the case, the work is informed not only by the artist's ongoing attitudes but also by his specific emotional tenor at a particular point in time. It seems safe to say that had he remade *Joe* several years earlier, he would have turned out a notably different picture. Spielberg made *Always* during that period when his relationship with Amy Irving was concluding, so the film is understandably bittersweet.

How else can one explain Spielberg's shift away from what the original *Joe* was about (the likeable dead flier guiding his young protégé to heroic stature), instead gravitating toward an emphasis on problems in the Pete-Dorinda relationship. The film can be interpreted as an "objective correlative" for Spielberg's own failed relationship, transformed into mass entertainment by paralleling the business of firefighting with filmmaking. Pete is completely taken with Dorinda; he does not dream about, much less consider experiencing, any other woman. But he is more committed to his profession than

Dreyfuss as Pete, the flyboy hero; Spielberg first heard romanticized tales of heroic flyers as bedtime stories from his father, who had served in World War II.

194

to her; firefighting allows Sandich to fly (physically) just as filmmaking allows Spielberg to fly (artistically).

Each man has a soft, sweet, tender spot for his woman; each man tries but cannot deny the fact that his professional obligations take precedence, something that Marion had to learn about Indy in *Raiders of the Lost Ark.* Let's not forget that when asked what he feared most in life, Spielberg once replied: "Relationships!" Is there any doubt Sandich would have answered the same? Dorinda talks about leaving this place and enjoying a more conventional lifestyle elsewhere, while Pete teaches firefighting. (Did Spielberg and Irving ever consider taking a year off together during which he would teach filmmaking, as his colleague Brian De Palma once did?) Pete talks, sometimes seriously and sometimes sarcastically, about what it would be like to go to a normal day job instead of being constantly on call. When Pete and Dorinda slip into bed to spend their day off together, he is happy until the phone rings. "Don't answer it," she begs. On the second ring, he does. It's a call for him to go fight a fire; it's not hard to assume that Spielberg and Irving played out precisely that moment, only with an "incendiary" problem in the editing room demanding his presence.

Richard Dreyfuss, who early on played Spielberg's alter egos on film, returned to the fold for this, one of Spielberg's most highly personal projects (photo by John Shannon, courtesy Amblin Entertainment and Universal City Studios).

"Tell me you love me, tell me!" Dorinda insists, though Pete cannot reply. Another Spielbergian theme is thus initiated, communication attempted (but not completed) through language. Pete does love Dorinda but has trouble putting it into words. He is too individualistic; to mouth those words would reduce his complex emotions to the level of cliché. In Spielberg, language always impedes rather than accelerates communication. At the last possible moment, as he is about to fly off and meet his fate, Pete does at last manage to say the words, calling after Dorinda, "I love you." We hear the words, but she does not; he is drowned out by one of those mechanical Spielbergian dins, emanating from his plane's engine. The film (as compared to *Joe,* which took its ghostly hero on a decidedly different journey) is about Pete's need to communicate (wordlessly, since words do not work their intended effect) his love to Dorinda.

He accomplishes this when, toward the end, she attempts to complete a flying mission. In the original, of course, the young male lead had to be guided on the dangerous mission by his ghostly father figure; the woman patiently waited at home. Spielberg's inversion adds a

The uneasy relationship between fathers and sons (foster or biological) became a key topic for drama in Spielberg's later films.

ideas are merely given lip service in this bit of failed whimsy.

That includes the movie-about-movies theme. Al initially approaches Dorinda in the manner of a man who cannot speak directly to women but can only talk to them by hiding behind the shield of a movie situation: "Gee, Miss Scarlett," he says with a sigh, acknowledging that she is something of a goddess by assuming the approach southerners took to Scarlett O'Hara in *Gone With the Wind*. Later, Ted will attempt to convey his "Aw, shucks" western attitude toward women by lapsing into a lame John Wayne imitation. It is difficult to tell, though, whether the awfulness of the mimicry derives from Ted's character as written or is merely due to the inadequacies of Brad Johnson as an actor.

Importantly, though, Dorinda ceases to reject Ted as

Holly Hunter as Dorinda, who in the remake actually flies the final mission; in the 1940s version of the story, she remained at home while the men took care of business (photo by John Shannon, courtesy Amblin Entertainment and Universal City Studios).

feminist sensibility, allowing the woman an active rather than passive role. It also adds, however inadvertently, a discomforting quality to Spielberg's concept of family values, continuing the Oedipal theme first suggested in *Empire of the Sun*. Though Spielberg does not delve deeply into the situation here, it is important to note that in the film's finale, Pete facilitates a romantic relationship between his adopted "son" and the woman he has been sleeping with.

The ending violates, rather than sums up, what came earlier: Why watch Pete counsel Ted if, at the moment of crisis, he will instead guide Dorinda to a successful flight? At one point, Pete and Ted visit an abandoned building. There they see an old hobo (Roberts Blossom), described as being "like a radio station," presumably receiving messages from God. But this theme is not developed enough to have the kind of impact here that it did in previous Spielberg films. In truth, most of his recurring nothing more than a superficially handsome hunk, seeing him instead as a viable man in her life when he stops to help a school bus in trouble, the driver having suffered a heart attack. Ever since Mann in *Duel,* Spielberg's heroes have identified themselves as positive by rushing to school buses in distress; save the children and you win the heart of the woman as well as the filmmaker. Also, Pete—while in the plane with Dorinda—will talk to her as he would to a child, a rather unsettling notion, since she's a grown woman and his own former lover. At least he is at last able to tell her that he loves her, admitting he should have said it while he was still alive. During her near-death experience after her plane crashes into a lake, she briefly sees him and understands the emotion without having heard the words. Though we in the audience see him all along, Dorinda can only see him when she believes he is there: once again, believing is seeing.

Communication does take place, on a deeper, nonverbal level. At one point, Pete even extends his hand to her, and the image, caught in close-up, recalls the similar one in *E.T.:* Spielberg's films are about the need to communicate through touch rather than words. "My boy," Pete says of Ted before turning and walking away, embracing the light. One of the many reasons this cinematic conceit doesn't work is the musical score by John Williams. Williams's music for Spielberg's films had indeed long since become a negative factor. Whereas his classically simple theme for *Jaws* had been instrumental in making

suspense sequences click and the mock-heroic orchestration for *Raiders of the Lost Ark* suggested and supported that film's delicate balance between revival and parody, Williams had since fallen into the trap of creating music that merely pumps up the visuals, already a bit too heightened to begin with.

The result was absolute overkill. Vincent Canby of the *New York Times* complained:

Always is filled with big, sentimental moments, [but] it lacks the intimacy to make any of this very moving. Though the story calls out for simplicity, it unfolds in an atmosphere of forced laughter and forced tears. Gentle and moving as it means to be, there is barely a scene that wouldn't have worked better with less fanfare.

That is particularly true in contrast to the original, directed in a modest, understated style.

In other words, *Always*—like *Raiders of the Lost Ark*—was not a movie about a real-life experience; it was a movie about a modern grown-up's warmly recalled childhood memories of watching Hollywood movies which glorified real-life experiences. So his films represent reality twice removed. Such an approach worked in *Raiders of the Lost Ark* in a way that it could not here, since *Raiders* was essentially an escapist adventure film, whereas *Always* is meant to be a serious-minded people-relationship movie with some adventure along the way.

Hook

A TRISTAR FILM, 1991

CAST

Dustin Hoffman *(Captain Hook);* Robin Williams *(Peter Banning/Pan);* Julia Roberts *(Tinkerbell);* Bob Hoskins *(Smee);* Maggie Smith *(Granny Wendy);* Caroline Goodall *(Moira);* Charlie Korsmo *(Jack);* Amber Scott *(Maggie);* Dante Basco *(Rufio);* Glenn Close, David Crosby *(Pirates);* Phil Collins *(London Bobby).*

CREDITS

Director, Steven Spielberg; producers, Kathleen Kennedy, Frank Marshall, and Gerald R. Molen; screenplay, Jim V. Hart and Malia Scotch Marmo, from a story by Hart and Nick Castle; cinematography, Dean Cundey; film editor, Michael Kahn; music, John Williams; songs, Williams and Leslie Bricusse; production design, Norman Garwood; costumes, Anthony Powell; Panavision, Technicolor and Dolby Stereo; running time, 131 mins.; rating: PG.

Throughout the 1980s, Spielberg tossed around concepts for his own version of James Barrie's 1904 classic *Peter Pan.* In many respects, it seemed the film—concerning a little boy who refuses to grow up, can fly, and believes in magic—he was born to make. On the wall of his Universal Studios office, an autographed *Time* magazine cover of Michael Jackson, Spielberg's leading con-

Director Steven Spielberg sets up an intricate shot visualizing the film's theme of time and what its passage does to the human personality; Julia Roberts, in the background, plays Tinker Bell (courtesy TriStar Pictures).

Spielberg guides Robin Williams, as Peter Banning/Peter Pan, through a key moment in which the character, after years of mundane living in the adult world, gradually gets back in touch with his "inner child" (courtesy TriStar Pictures).

Initially, Peter Banning—contemporary yuppie—has no recollection of his past life as Peter Pan (courtesy TriStar Pictures).

tender as child-man celebrity of a generation, was framed; speculation ran rampant that Spielberg would eventually direct Jackson as Peter Pan. But the years passed, and while Jackson remained frozen in time—then unable to move into an adult relationship, eventually scandalized by claims of sexually molesting children-playmates—Spielberg grew older gracefully. He was a husband and father now and had made serious movies.

As one friend put it, "*E.T.* was Steven's *Peter Pan.* The birth of his son shut off his excitement for the theme of the boy who refuses to grow up." Understandably, then, in 1987, Spielberg firmly announced that he had permanently abandoned the project: "I've had it up to here with 'I don't want to grow up.' " What happens, though, when a father entertains his little boy and rediscovers the sim-

ple pleasures of play? A few years later, the notion of a Pan picture resurfaced, though Spielberg still refused to retract his vow. As he explained on the eve of *Hook*'s release: "Seven years ago, I had wanted to make a Peter Pan story that was essentially a live-action version of the animated Walt Disney film, one as fanciful and spectacular as the cartoon but more faithful to the Barrie play." Instead, he made a movie that concerned itself with the ongoing allure of Barrie's story. As critic Brian D. Johnson of *Macleans* would eventually quip, "Spielberg has made a movie that is less about Peter Pan than the Peter Pan syndrome."

Such a script began its germination process when, in 1982, aspiring screenwriter Jim Hart's three-year-old son, Jake, drew a sketch of Hook escaping the crocodile.

199

Peter Banning, afraid of flying (much like Spielberg himself), is aghast when, during a stormy flight, his daughter (Amber Scott) draws a sketch of the plane crashing, her dad being the only one on board without a parachute (courtesy TriStar Pictures).

The seed for a sequel was planted but required nurturing. Four years later, Jake did just that during one of their regular "What if?" games at dinnertime: "What if Peter Pan did grow up?" That set his father to wondering: Could Peter have turned out like so many of his own friends, "suits" that had lost touch with the spontaneous little boys they had once been?

Hart sent his story around to the studios, but everyone passed. Then coproducers Craig Baumgarten and Gary Adelson read his treatment and felt that it had enough potential to team Hart with Nick Castle, an experienced writer. After working together for almost a year, with less than spectacular results, Castle was dropped. A parade of other people waltzed in and out, including actress-turned-writer Carrie Fisher, who penned the quasi-feminist Tinker Bell dialogue. The Indians (a major presence in Hart's first draft) were excised for fear that this might be misconstrued as racial caricaturing. Many critics eventually complained that the film appeared to have been written by a committee of politically correct types trying to please everyone.

At some point, Dustin Hoffman read the script and became enthused. He felt it was perfect for Spielberg, with whom he had originally hoped to do *Rain Man,* about an autistic man with childlike qualities whose optimism al-

most magically transforms his jaded brother, a perfect Spielberg premise. However, after five months of pre-production, Spielberg had begrudgingly dropped out to meet previous Indiana Jones commitments. Hoffman hoped *Hook* might be the film he and Spielberg were meant to do together.

To ensure box-office potential for a film initially budgeted at $40 million, soon soaring to more than $79 million, it was necessary to have star insurance. Spielberg had previously stated, "My major desire is not to make movies with people who have been on the cover of *Rolling Stone.*" Working with lesser-known people allowed him to avoid egos and salary demands, concentrating on elaborate set designs, special effects, and his

The elaborate flying and fighting sequences were all filmed on stylized studio set designs, which Spielberg hoped to locate at one of the Universal theme parks after filming was completed.

200

personal vision. Now, though, big names were obligatory. Hoffman's participation made it easier to sign others, though he brought with him his long-standing reputation as "difficult Dustin," the perfectionist. Deciding to base his characterization on conservative TV commentator William F. Buckley Jr., Hoffman brought along his own writer, Malia Scotch Marmo, to further develop his character. Hart would eventually claim that "Steven tends to use writers like paintbrushes. He wants this writer for this, this writer for that," literally "directing" assorted writers as well as his legion of actors.

Finally, Robin Williams agreed to play Peter. The film could only be green-lighted if Spielberg, Hoffman, and Williams agreed to work for no conventional salary at all.

Instead, they would split 40 percent of the box-office grosses (as compared to net profits, which are often nonexistent even with successful films), considered the richest participation deal ever. Julia Roberts—signed for $2.5 million, having emerged as the hottest actress in Hollywood thanks to *Pretty Woman*—would be Tinker Bell. Having signed to play the part, the twenty-three-year-old actress suddenly admitted herself to a hospital (claiming "sheer exhaustion"), called off her impending marriage to actor Kiefer Sutherland, then jetted off to Ireland to see her new boyfriend, actor Jason Patric. Rumors ran rampant that Roberts would fail to show up and be replaced by either Michelle Pfeiffer or Kim Basinger, though she in fact did report for work. Roberts's sequences were all completed over a tight, intense several days, during which the actress had little contact with other cast members. Mostly, she stood in costume with blue screens behind her, oversized props and forced-perspective sets around her, pretending to be seven inches tall while speaking to unseen people or reacting to things that were not there.

The other performers, however, shared the vast soundstages at M-G-M. *Hook* was the first Spielberg movie to be shot completely (exteriors as well as interiors) on soundstages. The film's Neverland set cost $8 million to build. The creation of individual sets (pirate ship, lost boys' camp, etc.) was jointly undertaken by Oscar-nominated production designer Norman Garwood *(Glory; Brazil),* collaborating with visual consultant John Napier, celebrated for such live-theater pieces as *Cats, Les Misérables,* and *Miss Saigon.* Basic to the success of those shows was Napier's glorious theatricality; the key question was whether such a patently artificial look

Rufio (Dante Bosco, *center*) and the other lost boys circle around the newly arrived Peter (courtesy TriStar Pictures).

would go over with a modern moviegoing audience, which has little in common with the audience for a Broadway play.

Certainly, such an approach had worked in the golden age: the Kansas farm where Dorothy lives, as well as the colorful Oz she is whisked off to, are equally theatrical. *The Wizard of Oz,* which had already influenced previous Spielberg movies, would certainly have an impact on *Hook.* Spielberg gleefully announced that Stage 27 at the Sony studio (previously M-G-M) where he was now working had been a key soundstage for Victor Fleming's film. The theme of flying off from the real world to a fantastic one is basic to both stories; Spielberg's film, like 1939's *Wizard of Oz,* concludes with a child asking to go home.

In *Hook,* that child was played by Charlie Korsmo, fresh from *Dick Tracy* with Warren Beatty. Children proved essential to Spielberg's film in theme as well as plot: Spielberg, Hoffman, and Williams had each discovered the joy of parenting, often swapping stories on the set about experiences with their own kids. Korsmo's child compatriots, the lost boys ranging in age from six to 15, were professional child actors and everyday kids who looked right for the parts. A few, such as skateboarding champion Frankie Hill, were cast owing to unique skills. Spielberg conceived of his lost boys as an ultramodern interracial mix. Hoffman's own son Maxwell was eventually cast as Peter the child in a flashback scene.

For adult pirate extras, 150 surly types were recruited at biker hangouts in and around L.A. Strictly forbidden to fraternize with actors, they were herded off to their own humble rest area between shots. When the bikers realized

The touch: As in such previous Spielberg films as *E.T.,* the ultimate communication takes place not during speech but in the action of an innocent touch. One of the lost boys believes Peter Banning really is Peter Pan, "seeing" him as such only after touching him (courtesy TriStar Pictures).

The theme of time as well as the desire to escape from the ravages of time (and the need to grow up) by flying away are emphasized by omnipresent clocks in the cabin of Captain Hook (Dustin Hoffman, *center*); he is flanked by Smee (Bob Hoskins) and Peter's son (Charlie Korsmo) (courtesy TriStar Pictures).

Character actors in tandem: Dustin Hoffman as Captain Hook takes the earnest advice of Bob Hoskins as First Mate Smee.

they were being fed pretzels and water while stars snacked on soup and chili, several all but mutinied. Two pirates, however, were actually big names: rocker David Crosby and (disguised as a male) Glenn Close.

Though the set designers had gone to work as early as August 1990, ultimately filling nine soundstages, Spielberg did not begin the shoot until mid-February 1991. Principal photography would continue for a whopping 116 days. For the complex flying sequences, Spielberg strapped actors into harnesses and crane-hoisted them, then employed a "flying camera" technique, Cablecam, to make the final results appear "without strings"; though realism was not an issue, believability indeed was. From there, the crew moved to

Stage 12 (for the tree house, which resembled the one in Disney's *Swiss Family Robinson*), then on to Stage 27 for the *Jolly Roger*. It had to be the pirate ship to end all pirate ships, emerging as a composite of various seventeenth-century wooden vessels, intermingling elements of a British frigate with Spanish baroque. Completed, the vessel ran 35 feet wide, 170 feet long, and 70 feet high at the mainmast. Originally, it was to continuously move, motored by huge truck inner tubes linked together hydraulically so that crew members could inflate or deflate each tire for the proper rocking sensation. Unfortunately, the chandeliers in Hook's cabin swayed to the point of distraction; Spielberg decided that the ship had dropped anchor and would remain still.

Extending from the *Jolly Roger* was the pirate wharf. A large working roller coaster, built on Sony Sound Stage 30, whisked the lost boys through their playground, which (being out of time) features favorite elements from each of the four seasons. "Every day it was like going to work at Disneyland," claimed Dante Basco, who played Rufio, oldest of the lost boys. Indeed, many critics would eventually complain that the film did not appear to have been shot on a movie set at all but at a theme park built to capitalize on the success of the movie. Fact is, following the completion of filmmaking, Spielberg approached Universal Orlando, hoping to relocate his set designs there. For Spielberg, this approach marked a return to the glory days of films and filmmakers he admired: "There hadn't been anything like these sets built in Hollywood since the golden era. Sets that seem extraordinary to us now were standard operating procedure in the 1930s and 1940s. We created an entire world here, just like [in] *Oz,* and on the same stages."

Next to the ship, an elaborate camera scaffold had been placed on wheels. It was capable of being raised and lowered several stories to capture stunts in which 175 bodies (the most ever for such a scene) would swing across on ropes. Spielberg instructed his stunt coordinator to watch old pirate movies like *The Sea Hawk* for inspiration, then to "outdo those classics, but do it safely!" The approach, clearly, was that if it's bigger, it will be better, though that does not always prove true. The enormity of the undertaking (compared to the budgetary restraint Spielberg had exercised on such intellectually stimulating projects as *The Color Purple*) caused a psychoanalyst, Dr. Harvey Greenberg, to write a six-page study of the director's state of mind, concluding: "*Hook* could be a sign of the failure of inspiration that has stricken many other artists at Spielberg's vulnerable age." There is evidence that at some point Spielberg himself began to wonder if the final result would prove entertaining or excessive. The filmmaker admitted to Ivor Davis of the *London Sunday Times:* "Every day I came on to the set, I thought, 'Is this flying out of control?'"

Principal photography at last ceased in September, at which point the enormous task of postproduction began, including addition of music, painstaking editing, and special-effects shots. When the movie premiered in mid-December, Spielberg had just turned forty-four, precisely the age Barrie had been when his play premiered at London's Duke of York Theatre in 1904.

Like *Indiana Jones and the Temple of Doom, Hook* announces its self-conscious artificiality in its first shot, a tight image of Peter and Wendy. Quickly, though, the camera pulls back to reveal that these are child actors, being coached (they forget their lines) by a nearby drama teacher. What we are watching, then, is a new film about an old play; that will be true not only of the first scene but also all of *Hook.* Even the brief dialogue, seemingly arbitrary, is significant: "I don't ever want to become a man. Always, I want to be a little boy and have fun."

With only the slightest alteration, this could be lifted from an early interview with Spielberg, speaking about why he chose to make escapist movies.

When I became a man, a profound line of poetry tells us, I put aside childish things. *Hook* can be viewed as a necessary film for Spielberg; with it, he attempts to put aside the Peter Pan myth by dealing, through the creation of a new drama about the old myth, with his own ongoing obsession with it. So we meet Peter Banning, in the audience of this grade-school show (his daughter plays Wendy), trying to concentrate even as a beeper sounds.

Spielberg reflected to interviewer Clifford Terry: "I'm part of a generation that is extremely motivated by career, and I've caught myself in the unenviable position of being Peter Banning from time to time. I've seen myself overworked and not spending enough time at home." The film is a highly personal autobiography disguised as mass-market entertainment. Peter is a cutthroat corporate raider, one of those upscale yuppie lawyers who were the dominant screen heroes of the Reagan era. Then, after Oliver Stone's *Wall Street,* the stock market crash of 1987, and the Boesky-Milken scandals, such "heroes"

Jack (Charlie Korsmo) and Maggie (Amber Scott) feel quite differently about their father after he has rediscovered his own inner child (courtesy TriStar Pictures).

were reassessed in life and art, now seen as (at best) questionable characters. However distracted, Peter at least managed to show up for his daughter's play; the following day, when he is supposed to attend his boy's baseball game, he arrives late.

Peter's dysfunctional relationship with his son reintroduces another key theme:

PETER: When are you going to stop acting like a child?
JACK: I am a child!
PETER: Grow up!

Jack has wisdom, which the highly educated Peter lacks. Once more, the child is father to the man.

"Well," Peter constantly tells people, "gotta fly," running off to his next business meeting. When the entire family boards a commercial jet and heads for London to visit Peter's grandmother, Wendy Darling, Peter looks suspiciously like John Lithgow in the "Nightmare at 20,000 Feet" segment of *Twilight Zone—The Movie,* ter-

rified to be aboard. That may sound ironic for a Spielberg hero. "Flying machines always represent transcendence in Spielberg's universe," Bob Strauss wrote in the *L.A. Daily News.* How fascinating to learn, then, that Spielberg once made a surprising confession: "I'm afraid to fly in real life." Spielberg is Peter; Peter is Spielberg.

The concept that life and theater cannot be neatly separated, however much we might try, is reestablished the moment they arrive. Whereas the initial scenes in the United States featured a harsh, realistic, contemporary look, Wendy's Kensington Street purposefully appears Victorian, as if (owing to her personality, having grown old gracefully without ever losing childlike wonder), time has virtually stood still here. It makes sense that when Peter's daughter Maggie asks if Granny is the Wendy of the old story, Moira answers, "Yes!" at the same moment Peter says, "No!" This time it is the female who remains open to magical connections.

Maggie, like her mother, instinctually *believes:* "I just played you in school," she tells Wendy upon meeting her. "One rule that must be obeyed in my house," Wendy insists. "No growing up!" She resembles one of those elderly people whose souls are still young in "Kick the Can." Wendy explains that Sir James Barrie lived next door when she was young, loved the adventure stories she and her brothers played, and so wrote them all down in a book. Wendy confides something even Mr. Barrie didn't know: "They were all true!"

Moira is an admirable adult: "How long do our children want us around? A few years, then it's over. You're not being careful—you're missing it!" Her husband fails to see that true magic is present in the most mundane activities, something Spielberg, Hoffman, and Williams all had learned through parenthood. At the hospital, where a wing is being dedicated to Granny Wendy, we learn that over the years she has adopted, then placed in foster homes, dozens of "lost" children (all in attendance as adults), including Peter. As he speaks in tribute, cross-cutting reveals that fabled Spielbergian light ("illumination!"), back at the Darling residence, into which his children are absorbed: we know, from previous experience, that this can result in the wondrous (Close Encounters of the Third Kind) or the horrifying (Poltergeist). We also note the magical connection between children and the elderly as Wendy psychically senses something is happening. She and the children are secret sharers: "My God!" Wendy invokes the Lord's name not blasphemously (as in Indiana Jones and the Last Crusade) but out of awareness of the spiritual aspect of what is transpiring.

Unlike the Poltergeist parents, the Bannings do call the police, though Wendy privately confides to Peter that this will accomplish nothing. She explains that he once was Peter Pan (he considers her mad or senile), who gave up perpetual youth when, visiting the mature Wendy, he fell in love with her granddaughter (Moira) and joined the real world, eventually forgetting everything. "Only you can save your children," Wendy insists. "Somehow you must go back; you must make yourself remember!"

In earlier films, Spielberg depicted mothers saving their children, while fathers stood around helplessly. After hitting the age forty, Spielberg changed his tune: in Indiana Jones and the Temple of Doom, Hook, and Schindler's List, father (biological or surrogate) brings the children home. Having become a parent, suffering through a divorce which caused him to be something of an absentee parent, Spielberg now had no choice but to empathize. He now respected what he earlier resented, as illustrated in the Jones Junior and Senior reconciliation of Indiana Jones and the Last Crusade. No wonder, then, onetime Spielberg agent now executive Mike Medavoy proclaimed: "If you look at Steven's body of work and you see [Hook], it's the culmination of all his work rolled into one." Peter also serves as a fitting portrait of the modern American male, intent on "rediscovering the lost child" within himself. In Peter's case, that nineties concept is taken literally.

When Tinker Bell appears, she is Disney's 1953 Monroe-like conception merged with the stage notion of a moving ball of light. She also introduces the idea of a movie about movies: Her flickering light makes her initial scene appear to be something out of a silent film.

"I'm dying," Peter cries as he's drawn to her white light; the theme of death, so significant in previous Spielberg films, will be further developed here. Yet Peter clings to his realism: "I do not believe in fairies," he tells Tinker Bell, echoing the words of Indiana Jones. Whether fairies, ghosts, or gods, the Spielberg protagonist must, during his hero's journey, overcome his limiting realism, learning to believe in something (anything) beyond the here and now. But Peter is not yet ready to fly (physically or spiritually), so Tinker Bell must carry him off to Neverland, forcing him to face Hook, who kidnapped the children to draw Pan back for one last duel. This paunchy, middle-aged man is no fit adversary, so Hook gives Tinker Bell three days to ready him.

The lost boys he encounters constitute a punk youth cult. They angrily turn on the adult Peter ("He's old!") for the same reason the hippie youth of a quarter century earlier (briefly glimpsed in Jaws's opening beach sequence) would have collectively stated: "Don't trust anyone over thirty!" As in Jaws, Spielberg does not accept their attitude at face value. Just as Peter must, from them, learn to recapture magic, they have much to learn, too. By the end, they will accept this post-thirty adult as friend and leader. First, though, they must help him "see" again (the

Hook, the false father figure, threatens Banning (Robin Williams), the lapsed but decent true father who, by film's end, will complete a hero's journey worthy of Joseph Campbell, redeeming himself in the process.

While Smee (Bob Hoskins, *center*) looks on, Captain Hook wears the adult glasses discarded by Peter (courtesy TriStar Pictures).

limited-perception theme); the logical first step occurs when they physically remove his glasses, Peter then sees once more with childlike wonder. Significantly, they accept Peter only after touching him, running their hands all over his face; for them, sight means nothing. They do not believe until they first experience tactilely. Fingers extended toward him, each appears a variation on E.T., with his own extended magical finger.

"Death is the only way to adventure," Hook confides to Smee in his cabin, even as (in a most bizarre moment) he lifts a pistol to his head, contemplating suicide. Death permeates this motion picture, culminating in the unexpected death of a child. In the meantime, Smee devises a plan to destroy Pan: make Peter's children like, even love, Hook. This allows for another key theme, the cautionary-fable warning against false father figures, who appear the ideals that lonely children wish their own flawed fathers could be. To win over the children would be the ultimate revenge.

Meanwhile, back at the lost boys' woodland hideaway, Peter is succeeding at unlearning all the baggage of his adult vision. He does this precisely as the Spielberg hero must, by rejecting the adult's seeing-is-believing approach. When the lost boys sit down for dinner and open huge pots, a disappointed Peter sees nothing there. Then he learns to communicate, trading quips in slang (which he previously did not use) with Rufio, prince of punks. "You're playing with us, Peter," another child happily announces. Peter realizes this is true. He has, like the adults in "Kick the Can," discovered that to play with children is to recover something of childhood that was in danger

207

of being lost forever. Sharing their perception, he believes; when he looks back at his dinner plate, it is full. Believing is seeing.

The food fight that follows is, as Richard Schickel noted in *Time,* "dismal and realized without conviction." Fortunately, Spielberg quickly moves on to more pertinent matters: "Do you remember your mother, Peter?" a boy asks, rekindling memories of Disney's *Peter Pan.* ("Your mother, and mine . . . ," surrogate-mother Wendy sang to the animated lost boys.) Spielberg then crosscuts to Jack, surrendering to the seductive charms of the false father figure, even as his sister (a potential mother, therefore more wise than the male) sighs sadly. Hook smashes watches, symbolically killing time; Jack

Peter Banning gets in touch with his own inner child and reverts back to Peter Pan.

Steven Spielberg shares the "dailies" with Julia Roberts (*left*) and Robin Williams (*right*) (courtesy TriStar Pictures).

mutters that his conversion to Hook is revenge "for (my father) never doing anything with me."

"My Jack!" Hook gloats at the baseball game he arranges, when the boy hits a home run. Peter, disguised and in the stands, sadly says: "My Jack?" However fabricated the setting, the scene's emotions sting: It is the horror every biological father must feel while watching his son's foster father cheer him on at some Little League ball game.

"Fly!" Peter keeps repeating, knowing that to actually take flight would complete his conversion. Peter peers into a lake, noticing a child's reflection staring back; just as in "Kick the Can," the adult physically becomes a child at that moment when he totally surrenders to child-like vision. Spielberg—through his surrogate Peter—finally forces himself to put into words the reason for his own attitudes during two decades as a moviemaker: "I was afraid . . . I didn't want to grow up, because everybody who grows up has to die someday." Clinging to childhood is a denial of death.

However, Spielberg also said, as he approached forty, that he wanted to stop being a child and instead have a child; the birth of that child ended his desire to make the movie Peter Pan or to go on being the movie business's own Peter Pan. Understandably, this situation is dramatized: in flashback, Peter witnesses the birth of Jack.

Moira hands him the baby, saying: "You're a father, Peter." The moment—so surprisingly realistic in the context of this fantastic film—can hardly be invented. It wouldn't be surprising to learn that this is precisely what his wife said to Spielberg when she handed him their child for the first time. When Peter then recalls the motivation for his transition, it is clearly autobiographical: "I know why I grew up—I wanted to be a father!"

Then what for many proved to be the most difficult moment in the movie occurred: The death of Rufio at the hands of Hook. It is worth noting that Peter initially interrupted the Hook-Rufio duel, planning to fight the captain himself but flying off when his daughter called out for help. The film's unexpected death of a child allowed Spielberg to at last artistically come to terms with, and by so doing put behind him, the most horrific moment of his career: the *Twilight Zone* accident. Just as Peter is not there when Rufio needs him, so was producer Spielberg not on the set that night. In saving one child, there will always be another left unattended. Though Spielberg was not on the set when that awful accident occurred and ultimately was in no way held legally responsible, there must have been a degree to which, deep down, he held himself accountable. That guilt, expressed through Schindler in the realistic movie to come, also informs Peter Banning's sense of loss.

Peter quotes Barrie, that dark, disturbing line eliminated from so many Pan adaptations: "To die would be a great adventure." Spielberg heroes have, for some time, learned to accept death as precisely that. When Peter says it, we are inclined to believe that Spielberg has at last convinced himself. Family values are also at the forefront: "Dad, I want to go home," Jack admits, helping the father realize that death, however great an adventure, is not something one should embrace too soon: Life, too, is a great adventure. Motherhood, less emphasized in this film than in others, is also an issue: "You need a mother very, very badly," Peter's daughter informs Hook.

Peter has at last emerged as a savior. "We *believe* in you," the lost boys tell him. As in previous Spielberg films, the ultimate goal of the adventure is to discover the divinity in each person. "Say it and mean it, Peter Pan," Tinker Bell insists; "I believe in fairies," he says, negating his own earlier realistic attitude and accepting the existence of a spirituality out there. Hook is apparently beyond hope. When the crocodile statue crashes down on him, he disappears into its mouth, the camera peering out from inside, echoing *Jaws.*

Generally, critics did not care for the film. Vincent Canby of the *New York Times* groused that "the movie's obviously expensive scale inhibits the fun instead of enhancing it." Pauline Kael of the *New Yorker* complained that "its tricks feel strained; we're constantly aware of the backbreaking effort it's taking to produce them, and that's no kind of magic at all," adding that the final assault on the pirate ship recalled "the rote, mechanical quality of hourly demonstrations at a theme park." David Ansen of *Newsweek* noted that the "Neverland sets are a letdown; overlit, they have the cheesy artifice of a run-down amusement Park. . . . *Hook* is a huge party cake of a movie with too much frosting. After the first delicious bite, sugar shock sets in." Peter Travers wrote in *Rolling Stone:* "The film has been engineered for merchandising potential and the widest possible appeal. What's missing is the one thing that really counts: charm."

Hook grossed $13.5 million during its first weekend, a total of $20 million for its initial week in 2,197 theaters. Ordinarily, that would be a considerable sum, though disappointing for a movie with three top stars by the world's most popular director. Though the film continued to draw in customers, most exited theaters feeling if not unsatisfied, then less than enthused. The film never came close to equaling in emotional appeal or box-office impact such Spielberg films as *Jaws, E.T.,* or *Jurassic Park.* Spielberg himself admitted: "Maybe *Hook* is going to be the last big show I put on. A lot of my movies in the future are going to have to scale down." The failure of the film keyed the end of an era not only for Spielberg but also for the movie business, which would soon regain a sense of fiscal responsibility.

Jurassic Park

A UNIVERSAL FILM, 1993

CAST

Sam Neill *(Grant);* Laura Dern *(Ellie);* Jeff Goldblum *(Ian Malcolm);* Richard Attenborough *(Hammond);* B. D. Wong *(Wu);* Samuel L. Jackson *(Arnold);* Wayne Knight *(Nedry);* Joseph Mazzello *(Tim);* Ariana Richards *(Lex);* Bob Peck *(Muldoon);* Martin Ferrero *(Donald Gennaro).*

CREDITS

Director, Steven Spielberg; screenplay, Michael Crichton and David Koepp, from the novel by Crichton; cinematography, Dean Cundey; editor, Michael Kahn; music, John Williams; production design, Rick Carter; dinosaur effects, Dennis Muren, Michael Lantieri, Stan Winston, Phil Tippett; producers, Kathleen Kennedy and Gerald R. Molen; running time, 123 min.; rating: PG-13.

Just as Peter Benchley's *Jaws* had been picked up by producers while still in galley form, so, too, would Michael Crichton's novel be spotted by Universal in May 1990, long before it reached bookstores. The studio made their $2 million bid on behalf of Spielberg, producer Kennedy later explaining that "it was one of those projects that was so obviously a Spielberg film." In many ways, she was right: a theme park in which dinosaurs break loose and run rampant was essentially *Jaws* reset at

Steven Spielberg envisions a shot *(left)*, then checks through the viewfinder *(right)* to make certain the final result will be precisely what he wanted (photos by Murray Close, courtesy Amblin Entertainment and Universal).

a futuristic Epcot Center. On the other hand, there was much in the novel that didn't seem Spielbergian. Crichton continuously ground his narrative to a halt, offering lengthy, unfilmable informational discussions about DNA cloning.

Many readers were shocked to hear that the "benign" Spielberg would make such a movie. He, meanwhile, remained deeply disturbed over the outcry against violence following the release of *Indiana Jones and the Temple of Doom.* Such concern became his operating principle for planning *Jurassic Park.* Spielberg at once made it clear

to Crichton that he had no intention of filming the book as written. Instead, he would take Crichton's basic concept and completely reinvent it as a Spielberg film. Though there would be scares aplenty (Spielberg emphasized in the media that he would not allow his own four children under the age of eight to see it), they would be "good scares," the lion's share of violence taking place offscreen.

John Hammond, owner and creator of the park, would be transformed from a nasty megalomaniac, interested only in acquiring power and making money, into a well-

John Hammond (Richard Attenborough, *second from left*), the park's creator, was transformed from Michael Crichton's greedy capitalist villain into an egalitarian democrat; here he joyfully welcomes Dr. Ellie Sattler (Laura Dern), lawyer Donald Gennaro (Martin Ferrero), chaos theorist Ian Malcolm (Jeff Goldblum), and Dr. Alan Grant (Sam Neill) (photo by Murray Close, courtesy Amblin Entertainment and Universal).

The miracle of birth: Ian, Hammond, Ellie, and Grant gaze on in amazement as a baby raptor pecks its way out of the shell (photo by Murray Close, courtesy Amblin Entertainment and Universal).

intentioned, charming old bumbler, tragically overeager to share a wonderful dream with the children of the world: Walt Disney by way of King Lear. Instead of the apocalyptic ending (in Crichton's novel, the island is bombed into oblivion), the more optimistic (and commercially savvy) Spielberg would allow *Tyrannosaurus rex* to remain alive, leaving the door open for a sequel. A purely practical decision was to reduce the book's fifteen species of dinosaurs to a more affordable six, which could be achieved within the considerable yet limited budget, $56 million, later updated to $65 million.

Though Crichton would, under Spielberg's guidance, streamline his own story, he would be joined by David Koepp, screenwriter for the dark comedy *Death Becomes Her.* As with *Jaws,* humor had to be added. Koepp created some of the film's memorable lines, including chaos theorist Ian Malcolm's comparison of their problem to Disneyland's disastrous opening day: "When the Pirates of the Caribbean ride breaks down, the pirates don't eat the tourists."

While Crichton and Koepp were collaborating, Spielberg and producer Kennedy began a two-year preproduction period, carefully planning the dinosaur effects that would either make or break the movie. First hired was Rick Carter, production designer on the second and third *Back to the Future* films. Again employing his sto-

ryboard approach, Spielberg carefully told Carter his vision for *Jurassic Park*'s ultrarealistic look. Carter then assembled a group of illustrators who created the initial tableaus for each of the film's images. These were then submitted to Spielberg, who gave his blessing or made suggestions for changes. When at last the vision in Spielberg's mind had been translated by Carter's team onto paper, the key reference for all the work to follow had been established. Hundreds of craftsmen who would work on *Jurassic Park* always referred back to this "Bible."

Lata Ryan was hired as associate producer, bringing together a "dream team" which could accomplish the goal. Just as with *Jaws* and *E.T.* (seemingly ambitious in their time, child's play in comparison to this) multiple models for the shark and alien were necessary, so, too, would they need various renditions for each of the film's dinosaurs.

Stan Winston (who had recently worked on *Aliens*) created life-sized action-model dinosaurs. He spent a full year on research, working with paleontologists to make certain that his creations were as true to what experts believe dinosaurs were really like as possible. Then his team created fifth-scale sculptures and, working from them, assembled full-scale creations, including a twenty-foot *T. rex* constructed from a frame of fiberglass and

Realizing Jurassic Park is in a state of emergency, computer expert Ray Arnold (Samuel L. Jackson; *left*) and John Hammond hope to restore order (photo by Murray Close, courtesy Amblin Entertainment and Universal).

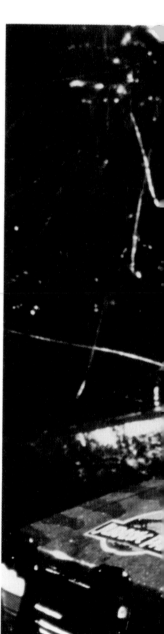

Dr. Alan Grant begins his hero's journey while taking his first step on the road to maturity and eventual fatherhood by rescuing the little girl Lex (Ariana Richards) from the *T. rex* (photo by Murray Close, courtesy Amblin Entertainment and Universal).

214

three thousand pounds of clay, covered with latex skin, mounted on a "dino simulator" composed of hydraulic technology. Once accomplished, this creature could be "actuated" (moved) through a computer control board. Winston and his craftsmen first rehearsed the necessary moves with their "Waldo" (smaller model), computer-recording the movements they wanted, then programming the full-size *T. rex* to repeat those actions. In addition, Winston's team of sixty artists, engineers, and puppeteers also created a *Velociraptor, Brachiosaurus, Triceratops, Gallimimus, Dilophosaurus* ("Spitter"), and a baby Raptor that hatches from an egg.

Initially, Spielberg had planned to use life-sized models and miniatures exclusively. All of that changed owing to a happy case of timing. Lucas's Industrial Light and Magic (ILM) entered the scene. Dennis Muren, ILM's effects supervisor, brought computer graphics to the mix, having just perfected a concept called "morphing" for the fluid transition sequences in *Terminator 2: Judgment Day.* Muren's team built the bones and skeleton of a dinosaur in a computer and from that created a walk cycle for the film's *T. rex.* Spielberg was initially wary of using computer-generated dinosaurs for his movie, since computer-graphics monsters had, in the past, appeared stilted and soulless, fully animated but somehow less than alive, with a zombielike quality that was off-putting.

According to Muren, Spielberg was absolutely blown away by what he saw: computer graphic creatures that

The classic confrontation: The resuscitated *T. rex* eyeballs an assortment of contemporary types in the theme-park movie to end all theme-park movies.

In the dinosaur world, there is good and bad, as in the human world; here Tim (Joseph Mazzello), Dr. Grant, and Lex feed a friendly "veggie" *Brachiosaurus*, who resembles a gigantic E.T. (photo by Murray Close, courtesy Amblin Entertainment and Universal).

Lantieri, responsible for surmounting mechanical challenges posed by the work of the other teams. Lantieri created exterior cranes and immense hydraulics systems to facilitate movement of full-size models, also designing camera riggings that were carefully customized to move in tandem with Winston's creations so that the final film would leave the viewer with a sense of sharing the actual movement that takes place on-screen rather than (as in previous dinosaur movies) watching the movement of the beasts from a safe distance, owing to an essentially static camera.

While all this was going on, numerous soundstages at Universal were being prepared for live-action filming. Four months of principal photography began on August 24, 1992, on the island of Kauai. Three weeks were spent filming in the lush tropical paradise until Hurricane Iniki flattened all the locations one day before completion.

The makeshift family unit: Though not biologically related, the man and woman become foster parents to the frightened children (photo by Murray Close, courtesy Amblin Entertainment).

were totally convincing in terms of life as well as movement. Muren himself admitted, "Six months before, we didn't think we could do that." A breakthrough software program called Matador, provided by a small British company, Parallax, provided animators with an automatic sense of perspective, "brushes" which allowed for easy creation of shadows or smears of mud on a creature's back, and 16.7 million different hues for full verisimilitude of color. ILM representatives had seen the product at a computer-graphics trade show and bought it. Now animator Steve Williams could create the illusion that the dinosaur's skin was moving and his belly swaying. One look and Spielberg knew he had just seen the future; his film would be the first to include it.

ILM created the stampede of frightened *Gallimimus*, several wide-angle shots of dinosaurs in herds, as well as a strikingly convincing computer-generated image of the *T. rex* walking in daylight. All in all, there are fifty-four computer-graphics sequences, totalling six and a half minutes of running time. The large models, originally set to dominate the filmmaking, were employed only for sequences in which actors and creatures mix, such as the scene in which Ellie nurses a sick *Triceratops*. For that, the dino model was flown to the Hawaii location; the others were all left behind.

The fourth effects unit was headed by Michael

Producer Kennedy pulled her crew together, and shortly they were all back in L.A., shooting the pursuit of the children by a pair of raptors through an industrial-size kitchen set on Stage 24. From there they moved to Red Rock Canyon State Park in the Mojave Desert, which subs for the Montana dinosaur dig site. Then it was back to Universal Studios, Stage 27, the sequence in which a car slowly slips from the tree branch on which it precariously hangs. Lantieri's team had created a series of steel cables that carefully controlled every movement during the seemingly random drop of the vehicle.

One somewhat insurmountable problem was finding a way to condense the wealth of scientific information Crichton's book included, explaining the nature of DNA cloning. Details would bog down the film in data, yet it would also be a mistake to allow the audience no semblance of understanding of what was taking place. Spielberg and his writers found a uniquely cinematic way

Family values: Grant reluctantly but gradually accepts his role as father figure to the lost children, insuring that his ongoing relationship with Ellie will work out.

Paleontologist Grant examines a dinosaur egg as the children—symbolically becoming his children—gaze on (photo by Murray Close, courtesy Amblin Entertainment and Universal/MCA).

around the problem. When John Hammond's invited guests arrive, before taking "the tour" they are first herded into an auditorium to watch a short film. Through the use of a cute cartoon, they (and we) are amused while also absorbed by this short form, simplified for the masses. Mr. DNA humorously explains that millions of years ago mosquitoes sucked the blood of dinosaurs, then were trapped in amber. Recently, scientists drew from those mosquitoes enough preserved dinosaur blood to clone one.

The cartoon approach works because the animated film is a precise rendering of ones used in Disney's theme parks to introduce such rides. The cartoon also allows for one of Spielberg's movies within a movie. The characters in his film watch this film, and we watch over their shoulders, breaking down the barrier between moviegoing audience and the film's characters. Also, it allows Spielberg an opportunity to create a homage. When Hammond runs the movie for guests, he stands by the screen, though he is also one of the live-action players in his miniature movie. While allowing us the first notion that Hammond is something of a dual personality (there he is, two of him, before our very eyes), Spielberg acknowledges the first filmmaker to put a dinosaur on-screen.

That was Winsor McCay, who created "Gertie the Dinosaur" around the turn of the century. Having completed a simple pen-and-ink limited-animation sketch-cartoon about *Brontosaurus* Gertie, McCay then combined cartoon with live-action footage of himself, Gertie seemingly interreacting with him. McCay also arranged for "personal appearances" in which he would step onto the stage of some auditorium, speak to his audience, then

Menaced children have always played a key element in Spielberg films, whether it's the child Tim (Joseph Mazello) hiding from beasties in this fun-chiller, or the little boy desperately hiding from Nazis in Spielberg's next (and most deadly serious) project, *Schindler's List.*

slip behind the screen as a filmed live-action image of himself interacted with the animated Gertie. More than a theme-park owner, then, Hammond represents every filmmaker, beginning with McCay and on up to Spielberg, who has ever presented the plausible impossible of a dinosaur coming back to life. Though there is no *Brontosaurus* in Jurassic Park (the place or the film), what we see in the cartoon is the enchantingly inimical Gertie. Gertie was (somewhat surprisingly for 1900) a female; all the dinosaurs in Spielberg's film are also female, a key plot point being that they learn to reproduce without the necessity of men. That introduces a quasi-feminist theme, a nod to Spielberg's upbringing in a house of strong women.

In Hammond's display, there's a banner proclaiming that the place offers a return to the time *When Dinosaurs Ruled the Earth,* the title of a Hammer film which pre-dated *Jurassic Park* in making the distinction between nasty meat eaters and gentle "veggie" dinosaurs. *Jurassic Park* is, then, not only a movie about dinosaurs but about dinosaur movies—and, for that matter, movies in general. Spielberg opens the film with an audience "hook": As one of the (as yet unseen) beasts is transported in a

seemingly impregnable cage, it nearly escapes, sucking a screaming worker into the darkness. The rapid-fire editing and dark-of-night setting likewise draw the viewer into the film, a variation on the sucking down of Susan Backlinie in the *Jaws* opening. Simply, it is Spielberg back in familiar territory—the monster movie—but returning as a mature filmmaker rather than a talented newcomer.

An important element in the opening is the hat Muldoon, big-game warden and guardian of this beast, wears. It is strikingly similar to the fedora that Indiana Jones sported, an indication of the Spielberg heroic figure in lighthearted adventures like *Raiders of the Lost Ark* as well as the upcoming ultraserious *Schindler's List.* Our initial impression, then, is that this man will fill that role, though we don't see him again for some time. Shortly, we meet Grant (like Jones, a professional digger), who also sports a hat, momentarily confusing us; since we only glimpsed Muldoon in the darkness, is this he?

With Grant is his quasi-fiancée Ellie, who also wears a hat, her brim turned up in the style of a cowboy's comic sidekick. In turn, as we meet the film's other "positive" figures, almost every one wears just such a hat: elderly park owner Hammond, mathematician Ian Malcolm. All are (with the possible exception only of near-perfect Ellie) in some way flawed; Muldoon makes mistakes of judgment, Grant fears commitments, Hammond is overzealous, Malcolm a bit too pushy. Yet every one has decent motives and, when the crisis is precipitated, attempts to behave correctly. Hats identify each as potential heroes, offering a satisfyingly new variation on a traditional Spielberg theme. Previous films have concerned some ordinary person who rises to heroic stature under extreme pressure. Here we encounter a virtual "collective" of candidates and must wait and watch to see which will finally rise to that occasion. Grant is the least likely, though circumstances eventually transform him into a "Prof. Henry Jones," who becomes *Indiana* out of necessity.

As the others drop out owing to injury or are killed, Grant emerges as the hero by natural selection, strikingly appropriate considering *Jurassic Park*'s Darwinian material. The social Darwinism in the human community serves as a perfect foil for the disastrous reverse Darwinism within the animal kingdom inflicted by Hammond's scientists. This parallel between modern, technocratic humans and once-extinct beasts is visually conveyed by the eating process, serving as a bridge between the two, much as it did in *Jaws.* When the visitors arrive on the island, they watch as a huge ox is lowered into an unseen carnivore's plant-filled cage; they recoil in horror at the sounds of carnage in the foliage below. Hammond, meanwhile, describes at length the dainty nouvelle-cuisine lunch his chef has prepared, smilingly inquiring: "Anyone hungry?" Much later, when Hammond fears his own lost grandchildren are being devoured in the jungle, he abstractly sits at his table and

eats. The early bit is more than just a gag; the latter, something other than textural business. Each visualizes a theme running through the film: Despite the superficial differences between man and beast, they are frightfully similar.

True, heroes are, like villains, to some degree motivated by money. Grant and Ellie agree to check out the park only after Hammond explains that in return he'll finance their archaeological dig for three years. Importantly, though, it's not money as money (an end unto itself) that interests them, but money as a means to an idealistic end, that being serious scientific research. There is a certain irony here: in the midst of what is undeniably a capitalistic endeavor (no one would ever mis-take the film *Jurassic Park* for an art-house flick), Spielberg nonetheless displays a social consciousness.

There is never any question that Hammond, however financially successful he'd like his park to be, is motivated less by potential profit than a desire to make his dream come true. At one point, when Gennaro speaks elatedly about the high price they could charge for tickets, the egalitarian democrat Hammond scolds the scurrilous fellow, insisting that ticket prices must be kept low enough so that everyone can come. This was always the attitude of Spielberg's idol Walt Disney when creating his own "land." It is the attitude of Spielberg in making a movie like *Jurassic Park* or the inevitable *Jurassic Park* attraction in Universal Studios. There is nothing wrong

Laura Dern as Dr. Ellie Sattler (photo by Murray Close, courtesy Amblin Entertainment and Universal/MCA).

with making a pile of money as long as the public's entertainment and education are foremost.

Stuart Klawans detailed *Jurassic Park*'s "self-reflexivity" in the *Nation:* Spielberg,

the noted director of roller-coaster movies, a director whose works have in fact been turned into thrill rides at Universal Studios theme parks, tells the story of a showman who is about to open—a theme park. Its main attraction is a tour, via computer-controlled Fords, past real-live dinosaurs. Your experience of the movie is pretty closely analogous to the characters' experience in the movie—much as the on-screen showman is analogous to the one offscreen. To portray Hammond, the creator of Jurassic Park, the creator of *Jurassic Park* chose Richard

Attenborough—another film director. Coyly, ironically, Spielberg trails his camera past a big display of items from the Jurassic Park gift shop. They are identical to the product tie-ins for *Jurassic Park.*

Spielberg's movies are like the rides in Disney's Epcot Center: However well designed the roller coasters may be for providing requisite thrills, they whisk the viewer past enough informational sights and sounds that it is virtually impossible not to learn something. Before the film is over, even the most oblivious audience has learned that according to current theory, dinosaurs are more closely related to birds than reptiles, were probably warm-blooded rather than cold-blooded, and capable of highly

Jeff Goldblum as Dr. Ian Malcolm, the chaos theorist who predicts that what can go wrong will go wrong (photo by Murray Close, courtesy Amblin Entertainment and Universal/MCA).

intelligent thought rather than the lumbering beasts with pea-sized brains. Hammond's ambitions for the park are identical to Spielberg's for the film.

The characters, as reinvented by Spielberg, identify themselves as good or bad in terms of their treatment of children. When the tour cars initially break down in *T. rex* territory, the lawyer leaps out, deserting the terrified kids, hiding in a nearby toilet; he's eventually discovered and gobbled up, much to the audience's delight. Malcolm, up to this point obnoxious, proves himself a worthy person. Selflessly, he grabs a flair ("illumination!") and purposefully leads the beast off in the other direction, calling back to Grant, "Save the children!" Grant extricates the children from their yellow buslike vehicle, recalling stalled buses in films dating back to *Duel* and adults who

achieve heroic stature by getting the kids out. Horrified by their experience with the lawyer, representing all adults who fail to meet their responsibilities, they scream: "He left us." Grant calmly replies: "That won't happen with me." At that moment, he has completed a significant stopgag on his hero's journey; his character has begun his arc. Earlier, he had no interest in children: "You actually want some of those?" he asks Ellie, Spielberg's happy compromise between traditional mother and modern career woman. Grant's experience with a child, back in the American West, appeared anything but hopeful. He went so far as to seize a dinosaur's claw, using it to frighten a sassy boy. He is standoffish even around Tim, a sweet child. The film charts Grant's moral education as he comes to understand what every male hero in Spielberg's later films must grasp: There is no greater reward than parenting, however limiting or exhausting it sometimes seems. If the young Spielberg made movies that glorified the joys of childhood while conveying an adult's uneasiness about leaving such pleasures behind, the mature Spielberg makes movies about the alternative delight of reclaiming that wonderful childlike way of perceiving the world by sharing it with one's own child, biological or foster.

Spielberg reached this realization before the movie begins; it is the lesson Grant will learn by film's end. The movie can be seen as one more emotional autobiography, employing crowd-pleasing entertainment to share a lesson the artist has learned about life. *Hook* suffered, owing to Spielberg's mistake of halting his story to allow for lengthy didactic statements expressing such attitudes. In *Jurassic Park,* he regains his status as the world's foremost showman—part Barnum, part DeMille, part Disney—expressing those ideas through Grant's body language and facial expressions rather than words.

Spielberg also proves himself the modern master of a technique created by the first true genius of cinema: D. W. Griffith's parallel editing between various points of equal interest as groups of sympathetic characters are thrown into uniquely fascinating, though widely varying, situations of peril. Ellie, hiding in the shed and menaced by other creatures, is about to pull the switch that will reintroduce electricity to the fence, where, unbeknownst to her, her loved ones are; Grant and the children, pursued by dinosaurs, crawl over that very fence; Muldoon, in the wilds, stalks and is stalked by a beast; Hammond, back at the main office, desperately tries to communicate over a speaker system. Spielberg sets up each situation and, at the moment when we are most involved, abruptly cuts away (purposefully frustrating us) to another area of interest, involving us deeply in that situation, only to cut away once again at that moment when the action becomes heightened. It works today as dazzlingly as it did in 1915's *Birth of a Nation,* for this is what movies, at their most visceral and emotionally involving level, have always been about.

Spielberg, like Griffith and all the popular (as compared to art-house) geniuses in between (notably, Ford, Hawks, Hitchcock, and Disney), understands the basic appeal of movies for the masses, knows in his gut that if a filmmaker wants to express ideas, he must slip them in so subtly that the viewer will not even notice. Previous close-textual studies have revealed that those earlier filmmakers did indeed have ideas, were more thoughtful and thought provoking than was at first obvious. The same is true of Spielberg, whose basic ideas are family values, illumination, and flight.

Spielberg's children are noticeably different from Crichton's. An early line of throwaway dialogue establishes the fact that in this version they are one more set of lost Spielberg children, on the island because their mother, Hammond's daughter, is "getting a divorce." Malcolm, meanwhile, all but rules himself out as a possible hero through his cynical attitude toward marriage; attracted to Ellie, he admits: "I'm always on the lookout for a future ex–Mrs. Malcolm." However attractive he may be, we must look elsewhere for the proper hero. However unlikely a candidate Grant seems, with Spielberg it is always such unlikely candidates who overcome all odds and rise to the occasion.

Ellie is anything but a retro-woman. When Muldoon goes out searching for the kids, she unhesitantly says, "I'll go with you," scoffing at Hammond's untenable words about doing a difficult job in her place: "I really should be the one . . . I'm a . . . and you're a . . ."

"Illumination!": Light has always played a key role in Spielberg films, symbolizing the projection of the very movie we are watching; here, Malcolm peers up in amazement, like so many other Spielberg heroes before him.

223

We giggle with her as Hammond, a genial chauvinist, attempts to be both "man" and "gentleman"; however, she is clearly the one who can get things done. Yet it is Grant who finds himself at the center of action, if for no other reason than that Grant has so much to learn. It is important, too, that the children are no mere ciphers, whining while waiting to be saved, but play an active role, including the salvation of the ever-dwindling group. In Grant's first sequence, it became abundantly clear that he has an aversion to computers, the old dog who cannot learn new tricks. Toward the film's end, it is obvious that the only way to keep the dinosaurs from gobbling up everybody is by putting the park's computer system back into operation, which the kids—modern, computer-age whiz kids—do, to Grant's amazement. He realizes, then, that he can't get along without kids—in more ways than one. Spielberg gave this act of salvation to the little girl Lex, whereas in the book, it had been the boy, Tim, who pushed all the right buttons. This placated feminists, who might otherwise have complained that the (human) females didn't have enough to do; it serves as not only social comment but also personal expression, Spielberg once again reasserting his belief, learned during childhood, in the strength of women.

Then they are all together in a helicopter, escaping. Spielberg shows us what he tried so awkwardly to express through words in *Hook:* a makeshift family, the mother sitting to one side, necessary catalyst, the camera framing her by herself, allowing the father figure to cuddle the two kids. Though Grant and Ellie may not raise these particular children, we know without being told that they will soon be surrounded by their own.

Illumination takes place in the amber that preserves the ancient mosquitoes, which in turn contain the blood from which dinosaur DNA will be drawn. Spielberg's choice of camera angles makes it clear that the filmmaker views these pieces as something more than relics. While touching the amber—whether for purposes of scientific perusal or personal affection—Hammond always holds them up to the light; most often, the amber, as set against the light, is allowed to dominate the screen in close-up, a light source shining through in much the same way that light is passed through the cels on a filmstrip to create the projected image on a screen. If Hammond is allowed to speak for the filmmaker, his theme park representing Spielberg's theme-park movies, then his illumination represents the projection process.

"How can we stand in the light of discovery," Hammond wants to know, "and not act?" What's contained in the amber has potential for glory or goriness; it is initially impossible to tell whether the characters will, as a result of what is found in the light, encounter something beautiful *(Close Encounters of the Third Kind)* or horrific *(Poltergeist).* The light consistently stands for the unknown, the mysterious and magical aspects of the universe, though whether they will provide Hitchcockian horror or Disney sweetness always remains to be seen. It

becomes clear that Spielberg has here split himself in two: If Grant represents Spielberg the person and parent, Hammond stands for Spielberg, moviemaker and entrepreneur.

Flight is a metaphor here, as it has been in previous films. From the earliest dialogue, the point is driven home that dinosaurs predated birds, creatures Spielberg inherits from Hitchcock. In addition to being in line with current scientific thought, this helps us understand Spielberg's ongoing interest in dinosaurs (he served as executive producer for the animated films *The Land Before Time* and *We're Back! A Dinosaur's Story*). In studying them, he is tracing the history of his beloved birds, animals that achieve what his heroes aspire to: "When did these guys learn to fly?" Grant muses aloud early on, during his dinosaur dig. At the film's end, Grant—having just escaped the island—peers out the helicopter (in slang, whirly*bird*) window, noticing a flock of birds just below him. He smiles, not so much ironically as optimistically. As always in Spielberg, idealism fails (Hammond's naive belief that the park can be perfected), but optimism wins the day: Though it took untold millions of years, nature or God or whatever you choose to call it did prove itself a benign force by turning dangerous, deadly beasts into dignified, delicate birds.

Grant and Ellie live out Spielberg's believing-is-seeing theme when they first arrive on the island and marvel—staring without speaking—at the *Brachiosaurus,* moving in herds across fields. For adults, seeing is believing. But for the children, believing is seeing: The kids don't believe in the friendly *Brachiosaurus* before them until they pet it, touch it. Grant and Ellie learn to believe without seeing, since they are positive characters. On the other hand, the villainous Nedry loses his glasses (his source of sight) at a key moment during his attempted escape. Nonetheless, he relies on sight, which will kill him: The *Dilophosaur* that stalks him appears, at first sight, to be as harmless as a puppy. Locked into the seeing-is-believing approach, he is unaware of the creature's killer instincts and suffers the consequences.

The *Brachiosaurus* faces resemble E.T.'s, extended on a long neck and immense body. Spielberg nods to other films as well as his own. The huge gate leading into *T. rex* territory looks like the one natives used to keep monsters at bay in the original *King Kong;* Malcolm goes so far as to caustically comment, "What have they got back there—King Kong?" As in previous Spielberg films, we view reality through the prism of past movies, which constitute our collective cultural consciousness; reality and film are not easily separated. The dinner table in Hammond's great room, where he is joined by Ellie, resembles the breakfast table in *Citizen Kane,* while the industrial kitchen in which the kids hide from raptors is identical to the one Steve McQueen retreated into in the original 1958 version of *The Blob.* But the greatest movie reference is the last: Fleeing the raptors, Grant and Ellie crawl over the top of a dinosaur skeleton on exhibit in the main hall. As it comes crashing down and they struggle to maintain equilibrium, the tone turns comic; they resemble Cary Grant and Katharine Hepburn in the climax of Howard Hawks's *Bringing Up Baby.*

The communication-beyond-language theme is also present. A key moment in Grant's arc occurs when, hiding in the treetop branches with the children, he hears the *Brachiosauri* and notes that they are not making mindless, meaningless noise but "singing" to one another. He then imitates their songs, and they respond; he realizes his potential to be the kind of man who can move beyond the limiting language barrier, like Neary in *Close Encounters of the Third Kind,* who opened up and responded to the music (the "singing") coming from star people. Evident, too, is the concept of the secret sharer: "Turn the light off," Grant keeps repeating when the children are menaced by the *T. rex* in the adjacent car; "Turn the light off," Tim thinks out loud, receiving the "radio message" from Grant, doing as he's told.

Malcolm briefly links what happens to Spielberg's metaphysical theme when he says: "God creates dinosaurs. . . . God creates man. . . . Man creatures dinosaurs. . . ." The chaos-theory expert, following the possibility through to its logical conclusion, sees the potential for tragedy when men play at being gods.

After a record-breaking opening, *Jurassic Park* quickly earned over $200 million during the next two months, while its foreign engagements at once estab-lished this as the most successful motion picture of all time. Critics were generally moderate in their praise. Terrence Rafferty of the *New Yorker* dismissed it as "just a creature feature on amphetamines," claiming the film was too familiar: "*Jurassic Park* is like an album full of new, slickly rearranged versions of the director's greatest hits." Richard Corliss of *Time* was kinder:

No film could be more personal to [Spielberg] than this one, a movie whose subject is its process, a movie about all the complexities of fabricating entertainment in the microchip age. It's a movie in love with technology (as Spielberg is), yet afraid of being carried away by it (as he is).

Almost all critics marveled at the technical virtuosity, admitting that the film clicked in a way *Hook* had not. Yet if it was clear this was a striking work of its type, that did not deter the ongoing concern that the human element was superficial. Peter Travers of *Rolling Stone,* hailing the film as "colossal entertainment," paused in his praise to note: "Compared with the dinos, the human characters are dry bones . . . flattened into nonentities on the trip from page to screen." Creating serious drama without resorting to charming trickery remained the last great challenge for Spielberg. Clearly, he felt ready to tackle that one: His next project would be the long-delayed *Schindler's List.*

Schindler's List

A UNIVERSAL RELEASE, 1993

CAST

Liam Neeson *(Oskar Schindler);* Ben Kingsley *(Itzhak Stern);* Ralph Fiennes *(Amon Goeth);* Caroline Goodall *(Emilie Schindler);* Jonathan Sagalle *(Poldek Pfefferberg);* Embeth Davidtz *(Helen Hirsch).*

CREDITS

Directed by Steven Spielberg; producers, Spielberg, Gerald R. Molen, and Branko Lustig; written by Steven Zaillian, from the novel by Thomas Keneally; cinematography, Janusz Kaminski; editor, Michael Kahn; music, John Williams; production designer, Allan Starski; Eastman black and white; running time, 185 mins.; rating: R.

In 1982, film critic Andrew Sarris admitted to enjoying *E.T.,* noting that the film evidenced Spielberg's movement beyond the pyrotechnics of cinematic action and, happily, toward a mature understanding of human relationships. Still, Sarris admitted to some qualms about the often-discussed "Spielberg optimism":

There is still too much of the world between the children's room and outer space left unexplored in the cinema of Steven Spielberg. He does not have to remake *The Grapes of Wrath.* All I ask is that sometime before he reaches the age of fifty, he should become somewhat more skeptical of his own self-induced euphoria.

Whether Spielberg ever read that comment is unknown; yet even as he approached that milestone birthday, the filmmaker set to work on precisely the kind of film Sarris had, some years earlier, respectfully requested.

The black-and-white social epic *Schindler's List* may not be a remake of *The Grapes of Wrath,* but it is another example of socially oriented cinema. Ford, adapting John Steinbeck's radical book to his own more mainstream purposes, had perceived the Great Depression as the ultimate testing ground for his fervent belief in family, tack-

Steven Spielberg, directing *Schindler's List* on location in Poland (photo by David James, courtesy Universal/MCA and Amblin Entertainment).

ing on an optimistic ending (controversial in its time) to Steinbeck's bleaker tale. Fifty years later, for Spielberg there likewise was an ultimate test of his own similar optimism: the Holocaust, alluded to in early films, even ones as seemingly escapist oriented as *Raiders of the Lost Ark* and *Twilight Zone—The Movie*. It was as if Spielberg had been sparring with the Holocaust all along, shadowboxing with an issue he gradually realized in time he would confront.

When he was a child in New Jersey, his grandmother

The poster for *Schindler's List*, reminiscent of the hands touching in the earlier *E.T.* logo.

taught English to an Auschwitz survivor who in turn taught Steven numbers using the brand that Nazis had tattooed on his arm. Had he grown up there, Spielberg might, like Woody Allen, have become a self-consciously Jewish filmmaker. But as a displaced preteen in Arizona, he had been the only Jew in his neighborhood. Generally accepted, he still felt like an outsider: The family's earlier orthodoxy had been abandoned, though they were the only house in the neighborhood without lights at Christmastime. Then, as a teenager in California, he had been denigrated by surfer-style anti-Semites, an experience he later repressed but never completely forgot. For psychological reasons, Spielberg avoided making Judaism an element in his films, in the way Martin Scorsese employed his Italian heritage for the basis of his work. The Norman Rockwell families Spielberg portrayed on-screen (perhaps filming the early life he wished

he had led rather than the one he actually did) caused *Newsweek*'s David Ansen to marvel: "The fantasies he concocted in his spectacular career were the ultimate triumph of assimilation: he colonized the world with his imagination."

But the heritage passed on by parents and older relatives was stored away in his memory buds. On a personal level, second-wife Kate Capshaw converted to Judaism. Artistically, the ever-growing presence of Nazis (including Hitler himself in *Indiana Jones and the Last Crusade*) testified that despite his early insistence that he was not someone who wanted to make serious films, he was moving in precisely that direction. Forcing himself to visit concentration camps, he surprised himself by not crying; he was instead consumed with anger and a sense of helplessness: "There was nothing I could do about it, yet I thought, there is something I can do about it." Being

Schindler is initially presented as a friend of the Nazis, immersed in "the good life"; almost against his own will, he will be transformed by circumstances into the El Cid of the Holocaust (photo by David James, courtesy Universal Pictures and Amblin Entertainment).

a moviemaker, he could make a movie. When Spielberg read Thomas Keneally's 1982 novel shortly after its publication, learning of Oskar Schindler and "the list," he immediately determined to film it.

The way in which that book came to be written is, in itself, a remarkable story. A Catholic from Australia, Keneally was in Beverly Hills to publicize *Confederates,* a novel, at Brentano's. The month was October, but the heat had risen to an unseasonable 100 degrees; staggering around after leaving the bookstore, Keneally stepped into an air-conditioned leather-goods shop to cool off. Feeling anxious about being there so long without buying anything, the author noticed a handsome briefcase and decided to purchase it, mentioning he could use it to carry manuscripts.

The elderly owner, who called himself Leopold Page, was intrigued to have an author in the store, replying:

"Have I got a story for you." While they waited for American Express to clear Keneally's charge, Page explained that his real name was Poldek Pfefferberg. He and his wife, Mila, were concentration-camp survivors, owing their lives to a onetime Nazi turned savior of Jews. Keneally insisted that as a Gentile who knew little of the Holocaust, he was hardly the proper writer to tell this story. His host vehemently insisted that this was precisely what qualified him: It was the job of every decent, caring human being to get involved, to learn from history and share such knowledge. Keneally found himself entranced by the tale, canceling his flight home to Australia and moving into Pfefferberg's home. There he was given full access to documents which served as jigsaw pieces in composing a portrait of Schindler.

Three weeks later, he decided that he absolutely wanted to do the project. After much painstaking work,

Keneally created a book filled with vivid detailed information about the events surrounding a German-Catholic playboy-entrepreneur and Nazi party member who moved to Poland in 1939, hoping to capitalize on Hitler's conquest of that country. Schindler opened an enamelware factory, hiring Jews as workers to exploit them as cheap labor. However, his close proximity to the suffering people eventually moved him so intensely that in time Schindler used his vast fortune to "buy" his Jewish workers (now marked for deportation to the Auschwitz death camp), spiriting them away to a safe haven near his hometown, where they remained until the war was over. Those Jews—more than eleven hundred—came to be called *"Schindlerjuden"* (Schindler's Jews). Decades later, they made certain Schindler was buried in Israel as a "righteous Gentile" following his death in 1974.

For a brief time after publication, it appeared that M-G-M would pick up the film rights. The project suddenly moved to Universal, purchased as a possible six-part TV miniseries; Keneally himself wrote the script for that proposed rendering. Then Kurt Luedtke (who won an Oscar for his impressive screenplay *Out of Africa,* based on Karen Blixen's seemingly unfilmable memoirs) attempted an adaptation. Spielberg had such immense respect for this writer's talents that when Luedtke finally admitted he could not find a way to lick the problem of adaptation, Spielberg briefly became convinced that no one would be able to do so, temporarily abandoning the project.

On a gut level, Schindler and the list never went away. One reason why Spielberg stuck with it was the realization that without his name attached, *Schindler's List* would probably not get made. One studio executive, upon hearing Spielberg describe the project, suggested (without irony) that the filmmaker ought to merely take the money it would cost to film *Schindler's List* and contribute that amount to the Holocaust museum rather than wasting it on a film no one would ever pay to see. Though intended as helpful advice, Spielberg took the statement as a gauntlet across the face, sensing that with the power of his position came a certain responsibility: At least once he ought to do something that touched his human conscience and Jewish consciousness.

So Spielberg reconsidered. Then, in 1989, he—older now, more confident he could not only do it but also do it right—came to believe that Steven Zaillian might be the proper writer. Zaillian had been drawn into the project by Scorsese at a time when, after Spielberg backed off, Scorsese briefly considered doing it. Zaillian had successfully adapted another disturbing story, *Awakenings,* whittling the complex material down to manageable size. Moreover, he had in that script managed to take a dark subject (an incurable sleeping disease in which patients are temporarily brought back to consciousness, only to eventually drift back into their comalike state), miraculously turning what could have been a depressing, downbeat movie into a life-affirming work.

Most important, Zaillian found a way to lick what Luedtke had considered the formidable "problem" posed by the Schindler story: *Why* Schindler did what he did. Luedtke had felt the need to understand, then dramatize, the essential reason for Schindler's transformation from card-carrying Nazi to El Cid of the Holocaust. This was not to be found in Keneally's book, which documented in detail what the man did without speculating about motivation. Luedtke had toyed with the idea of inventing dramatic scenes to make Schindler's psychology clear, but that struck him as melodramatic. Without this, *Schindler's List* would remain a docudrama, showing the surface of events rather than allowing the audience a comprehension of them. Zaillian, on the other hand, proposed a "Rosebud" theory, drawing the phrase from one of Spielberg's own favorite films, *Citizen Kane,* referring to the title character's final word. Kane's childhood sled is an "open" symbol, suggesting different things to different viewers. Zaillian's invocation of "Rosebud" had an immediate impact on Spielberg, who, lest we forget, is

Dealing with the devil: Like so many previous Spielberg heroes, Schindler is anything but an innocent or an idealist, choosing to befriend the monstrous Amon Goeth (Ralph Fiennes) in order to secure the safety of his Jews (photo by David James, courtesy Universal Pictures and Amblin Entertainment).

today the proud owner of the last remaining Rosebud sled prepared for that 1941 classic.

Spielberg and Zaillian immediately began work on the creation of their own Rosebud. Not wanting to cheapen the material by invention, they searched for a historical object they could transform into their own open cinematic symbol. Keneally had vividly described an incident in which several hundred families were evicted from their ghetto apartments by SS men, then shot down on the streets. Observing this was a little girl, who happened to be wearing a scarlet dress. Schindler, if his recollections of years later are to be trusted, had at the time been stunned by the sight: a beautiful child, blithely passing through the grotesque scene as if sleepwalking, perhaps so stunned by the nightmarish incident that she couldn't accept it, instead assuming she must be dreaming. This suggested Spielberg's own believing-is-seeing theme: The child refuses to believe what's happening, so she doesn't see it. In their story conferences, the idea was discussed and developed until writer and director deter-

Having assembled the list, Stern approaches Schindler, who initially only wanted to exploit cheap Jewish labor but now finds himself on a mission of hope (photo by David James, courtesy Universal Pictures and Amblin Entertainment).

mined this sight could, like Rosebud, serve successfully as a prism, suggesting all sorts of possibilities going on within Schindler's mind without insisting on any. Schindler, an adult, is conversely a seeing-is-believing person. He has heretofore denied the horror of the Holocaust, but when it is there before his eyes, he must admit its existence.

Since Spielberg had already determined that the film must be shot in black and white to convey the proper gritty atmosphere, he then made the decision—unpopular in some quarters—to employ color for the dress. It is a device that strikes observers as brilliant or patently offensive. Those who defend the director's decision believe the color red, marbled into the black-and-white image, is necessary to make clear, without reliance on the crutch of words, that this is what impresses Schindler; we see as he sees, selectively, the color forcing us to concentrate on this single element. Others complain that any sudden intrusion of color into what we have accepted as the black-and-white world of this film draws too much attention to itself, making us consciously aware that what we had accepted as "truth" is, after all, only a movie.

Polish-born cinematographer Janusz Kaminski went so far as to argue, during the actual shoot, that the film was not shot in black and white, in any 1993 state-of-the-art sense, but black and white of the Italian neorealist order: "We were aiming for a naturalistic look, not using things like bright lights. I'm trying to imagine myself being here fifty years ago with a small camera without

Poldek Pfefferberg (Jonathan Sagalle) and his wife, Mila (Ada Nitzan), are among the more than eleven hundred Jews saved by Schindler; some forty years later, the real-life Pfefferberg accidentally met writer Thomas Keneally, told the novelist of his wartime benefactor, then persuaded the Australian Catholic to author a book that inspired Spielberg's film (photo by David James, courtesy Universal Pictures and Amblin Entertainment).

lights. We're favoring long lenses, doing a lot of hand-held shots. We want people to see this film in fifteen years and not have a sense of when it was made." So seemingly artless is the desired and achieved newsreel effect. Spielberg concurred, insisting that *Schindler's List* was "probably the sloppiest film [I] ever [made]," that being an aesthetic choice, not an accident. On location, Spielberg told interviewer David Gritten: "Certain scenes have more impact if the camera's not on wheels or steel tracks. It makes it a little messy and adds to the documentary style. Most scenes we're shooting in two or three takes, and we're working real fast. I think that gives the film a spontaneity and also serves the subject."

Such major names as Kevin Costner and Mel Gibson were passed over in favor of virtual unknown Liam Neeson, Spielberg feeling it was best to have an actor who brought no movie-star baggage with him to the role. Still, casting was hampered by the fact that he had watched numerous documentaries about Schindler. A sense of the man's face, weight, and mannerisms made choosing all the more difficult; no one was precisely right, though Neeson came closer than most. Spielberg noted the real Schindler's commanding presence and "cigarettes-and-cognac voice" as well as his quietly dynamic impact on women. Neeson was tested early on, then didn't hear back for six months. While appearing in Eugene O'Neill's *Anna Christie* on Broadway, Neeson learned that Spielberg, his wife, Kate Capshaw, and Capshaw's mother were in the audience. It wasn't so much the actor's commanding on-stage performance as the backstage meeting that cinched the role. When Neeson noticed that Capshaw's mother had been deeply moved by the play, he impulsively hugged her. Afterward, Capshaw reportedly said to her husband: "That's exactly what Schindler would have done."

Ben Kingsley, on the other hand, was chosen less for physical resemblance to the real Itzhak Stern than acting ability. There is no documentary record of Stern (a relatively minor character in Keneally's book) for a frame of reference. So many Jews worked for Schindler in various executive capacities that to include all would have confused viewers. Instead, the composite figure called Stern allowed Spielberg to build the character not only dramatically but also symbolically: the film's Stern becomes, in Spielberg's own words, "Schindler's subconscious." He articulates important ideas Schindler would never put into words but on some instinctual level responds to: Stern is Schindler's Spielbergian secret sharer.

Despite such artistic license, the surface had to appear as authentic as possible. For the sake of visual realism, *Schindler's List* was filmed in Poland, often on the Krakow sites where events occurred. The filmmaker arrived on March 1, 1993, and set to work on what would be a seventy-five-day shoot, with six-day workweeks. Spielberg was informed that he would not be permitted to film in Auschwitz or Birkenau, located thirty miles from Krakow, owing to objections by the World Jewish Congress, which insisted that the area was hallowed ground. It would have been easier for Spielberg to accept this had nine previous film crews (including *Triumph of the Spirit* one year earlier) not been granted permission; he couldn't help but believe that authorities feared that Spielberg, "the modern Disney," would trivialize the Holocaust.

Spielberg chose not to argue the point. Production designer Allan Starski constructed 148 separate sets at thirty-five locations, all completed within the limits of

Making voyeurs of his audience, Spielberg places his camera outside the window as Schindler confronts Goeth about the Jews (photo by David James, courtesy Universal Pictures and Amblin Entertainment).

Liam Neeson as Oskar Schindler, a man of "expensive cognac and imported cigarettes" (photo by David James, courtesy Universal Pictures and Amblin Entertainment).

the film's tight $23 million budget. Since Starski had previously worked on Andrzej Wajda's *Korczak* and Agnieszka Holland's *Europa, Europa,* both with Holocaust-related themes, Spielberg knew he could be trusted to create the necessary sense of horrific vividness. Often Starski brought historical details into his construct: The front gate to the concentration camp shown in the movie is the actual gate, though the camp itself is a detailed reconstruction. They did shoot exterior scenes just outside Auschwitz's grotesque fences for a sequence in which prisoners are herded off a train and into the camp. Even the clothing people wear is authentic. Costume designer Anna Biedrzycka-Sheppard advertised in the local papers that she wanted to buy old items left over from the 1940s, hoping some residents would pull stuff out of mothballs. She was stunned and saddened to realize that the largely poor population wanted to sell the old clothing off their backs for any money they could get.

Spielberg hired a largely Polish crew to assist the small coterie of Americans (as well as Brits, Israelis, Croats, Germans, and Austrians) he brought with him. The team was assembled by Spielberg's Polish coproducer, Lew Rywin, at Heritage Films. Rywin located the actual apartment building near Wawel Castle where Schindler had lived. Scenes were subsequently shot there, as well as at Schindler's factory (still functioning) and the actual train station, which had changed surprisingly little over more than half a century. Coproducer Branko Lustig had himself been interned at Auschwitz as a boy; his vivid memories made their way into the film's grim texture.

One unexpected and awful experience was the realization that anti-Semitism is still alive in Poland. British actor Ralph Fiennes plays Amon Goeth, a real-life Nazi officer who in the film is dramatically transformed into Schindler's evil twin–Doppelgänger. Fiennes recalls standing around in a Nazi uniform, waiting to shoot a scene, when an elderly woman passing by rushed up and, apparently under the impression that the Nazis had returned, thanked him for killing so many Jews in the past, hoping they'd get "the rest of them" this time. In fact, fewer than five hundred Jews choose to live in Krakow today, though five thousand were there at war's end; there had been nearly seventy thousand Jews in the city before the Holocaust began.

Rywin found Spielberg and the Americans a hotel with the capacity for a satellite link to the United States, bouncing its signal from Poland through Washington, D.C., to San Francisco, where special effects for *Jurassic Park* were simultaneously being created at Industrial Light and Magic. After each day's shooting, Spielberg would then watch as friends back home waved "hi," beaming him the F/X shots and music for his approval,

Schindler's wife, Emilie (Caroline Goodall), surprises her husband with a visit to Krakow (photo by David James, courtesy Universal Pictures and Amblin Entertainment).

allowing Spielberg to edit the blockbuster from his Krakow hotel room. Three weekends in a row, he also flew from Poland to Paris to work on postproduction of *Jurassic Park* in a dubbing room. Fortunately, wife Kate and their five children were there, offering support, which helped carry him through the exhausting schedule. In addition to the grueling time demands, the experience was difficult for the director emotionally: By day, he was embracing his own future, filming (often weeping as he did) the first overtly serious work of his career; by night, he was finishing off the past, completing his greatest "show."

"My films have been made for you," Spielberg later told *Newsweek*'s Cathleen McGuigan, "you" of course referring to the public at large.

Just like somebody makes a hamburger the way you want it. That's been my modus operandi. Now I go to Poland and I get hit in the face with my personal life. My upbringing. My Jewishness. Jewish life came pouring back into my heart. I've often protected myself with the movie camera. The camera has always been my golden shield against things really reaching me. I came to realize the reason I [made] the movie is that I have never in my life told the truth in a movie. My effort as a moviemaker has been to create something that couldn't possibly happen. So people could leave their lives and have an ad-

venture and then come back to earth and drive home. One of the things I thought [was], if I'm going to tell the truth for the first time, it should be about this subject. Not about divorce or parents and children, but about this.

The Holocaust is the heritage that defines him rather than the alternative, idealized Middle American lifestyle he previously dreamed of disappearing into, assimilating in order to deny his own reality as a Jew.

It was soon apparent, however, that the evolving film was, in addition to a contemporary Jewish artist's portrait of the Holocaust, a Steven Spielberg movie. He had transformed, shaped, rearranged, even reimagined the story in such a way that it was now as much an expression of his worldview as anything that had gone before. A reporter for the *L.A. Times/Calendar*, visiting the set, recalls approaching Liam Neeson, standing near a period car with wide running boards, looking absolutely dapper in a beautifully cut suit and wide-brimmed fedora. Before the journalist could even utter a word about Neeson's striking resemblance to Harrison Ford in Spielberg's trilogy, Neeson beat him to the punch: "No Indiana Jones jokes, okay?"

When the movie was completed and before the public, Jeff Stickler of the *Minneapolis Star-Tribune* pointed out that "Goeth is to this film what the insatiable shark was to *Jaws,* and the deadly velociraptor was to *JP.*" Frank Rich of the *New York Times* commented that when "the Jewish factory workers" appear before Schindler, they "look up at him awe-struck, as if he were the levitating mother ship in *Close Encounters of the Third Kind.*" Henry Sheehan of the *Orange County Register* commented that in many respects Schindler resembles E.T., who is "old but childlike. E.T. is a child's fantasy about what a grown-up should be, powerful but kind," the film's Oskar Schindler yet another variation on that theme. J. Hoberman of the *Village Voice* felt that Schindler's chosen Jews, smiling as they were spirited away to a safe haven, reminded him of "a transport of under-privileged waifs (on) a special trip to Disneyland" or perhaps the Indian children returning to their village in *Indiana Jones and the Temple of Doom.*

No one reading Crichton's *Jurassic Park* or Keneally's *Schindler's List* would ever in a million years think that these books tell the same story, one as an escapist fantasy, the other as realistic drama. But that is precisely the case with the Spielberg films of those books. The early conversations between Schindler and his visiting wife reveal that their relationship is incomplete because he can't commit to a family; his words recall what Grant tells Ellie in the *Jurassic Park* opening. In each, a man in a hat, so deeply involved with his own affairs that he has no time for children, eventually rises to heroic stature by reuniting lost kids with their families even as monstrous beasts (dinosaurs/Nazis) attempt to stop him. The communication theme is there: Schindler relies on Stern to translate for him when he speaks to Jewish businessmen until he breaks the language barrier and learns Yiddish himself. So is the concept of "illumination," Spielberg's personal symbol for optimism here melding beautifully with the generalized Jewish symbol for optimism, the Eternal Light, which opens and closes the film. His beloved period, the 1930s and 1940s, are re-created; the mark of his newfound maturity is that this time, he does not romanticize the era, but he treats it realistically.

One previous Spielberg theme is notably missing: the notion that his movie is less concerned with the subject matter at hand than with the old movies he knows and loves. Though *Schindler's List* may be to his career ̣vhat *The Grapes of Wrath* was to Ford's, there are, thankfully, no homages to Ford of the type that made *The Color Purple* seem an elaborate artifice rather than a true adaptation of Walker's work. Spielberg self-consciously denied himself that crutch and, in so doing, finally found his own voice. As he told *Newsweek:*

My problem is I have too much of a command of the visual language. I know how to put a Cecil B. DeMille image on the screen. . . . But I've never really been able to put *my* image on the screen, with the exception of *E.T.,* perhaps. And certainly not until *Schindler* was I really able to *not* reference other filmmakers. I'm always referencing everybody. I didn't do any of that on this movie.

As an expression of Spielberg's sensibility, *Schindler's List* had to portray the family unit as a source of faith. No wonder, then, that of the numerous details chronicled in Keneally's novel, Spielberg—forced to select, even for a film as lengthy as this one—consistently did so in a way that expresses his own long-standing priorities. Understandably, the most horrific images in his film are not what one might expect (the workings of the crematoria, surprisingly enough kept offscreen) but of families torn asunder by the Nazis. Correspondingly, the most awe-inspiring moments are ones in which some families are happily reunited.

Shifting to a related theme, the mother-child bond, Spielberg created a dramatic subplot involving a specific mother and daughter. The little girl is easily recognizable owing to glasses she always wears. (Indeed, if there is a single "reference" in *Schindler's List,* this is it: the child in *Jules and Jim* (1960), one of Spielberg's favorite Truffaut films, wore identical glasses.) When the Nazis search for victims, the mother gives up her daughter to another woman who will hide her; consider how many Spielbergian mothers are separated from their children in films as diverse in tone and intent as *The Sugarland Express, Poltergeist,* and *Empire of the Sun.* But the child—wiser in a way than her parent—insists on remaining with her mother, though they are headed for a death camp. The girl is mother to the woman.

The film actually tells two parallel stories: father-figure Schindler, trying to save all the children; mother and daughter, attempting to remain together. Toward the end, one of the most harrowing moments occurs when Schindler has saved his Jewish workers, only to realize that the Nazis plan to separate mothers from daughters. The camera immediately focuses on this specific mother and daughter, vividly representing the generalized horror of them all. Schindler's ultimate heroic act is the reuniting of parents and children, particularly these two. At last, the reluctant hero-father and the mother-child theme are fused, in a scene that has some basis in history, dramatized as only Spielberg would have thought to dramatize it.

Though the *Jerusalem Post* had tagged *Schindler's List* "a radical departure" for the director, they were correct only in tone, not theme. Sheehan perceptively noted that "*Schindler's List* is less a departure than a continuance . . . we see a familiar confrontation being played out here, although certainly with its own unique variations." Most responses were raves, even from critics who ordinarily save their most savage comments for Spielberg. John Simon of *National Review,* who despised even the most loved Spielberg blockbusters, used such words as "art," "impeccable," and "perfect," while Stanley Kauffmann of the *New Republic* noted:

Much of his previous work has been clever but *Schindler's List* is masterly . . . a welcome astonishment from a director who has given us much boyish esprit, much ingenuity, but little seri-

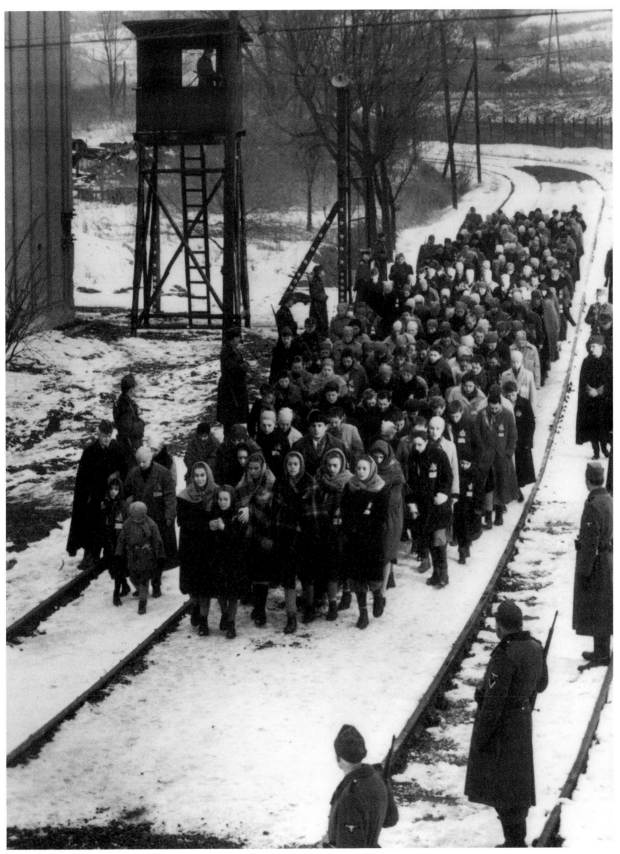

Despite the carefully planned strategy, three hundred women and children are accidentally rerouted to the Auschwitz-Birkenau concentration camp; when Schindler determines to find a way to get them out, he follows the ritualistic hero pattern of such previous Spielberg projects as Indiana Jones in *The Temple of Doom* (photo by David James, courtesy Universal Pictures and Amblin Entertainment).

Schindler rescues his Jews and, beaming paternally, welcomes them to the safety of his new factory at Brinnlitz (photo by David James, courtesy Universal Pictures and Amblin Entertainment).

ousness. His stark, intelligent style here, perfectly controlled, suggests that this may be the start of a new period in Spielberg's prodigious career—Part Two: The Man.

Schindler's List won awards for Best Picture from all three major film critics' societies and would eventually win the Academy Award for Best Picture of the Year.

When critics did pause in their praise to point out a flaw, it was inevitably the one that had driven Luedtke from the project. David Denby in *New York,* though lauding the film as "an astounding achievement," did insist that

one of the few failings is that Schindler's transformation from profiteer to saint isn't made psychologically clear. Liam Neeson puts his bulky body and leathery voice into the performance, but as the film goes on, he gives this decent man a look of increasing bewilderment, as if Schindler were amazed not only by the Final Solution but by his own acts.

However, Terrence Rafferty of the *New Yorker* applauded this very approach. Calling the film "a great movie," he insisted

The triumph of the book is that Keneally never fully answers the question "Why?" and, besides, persuades us that it would be foolish to try; heroism of this magnitude is, at its heart, inexplicable. Spielberg also respects the mystery of Schindler's personality, and part of what makes the film so moving is that ambiguous, complex hero. . . . Spielberg's rigorous refusal to simplify his protagonist's motives seems to connect him, in a minor but distinct way, to Schindler himself.

Schindler as Spielberg's latest autobiographical character is noteworthy. Like Spielberg, Schindler early on is interested only in escapism; like him, he learns to appease sharks in order to survive; like him, he views the Holocaust (Schindler firsthand; Spielberg as a visitor to the historical setting) and knows he must do something about it. Spielberg was enraged that as an artist of a later era all he could do was make a movie; he made a movie about a man not unlike himself who did what he would have liked to have done had he been there as a non-Jew.

There were, it is worth noting, dissenting voices. In the *Village Voice,* J. Hoberman complained that Spielberg had made "a feel-good entertainment about the ultimate feel-bad experience of the 20th Century," insisting that the subject matter had been "Spielbergized—the poster of a father grasping a child's hand is not the only aspect of *Schindler's List* that recalls *E.T.*" That last statement opens a fascinating critical Pandora's box: Hoberman and Sheehan noted the same thing—the imprint of Spielberg's artistic sensibility on the subject matter—but drew totally different conclusions, one lauding the film even as the other attacked it for precisely the same reason.

In the *L.A. Times,* a high school graduate about to attend Brown University named Robbie Kinberg argued that Spielberg had failed to find the proper balance between historical reality and personal expression: "Although his style and subject matter may have matured, his thematics remain in Never-Never Land." In particular, Kinberg cited a single sequence, brilliantly devised and executed, though emotionally dubious:

A group of women who were supposed to go to Schindler's camp are instead herded into the gas chambers. The camera follows as the suspense is elongated with close-ups of horrified faces and threatening shower heads. But to my horror the gas chambers had been "Spielbergized," and water poured down. Spielberg has reduced the gas chambers to a dramatic device so that Schindler can single-handedly save these women. True, this scene is based on events recalled by survivors, but there is not another scene in the film that shows the gas chambers. From this film, how are we to know that gas ever came down?

Spielberg effectively employs his *Psycho*-inspired manipulation of the audience's ongoing fear of showers, acceptable enough in the middle of an escapist film, perhaps less so when the material is of such a highly serious nature. Hoberman likewise complained about the theme-park quality of the "thriller suspense and last-minute rescue" here, though Peter Rainer spoke eloquently in defense: "So now Spielberg's narrative gifts are being held against him. Charles Dickens employed suspense and last-minute rescues for emotional effects too [in his hard-hitting novels of social conscience]. Why the double standard?"

Simply, Spielberg was in a bind from which there was perhaps no escape. His hero, Oskar Schindler, never visited the gas chambers in operation. If the point of the movie is to tell his story, was it necessary (or even right) to show those gas chambers in order to set the hero's story in its proper context? In 1989, our most consistently serious minded filmmaker, Oliver Stone, had in his Vietnam War–era *Born on the Fourth of July* depicted a student versus police riot on the Syracuse University campus which never occurred. Admitting he had invented the incident which most audiences accepted as absolute truth, Stone defended his approach by insisting that the campus confrontation represented those in other places (including Kent State) which his hero Ron Kovic (Tom Cruise) had not been involved with but which his moviegoing audience must see to fully understand the context of that period. Stone had been widely criticized for playing fast and loose with facts to convey his own sense of the larger, greater truth; now Spielberg was ironically being criticized for not following suit. Spielberg stated: "I'm not known as a conscientious sociological filmmaker who makes movies, like Oliver Stone. I respect and admire many of Oliver Stone's movies, but I haven't had an appetite to make movies that have messages and can change the world."

Frank Rich made it a point to identify himself as a Jew

for the first time ever before admitting that he found the film "more often numbing than moving," complaining about

the anonymity of the film's Jews. Mr. Spielberg has found hundreds of evocative faces to populate his simulated Holocaust, but their souls are skin-deep. (They) have the generic feel of composites, and are as forgettable as the chorus in a touring company of *Fiddler on the Roof,* or, for that matter, the human dino-fodder of *Jurassic Park.* They blur into abstraction, becoming another depersonalized statistic of mass death.

However, the filmmaker insisted early on that he was "not making a movie about the Holocaust, but about one man who saved lives" with the Holocaust as its setting. Anyone who understands Spielberg as an artist, based on a close study of his previous pictures, must realize that what emerged is the Spielberg morality play, the story he tells and retells in varying situations.

Other artists could and would have chosen to make movies about the darker aspects of the Holocaust, the 6 million who did not escape, as compared to the thousand who did. The point is, a popular storyteller emerges as a true artist by demonstrating that he does indeed possess an organized, ongoing vision, one which matures even as the filmmaker does on a personal level, yet remains fundamentally consistent. On any large subject (in this case, the Holocaust) he considers many stories and finally chooses the one in which he perceives a potential for expressing himself. There is a generalized Spielberg way of viewing the world; the film he made of *Schindler's List* stands as one more specific illustration/dramatization of that view. Spielberg (the filmmaker), being Spielberg (the person), chose precisely the right Holocaust story for his own ongoing optimism, the Holocaust story that acknowledges evil in the world but insists that it can be overcome.

Spielberg refuses to surrender to *nada,* will not give in to the encroaching darkness, clings to a positive vision despite mounting evidence to the contrary. Perhaps that helps explain why Spielberg has over the years become the world's most popular filmmaker; in addition to remarkable talents for providing entertainment, he more importantly reassures his audience, again and again, that there is hope, something we sorely need at a time when such belief is constantly tested by everyday events. The 1990s is a decade in which the quality of life, in our country and worldwide, appears to be constantly diminishing: the AIDS epidemic, an ever-escalating crime rate, intensifying pollution, worldwide economic woes, ethnic cleansing, fear that the family unit is doomed, the reemergence of rampant racism and anti-Semitism, increasingly violent acts of international terrorism, the preeminent drug culture, political corruption, generalized cynicism.

Aware of this, Spielberg admitted that he was glad that he had not been able to make *Schindler's List* right after completing *E.T.* In an interview conducted in Krakow, he explained that whatever one thought of the eighties while living through them, they were vastly superior in all respects to the nineties: "I think *E.T.* was a success not just because it was a good film but because the world was ready for a peace-loving film of that ilk" at a time when we were on the brink of perestroika and the wonderful, hopeful sense that, at least temporarily, emanated from the decimation of the Berlin Wall. "There was hope out there, and *E.T.* enjoyed all the economic benefits of a healthy country. It would have been the wrong time to release *Schindler's List.* Now it seems to me the story is more relevant. The world is more contradictory, complex, a darker place, and this is a complex story," one which proves through its dramatic example that hope is possible even in the worst of times.

Without optimism, civilized life as we know it would cease to be. People—good, decent people—have to believe in something, or they cannot go on. *Schindler's List,* like *E.T.* and a dozen and a half other Spielberg movies, provides an audience with a convincing illustration of such guarded optimism. The film insists that, however horrific things may be, there are always straws we can grasp at if only we search long and hard enough to find them. While some may scoff at the very act of grasping for straws in the middle of an all-encompassing storm, Spielberg would probably answer that, however fragile, they are sometimes all we have.

Miracles can and do happen: If you can't believe that the Christ-like alien *E.T.* will share a flight into the night sky, how can you deny that the historic Oskar Schindler saved those who would otherwise have been doomed? Certainly, the immense international audience attending Spielberg's films attests to the fact that countless millions of people want, perhaps more importantly need, to go on believing what he, in the universal language of the cinema, so artfully employs, and steadfastly/reassuringly continues to tell us.

The Lost World: Jurassic Park 2

A UNIVERSAL RELEASE OF AN AMBLIN PRODUCTION, 1997

CAST

Jeff Goldblum (*Dr. Ian Malcolm*); Julianne Moore (*Dr. Sarah Harding*); Pete Postlethwaite (*Roland Tembo*); Arliss Howard (*Peter Ludlow*); Richard Attenborough (*John Hammond*); Vince Vaughn (*Nick Van Owen*); Vanessa Lee Chester (*Kelly Curtis*); Peter Stormare (*Dieter*); Richard Schiff (*Eddie Carr*); Thomas F. Duffy (*Burke*).

CREDITS:

Director, Steven Spielberg; producers, Gerald Molen and Colin Wilson; screenplay, David Koepp, from the Michael Crichton novel; cinematography, Janusz Kaminski; editor, Michael Kahn; music, John Williams; production design, Rick Carter; computerized dinosaur effects, Dennis Murren; live-action dinosaurs, Stan Winston; special dinosaur effects, Michael Lantieri; running time, 134 mins.; rating: PG-13.

On Oscar night 1994, Steven Spielberg's great dream finally came true when *Schindler's List* won seven awards, including Best Picture and Best Director; *Jurassic Park* picked up another three in technical categories. The then forty-seven-year-old filmmaker had at last proven the possibility of balancing a career between escapist fun and serious social cinema.

Taking a behind-the-scenes role, Spielberg oversaw such Amblin hits as *The Flintstones, Casper,* and

The Stegosaurus, not included in the first film and sorely missed by many dinosaur buffs, is encountered early on in *Lost World;* though the scene is bright and suggests the sense of wonder of the first movie, *Lost World* will shortly turn dark (courtesy Amblin/Universal).

The master at work: Spielberg sets up a shot (top left), shares his concept with cast and crew (right), then confers with screenwriter David Koepp (bottom left) (courtesy Amblin/Universal, photo credits, David James).

Twister. He moved into the theme restaurant business with a submarine sandwich shop designed in the style of an underwater craft and called, tongue firmly in cheek, Dive! The Universal theme parks in California and Florida were all but transformed into Spielberglands. As co-creator of the DreamWorks SKG studio with Jeffrey Katzenberg and David Geffen, Spielberg threatened to become—like lifelong idol Walt Disney and longtime friend George Lucas—an idea man, a reigning presence rather than a hands-on filmmaker. Amassing a wealth estimated (by Forbes) at $1 billion, he could well afford to take a break from the nuts and bolts of directing.

As he neared fifty, he began to follow more mature pursuits. Spielberg founded the Survivors of the Shoah Visual History Foundation to record memories of Holocaust survivors. Closer to home, he put in daily duty as husband to Kate Capshaw Spielberg and father to their seven children (including Max, his son with Amy Irving, Kate's daughter Jessica, and the couple's three biological

and two adopted African-American children). Carefully avoiding the work-home dichotomy that contributed to the break-up of his first marriage—not to mention the marriage between parents Leah and Arnold—Spielberg consciously avoided the Charles Foster Kane trap. The Rosebud sled still held a place of honor in their Pacific Palisades mansion. Unlike *Citizen Kane*'s isolated anti-hero, who blows his second marriage as surely as he did the first, Spielberg learned from early mistakes. He appeared determined to follow the path of his alter-ego (played by Robin Williams) during the final moments of *Hook*. So the filmmaker became, in his own words, "Mr. Carpool"—spending time with the children, eating three meals a day with them, every day, between 1993 and 1997. Family was clearly his priority. Still, moviemaking—what Orson Welles once tagged "the greatest Erector Set a kid could ever hope to play with"—would always call to the director dormant within him. Besides, Kate occasionally found time to act in

243

movies, including Warren Beatty's remake of *An Affair to Remember.* So in the Fall of 1996, Spielberg gave in to his mistress, moviemaking, directing the *Jurassic Park* sequel for Universal, then moving on to *Amistad* for DreamWorks.

As with *Jurassic Park,* Spielberg immediately scuttled everything in Michael Crichton's *The Lost World* (still unpublished when pre-production began) except the concept of a second island with DNA dinosaurs and the all-important *T. rex* vs. trailer on the edge of a cliff sequence. Spielberg was far more insistent that, in preparation for this project, screenwriter David Koepp watch the 1925 film of Sir Arthur Conan Doyle's *The Lost World* than he read Crichton's book, though Koepp did both. During an early meeting-of-the-minds, Spielberg determined that while the central conflict of the first film had pitted "veggies" against "meat-eaters," Koepp's new script should pit "gatherers" (well-meaning observers) vs. "hunters" (who capture creatures for a zoo), as well as the dinosaur kingdom's counterparts to both social groups.

A second Costa Rican island—Site B, eighty-seven miles southwest of the one housing John Hammond's aborted theme park—turns out to have been the spot where a scientific team developed DNA dinosaurs. Though a hurricane had demolished the lab, dinosaurs somehow survived, reproducing despite a missing chromosome—which was supposed to keep that from happening. Chaos theorist Ian Malcolm (Jeff Goldblum), in disgrace for his supposedly outrageous stories (government and corporate interests hushed up the incident), initially turns down Hammond's invitation to lead an observational party. But Malcolm becomes a white knight after learning current girlfriend Sarah Harding (Julianne Moore), a paleontologist eager to engage the creatures, is already there.

This "gatherer" group includes a seemingly flippant but committed to causes photographer, Nick Van Owen (Vince Vaughn) and a softspoken operations specialist, Eddie Carr (Richard Schiff). Complicating matters for Malcolm—this time, reluctant hero rather than wisecracking one-man chorus—is a competing group arriving in full force to round up the animals, led by Hammond's less-pleasant, more mercenary nephew, Peter Ludlow (Arliss Howard) and the obligatory man in the hat, big game hunter Roland Tembo (Pete Postlethwaite). Adding to the mix is Malcolm's daughter Kelly (Vanessa Lee Chester), who stows away to join the adventure—providing that mandatory element for a Spielberg crowd-pleaser, the precocious child.

Up until three weeks before shooting commenced, Spielberg planned to save the San Diego sequence for a third film in a planned trilogy. *Lost World* would end with an extended chase of the heroes by raptors, and—as they fly off in a helicopter toward seeming safety—a surprise attack by flying pterodactyls. Always the savvy businessman, however, Spielberg knew competing film-makers were already at work on remakes of *Godzilla* and *Mighty Joe Young;* were he to wait, those movies might render his third film irrelevant. Spielberg made sure he got there first. Then again, perhaps not so savvy. Brian D. Johnson of *Maclean's* would eventually tag this "a cumbersome spectacle, a sequel that tries to bite off more [story] than it can chew."

But such considerations remained far in the future. First, Spielberg began elaborately storyboarding each individual sequence—child on the beach, raptor chase through long grass, trailer on cliff, *T. rex* vs. suburbia—that caught his fancy; Koepp's job, like those writers who scripted for Hitchcock, was to provide narrative glue that would hold together a half-dozen fully realized Spielberg moments.

While Koepp burned his way through nine drafts, Spielberg and Universal agreed the movie's total budget would approach $75 million, considerable, but not staggering when one recalls that at the same time *Speed 2: Cruise Control* and *Titanic* were each being shot for more than twice that amount. One way to cut costs was shooting close to home. Eureka, California provided a stand-in for the jungle location needed to create a seeming Shakespearean Green World that turns dangerously dark for the characters; at the advice of a location scout, Spielberg had visited and been overwhelmed by the primordial beauty of the giant redwoods.

The first week of September, 1996, Spielberg's crew of 150 arrived and began augmenting 125 million year-old redwoods with palm trees to create a fictional environment. Three weeks of location work was followed by shooting on sound stages and an elaborate set, on Universal's backlot, representing the dinosaur's graveyard and ruined laboratory. The Walt Disney in Spielberg was thrilled with the idea that he and his designers were creating not only a movie set but an upcoming stop for the thrill ride at Universal's theme park; when the moviemakers moved on, the visitors' tour was rerouted to include this attraction.

A few weeks after Kate Capshaw gave birth to their third child, Destry, Spielberg was aboard *Gulfstream 4* and on his way to Hawaii. There, during the week before Christmas, he shot exteriors on Kauai's lush green leeward side. These included the scene of an attack on a little girl, the film's unforgettable opening, filmed at the tail end of shooting.

Long before and throughout location shooting, f/x people were hard at work. In the intervening years between *Jurassic Park* and *Lost World,* digital technology—dazzling and groundbreaking in 1992—had been further refined as computer craftsmen honed their skills on forgettable fare like *Jumanji.* That, of course, allowed for the gradual perfection of product before *Lost World*'s cameras (and computers) rolled. *Jurassic*'s commercial success (worldwide box-office receipts topped one billion dollars, before counting video, TV, etc.), coupled

Self-allusions, notably absent from *Schindler's List,* return with a vengeance in *Lost World;* here, the heroes are treated to imagery reminiscent of *Jaws* (courtesy Amblin/Universal).

"The Touch" returns, only with a new twist; as Sarah (Julianne Moore) maternally touches the baby Stegosaurus, she upsets the balance of nature, initiating a new, more complex attitude toward women in Spielberg films (courtesy Amblin/Universal).

with raised audience expectation, caused Spielberg to pull out all the stops: Compared to five species in the first film, the sequel featured nine; rather than fifty-two effects shots appearing on screen, a whopping eighty-five would now keep the action constant.

In addition to computer graphics, enhanced dinosaur robots—each weighing nearly ten tons—cost as much as $1 million apiece to create. Stan Winston, in charge of these robotic puppets, designed forty-four this time, each able to (believably) interact with actors. In fact, creatures and humans interact more often than in any previous example of special effects cinema. Michael Lantieri, special-effects supervisor assigned to create a seamless mix between computer graphics and life-size models, was thrilled to note that almost every shot in the movie contained some sort of special effect; in *Jurassic Park,* such sequences did not appear until nearly halfway through, and then only occasionally.

Since audiences had been disappointed that no *Stegosaurus* appeared in *Jurassic Park,* Spielberg obliged by providing an entire herd. One particularly happy addition: A little creature called *Compsognathus* (Compy for short), a cross between a chicken (in size) and a piranha (in attitude), is introduced in the opening; later,

the pack dispatches an unsavory villain, Dieter. Attention to detail is impressive: Each little Compy (there were forty) was given its own varied way of moving to suggest unique personalities.

There were, of course, plenty of powerfully rendered Spielbergian set pieces. The best was borrowed from Crichton's book: Malcolm, Sarah, and Nick swinging from ropes attached to the remnants of a trailer precariously hanging from a cliff, as a *T. rex* attempts to shove them off. It would be hard to believe any filmmaker—current or classic—could have staged this remarkable ten-minute mini-masterpiece of suspense, horror, and comedy half as effectively as Spielberg. Still, its very impressiveness opened him to to the criticism once visited upon his idol Hitch: Was this merely a talented technician masterfully manipulating an audience's obvious motor responses, or a true artist able to intelligently engage with an ensemble of believable characters, even within the context of crowd-pleasing entertainment—as auteurs Hitchcock, Hawks, and Ford all did in the old days?

Was Spielberg their contemporary equivalent, or only another Brian De Palma, aping the surfaces of greatness without offering anything important underneath, mere

246

style without substance? Spielberg's own words seem significant: "I feel I'm all over my movies," he stated in 1997. "I know my movies are all over me." His own, and other people's: Allusions—purposefully kept to a minimum in *Schindler's List*—run rampant here. Early jeep chases recall Howard Hawks's 1962 classic *Hatari!;* a parent dinosaur protecting the child derives from the forgotten British gem *Gorgo* (1961). The dinosaur breaking loose from a supposed show to terrorize the populace recalls an entire tradition of films from *King Kong* (1933) through *Mighty Joe Young* (1949) to *Valley of Gwangi* (1969). "Our last chance at redemption," Hammond's early description of Malcolm's return visit, implies Spielberg is again working in the deep Catholic consciousness of idols Hitchcock and Ford. In fact, though, the film's redemption is uniquely Spielbergian, initiating a third stage in his ongoing development as a dramatist.

Familiar Spielberg stock characters return, with an original twist. Among the hunter faction, the most likeable is Dr. Burke (Thomas E. Duffy), a bearded, aging hippie who recalls early Richard Dreyfuss characters, such as Neery in *Jaws*. Spielberg rewrote Peter Benchley's book to spare that nice goofball's life, but here he goes the other route. Burke suffers the film's most horrible death: A poisonous snake slithers down his neck, sending him rushing into the mouth of a *T. rex.*

The film's man in the hat, Roland, initially appears no different from his predecessors, but when Roland removes the hat and to reveal he's bald, Spielberg is providing a less than romantic (even comical) motivation for his wearing it. We deduce—as the filmmaker already has—that all previous macho men wore hats less as obvious badges of courage, more to cover some similar undercurrent of insecurity. At last, Spielberg appears to have realized that beneath the surface of any hero beats the heart of a normal man.

Understandably, then, the man in the hat is presented from an ambivalent point of view: too courageous to be lumped with Ludlow as one of the villains, yet failing to grow beyond his initial amoral attitude (hunting for the pure blood sport of it), unlike Indiana and Schindler on their respective physical and spiritual treks toward heroic stature. The last time we see Roland, he's virtually defeated, his cold-blooded (though, significantly, non-monetary) reason for making the journey denied when Nick of Greenpeace removes the bullets from Roland's gun. "I've spent enough time in the company of death," Roland mutters before walking away; we're left with the sense he's been enlightened by this experience, realizing his old John Wayne mentality has been displaced by a new, politically correct type of hero, Nick.

But Malcolm, not Nick, dominates the film. He, Nick, and all the gatherers (particularly Sarah) set out to prove dinosaurs are not dangerous, dumb creatures but nurturing parents. "It's a story about families," Julianne Moore noted on the eve of the film's premiere, setting *Lost World* squarely in the center of Spielberg's oeuvre. More specifically, *Lost World* is about Spielberg's own family: Malcolm's stowaway daughter (Vanessa Lee Chester) is, without explanation, African-American. This revives Spielberg's ongoing integration theme, first hinted at with *The Twilight Zone's* Jewish person of color, Bloom. Now, though, such a situation also reflects on Spielberg personally as the adoptive father of a black girl. Kelly sneaks on-board after her dad chooses work over quality time together; such choices, always pressing on filmmaker-entrepreneur Spielberg, render Malcolm an autobiographical figure.

These autobiographical treatises disguised as mass entertainment reflect changes occurring in Spielberg's own life. The transitional piece was *Last Crusade,* in which Spielberg's alter ego, Indiana Jones, reconciled with his own long-absent father. Spielberg's mixed emotions about Arnold have always been essential to the fascinating tension in his work. On one hand, his father had inspired him with storytelling in general and filmmaking in particular, and initiated his interest in science-fiction and the WWII era, but, he had not been there when the insecure child needed a father most. "Bernie [Adler, Leah's second husband] didn't want me around," Arnold told *Time* in 1997, so "it became an uncomfortable situation. The kids [including Steven] suffered, and I just had to ride it out. At the premiere of *Jaws,* we sat at separate tables."

Arnold now admits to jealousy—while watching Steven receive an honorary degree at Brandeis—of Steven J. Ross of Warner Bros., in attendance as Steven's foster-father; that real-life moment finds artistic expression in *Hook,* when Peter Banning attends a baseball game his biological son plays under the guidance of the pirate. (Banning was central in that film, the intended source of audience empathy.) Then, Ross and Adler died, leaving Steven without surrogate father figures. The director contemplated his own failed first marriage and occasional time spent with first-born son Max, realizing a terrible truth about himself: "I didn't want to be as wrapped up in my work as my dad, and yet inexorably I was becoming my dad."

So, like Harrison Ford and Sean Connery on screen, Steven and Arnold finally reached out to each other. "It was like coming home again," Spielberg said, "making up for lost time—and we have a lot of lost time between us."

In the films that followed, long-absent father figures are fully embraced rather than cautiously reapproached. So the injured *T. rex* is now rescued at mid-movie by father and mother working in tandem. "Mommy's very unhappy," Malcolm sighs at the first sound of trouble, his initial reaction expressing the old Spielberg. In fact, it's Daddy who attempts to push Malcolm off the cliff. The dinosaur couple is not hunting, but searching for their child, not unlike the lovable rednecks in *Sugarland Express.*

CUT TO .. Thorne flies forward!..

PUSH-INT ends OTS Thorne..

cont'd next pg

Thorne dives for hook..

CRANE-OUT as Jeep arrives..

..trailer shakes - Thorne spins around..

Thorne just misses!..

..Thorne "HELLO!"

cont'd next pg

WIDE trailers slide forward..

TILT-UP CRANE-DOWN

..REVISE

trailer slowly shifts!..

Sarah, "We're sliding!"

CAM WHIP PAN

cont'd next pg

cont'd ..REVISE

Sarah & Ian reach the end of their rope!..

.. to Jeep..

cont'd next page

wheels run - Thorne heads for Jeep..

WIDE they swing back & forth..

steadi CAM PUSH-IN

cont'd next page

long shot over winch cable..

Jeep strains to hold trailer..

Within this altered context, the "touch" still exists, though less simple and less of an unqualified good. "She can't not touch," Malcolm complains about Sarah when she approaches the baby *Stegosaurus;* however well-intentioned, it's Sarah—the film's woman—who disturbs this friendly gatherer of the dinosaur kingdom, causing creatures to stampede. Conversely, it's a man—Eddie Carr—who proves sensitive, refusing to fire ("They're just protecting their baby!") when ordered to do so. "So am I," Malcolm chides, referring to Sarah—who is, in fact, more overgrown child than traditional Spielbergian earth-mother, despite her intellectual mastery of paleontology. When she and Kelly hide from raptors, they appear—despite the age difference—like an interracial re-rendering of the Gish sisters, Lillian and Dorothy, innocently embracing as they hide from figures of menace in D.W. Griffith's pre–World War I melodramas.

Florid melodrama certainly describes the tone of *Lost World's* unnecessary "second" third act. However dramatically negligible this portion may be, it's thematically linked to everything that preceded it. *Gorgo* featured an angry mother, something Spielberg most likely would have featured had he told such a story a decade earlier, during the period when *Poltergeist* sent Jobeth Williams into the void to recoup her little girl. The new Spielberg has the father visit San Diego and tear up the city before being reunited with his baby. Like Indy and Schindler, he gets the child out safely; that baby, heading home at last, invokes other lost Spielberg heroes ranging from the unforgettable E.T. to the upcoming Cinque.

"Our other title for *Jurassic Park* was 'Eat the Lawyer,'" Spielberg half-kidded. "This time, it's gonna be 'Eat the Rich.'" During the film's opening, a yacht has stopped by the island of Isla Sorna; as the crew prepares an elaborate luncheon, English accents identify the classy husband and wife. The sequence begins typically: Protective mother worries the child may wander into danger, oblivious father incorrectly insists everything's safe. As racks of lamb are dutifully carried past the camera, a glimpse of the father's newspaper—the *Financial Times*—visually links meals to money. Shortly, the little girl encounters a Compy; she feeds the creature, causing an attack. Spielberg paints the child's cameo-portrait in convincing strokes: She's sweet, not some spoiled brat, so there's no sense of poetic justice. As everyone responds to her screams, Spielberg's camera picks out and focuses on the father running to help. The camera does not follow him, though; as he rushes by, it lingers instead on the mother, who halts—screaming at what she sees (but we do not).

Still, the "eat the rich" theme is not exclusive; despite this initial attack and the rich villain's death at film's end, many victims sandwiched in-between (no pun intended) are decidedly middle-class—counterparts to audience members. If *Poltergeist* was, as Spielberg put it, his "revenge against television," then *Lost World* could similarly be considered his revenge against suburbia. When daddy *T. rex* tears lose, he goes straight for the kind of neighborhood sacrosanct in earlier Spielberg movies, even gobbling up a faithful, adorable doggie in a bit of black humor the director would not have included earlier in his career. Clearly, the film's morality is

249

Godzilla revisited: Spielberg's revenge against suburbia (courtesy Amblin/Universal).

different—and darker—than anything preceeding, *Hook* notwithstanding.

What we encounter in his portrayal of nature here is, if not an outright rejection of the values present in earlier films, at least a reconsideration of such notions from a more mature viewpoint. The film's thematic subtext offers, under the surface sheen of entertainment, a harsh vision that drastically differs from the conventional moral scheme of *Jurassic Park*—making clear how far Spielberg has progressed as a thinking person, for better or worse. While *Jurassic Park* marveled at modern science's possibilities while cautioning of inherent dangers, this sequel undermines such attitudes. *Lost World* stands not all that far from Joseph Conrad's *Heart of Darkness* and Francis Coppola's cinematic version *Apocalypse Now,* insisting that civilization is an illusion, with raw nature reclaiming the world. Thus, man—seemingly at the top of the food chain—is about to be undercut, as survival of the fittest dominates the natural world, just as Social Darwinism rules in the world of men.

"If we can only step aside," Hammond says in the final voice-over—accompanied by an image of a pterodactyl stretching his wings—"and trust in nature, life will find a way." The words may seem nothing more than a jingoistic coda familiar in Spielberg, the last great cinematic sentamentalist in the tradition of Disney, DeMille, Ford, and Capra. Actually, those words, closely examined, imply a revision (for the filmmaker, as well as his autobiographical entertainer-entrepreneur) of everything that's gone before. *Lost World* is noticeably void of the light we associate with Spielberg's notion of a religious truth, suggesting the movie's darkness was intended for metaphorical as well as textural purposes. Indeed, the only time the light appears is while Malcolm gazes at a map; brightness radiates from behind the chart, deriving from Isla Sorna: Spielberg's way of visually stating that the island itself holds the key to the truth—the meaning of life.

The final shot is so brightly lit that the image literally hurts the viewer's eyes. With the pterodactyl's appearance, optimism—albeit guarded—has returned to the scene; once man is gone, life once more becomes a positive experience. *The Lost World* is Spielberg's near-nihilistic statement about the arrogance of all men (himself included) who, like Hammond, believe their well-intentioned interference in the natural world can have happy consequences; the voice calling out in this cinematic wilderness insists on, of all things, benign neglect. That represents a radical—and radically conservative—approach to life from a filmmaker who, by all accounts, ostensibly remains a political liberal.

Most critics, however, did not see it that way; it wasn't so much that they disagreed with the film's ideas as they failed to notice the presence of ideas at all. "It's just spectacle and nothing else," David Denby complained in *New York*. "Spielberg and Koepp seem both timid and exploitative, afraid to offend the animal rights movement even while using animals to rip humans to shreds." Leonard Klady of *Variety* concurred: "Schematic and largely predictable... Like popcorn, it's a tasty, fun ride without a great deal of nutritional value."

Whatever its merits and flaws, the experience of digging in and doing *Lost World* whetted Spielberg's appetite for *Amistad*: "It made me wistful about doing a talking picture," he admitted, agreeing at least in part with his critics, "because sometimes I got the feeling I was just making this big, silent-roar movie." As critic Jack Kroll noted, "Spielberg [remains] the great double personality of modern movies... he's turned over his pop [projects] to the technologists, at the expense of story and character. At fifty, he's clearly tempted by the lure of being the greatest moneymaker in movie history, and also [drawn by the desire to be] an artist who tackles the great themes" in serious pictures. The problem: *Lost World* rang hollow even with those *Jurassic Park* buffs who couldn't resist flocking to the follow-up.

On the eve of the film's release, Spielberg made the cover of *Time;* can Man of the Year be far off? (courtesy Time/Warner)

Amistad

A DREAMWORKS PICTURES RELEASE,
1997

CAST

Morgan Freeman (*Theodore Joadson*); Anthony Hopkins (*John Quincy Adams*); Matthew McConaughey (*Baldwin*); Nigel Hawthorne (*Martin Van Buren*); Djimon Hounsou (*Cinque*); David Paymer (*Secretary Forsyth*); Pete Postlethwaite (*Holabird*); Stellan Skarsgard (*Tappan*); Anna Paquin (*Queen Isabella*).

CREDITS

Director Steven Spielberg; producers, Spielberg, Debbie Allen, and Colin Wilson; screenplay, David Franzoni and Steve Zaillian (*uncredited*), cinematography, Janusz Kaminski; editor, Michael Kahn; music, John Williams; production design, Rick Carter; visual effects, Scott Farrar/Industrial Light & Magic; sound, Dolby; running time, 152 mins.; rating: R (for realistic violence).

"It's always tough to get an audience interested in history," Steven Spielberg lamented to a visitor on the set, halfway through his *Amistad* shoot. Though *The Color Purple* and *Schindler's List* had both been box-office successes, *Empire of the Sun* didn't register. And while the director hoped his upcoming film—his first thematically ambitious project in five years—would fall into a class with the former, something in Spielberg's gut warned him that *Amistad* would more likely be a case of

Cinque (Djimon Hounsou) is brought to America in chains; for total authenticity, Spielberg insisted on using actors of African ethnicity rather than popular black American stars (courtesy DreamWorks SKG).

John Quincy Adams (Anthony Hopkins) meets with Cinque and translator James Covey (Chiwetel Ejiofor); though there is no historical evidence to support such a meeting, it is essential to the drama (courtesy DreamWorks; photo credit, Andrew Cooper).

the latter. Far more hurtful, however, were lukewarm reviews in major publications: "Stiff but powerful," (David Denby, *New York*); "not always dramatically exciting," (Emanuel Levy, *Variety*); "falls short of Spielberg's highest accomplishments," (David Ansen, *Newsweek*); "incomplete and hyperbolic," (Stanley Kauffmann, *The New Republic*).

What went wrong? The answer to that is complex. Certainly, the material was inherently powerful. In 1839, fifty-three Mende tribesmen, abducted from their homeland in Sierra Leone by Africans of an enemy tribe, were held hostage in a seacoast prison illegally used as a slave trading outpost. Turned over to Portuguese sailors, the Mendes were shipped to Havana, purchased there by a pair of Spanish planters eager to ship this "chattel" to their Caribbean plantation. The Mendes found themselves shackled aboard *La Amistad* (Spanish for "friendship," ironically), a coastal schooner occasionally illegally used as a slave ship.

On July 1, 1839, during a storm off the coast of Cuba, Cinque—a prince's son and rice farmer—slipped loose from his shackles and led an attack resulting in the death of all crew members except the planters, spared to navigate the boat back to Africa. Instead, they purposefully veered toward North America. After nine weeks of floundering about at sea with little food or water, *La Amistad* arrived off the Long Island coast, near Culloden Point. *La Amistad* was—at the prodding of the planters—seized by a U.S. Navy brig, the *Washington*. Towed to New Haven, it was placed in salvage. The Mendes, summarily charged with murder, were incarcerated in the local jail. A local real estate lawyer named Baldwin soon convinced Hartford's U.S. district court that the Mendes must be returned to Sierra Leone.

Instead of providing closure, however, this ruling set the scene for two additional courtroom confrontations.

Conservative forces moved the case to the circuit court, which upheld the original decision. President Martin Van Buren, fearful of alienating the South during an election year, then insisted the case be heard before the U.S. Supreme Court. Quietly, Van Buren appointed a judge he believed would find in favor of extradition.

In 1841, former president John Quincy Adams, speaking eloquently for nine hours over two days, secured the Mendes' freedom. Finally, the thirty-two surviving tribesmen (twenty-one had died at sea or in prison) were again free men. The case was a legal landmark: For the first time, the Supreme Court had unequivocably come out in favor of civil rights.

At the time, *La Amistad* became the Alamo of the abolitionist movement; the rallying call was now "Remember the *Amistad*!"

In our century, though, the *Amistad* story was largely overlooked by the entertainment industry; no movie or TV version appeared, even on shows dedicated to historical tales with a leftist bent. Why did Hollywood avoid the issue? In the minds of some observers—particularly African-American cultural critics—producers were leery of any story in which blacks killed without receiving punishment.

In the spring of 1988, Jacqueline Kennedy Onassis, then an editor at Doubleday, was taken with a still-unpublished manuscript called *The Summer Triangle*. The material, Mrs. Onassis believed, might appeal to the man who'd made *The Color Purple,* and she overnighted it to Amblin. No question they were interested: Shortly, author Barbara Chase-Riboud was, at Amblin's expense, flown from her home in France to Los Angeles. On the Universal lot, she pitched the project to several execs; Spielberg himself was not present. Chase-Riboud then returned home, hoping for the best. Instead, she received a regretful rejection letter dated April 25, 1988,

Young attorney Roger Baldwin (Matthew McConaughey) argues Cinque's case, transforming in the process from disinterested attorney to committed friend; in real life, Baldwin was a middle-aged man, but Spielberg transformed the historical personage into an audience-surrogate for youthful viewers (courtesy DreamWorks; photo credit, Andrew Cooper).

explaining only that "we see too many obstacles"; what the obstacles might have been remained vague.

Perhaps Amblin's true "obstacle" was a carry-over fear from *The Color Purple:* Someone would eventually question whether a white filmmaker, however talented, should tell a tale of African-American history. That discussion—if valid at all—was more appropriate for the Alice Walker adaptation, as every major character in her book is black. Despite the obvious centrality of Cinque and other Mendes, the *Amistad* story is as much about the whites who became involved. As Spielberg himself would rightly state in 1997, "This is not about African-American history so much as American history." Or, in the words of Sierra Leonian actor Sheriff Kargbo, picked by Spielberg to play a Mende: "It's a fight song for unity and togetherness." The story is a portrait of right-minded whites working together with victimized blacks for justice.

Such a vision would generally endear the concept to mainstream audiences of any color, but it hardly sits well with black nationalists, who vocally object—as vehemently as do white racists—to any work glorifying the integration of blacks into the company of whites. Haki Madubuti, owner of the Third World Press publishing house, took the separatist approach: "We have to be in control of our own stories." Conversely, mainstream integrationist Orlando Patterson, a Harvard sociology professor, insisted, "What's important is that [an *Amistad* movie is] finally getting made—no matter who made it, as long as it's quality work."

In 1988, such discussions were a decade away. Chase-Riboud's manuscript was never returned, either to her or Mrs. Onassis, though to do so is general practice. As far as anyone knew, it remained somewhere at the Amblin offices. Chase-Riboud accepted the bad news, shifting her attention to the forthcoming publication of her book, now called *Echo of Lions*.

Amblin moved on to other projects, but there remained one great champion for an *Amistad* film. In 1978, two years before hitting it big in *Fame,* Debbie Allen was a struggling actress-choreographer criss-crossing America on tour. On the Howard University campus she spent a free hour browsing in a bookstore, happening upon a collection of essays about African-American history that she bought to read on the bus. The first story, and accompanying illustration, retold the story of *La Amistad.* Devastated by what she read, Allen was disturbed that—though African-American and aware of her cultural history—she'd never before encountered this tale.

Producing a film about *La Amistad* became a cause celèbre that Allen pursued between stage, film, and TV commitments. Learning of William A. Owens's book *Black Mutiny,* she took out an option on the old tome, hoping to interest one of the newly prominent black filmmakers. Spike Lee's younger brother is named after Cinque; yet Lee, whose Thousand Acres and a Mule company supposedly exists to tell such tales, gave no indication of interest—the case with every other black filmmaker Allen approached. "The opportunity was there for them to make *Amistad,*" Allen bitterly insists when asked why she eventually worked with white moviemaker Spielberg, "and they didn't." Lee and the others were less frightened by incendiary material than—like their white counterparts—the prospect of box-office failure. *Glory* (1989) and *Rosewood* (1997) are among prestigious, acclaimed films of black interest that returned no profit.

Spielberg, meanwhile, had gone into business with David Geffen and Jeffrey Katzenberg, forming the much ballyhooed DreamWorks SKG studio. There would, of course, be bread-and-butter films to pay the bills, but they were also on the lookout for some high-prestige product to make everyone aware DreamWorks had truly arrived. Staffer Laurie MacDonald was assigned to find suitable material for development. As it happened, MacDonald's children attended the same elementary school as Allen's. One morning, the two women met at

Santa Monica's Broadway Deli for breakfast. Initially, talk was of kids, but the conversation soon turned to the current scarcity of strong story material, at which point Allen thought of her half-forgotten *Amistad* project, which she casually mentioned.

MacDonald's interest was piqued. Three days later, Allen was whisked into the DreamWorks office, where she pitched the project directly to Spielberg. "She was very compelling in her arguments to convince me to look beyond [issues of] color and race," Spielberg later said. During their meeting, he gave Allen no indication of ever having heard the concept before. Ironically, David Franzoni, who had been hired by Dustin Hoffman to adapt Chase-Riboud's novel, was assigned to create a screenplay Spielberg would produce, if not necessarily direct. Franzoni's script included Theodore Joadson, a

Morgan Freeman as a fictitious black abolitionist; legal questions would arise as to why this character, present in the historical novel that the film supposedly was *not* based on, appeared in the film (courtesy DreamWorks).

"Give us free!"; Cinque stands in a long line of strangers in a strange land who dominate such varied Spielberg films as *E.T.* and *Jaws* (courtesy DreamWorks, photo credit Andrew Cooper).

sophisticated black abolitionist eventually played by Morgan Freeman. The character does not exist in history, but a similar character—Braithwaite—is central to Chase-Riboud's novel.

All that, however, would explode later. For the time being, Spielberg expressed general satisfaction with Franzoni's story structure, not caring much for his bald language. He assigned Steven Zaillian (*Schindler's List*) to redo the dialogue. Zaillian also added a fictitious involvement of Queen Victoria in the proceedings.

Spielberg was smart enough to learn from past experience. Critics had complained that *The Color Purple* played as "compromised" and "sanitized," the work of a well-meaning white boy unaware of his own arrogance in trying to relate a chapter from African-American history. Still burned by the controversy—and understanding that in our day, perception is indeed reality—he craftily set about defusing any such criticism before it could occur. An African-American executive at Dream-Works, Cinque Henderson, named after the story's hero, was assigned to sell the still-in-embryo project step by step; by release date, any potential hostility should have been long since assuaged. Prominent black opinion makers, including historian Henry Louis Gates Jr. and poet Maya Angelou, were courted to serve as consultants. Major movie stars—Will Smith, Denzel Washington, Wesley Snipes—were passed over for Cinque in favor of an unknown actor of native African origin. (Though Benin-born, Djimon Hounsou was in fact raised and educated in France.) Gates, now a member of "the

team," spoke in Spielberg's defense: "It's important that our stories *not* be ghettoized—they have to be a part of (mainstream) American history." This, of course, is the middle-of-the-road view, black or white. Certainly, no contemporary American filmmaker is more squarely middle-American than Spielberg, who insisted, "I am making this film for my black children (adopted African Americans Theo and Mikaela) *and* my white children"—and, by implication and extension, all the children in the world. Brave words aside, Spielberg—following his long absence as a hands-on filmmaker, if not entrepreneur—reverted to precisely the pattern he'd employed before the big Oscar win: first mounting a surefire box-office hit with *Lost World,* then moving on to the more modest (estimated at anywhere from $36 to 40 million) socially conscious film. *Amistad* was (like *Schindler's List*) made on such a tight budget that, whatever happened theatrically, when home video, cable and network TV, and foreign rights were taken into consideration, it could not fail to break even.

At last, shooting commenced. Sea scenes were shot near Puerto Rico. In March, 1997, Spielberg arrived in Newport, Rhode Island, accompanied by actor Anthony Hopkins (cast as Adams). The city's historic district would provide the New Haven courtrooms, as well some New England exteriors. By mid-April, Spielberg and company had relocated to Mystic, Connecticut—made famous by a movie immortalizing its pizza shop—where the historic harbor and authentic environs could sit in for Long Island's Montauk Point. Spielberg's researchers peered into New Haven business records dating back to the mid-1830s, discovering names of stores and shops in operation at the time. Then, set designers set about creating signs ("Chaz Kirby, Sailmaker"; "S. Babcock, Stationery"; "Schaefer's Tavern") that were historically accurate down to the smallest detail.

At Seaport Streetwharf, *The Pride of Baltimore*—with its tall twin masts, dark hull, and weathered sails—could "play" the part of *La Amistad* itself. So that the filmmaking process, as well as resultant movie, would appear politically correct, Spielberg insisted only African-American crew members shackle black actors playing slaves in bondage.

Janusz Kaminski's cinematography visualizes Spielberg's theme: Cinque's body all but glows, suggesting he is the light and wisdom. Cinque's homeland is also a place of such light; immediately after the mutiny, Cinque instructs the surviving sailors to take his people home—"East to the sun." Spielberg quickly cuts away to a blinding light. What most attracts Cinque to the image of Jesus in an old Bible is the light that surrounds his head; from the image in the book, Spielberg then cuts to a shot of Cinque filmed in just such a way, with halo effect dominant.

Spielberg's theme of language impeding, rather than facilitating, communication appears when Cinque cannot explain to oblivious Americans that he and his tribesmen are freeborn. The motherhood theme is also present: An African woman, holding her baby, slips over the *Amistad*'s side and into the sea, a stunning, powerful, and notably Spielbergian vision of menaced madonna and child surrendering to the tragic peace of the great watery mother. Yet the movie also continues the de-feminization of Steven Spielberg so prominent in *Lost World:* the movie's heroes are all men, and Adams is seen as something of a father to his country.

Religion remains a potent theme. The Cinque of Spielberg's imagination is, in jail, exposed to the New Testament for the first time; he unofficially converts to Christianity without turning away from African religion and culture. In the filmmaker's eyes (here, as in previous pictures), "good" religions offer unique, appealing approaches to a single moral theme: integration (religious as well as racial), always possible in the world according to Steven Spielberg. As David Denby noted in *New York,* Spielberg—always, at heart, a religious filmmaker in the broadest, least parochial sense—viewed "the *Amistad* affair as Armageddon in the New World—the trial of Christian faith, of humanity's right to be saved." No wonder, then, that Spielberg's incarnation of the

Cinque's mid-movie recollection of the Middle Passage includes being sold in the slave market in Havana (courtesy DreamWorks; photo credit, Andrew Cooper).

257

The film's heroes, both black and white, make clear that this is one of Spielberg's integrationist essays conveyed through cinema; "I made the movie not only for my black children," Spielberg said, "but for *all* my children!" (courtesy DreamWorks).

young white judge steps into a church for guidance (he's intercut with Cinque praying) and subsequently makes the right choice.

As the child queen Isabella II of Spain, Anna Paquin angrily bounces up and down on her bed, having a fit after learning one of her ships is missing—a period-piece variation on the out of control child as all-powerful monster from *Twilight Zone—The Movie*. Avoiding the extremes of abolitionists and opposing conservatives,

Adams is, as *Variety* tagged him, "a reluctant hero"— this film's old, intellectualized Indiana Jones, coming to the rescue at the last possible moment. Miracles still come true in Spielberg's reality, just as they did in the films of his idols Walt Disney and Frank Capra. The final saving of the slaves can be seen as an act of God or an act of man. Either way, it is the act of a father—the Lord in heaven or Adams in the courtroom. Understandably, when Cinque is marched into the courtroom

Djimon Hounsou as Cinque; *Amistad* continued the "de-feminization of Spielberg" begun in *Lost World*, as male heroes dominate the tale (courtesy DreamWorks; photo credit, Andrew Cooper).

for the final confrontation, he senses everything will be all right when he glances over to the harbor and sees a ship's masts, which appear to him to be crosses—a sign.

The theme initiated in *Lost World*—the very rich as self-absorbed and oblivious—continues here, most often indicated by music; from the shipboard concert taking place on a yacht that the *Amistad* early on passes in the night, to Van Buren tuning his harp alone after losing the election. Another element that, as in *Lost World,* characterizes the rich is their propensity for overeating. The concert is also a dinner cruise; at mid-movie, Southern senator Calhoun intimidates Van Buren during an elaborate dinner party. In contrast, there's the extremely simple food seen being consumed by the heroes, from Cinque to Baldwin.

Once again, Spielberg—working in a tradition that stretches from Sophocles through Shakespeare to Cecil B. DeMille and John Ford—got much of the history right while imposing his own artistic stamp on the material.

Schindler's List had won over many critics—even staunch Spielberg opponents—by playing down the horrors of the Holocaust with a surprising, effective low-key approach from the current master of crowd-pleasing. Here, Spielberg reverted to pulling out all the stops: encouraging actors to play their scenes at a heightened level, filming from the most self-conscious camera angles, allowing John Williams to provide an over-inflated symphonic score that threatened to drown potentially powerful moments in bathos. Perhaps Spielberg

had grown rusty, having remained behind the scenes too long, creating DreamWorks SKG rather than continuing to hone his craft. Then again, *Amistad* was only the second film to be released by DW, and its first "prestige" item; in addition to a director's critical reputation, a new studio's future was at stake. It's easy to understand why Spielberg—admittedly fearful about box-office potential—took *Amistad* to extremes.

What made *Schindler's List* impressive was not only the desire to tackle stories with substance, but Spielberg's courage to back away from his previous crowd-pleasing approaches. In view of this, *Amistad* has to be considered a giant step backward. The great (and sad) irony: Despite a concerted technical effort to make the audience personally involved with the proceedings, most ticket-buyers (not that there were many) left with the distinct sensation all the technical overkill was for naught. The subtler approach of *Schindler's List* had done the job much more effectively.

What gradually unwound was a detached "thesis" film. Whereas *The Color Purple*, despite its faults, had succeeded with the public by emphasizing the human relationships in Alice Walker's story—woman to man, woman to woman—while providing a historical backdrop, *Amistad* emphasizes historical events rather than the personalities involved. The result is a film that plays better as history lesson than as human melodrama; while this might qualify it for classroom use, it is hardly what the public hankers for in a holiday release. Even the finest actors were stymied. Morgan Freeman's underdeveloped role was, at best, perfunctory, existing more for reasons of political correctness—introducing at least one black character who wasn't a slave—than for narrative purpose. Anthony Hopkins offered a stereotypical curmudgeon, Adams as lovable Grumpy Old President. Matthew McConaughey continued to suggest he has the star look but lacks the talent to back it up, sharing more in common with Tab Hunter than Robert Redford.

The ever-shifting point of view—Cinque, Joadson, Baldwin, Cinque again, etc.—results in a film lacking any clear focus. Everyone had hoped to avoid making what *Entertainment Weekly* once tagged "limousine-liberal flicks": *Mississippi Burning, Ghosts of Mississippi,* and *A Time to Kill* (starring McConaughey in a similar role) all have been attacked by the African-American intelligentsia for presenting black history from over the shoulder of some noble white "lone ranger" who steps in to save the day. Considering the *Amistad*'s historical outcome, this was almost unavoidable; the facts demanded the very approach that the filmmakers had determined to avoid at all cost.

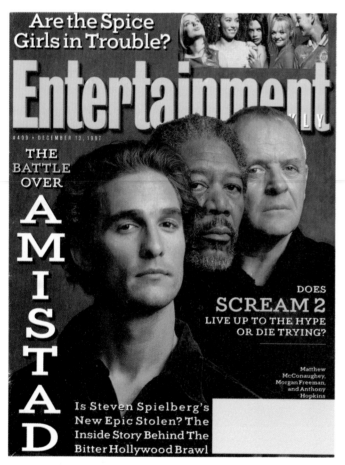

When *Amistad* made the cover of *Entertainment Weekly*'s December 12, 1997 issue, the focus was on the ensuing legal battle rather than the movie itself (courtesy Time/Warner Publications).

Then, despite the best laid plans of mice, men, and Spielberg, all the careful jockeying to present a public image of an enlightened multicultural crew working in perfect harmony threatened to blow sky high. One year earlier, Chase-Riboud had spotted a *Variety* article announcing Spielberg was indeed going to work on an *Amistad* film, though no mention was made of *Echo of Lions*. Upset, she contacted DreamWorks, growing more concerned when they refused to acknowledge her missives.

What occurred next was, as journalist Jeff Gordinier noted, an awkward situation involving "a black author going to war with a white filmmaker for allegedly ripping off an African-American tale." On October 17, the novelist filed a $10 million lawsuit in U.S. district court in Los Angeles, accusing Spielberg's company of stealing elements from *Echo of Lions*. Hers was one of the few books, fictional or historical, to mention that Cinque's actual name was Sengbe Pieh, which is in Spielberg's film. She invented an upscale black abolitionist, Braithwaite, as well as a memorable meeting between Cinque and Adams—seminal to the story as drama—though there's nothing factual to suggest the two ever came face to face, nor does this occur in any historical version.

It does, however, take place in the novel *Black Mutiny,* which Chase-Riboud may have read—and which Allen had optioned as the basis for her project. Spielberg's lawyer Bert Fields turned the tables, suggesting Chase-Riboud may have been the plagiarizer. As the situation swiftly grew uglier, Fields's language turned nasty, suggesting Amblin had rejected her book a decade earlier owing to artistic incompetence and labeling *Echo of Lions* "wordy, dull, confusing, and phony." The heart of the legal issue was, as Rebecca Mead noted in *The New Yorker,* whether there was "substantial similarity [between Chase-Riboud's book and Spielberg's film] that *doesn't* flow from history."

Diffusing Chase-Riboud's case, Dr. Clifton H. Johnson—founder of the Amistad Center located at Tulane University—explained that, as paid consultant on the project, he'd provided information about W.C. Pennington, a Hartford-based black abolitionist minister who had indeed become involved in the *Amistad* case.

Chase-Riboud's suit went so far as to request an injunction that would keep the film from being released in early December; in an eleventh hour decision, the judge refused to grant this—which would unnecessarily damage everyone involved—while leaving the door open for Chase-Riboud to continue her civil suit for damages, including a portion of the film's box-office receipts. Those, however, turned out to be all but negligible; by mid-March, 1998, *Amistad* had fallen off the top twenty films-in-current-release list after bringing in a paltry estimated box office take of $41 million—adjusted for inflation, one of the smallest ever for a Spielberg film.

The master at work; Spielberg directs Hopkins and Freeman (courtesy DreamWorks).

Saving Private Ryan

(PARAMOUNT–DREAMWORKS, 1998)

CAST

Tom Hanks (*Capt. John Miller*); Edward Burns (*Private Reiben*); Tom Sizemore (*Sergeant Horvath*); Jeremy Davis (*Corporal Upham*); Vin Diesel (*Private Caparzo*); Adam Goldberg (*Private Mellish*); Barry Pepper (*Private Jackson*); Giovanni Ribisi (*Medic Wade*); Matt Damon (*Private Ryan*); Dennis Farina (*Colonel Anderson*); Ted Danson (*Captain Hamill*); Harve Presnell (*General Marshall*); Harrison Young (*Old Ryan*).

CREDITS:

Director, Steven Spielberg; producers, Spielberg, Ian Bryce, Mark Gordon, Gary Levinson; writer, Robert Rodat; cinematography, Janusz Kaminski; editor, Michael Kahn; music, John Williams; production design, Tom Sanders; supervising art director, Daniel T. Dorrance; costume design, Joanna Johnston; sound, Dolby; running time, 169 mins.; rating: R.

Todd McCarthy of Variety, like most reviewers, hailed the latest Spielberg film as the director's masterpiece. He casualty pointed out something other critics missed: "*Saving Private Ryan* relates the kind of wartime stories that fathers never tell their sons." In addition to being true—in retrospect dads tend to romanticize rather than realistically describe war, particularly World War II— the comment is incredibly revealing about the *auteur*. As a youth, Spielberg had thrilled to his own dad's tales; as an adult, he had romanticized almost all of his early subjects. His ability to brilliantly accomplish that ro-

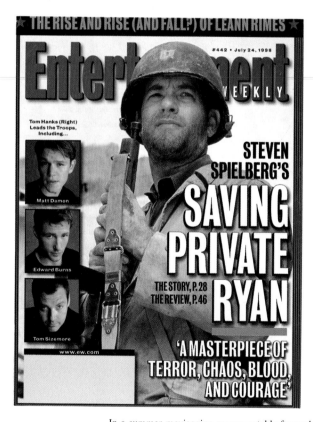

In a summer moviegoing season notable for such embarrassingly overwrought trivia such as *Godzilla* and *Armageddon*, the media had a field day hyping a film of substance that was clearly an artistic triumph; both *Entertainment Weekly* and *Newsweek* featured cover stories on *Saving Private Ryan*'s release. (Courtesy Time/Warner and Newsweek)

manticization proved to be his major liability as well as his greatest strength. Then, with films like *Schindler's List* and *Amistad*, Spielberg attempted to become more attuned to the real world. When he finally tackled the Big One, as veterans call it, he surprised everyone by avoiding what was expected—a cinematic canvas that conveyed his own dad's fables—and proceeded to make the most honest film possible. *Saving Private Ryan* completed the demythologizing process that had been basic to Spielberg's career for some time, leading him ever further from his roots as a maker of escapist entertainment. Meanwhile, the film's box-office success (it topped the lists during its first two weeks in release) made clear that, rather than abandoning Spielberg when he turned away from fantasy, his audience was willing to join him for the transition—from popcorn-style movie-maker to serious-minded filmmaker.

In almost every statement to the press about *Saving Private Ryan*, Spielberg directly stated (or carefully implied) his desire to consciously avoid film referencing, despite numerous pictures on the subject: World War II movies in general and D-Day movies such as *The Sixth of June* (1955) in particular. You don't die "in slow motion, with a blood bag coming out of the front of your chest and a huge fireball behind you," the filmmaker was quoted as saying, "shattering a plate of glass and then tumbling almost acrobatically into a perfect air-bag landing. That's not how it is." However, that's precisely how it seemed to be in the movies he and the entire generation that came of age in the second half of the twentieth century watched in theaters and on TV. The entire John Wayne tradition of World War II flicks presented a decidedly mythical portrait of combat, from thinly disguised propaganda pieces shot during the war itself (*Back to Bataan, The Fighting Seabees*) to supposedly more cynical reflections fashioned during the decade following what James Jones (*From Here to Eternity*) tagged "the last good war" (*Sands of Iwo Jima, Flying Leathernecks*) to what was widely considered in its time the first "realistic" reassessment of World War II, Darryl F. Zanuck's *The Longest Day* (1962). *Day* was a well-intentioned epic that nonetheless violated its own sense of docudrama by allowing John Wayne, Robert Mitchum, Henry Fonda, and other immediately recognizable but aging superstars to strut their traditionally heroic stuff.

That was precisely how that war looked in Spielberg's first World War II epic (or, more correctly, mini-epic), *Escape to Nowhere*, filmed by the fourteen-year-old writer-director (using his father's 8-mm home-movie camera) in a suburban Arizona backlot. Neighborhood kids were costumed to look as much like soldiers as possible, while gobs of Heinz ketchup made do for blood. By 1961, "the movies" had long since captured this gangly young outsider's imagination, with World War II films already exerting a special influence. His father had, after all, served in that war and, for bedtime

stories, related ever more exaggerated yarns about that fading era to his spellbound son. At that early point in the emerging *auteur's* history, fact was fused with fiction in the overactive adolescent imagination of a person who, in due time, would grow up to be the world's most famous storyteller since Shakespeare.

Had Spielberg shot a World War II epic early in his career, the mythical, rather than the realistic, conception is how combat would probably have appeared onscreen. Which may explain why he didn't make such a movie, though with his ever growing clout, Spielberg could easily have found financing. Instead, he danced around the issue, filming *1941*, a massive (and failed) comedy offering strained screwball sentiment instead of insight. Later, he approached the lingering impact of that war from a side angle in the Indiana Jones trilogy, with its two-dimensional Nazi villains menacing a comic book hero. Spielberg's instincts were sharp enough to tell him he yet lacked the perspective to do justice to such a monumental subject.

When he began mounting more serious films, Spielberg once more depicted World War II from its edge; *Empire of the Sun* dealt with the war's impact on a child who remains far from actual combat zones. True, there was "The Mission," a notable one-hour episode of *Amazing Stories* starring Kevin Costner as the captain of a bomber not unlike the one his father helped to man. However, the characters came off as overly familiar stereotypes, lifted from dimly remembered movies like *Thirty Seconds Over Tokyo* rather than from life itself. Characteristically, the young Spielberg chose to end that episode by having a threatened airman (D. B. Sweeney) saved by a metaphysical miracle worthy of Walt Disney or Frank Capra, rather than follow the story through to its grisly logical conclusion. Thus, an ongoing combination of attraction to and fear of World War II as subject matter caused Spielberg to shift the scene of *Always* from its original 1940s setting to a contemporary situation, diluting its dramatic possibilities in the process. There was no question that a major epic about World War II was in his future, though Spielberg would set about making it only when he felt secure enough in his vision.

Other moviemakers, meanwhile, were presenting diametrically opposed sides of the country's schizophrenic vision of war. Combat veteran Samuel Fuller wrote and directed *The Big Red One* (1980), a masterpiece of World War II realism that won rave reviews but suffered an ignominious fate at the box-office; draft-dodger Sylvester Stallone mounted *Rambo* (1985), a cartoonish portrait of Vietnam combat hooted by critics yet adored by the ticket-buying public. Then, combat veteran Oliver Stone entered the foray, forever changing the way in which Hollywood portrayed war with his sobering insider's view of Vietnam in *Platoon* (1986) and *Born on the Fourth of July* (1989). Originally, the latter film contained a scene (cut shortly before release) in which youthful Ron Kovic watches John Wayne on TV, rushes

out to play war games with neighborhood kids, and eventually signs up for Vietnam, where he learns the hard way the discrepancy between combat in the reel and real worlds.

That missing scene should have remained in the finished film; in a single sequence, Stone conveyed the ongoing danger lurking beneath the seemingly benign surface of Hollywood's romanticized battles. Like Stallone, Spielberg knew war only through an earlier era's aggrandizements. Unlike Stallone, Spielberg wisely kept his mouth shut on the subject, sensing all he could provide would be state-of-the-art imitation of stale cliches from other people's pictures. Whereas Stallone remained forever frozen as an icon of mock heroics for mindless moviegoers, Spielberg steadily grew as a person and filmmaker. Though *The Color Purple* was rightfully dismissed as a naive misconception of what it was like to be poor and black in the deep south during the Depression, the film could generously be considered a necessary (mis)step on Spielberg's difficult if deter-

264

Oscars for Best Director and Best Picture is, at the time of this writing, uncertain; what is clear is that at some point in the future, it is *Saving Private Ryan*, not *Schindler's List*, that will be recalled as his first masterpiece of realism, equaling in its virtual perfection that of *E.T.*, his initial masterpiece of fantasy filmmaking. "Fairly or not," industry analyst Jeff Gordinier wrote, "Spielberg is known as our Merlin, the man who conjured up the 'sense of wonder' school of filmmaking" in "giddy, saucer-eyed, gold-dusted fantasias" that established Spielberg as a "wizard of the box office." But by 1998, that was only partly true; mention Spielberg and the name now conjures up memories of *Schindler's List* and *Amistad* as readily as it does E.T. and Indiana Jones.

"I think people stopped trusting me about ten years ago," Spielberg told *Entertainment Weekly* on the eve of *Saving Private Ryan*'s release. "I really don't feel people expect from my movies the same kind of Disney enchantment that ascribed to me back in the seventies and first half of the 1980s." In large part, this was because he had slowly but surely distanced himself from charming fluff via the serious-minded movies that now alternated with box-office bonanzas. No doubt, in addition to his growing canon of ambitious work, this was the right time to eyeball World War II as a subject because of a recent reconciliation with Arnold Spielberg, the biological father so long missing from his life. In the third Indiana Jones flick, their cinematic counterparts—Professor Jones (Harrison Ford) and his estranged dad (Sean Connery)—belatedly joined forces to fight Nazis. Spielberg—his insecurity relieved by an acceptance of the long absent dad as a flawed but worthwhile human being—could deal with his father's war in an honest way that would not have been possible a decade earlier.

Thus, the "new" Spielberg emerged from the crippling cocoon of constant Hollywood homage to Hitchcock and others. He now hoped to do what his most important contemporaries—Oliver Stone, Martin Scorsese, Spike Lee, and Francis Coppola—had been trying to achieve from the beginning; to create a complex post-Hollywood cinema. "I wanted to achieve reality," Spielberg admitted about *Saving Private Ryan*. By again attempting (and finally succeeding) at such an ambition, Spielberg at last liberated himself from the crowd-pleasing artistic corner he had earlier painted himself into.

As with every project from a filmmaker who insists "if it isn't on the page, it won't be on the stage," *Saving Private Ryan* began with a script containing a great idea. A squad of soldiers must find and relieve a G.I. before

mined journey toward more mature moviemaking. *Schindler's List* was far from the masterpiece many considered it, but it marked a further step in the right direction as Spielberg continued to focus his unparalleled moviemaking skills on ever more serious subjects in his ardent desire to become a filmmaker of substance—as *Amistad*, one more worthy failure, made clear.

With *Saving Private Ryan*, Spielberg's artistic arrow finally hit the bullseye. Whether he will again win

Spielberg discusses an upcoming sequence with Matt Damon. (Courtesy DreamWorks/Paramount Pictures)

he's killed in combat after the deaths of his three brothers in other recent military actions. It isn't hard to understand why that story would appeal to the man who made *Schindler's List*: One is able to derive an abiding sense of optimism from the few who are saved, despite the possibilities for pessimism when considering the many lost.

Thirty-nine-year-old screenwriter Robert Rodat (*Fly Away Home*) was inspired to begin work on the script when he noticed an ancient monument to Civil War soldiers in the village of Putney Corners, New Hampshire, honoring a family that lost eight members during that conflict. Though the Sullivan Act (following the death of four sailors during the torpedo-bombing at Guadalcanal of the vessel on which they all served) assured no siblings would ever again be assigned to the same unit, Rodat's work of fiction remained entirely possible. Indeed, historian Stephen Ambrose's book *Band of Brothers* relates the similar, though true, tale of Fritz Niland, a member of the 101st Airborne. Niland's three brothers were all killed in separate combat zones during June of 1944; an army chaplain, Father Francis Sampson, was assigned to locate and remove the surviving Niland son from the battlefield after the boy's mother received three telegrams from the War Department on a

single day; Ambrose, it's worth noting, is listed as a consultant in *Saving Private Ryan*'s credits.

Spielberg, considering his ongoing fascination with the concept of family in general and mother-love in particular, could hardly help but be moved by such a premise. So his DreamWorks studio joined forces with Paramount, where the project was already in development under the guidance of *Speed* producer Mark Gordon. The moment the world's premier director attached himself, the film's future was as certain as anything can be in today's highly-dynamic movie market. To keep the tab down to a hefty though practical $65 million, Spielberg agreed to forego his usual salary (as he'd previously done on *Schindler* and *Amistad*), settling instead for a share of the profits. This, clearly, was one of those films he made for himself—his fulfillment as a creative person—as opposed to *The Lost World*, which was for the industry and the audience.

Though Spielberg likes to make statements on the order of "I am not an *auteur*; I am a team player," he immediately set about Spielbergizing the production with his by-now perfected system of old-fashioned studio-style efficiency. (An *auteur*, as Spielberg should know, is *always* a team player and first among equals owing to his central conception; "one man, one movie" refers not to the workload but a film's overriding vision). Though Rodat had already completed a dozen drafts, Spielberg directed the writers long before he'd initiate similar service with actors. He created a committee of talents, including writers Scott Frank (*Out of Sight*) and Frank Darabont (*The Shawshank Redemption*) neither of whom would receive screen credit, to work with Rodat on a final draft. Every plot possibility—including whether Ryan would be wounded when the film's eight heroes come across him, and the nature of Ryan's personality, which, during discussion, alternated between saint and sinner—was considered on the way to a shooting script.

Essential to the committee, as well the film's heart and soul, was star Tom Hanks. Of the relatively young actors who achieved superstardom during the nineties, Hanks has virtually no competition (with only the exception of Denzel Washington) at playing the kind of decent, strong, quiet heroes immortalized on-screen a half-century ago by Gary Cooper, James Stewart, and Henry Fonda. If Spielberg is (along with his onetime protege Robert Zemeckis) the nearest thing to a Frank Capra populist we have behind the cameras today, then Hanks is our contemporary incarnation of Capra's common-man protagonists. Surprisingly, director and star had not worked together before, although the two were close friends. Actually, that explains why: So many relationships have been destroyed during the difficult process of bringing a film to fruition that Spielberg and Hanks unofficially agreed to avoid such a possibility by maintaining a professional distance, but *Saving Private Ryan* proved too tempting to resist.

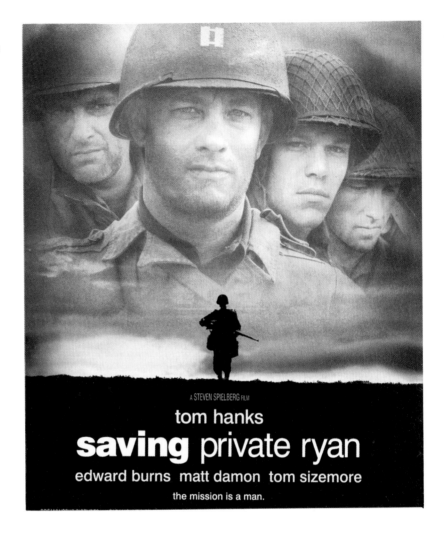

Advance advertising for *Saving Private Ryan* emphasized the humanity of the characters and the starkness of Spielberg's vision. (Courtesy DreamWorks Pictures/ Paramount Pictures)

Hanks was instrumental in holding Spielberg's cast together when a moment of crisis occurred. Insisting on total authenticity, Spielberg had hired fifty-three-year-old Captain Dale Dye, a retired marine combat veteran who served as an historical consultant on Stone's *Platoon*, to run his cast members—Hanks, Tom Sizemore, Edward Burns, Jeremy Davies, Barry Pepper, Giovanni Ribisi, Adam Goldberg, and Vin Diesel—through an agonizing week of boot camp. Always referring to the eight as "turds," Dye (whose company, Warriors Incorporated, serves as an independent contractor to insure authenticity for combat films) pushed the squad through such a horrific array of calisthenics (push-ups, sit-ups, five-mile runs) that the younger cast members were, halfway through, about to call it quits. (Thirteen years earlier, Charlie Sheen and other *Platoon* cast members considered walking rather than face any more of Dye's abuse). It was Hanks—the actor performing precisely the role in real life that his character does on-screen—who opted to stick it out; the others begrudgingly followed suit.

The only key cast member not included in such preparation was Matt Damon, cast as Ryan long before *Good Will Hunting* made him 1998's flavor of the year. Spielberg, believing like great directors of the past that the actor's feelings would translate into their performances, wanted his starts to resent the special treatment accorded Damon as much as their fictional counterparts become bitter about being ordered to risk their lives to insure some other soldier's survival. All the while, line producer Ian Bryce scouted locations, visiting virtually every inch of beachfront in Western Europe, searching for a stretch of land that could stand in for Omaha. Finally, he settled on a place called Wexford, on the east coast of Ireland, where some troops who participated in the D-Day invasion had rehearsed for the coming combat.

The location had to be okayed by Spielberg, who had a personal connection with the assault on Omaha Beach. In 1972, while hyping his first hit, *Duel*, in Europe, Spielberg spent a free day visiting the invasion site. The experience made a lasting impression. Walking ahead of the twenty-four-year-old director, a middleaged man—likely a combat veteran, returning with his family to the sight of his own longest day—fell to his knees, sobbing. The filmmaker, touched deeply, filed that image away; a quarter-century later, he pulled it out of his mental computer, employing the instance as *Saving Private Ryan*'s opening image.

Thanks to this signature shot, *Saving Private Ryan* becomes one more chapter in the ongoing cinematic autobiography of a director who, despite a reluctance to admit it, is a true *auteur*. Always, Spielberg exerts the creative force which shapes diverse pieces of material into works of persona expression, resulting not only in consummate craftsmanship but true art. Nonetheless, it's worth noting that, to one reporter, Spielberg described his approach to *Saving Private Ryan*'s visual scheme as a purposeful backing away from "the role of an artist," since he wanted "to achieve reality." Or, more correctly, the *illusion of actuality* that marks the best "realistic" films, though the event seemingly being "reported" had to be constructed after the fact. To achieve this effect, Spielberg would take the self-consciously "sloppy" approach he'd experimented with in *Schindler's List* to the point of perfection. Ironically, this was achieved by opting *against* the highly schematized visual perfection that dimmed the impact of *The Color Purple* and *Empire of the Sun*. "More matter," a character in *Hamlet* demands of a storyteller enraptured by his own purple prose, "and less art." It's a lesson Spielberg had at last learned. Rather than imitating take-your-breath-away tableaus of great Hollywood war films, Spielberg studied on-the-spot documentaries created by John Ford, Frank Capra, and John Huston during the conflict—particularly the latter's remarkable work of poetic-realism, *The Battle of San Pietro* (1944).

To achieve such an end, Spielberg would forego his beloved storyboards, instead improvising on the spot with hand-held cameras. The onscreen effect is, in the words of critic David Ansen, to "plunge us into the carnage" on a direct-impact level not ordinarily associated with a filmmaker whose movies ordinarily boast images that call attention to their own artistry. Such an approach once marked Spielberg as a postmodernist, the experience of watching one of his movies being something an audience remains aware of, resulting in a kind of hip, knowing artificiality. Here, though, he takes a step backward in terms of technique while managing a giant leap forward in emotionally involving his audience. There are, thankfully, none of the strikingly visual moments like those in *Schindler's List* (the small child hiding in the sewer) that pull us out of the picture; here, we forget we're watching a movie, instead going along with its flow, always at one with the film's created reality. By not striving for artistry, Spielberg managed to finally achieve true art rather than his previous examples of impressive artifice.

No wonder, then, that *Saving Private Ryan* drew impassioned reviews from critics who, in the past, often patronized Spielberg. "A movie of staggering virtuosity and raw lyric power," Owen Glieberman raved, "a masterpiece of terror, chaos, blood, and courage. More than Coppola (*Apocalypse, Now*), Stone (*Platoon*), or Kubrick (*Full Metal Jacket*), all of whom apotheosized the druggy morass of Vietnam, Spielberg has captured the hair-trigger instability of modern combat. He puts us directly inside the consciousness of men in battle" by using "his unparalleled kinetic genius" (so often, in the past, squandered on minor projects) "to create an excruciatingly sustained cataclysm of carnage, nausea, and death."

Nonetheless, it was impossible for Spielberg not to be influenced by past masterpieces. Wisely, he avoided any specific references to other people's movies that for three decades kept him from emerging as a unique voice in his own right. Yet it would be equally wrong to pretend those important films didn't exist—or influence his sensibility. In an article written specifically for a special film-oriented issue of *Newsweek*, Spielberg insisted the film that had the most impact on him was William Wellman's *Battleground* (1949), which earned Oscars for its stark black-and-white photography by Paul C. Vogel and an original screenplay by Robert Pirosh. *Battleground* focused on grunt-infantrymen, fighting the Battle of the Bulge without any true sense of what they were doing or why (other than trying to survive from day to day), rather than the commanding officers whose perception of the event had been the basis for most films. Yet as film historian Leonard Maltin noted, *Battleground* is a far-from-great movie owing to "a lack of genuine insight into the characters." Far more impressive—and, one might guess, one that has had more impact on Spielberg—was an earlier Wellman vehicle, *The Story of G.I. Joe* (1945), which told the story of average infantrymen through the eyes of war correspondent Ernie Pyle (Burgess Meredith). It achieved a heightened sense of documentary realism not in view in the better known, but less impressive, *Battleground*.

By far, the greatest World War II film (and, whether he acknowledges it or not, the one that made the greatest impression on Spielberg) was Lewis Milestone's *A Walk in the Sun* (1945). Screenwriter Robert Rossen adapted a script from Harry Brown's book in a manner that owed much to the Group Theater's liberal-social dramas of the 1930s. Like that classic, Spielberg's modern masterpiece focuses on eight men who embark on a specific mission, under the leadership of a compassionate if all-too-human officer (Dana Andrews). The discussions between men about everything from their favorite pastimes back home to the dubious purpose of their current objective to the future of mankind following the war's end are highly perceptive, as are the parallel philosophic debates in *Saving Private Ryan*. The film's squad members, like those in Spielberg's film, are drawn in admirably subtle and specific strokes, rather than the broader characterizations in *Battleground*.

Whichever film (or films) was most influential, *Saving Private Ryan* features something unimaginable when they were made: Gruesome images of combat of the type that first appeared onscreen in 1967. Cornel Wilde's *Beach Red* featured the image of a soldier lying face-down who slowly rises, his arm (severed, without his knowledge) remaining where it was. Ostensibly "about" WWII, Wilde's film was "informed by" the Vietnam conflict just then escalating out of control. Though all but forgotten today, *Beach Red*—loudly debated between those critics who hailed its graphic violence as a new form of honesty and those who damned it as exploitive and sensational—preceded (and set the pace for) such better-known ultraviolent films as the rural gangster epic *Bonnie and Clyde* (1967) and Sam Peckinpah's revolutionary western *The Wild Bunch* (1969), both—despite historical settings—reflecting the then-current (and highly-televised) violence raging in Southeast Asia.

The new American cinema of the seventies and beyond, spearheaded by those landmark movies, continues today. While George Lucas remains enshrined in the fantasyland of Industrial Light and Magic, Spielberg has belatedly chosen to join Coppola, Scorsese, Stone, and Lee in the real world. "His unsparing vision of D-Day wouldn't have been possible before Vietnam," *Newsweek* duly noted; Spielberg himself added, "In the 1940s, realism in war movies didn't really matter. After Vietnam, it was all that mattered." In *Saving Private Ryan*, that 'realism' translates into frightful bloodletting (images of wounded soldiers with their guts literally hanging out) that seems uncharacteristic of Spielberg; this is, lest we forget, the director who sniffed "I don't make R films" when *Poltergeist* was threatened with something stronger than a PG. In retrospect, though, *Amistad*'s unsparing opening seems a dry run for this film's thirty-minute D-Day prologue. Indeed, numerous industry insiders insist that had any other director dared offer such shocking imagery, the movie would have been labeled NC-17.

Thirty years ago *The Wild Bunch* was the most hotly debated of all movies from the Vietnam era, largely because of Peckinpah's complex treatment. His cross-cutting, oblique editing, slow-motion, and offbeat angles resulted in crazed kinetic choreography, a virtual ballet of blood that simultaneously fascinated and repulsed viewers. Some interpreted *The Wild Bunch* as a pacifist statement, telling the truth about the horror of gunplay in a way American movies had never before dared; others contrarily understood it as a Hemingwayesque tribute to the horrific, hallucinatory grandeur of macho combat. For his Omaha Beach sequence, Spielberg opted for just such an approach. Though he and cinematographer Janusz Kaminski aimed for an artless sense of reality

Edward Burns and Tom Sizemore as soldiers ordered to risk their lives so that another man might live. (Courtesy DreamWorks/Paramount Pictures)

during shooting, they stylized the sequence afterwards, in the editing room. The final result is a bizarre phantasmagoria, as images that appear lifted out of old newsreels are aesthetically juxtaposed into a mesmerizing montage. As journalist Jon Meacham reported, "Summer-moviegoers may slip into the multiplex looking for an escape into a simpler universe. They won't find one."

Ansen insisted this treatment of violence was essential to *Saving Private Ryan*'s "meaning," that being a consideration of "the [motion picture] medium's ambiguous relationship to violence. War, as a dramatic subject, is exciting, and the battles are the most exciting part [of any war film]. How do you depict violence without, in some way, promoting it? How do you take the thrill out of danger?" The answer is, of course, that you don't—if only because you can't.

This was, after all, Spielberg's father's war, the "good war," as General Eisenhower tagged it, the Crusade in Europe, crushing Fascism. There was never any question, at least for those who kept close watch on the emerging pattern of Spielberg's career, that sooner or later, he would approach World War II in a big way. The only question was whether he would do so too soon, while still an overgrown adolescent, resulting in a movie that reduced the complexity of that conflict, and war in general, to the entertaining infantilism of Indiana Jones. Wisely, Spielberg put off his World War II film until he was ready to do it right, and knew in his heart the proper time had arrived. This explains why he was able to create not only the best American film of 1998, and the crowning achievement of his career to date, but what may be the greatest war film ever made. As such, *Saving Private Ryan* proves that Steven Spielberg has at last "arrived" as the most important filmmaker of the century.

Spielberg directs Hanks and the rest of the group to "try it once more."

Appendix I: The Other Films of Steven Spielberg
THEATRICAL FEATURES WHICH SPIELBERG WAS ASSOCIATED WITH
BUT DID NOT WRITE OR DIRECT:

ACE ELI AND RODGER OF THE SKIES, 1973

Spielberg's credit: original story
DIRECTOR: Bill Sampson (John Erman)
STARS: Cliff Robertson, Pamela Franklin, Eric Shea
THE FILM: post–World War I stunt flier and son barnstorm the country. Early Spielberg story features two key themes—aviation and dysfunctional father-son relationship—but was botched by hack filmmaking approach.

I WANNA HOLD YOUR HAND, 1978

Spielberg's credit: coexecutive producer
DIRECTOR: Robert Zemeckis
STARS: Nancy Allen, Theresa Saldana, Eddie Deezen
THE FILM: ensemble comedy about cute teens on the night when the Beatles first appeared on Ed Sullivan. Shrill and over-played, notable nostalgia for an earlier, more innocent era.

USED CARS, 1980

Spielberg's credit: coexecutive producer
DIRECTOR: Robert Zemeckis
STARS: Kurt Russell, Jack Warden, Deborah Harmon
THE FILM: Spielberg's longtime association with cars crashing crystallizes in this off-color item from writing team of Zemeckis and Bob Gale, a kind of rube *1941* on a considerably smaller scale.

THE BLUES BROTHERS, 1980

Spielberg's credit: actor
DIRECTOR: John Landis
STARS: John Belushi, Dan Aykroyd, Carrie Fisher
THE FILM: elaborate, over-the-top, incredibly expensive comedy combines *Saturday Night Live* favorites with classic rhythm and blues, plus plenty of cars crashing. Spielberg's cameo attests to his then strong friendship with Landis.

CONTINENTAL DIVIDE, 1981

Spielberg's credit: coexecutive producer
DIRECTOR: Michael Apted
STARS: John Belushi, Blair Brown, Allen Goorwitz (Garfield)

THE FILM: Lawrence Kasdan *(Raiders)* scripted this charming, low-key romantic comedy involving a tough-guy journalist with a liberated environmentalist. A 1940s lighthearted-relationship movie updated for today.

GREMLINS, 1984

Spielberg's credits: coexecutive producer, actor
DIRECTOR: Joe Dante
STARS: Zach Galligan, Phoebe Cates, Hoyt Axton
THE FILM: magical pet spawns a killer brood at Christmastime.

Billy Peltzer (Zach Galligan) cuddles his lovable little creature Gizmo in the second *Gremlins* film to be directed by Joe Dante (courtesy Warner Bros.).

Brilliant combination of horror and comedy, boasting tone that was attempted (and just missed) in *Poltergeist*. Modern fairy tale includes homage to every great old Hollywood movie ever made.

BACK TO THE FUTURE, 1985

Spielberg's credit: coexecutive producer
DIRECTOR: Robert Zemeckis
STARS: Michael J. Fox, Christopher Lloyd, Lea Thompson
THE FILM: modern teen returns to 1950s, ensures that Mom and Dad fall in love. Delightful comedy-fantasy with strong relationship element and troubled-family theme Spielberg so often returns to.

Spielberg protégé Robert Zemeckis directed Bob Hoskins as Eddie Valiant and "Roger Rabbit" in *Who Framed Roger Rabbit*, the 1988 film that revitalized Disney's commitment to ambitious animation (courtesy Walt Disney Company and Amblin Entertainment).

WHO FRAMED ROGER RABBIT: Never forgetting the importance of the breaks that other people gave him, Spielberg has consistently supported eager and talented young filmmakers, most notable among them Robert Zemeckis. Spielberg allowed his name to grace their dream-projects as "executive producer," which was enough to ensure that the movie would get made. His influence was crucial to the making of Disney's *Who Framed Roger Rabbit*, the film that caused the animation Renaissance, with Roger, Baby Herman, and Jessica—all seen here in their later short *Tummy Trouble* (photo courtesy Walt Disney Pictures).

THE GOONIES, 1985

Spielberg's credits: coexecutive producer, story
DIRECTOR: Richard Donner
STARS: Sean Astin, Josh Brolin, Ke Huy Quan
THE FILM: contemporary group of Little Rascals go in search of Treasure Island. Surprisingly unappealing in all respects, lacking intended charm and magic, played at an off-putting fever pitch.

YOUNG SHERLOCK HOLMES, 1985

Spielberg's credit: coexecutive producer
DIRECTOR: Barry Levinson
STARS: Nicholas Rowe, Alan Cox, Sophie Ward
THE FILM: as the title says, first case solved by a diminutive Holmes and Watson, with ultramodern special effects as a bonus. Highly appealing film never found its audience, awaits rediscovery.

FANDANGO, 1985

Spielberg's involvement: Amblin presents
DIRECTOR: Kevin Reynolds
STARS: Kevin Costner, Judd Nelson, Glenne Headly
THE FILM: young Reynolds expanded his student-film to feature length, with Spielberg's formidable support. Quintet of college

Dennis Quaid, as test pilot Tuck Pendelton, braces himself for a miniaturized flight into the human body in *Innerspace*, a comical redux of *Fantastic Voyage* (courtesy Warner Bros.).

Don Bluth, who had once worked at Disney, directed *An American Tail*, the animated feature in which Spielberg was able to employ a Mickey-like mouse to communicate two themes near and dear to his heart: the Jewish immigrant experience and the separation of a child from parents (courtesy Amblin Entertainment and Universal City Studios).

buddies on a final fling before growing up; often involving, if less than fully satisfying.

AN AMERICAN TAIL, 1986

Spielberg's credit: coexecutive producer
DIRECTOR: Don Bluth
STARS: Dom DeLuise, Christopher Plummer, Madeline Kahn (voices only)
THE FILM: animated adventure of Disney's Mickey, here reimagined as a Jewish immigrant coming to America. Notable Spielberg theme of vulnerable child separated from family unit.

THE MONEY PIT, 1986

Spielberg's credit: coexecutive producer
DIRECTOR: Richard Benjamin

STARS: Tom Hanks, Shelley Long, Alexander Godunov
THE FILM: yuppified redux of *Mr. Blandings Builds His Dream House*, only nothing clicks; elaborate situations that should have been funny simply aren't.

*BATTERIES NOT INCLUDED, 1987

Spielberg's credit: coexecutive producer
DIRECTOR: Matthew Robbins
STARS: Hume Cronyn, Jessica Tandy, Elizabeth Pena
THE FILM: E.T. meets "Kick the Can" as cute aliens visit a New York City tenement. The kind of cookie-cutter imitation Spielberg you'd expect some rip-off artists to have made, not Amblin.

INNERSPACE, 1987

Spielberg's credit: coexecutive producer
DIRECTOR: Joe Dante
STARS: Dennis Quaid, Martin Short, Meg Ryan
THE FILM: *Fantastic Voyage* as a comedy, about miniaturized man entering another person's body. Dante attempts to rekindle his *Gremlins* magic and fails. Great special effects, though.

HARRY AND THE HENDERSONS, 1987

Spielberg's involvement: an Amblin Entertainment Production
DIRECTOR: William Dear
STARS: John Lithgow, Melinda Dillon, Don Ameche
THE FILM: a typically Spielbergian family meets Bigfoot while camping, takes him home, discovers he's as gentle as E.T. Middling, overly familiar movie has Spielberg themes without Spielberg's magical touch.

THE LAND BEFORE TIME, 1988

Spielberg's credit: coexecutive producer
DIRECTOR: Don Bluth
STARS: Pat Hingle, Helen Shaver (voices only)
THE FILM: animated tale of young dinosaur searching for new home and family, a familiar Spielberg theme. Okay animation,

*BATTERIES NOT INCLUDED: Like Walt Disney before him, Spielberg moved beyond the making of individual films, becoming overseer of a vast entertainment empire, delegating the responsibility of making Spielberg-style entertainment to younger directors. Their work may have been in Spielberg's tradition, but it rarely boasted his magic, as this modest blend of sentiment and sci-fi (starring Jessica Tandy and her husband Hume Cronyn) proved.

Lawrence Kasdan, who had penned *Raiders of the Lost Ark,* went on to direct John Belushi and Blair Brown in *Continental Divide,* a revival of the 1940s Tracy-Hepburn romantic comedies between strong-willed men and women, here given a contemporary ecological spin (courtesy Universal Pictures).

mediocre songs, mildly pleasant for kids. Notable as Spielberg's first dino movie.

WHO FRAMED ROGER RABBIT, 1988

Spielberg's credit: coexecutive producer

DIRECTOR: Robert Zemeckis
STARS: Bob Hoskins, Christopher Lloyd, Joanna Cassidy
THE FILM: live-action detective visits fantastic Toon Town to solve 1940s movieland murder mystery. Affection for old animation makes for contemporary classic that revitalized Disney's animation unit. Brilliant in all respects: The *Citizen Kane* of cartoons.

BACK TO THE FUTURE II, 1989

Spielberg's credit: coexecutive producer

DIRECTOR: Robert Zemeckis
STARS: Michael J. Fox, Christopher Lloyd, Lea Thompson
THE FILM: further adventures of the time-traveling team in their DeLorean. Frenetic pace and dazzling effects can't compensate for fact that original's charm is not present.

DAD, 1989

Spielberg's credit: coexecutive producer

DIRECTOR: Gary David Goldberg
STARS: Jack Lemmon, Ted Danson, Olympia Dukakis
THE FILM: muddled melodrama, as dysfunctional father-son re-

lationship takes a turn for better when Dad is dying. Spielberg handled that situation far better in *Indiana Jones and the Last Crusade.*

JOE VERSUS THE VOLCANO, 1990

Spielberg's credit: coexecutive producer

DIRECTOR: John Patrick Shanley
STARS: Tom Hanks, Meg Ryan, Lloyd Bridges
THE FILM: acclaimed writer Shanley turned director for this pretentious dud about a man who will become a millionaire if he leaps into a live volcano; awkward attempt to combine modern morality play, romantic comedy, and Kafkaesque fable.

ARACHNOPHOBIA, 1990

Spielberg's credit: coexecutive producer

DIRECTOR: Frank Marshall
STARS: Jeff Daniels, Harley Jane Kozak, John Goodman
THE FILM: Spielberg's longtime collaborator made directing debut with this good-natured, appealingly creepy redux of a fifties B–horror movie, as deadly spiders invade a small town. Surprisingly enough, a box-office disappointment.

GREMLINS 2: THE NEW BATCH, 1990

Spielberg's credit: coexecutive producer

DIRECTOR: Joe Dante
STARS: Zach Galligan, Phoebe Cates, John Glover

In *Back To the Future* and two popular sequels, Zemeckis and Spielberg were able to explore time travel and the theme of family values, as Marty McFly (Michael J. Fox) must (in the company of Christopher Lloyd as Doc Brown) ensure that his own parents will meet and wed (courtesy Amblin Entertainment and Universal Pictures).

THE FILM: the ghoulies move to New York City. More of the same, but with none of the old magic. Major disappointment.

BACK TO THE FUTURE III, 1990

Spielberg's credit: coexecutive producer

DIRECTOR: Robert Zemeckis
STARS: Michael J. Fox, Christopher Lloyd, Mary Steenburgen
THE FILM: this time, it's back to the Old West, a most appealing choice since westerns were not (then) being made anymore. A huge improvement over *Back to the Future II;* almost as good as the first.

LISTEN UP: THE LIVES OF QUINCY JONES, 1990

Spielberg's credit: interviewee

DIRECTOR: Ellen Weissbrod
THE FILM: documentary about famed musician and composer who collaborated with Spielberg on *The Color Purple,* features interviews with numerous celebrities, Spielberg included.

AKIRA KUROSAWA'S DREAMS, 1990

Spielberg's involvement: "Spielberg presents"

DIRECTOR: Akira Kurosawa
STARS: Martin Scorsese, Akira Terao
THE FILM: Spielberg, Scorsese, and other A-list American moviemakers facilitated this highly personal anthology film in eight installments of varying quality, from Japan's most acclaimed director. Lucas's Industrial Light and Magic provided the striking special effects.

CAPE FEAR, 1991

Spielberg's involvement: Amblin Entertainment in Association with Universal

DIRECTOR: Martin Scorsese
STARS: Robert De Niro, Nick Nolte, Jessica Lange
THE FILM: Spielberg was slotted to direct this remake of the Florida-based thriller, originally done in 1962; had to leave when schedule conflicted with *Hook.*

AN AMERICAN TAIL: FIEVEL GOES WEST, 1991

Spielberg's credit: producer

DIRECTORS: Phil Nibbelink, Simon Wells
STARS: James Stewart, Amy Irving (voices only)
THE FILM: Spielberg goes it without Don Bluth for this entertaining and colorful sequel, which places the cute mouse in an Old West setting which resembles an animated version of the one in *Back to the Future III.*

NOISES OFF, 1992

Spielberg's involvement: Amblin Entertainment Presents

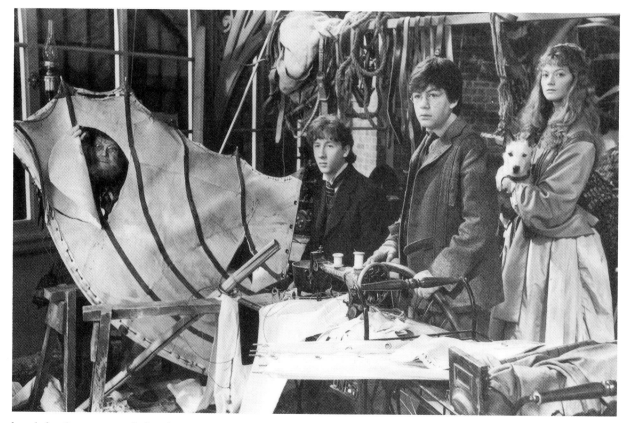

Long before there was young Indiana Jones on TV, there was *Young Sherlock Holmes* at the movies, an appealing and underrated film about the great detective's first case; Nicholas Rowe as Holmes, Alan Cox as Watson, and Sophie Ward as Sherlock's doomed inamorata (courtesy Amblin Entertainment and Paramount Pictures).

DIRECTOR: Peter Bogdanovich
STARS: Carol Burnett, Michael Caine, Nicollette Sheridan
THE FILM: charming theater piece about stage performers in the midst of a British sex farce in which their timing is always slightly off; does not work when the "live" quality is gone. Played with great gusto, though.

A FAR OFF PLACE, 1993

Spielberg's involvement: Amblin Entertainment Presents
THE FILM: Spielberg and Touchstone collaborated on this satisfying ecologically oriented update of the appealing 1950s Disney live-action films involving children, nature, and animals.

THE FLINTSTONES, 1994

Spielberg's "credit": "Steven Spielrock Presents"
DIRECTOR: Brian Levant
STARS: John Goodman, Rick Moranis, Elizabeth Perkins
THE FILM: though the "presents" credit may be facetious, longtime Spielberg collaborator Kathleen Kennedy is indeed listed in credits of this live-action comedy version of Hanna-Barbera's dino-era cartoon.

278

Sometimes the Spielberg formula was repeated without the Spielberg magic; here Ally Sheedy, lost, drives as her robot companion checks a map (a recurring image in Spielberg films, dating back to *Close Encounters* and *1941*) in the innocuous, infantile comedy *Short Circuit* (courtesy Amblin Entertainment).

As we go to press, Steven Spielberg is serving as executive producer for *The Bridges of Madison County*, directed by Clint Eastwood, starring Eastwood and Meryl Streep. Spielberg has also announced plans to begin a new film company, to be headed and run by himself, Jeffrey Katzenberg, and David Geffen.

In *The Money Pit*, Tom Hanks returns home to find that the construction of his dream house is not going well; the film was intended as a contemporary version of *Mr. Blanding Builds His Dream House*, though the results were not so happy (courtesy Amblin Entertainment and Universal Pictures).

Appendix II: Spielberg on TV
STEVEN SPIELBERG PERSONALLY DIRECTED THE FOLLOWING TV WORK:

ROD SERLING'S NIGHT GALLERY

ORIGINAL BROADCAST: 11/8/69, NBC
SEGMENT TITLE: "Eyes"
STARS: Joan Crawford, Barry Sullivan, Tom Bosley
Pilot for 1970–73 series, a variation on Serling's beloved *Twilight Zone*. In Spielberg's episode, a rich woman buys a poor man's eyes to see her beloved New York City one more time, only to witness the famed Manhattan total power blackout of 1965. Interesting starting point, as Serling, like Spielberg, was a Jewish writer who assimilated into mainstream America.

MARCUS WELBY, M.D.

ORIGINAL BROADCAST: 3/17/70, ABC
SEGMENT TITLE: "Daredevil Gesture"
STARS: Robert Young, James Brolin, Elena Verdugo
A teenage hemophiliac (Frank Webb) is treated by the title character. Interesting in that it allowed Spielberg to deal with relationship material centering on a youngster who feels very much an outsider from normal life.

ROD SERLING'S NIGHT GALLERY

ORIGINAL BROADCAST: 1/6/71, NBC
SEGMENT TITLE: "Make Me Laugh"
STARS: Godfrey Cambridge, Jackie Vernon, Al Lewis
A miracle worker, not unlike the one in "Kick the Can," approaches a down-and-out comic who is unable to get a laugh out of audiences and desperately needs a shot of optimism. Strikingly in tune with Spielberg's later work.

THE NAME OF THE GAME

ORIGINAL BROADCAST: 1/15/71, NBC
SEGMENT TITLE: "L.A. 2017"
STARS: Gene Barry, Barry Sullivan, Edmond O'Brien
This ordinarily realistic series about journalists took a turn for the fantastic with Spielberg's cautionary fable about a 1984ish Brave New World of the near future.

Young Steven Spielberg directs Joan Crawford in the pilot film for Rod Serling's *Night Gallery,* while the 1969 winner of the Lyndon B. Johnson lookalike contest peers on (courtesy Universal-TV).

Steven Spielberg created an anthology for NBC-TV's *Amazing Stories*, which sometimes featured Disney-like family entertainment broadcast early on a Sunday evening, at other times switching to a later hour for Hitchcock-type thrillers or Serling-style sci-fi. Sadly, Spielberg did not host each episode, as his idols had; his presence might have been the element that made the show click.

THE PSYCHIATRIST

ORIGINAL BROADCAST: 2/10/71, ABC
SEGMENT TITLE: "The Private World of Martin Dalton"
STARS: Roy Thinnes, Jim Hutton, Kate Woodville
Two of Spielberg's favorite themes, children's fantasy lives and parental abuse within dysfunctional families, are explored as the title character (Thinnes) analyzes a withdrawn child (Stephen Hudis). Spielberg often cited this serious-relationship chamber drama when critics accused him of overreliance on F/X.

THE PSYCHIATRIST

ORIGINAL BROADCAST: 3/10/71, ABC
SEGMENT TITLE: "Par For the Course"
STARS: Clu Gulager, Joan Darling, Michael C. Gwynne
Gulager is a pro golfer who learns he has cancer, can't cope, and turns to the title character. Another early example of character-driven drama from Spielberg.

COLUMBO

ORIGINAL BROADCAST: 9/15/71, NBC
SEGMENT TITLE: "Murder by the Book"
STARS: Peter Falk, Jack Cassidy, Martin Milner, Rosemary Forsythe
The first regular installment of the *Columbo* show (preceded by two made-for-TV movie pilots), which set the pace and the standard for all that followed: mystery writer Cassidy kills off his onetime collaborator as "the perfect crime."

NBC WORLD PREMIERE MOVIE

ORIGINAL BROADCAST: 11/13/71, NBC
SEGMENT TITLE: "Duel"
STARS: Dennis Weaver, Lucille Benson, Eddie Firestone
The original TV version that established Spielberg's virtuosity with men and machines.

CBS FRIDAY NIGHT MOVIE

ORIGINAL BROADCAST: 1/21/72, CBS
SEGMENT TITLE: "Something Evil"
STARS: Sandy Dennis, Darren McGavin, Ralph Bellamy
An American family, not all that different from the one in *Poltergeist,* moves into a Bucks County farmhouse that, like the one in the later movie, is cursed. First fling with highly spiritualistic material.

NBC WORLD PREMIERE

ORIGINAL BROADCAST: 3/31/72, NBC
SEGMENT TITLE: "Savage" (a.k.a., "Watch Dog"; "Savage Report")
STARS: Martin Landau, Barbara Bain, Will Geer

Spielberg directed two episodes of his *Amazing Stories* NBC-TV series, including "The Mission," a WWII aviation tale starring Kiefer Sutherland (*background, left*), Casey Siemaszko, and Kevin Costner (courtesy Amblin Entertainment).

TV journalists attempt to learn why a Supreme Court nominee (Barry Sullivan) is being blackmailed. Pilot for a proposed Landau-Bain series that never materialized.

AMAZING STORIES

ORIGINAL BROADCAST: 9/29/85
SEGMENT TITLE: "Ghost Train"
STAR: Roberts Blossom
Small children believe that the title object will come roaring into their home and yank them out of bed; similar to the child in *Poltergeist* fearing the tree outside his house.

AMAZING STORIES

ORIGINAL BROADCAST: 5/15/87
SEGMENT TITLE: "The Mission"
STARS: Kevin Costner, Casey Siemaszko, Kiefer Sutherland
A flier heads off into a 1940ish wild blue yonder. Nostalgia for the past and affectionate attitude toward aviation characterize this as Spielberg stuff.

ABOUT THE AUTHOR

Douglas Brode teaches the film directors course at Syracuse University's Newhouse School of Public Communications, Department of Television/Radio/Film. Beginning in January 1995, Professor Brode will offer a course on the films of Steven Spielberg, the first such course to be taught at any major university in the United States. Professor Brode is also the coordinator of cinema studies programs at Onondaga College in Syracuse. His previous books include the college text *Crossroads to the Cinema* and for Citadel Press: *Films of the Fifties, Films of the Sixties, The Films of Dustin Hoffman, Woody Allen: His Films and Career, The Films of Jack Nicholson, Lost Films of the Fifties, Films of the Eighties, The Films of Woody Allen,* and *The Films of Robert De Niro;* he is currently completing work on *Money, Women, and Guns: Crime Movies From* Bonnie and Clyde *to the Present.* Brode's articles have appeared in such popular magazines as *TV Guide* and *Rolling Stone* as well as more esoteric journals, including *Cineaste* and *Television Quarterly.* His play *Heartbreaker* has been professionally produced, and three of his original screenplays are currently under option at independent Hollywood filmmaking companies.